Police Powers
Law, Order and Accountability

Police Powers
Law, Order and Accountability

Bill Van Allen
*Georgian College of Applied
Arts and Technology*

PEARSON

Prentice
Hall

Toronto

Library and Archives Canada Cataloguing in Publication

Van Allen, Bill
    Police powers : law, order and accountability / Bill Van Allen.

Includes bibliographical references and index.
ISBN 978-0-13-242982-5

    1. Police power—Canada—Textbooks.   2. Criminal procedure—Canada—
Textbooks.   I. Title.

HV8157.V35 2009   345.71'052   C2007-905486-2

ISBN-13: 978-0-13-242982-5
ISBN-10:   0-13-242982-9

Vice President, Editorial Director: Gary Bennett
Senior Acquisitions Editor: Laura Paterson Forbes
Signing Representative: Joanne Venditto
Marketing Manager: Sally Aspinall
Developmental Editor: Emily Jardeleza
Production Editor: Pearl Saban
Copy Editor: Shirley Rennie
Proofreader: Patricia Jones
Production Coordinator: Avinash Chandra
Composition: Laserwords
Art Director: Julia Hall
Cover and Interior Design: Anthony Leung
Cover Image: Veer Inc.

1 2 3 4 5   12 11 10 09 08

Printed and bound in Canada.

To my daughter, Provincial Constable Jennifer Van Allen, Badge #11561, Southern Georgian Bay detachment, Ontario Provincial Police. I am honoured to see professionalism and respect for individual rights reflected in the manner in which you carry out your duties.

And to my students at Georgian College, it is a privilege for me to be able to instruct you on matters of law and proper investigative techniques. As you join the ranks of police services following your graduation, always be mindful of a police officer's responsibility to treat every person with dignity and respect.

WVA

Brief Contents

Contents

Chapter 3   **Arrest Procedures**   **53**

Chapter 4   **Use of Force**   **83**

Chapter 10   **Admissibility of Seized Evidence**   **249**

Appendix   **271**

As a former police officer with 29 years experience, 18 years of which were full-time major crime and homicide investigative duties, it was my privilege to have worked with many excellent police officers. Several of those officers served as role models for me at various stages throughout my career. As I look back over my policing career, the very best police officers I encountered, from a variety of police services – municipal, provincial, federal and international—all shared a number of common characteristics.

Without exception, the finest police officers were passionate about policing and they exemplified excellence in the manner in which they carried out their duties. They made career-long efforts to improve their knowledge of case law, statute law and investigative techniques. They strived to attend training courses and seminars and they devoted countless hours of their own time to researching legal issues and honing their investigative skills. They gained prominence within their respective police services by rising to supervisory positions or to specialized units.

The very best police officers always found a way to be effective – even during the most difficult of cases. They were seen as the "go to" officers who were assigned to take charge of intricate situations and were relied upon to provide solutions to complicated problems because they possessed expert knowledge. They enjoyed high conviction rates and were frequently recognized by their superiors and their peers as exceptional police officers. They were also highly respected by members of the judiciary, prosecutors and defence bar. They inspired public confidence in the policing profession.

I came to realize that in addition to their honesty, fairness, determination and empathy for others, the finest police officers treated each and every person with whom they dealt, with common respect and dignity. The best of the best not only enforced the rules of society – they also played by the rules. This elite group of police officers didn't follow the rules simply because they had to – they did so out of a sense of honesty, duty and fair play. The finest police officers always played by the rules for no other reason than because it was just the right thing to do.

Canadian courts and legislators have granted police officers all of the necessary tools with which to investigate crimes, gather evidence and apprehend offenders. The extraordinary powers given to the police to deprive individuals of their liberty, to use force and to search for evidence were all granted with the expectation that these powers would be used responsibly, fairly and judiciously.

Whenever a criminal court excludes improperly obtained evidence, or acquits an accused person, or stays a criminal proceeding as a remedy to a successful *Charter* challenge, it is not the intention of the court to punish the police. Nor is it the court's intention to reward the offender for his actions – nobody in our society benefits from that.

Canadian courts do not condone incidents of police wrongdoing for the very same reasons they do not condone law-breaking conduct on the part of offenders. The purpose of having rules of evidence is to strike an appropriate balance between society's right to effective law enforcement and an individual's rights to be free from unwarranted interference by the state. That doesn't mean that individuals are always free from interference from law enforcement agencies – just free from unjustified interference.

The laws that protect the rights of wrongdoers protect each and every one of us. In Canada, the police are appointed to safeguard and protect the individual rights that our society holds important for us all. If you, as a private individual, value your own personal rights, then you must value them for everyone – in every situation.

Police work can be a challenging and rewarding profession. Police officers are very well equipped to carry out the difficult tasks they encounter during the course of their duties. I have attempted, throughout this textbook, to give you information you will need to become a highly-effective police officer while stressing the need to respect the rights of all individuals.

"You cannot enforce the law, if you don't know what the law is." This is a message that I continually strive to deliver to my Police Foundations students. In order to become an effective police officer, you must always respect not only the scope, but also the limitations of your powers of arrest, use of force, powers of search and seizure and the use of discretion. Every time that police misconduct results in the exclusion of evidence or an acquittal or staying of proceedings, bad case law is created that makes it more difficult for the over 40 000 other police officers in Canada to do their job.

Professional police officers exercise their powers of arrest, use of force, discretion and search and seizure – not just because they can, but because legal justification exists for them to do so. Always remember that, as a police officer, you will be held accountable for the manner in which you exercise the powers that have been entrusted to you.

You must never abuse your position of authority nor take your responsibilities for granted. Treat everyone equally, fairly and honestly – the way that you would like to be treated if you were in their position.

It's the right thing to do.

Bill Van Allen, Orillia, 2007

SPECIAL FEATURES:
Decimal Numbering System:

- The content of this text is structured utilizing a uniform system of subordinate decimal numbering, which is consistent with what legislation students are exposed to throughout the Police Foundations Program, such as the frequently referenced *Criminal Code* and various other statute laws. This allows the student to navigate between topics and subtopics in a systematic, logical manner.

Ontario Use of Force Model (2004) ©

- This text promotes the Use of Force continuum currently in use in Ontario and reflects the adopted use of force guidelines developed for use by police services within the Province of Ontario. In Ontario, police officers are instructed regarding use of force response options using an assessment tool in the form of a wheel-shaped continuum that graphically illustrates proportional responses to various suspect behaviours.

- The Use of Force Model (2004) is intended as a learning tool to complement, not replace, departmental policy or statutory requirements. Police officers and others employed within the administration of justice are civilly and criminally responsible for any excessive use of force during the conduct of their duties.

- For the convenience of students and instructors, a full colour version of the Use of Force model has been reproduced on the rear inside cover of the text. The Ontario Use of Force Model (2004) © Queen's Printer for Ontario, 2004. Reproduced with permission. The Ontario Use of Force Model (2004) was developed through consultation between the Ministry of Community Safety and Correctional Services and its stakeholders. The Model has been amended by and is endorsed by the ministry.

- Different use of force models may currently be in use in jurisdictions other than the province of Ontario.

Boxed Inserts:

- Investigative Relevance boxes provide students with practical advice on procedures and concepts that relate to a police investigation. Drawn from the author's vast experience as a police officer, these boxes give aid on what to consider or be aware of in specific investigative situations.

- Investigative Hypothesis boxes supply students with an excellent visual of a deductive equation or linear hypothesis derived from a criminal event.

Reality-based Situations:

- Actual investigations are recounted to emphasize what occurs in actual police investigations based on the author's real-life experience as a career law enforcement officer.

Appendix:

- This textbook includes samples of selected legal forms and reports, which are discussed throughout the textbook.
- Samples are included of an Information to Obtain a Search Warrant, a search warrant and a Report to a Justice, reflecting a fictitious case to demonstrate how reasonable grounds are developed and properly presented to a justice in order to conduct a legally pre-authorized search for evidence in a criminal case.

SUPPLEMENTS:

The following instructor supplements are available for downloading from a password-protected section of Pearson Education Canada's online catalogue (vig.pearsoned.ca). Navigate to your book's catalogue page to view a list of those supplements that are available. See your local sales representative for details and access.

Instructor's Manual: This manual, available in PDF format, includes learning objectives for each chapter, a brief chapter outline, lecture plans and sample documents to supplement the PowerPoint Presentations.

Test Item File: Available in Microsoft Word format, this comprehensive test bank features multiple-choice and true-false questions with references to text page numbers, level of difficulty and skill level.

PowerPoint Presentations: Each chapter of the text is outlined in a series of PowerPoint Presentations, which include key points, figures, and tables.

Acknowledgments

I am sincerely grateful to all those who so generously assisted, guided and inspired me, throughout my career and during the writing of this book. Without their individual contributions, this book would never have been written.

I have had no shortage of role models throughout my policing career who, by their example, impressed upon me the importance of understanding the scope and limitations of my powers as a police officer. The past and present members of the OPP who taught me those lessons include: Detective Inspectors Jack Welsch, Dennis Olinyk, Jim Hutchinson, D/C/Supt. Dave Crane, D/Superintendent C.F. (Bud) Brennan, D/C/Supt. Wayne C. Frechette, D/Sgt. Tom Wright; and D/S/Sgt. Morgan Pitfield.

I also wish to acknowledge the positive impact that several past and present members of the Ministry of the Attorney General, Crown Law Office (Criminal) had on me and my subsequent interest in the proper drafting of search warrant informations. They include the Hon. Mr. Justice Casey Hill, Mr. Scott Hutchinson, and Ms. Renee Pomerance.

I am indebted to all those who generously assisted me during my research for this book including: Provincial Constable Jennifer Van Allen, Southern Georgian Bay OPP, D/Sgt. Jim Van Allen, O.P.P. Behavioural Sciences Unit. Sincere thanks are also extended to my colleagues at Georgian College of Applied Arts and Technology, Orillia campus, who teach Police Powers. S/Sgt. Gary Skelding, O.P.P. (retired) and S/Sgt. John Anglin, Barrie Police Service both freely shared their knowledge and teaching resources, and contributed worthwhile suggestions for meeting the needs of students.

I am grateful for the efforts of the representatives of those agencies who supplied photographs and permissions for use in this textbook, including Rose Bliss, Communications Manager, Special Investigations Unit (SIU); Sherrie Tonks, Administrative Assistant to the Director of the Ontario Police College (OPC); Jeannette Lejeune, Community Relations and Visual Identity Coordinator, Corporate Communications Bureau, OPP, Superintendent Sue Laverty, Regional Director, Support Services, OPP Central Region and Inspector Terry Wright, OPP Orillia detachment.

Very special thanks are extended to Mr. Dave Tamblyn, Principal, Schreiber-Terrace Bay Public School, for his generous permission to publish a much-wanted photograph and for going above and beyond the call of duty to obtain the required releases that enabled me to do so.

I wish to express my very sincere thanks to my former Georgian College student, Mike Downing, and also to Constable Scott Anthony, OPP Orillia detachment, for volunteering their time to participate in the simulated use of force photographs consistent with the Ontario Use of Force Model. Thanks also to Dean Dave Dubois, Community Studies Department, Georgian College of Applied Arts and Technology, Orillia campus, for the gracious use of Georgian College property for the taking of these photographs.

I would like to thank the following reviewers: Dino Doria, Humber College; James MacMaster, Algonquin College; Scott Nicholls, Humber College; Oliver Stoetzer, Fanshawe College; Peter Thompson, Algonquin College; Robert Tucker, St. Lawrence College.

I wish also to acknowledge the staff of Pearson Education who were involved in the conceptualization, writing and production of this textbook, including Ky Pruesse and Laura Paterson Forbes, Acquisitions Editors, Emily Jardeleza, Developmental Editor, and Pearl Saban, Production Editor.

Finally, thanks to my wife Emily, for your patience and understanding during the many months I spent writing this book while competing demands went unattended.

Bill Van Allen, Orillia, 2007

Police Powers

Sources of Police Powers

"To whom much is given, much is expected."

Luke 12:48.

After reading this chapter, students should be able to:

- Describe the terms powers of arrest, use of force, and search and seizure.
- Explain the differences between statute law, common law and case law.
- Name the five mandated core responsibilities for police services in Ontario.
- Explain what is meant by the term "facts in issue".
- Describe six differences between indictable and summary conviction offences.
- Analyze how the actions of police officers can conflict with individual rights guaranteed by the Canadian Charter of Rights and Freedoms.

1.1   INTRODUCTION

The implied notion of the expectation of a debt owed by someone who has been granted extraordinary or special privileges implied by the opening quotation of this chapter is fitting to any discussion of the powers which are entrusted to law enforcement officers. Take a brief moment to consider the exceptional powers which are granted to law enforcement officers (police, corrections, the Canadian Security Intelligence Service [CSIS], regulatory agencies, etc.) under statute and common law. Peace officers possess extraordinary powers which are entrusted to no other professions within our society.

No other single occupation within our society is entrusted with the power to make split-second decisions regarding the lawful restriction of the liberty of other human beings – in a wide variety of operational situations. Law enforcement officers are authorized to take persons into their custody, often against their will and often without any court ordered justification for their actions. The same actions by anyone else, acting outside of the legal authority to perform such actions in similar circumstances, could constitute a criminal offence.

Nor is any other profession authorized to seize a person's property or possessions with or, on many occasions, without some form of prior court order directing them to do so. In a variety of situations, police officers may seize an individual's personal property as evidence, without a warrant. Police officers are also authorized to obtain a variety of court orders (search warrants, etc.) that allow them to enter private premises to search for evidence and to seize any thing that would afford evidence of an offence or which was obtained by or used in the commission of offences.

Police officers possess a variety of other invasive evidence-gathering mechanisms to expedite the production of documents from third parties (general warrants, production orders, etc.) and judicial authorizations to intercept the private communications of named and unnamed persons in the investigation of designated offences.

Only in exceptional circumstances, such as self-defence situations, are everyday citizens legally entitled to use physical force against another person. Peace officers are justified in using as much force (interpreted as meaning the minimum, or least amount of force) as is reasonably necessary to carry out any duty where the use of force is required.[1]

Peace officers are legally justified in unleashing lethal force – the intentional taking of the life of another human being – in extreme situations when it is necessary to preserve their life or the life or another person or to protect against grievous bodily harm.[2] Responsibility for the use of these wide-reaching powers, which are entrusted to no other profession, can and should seem more than just a little daunting to anyone aspiring to become a peace officer in Canada.

It is small wonder that these awesome powers society has granted to police officers, through our legislative policy makers, also come with a formidable expectation that they will be used judiciously, responsibly, wisely and ethically. For example, to ensure accountability for the use of force, the *Criminal Code* provides that if peace officers use their powers improperly, they will be held accountable for that misuse:

> "Every one who is authorized by law to use force is criminally responsible for any excess thereof according to the nature and quality of the act that constitutes the excess."[3]

In addition to the potential criminal liability for excessive use of force, police officers and their police services might also incur considerable civil liability in cases in which an individual suffers financial loss due to damage or injury due to the improper exercise of an officer's authority.

Past abuses, real or perceived, have resulted in certain powers being limited and even taken away, making every peace officer's job more challenging than before. Prior to 1985, for example, designated members of the RCMP were issued with a "writ of assistance" and were authorized to enter premises, including dwelling houses, to conduct

---

[1]*Criminal Code*, R.S. 1985, c. C-46, s. 25(1).

[2]*Criminal Code*, R.S. 1985, c. C-46, s. 25(3) and R.R.O. 1990, Reg. 976, s. 9, *Police Services Act* R.S.O. 1990 c. P.15.

[3]*Criminal Code*, R.S. 1985, c. C-46, s. 26.

carte blanche warrantless searches under the *Narcotic Control Act*.[4] In the face of numerous legal challenges as to the constitutionality of evidence seized as the result of writs of assistance, the relevant legislation was repealed (cancelled).[5]

Always remember that those who are employed in law enforcement professions owe society an enormous debt, both in terms of responsibility and accountability for the use of these awesome powers of arrest, use of force and search and seizure. Responsible police officers exercise their powers of arrest, use of force, discretion and search and seizure not just because they can – they exercise these powers only when legal justification exists to do so.

1.2   A BRIEF HISTORY OF POLICING

Policing, as we know it today, is still a relatively recent historical development that has only been with us for some 200 odd years. In ancient times, long before the creation of laws and prior to the formation of organized police services, victims of wrongdoings and community members were responsible for the apprehension and punishment of offenders. As societies became more and more complex, formalized laws were developed in order to communicate the society's standards of acceptable behaviour to its members.

Following the Norman invasion of England in 1066, Sheriffs were appointed by kings and were made responsible for law enforcement within appointed jurisdictions. Citizens of this era were still largely expected to police themselves, resulting in law enforcement that was, at best, both inconsistent and ineffective.

During the Industrial Revolution, private police forces were established to ensure security of the shipping and commerce that occurred along the waterfront area of the River Thames. These forces were very successful in dealing with crime and were officially taken over by the City of London in 1800. During the eighteenth and nineteenth centuries, European cities began to form police services to combat growing lawlessness and to achieve fair and consistent enforcement of criminal and quasi-criminal law.

During the 1700s in London, England, author and Justice of the Peace Henry Fielding established a body of men, known as the "Bow Street Runners", who were responsible for law enforcement and crime prevention within a portion of the city. In 1785, William Pitt, a member of the British parliament, put forth a bill to create a police service for the City of London with a mandate similar to the "Bow Street Runners". Pitt's bill was eventually withdrawn due to strong opposition from those who felt that such an organization could be used to strengthen an already unpopular government.

Only as recently as 1829 did Sir Robert Peel, a British politician, successfully propose legislation that created a model of a police force after which present-day Canadian police services are modelled. Peel also successfully proposed a division of responsibility between the police, (the detection and prevention of crime) and the courts, (the prosecution of crime) that remains virtually unchanged in Canada today.

---

[4]*Narcotic Control Act*, R.S. 1985 c. N-1 [repealed 1996 c. 19, s. 94].

[5]S.C. 1985, c.19 s. 200 as cited in *R. v. Hamill*, [1987] 1 S.C.R. 301, 1987 Can LII 86 (S.C.C.).

Early policing lacked sophistication by any modern standards. The first police officers were poorly paid and received little, if any, formal training. The role of early policing was fundamentally to control crime and maintain public order. The twentieth century saw the role of law enforcement being expanded to reflect the "Serve and Protect" model of policing. This model incorporated a secondary role of combined social assistance and referral services to the community in addition to the principal role of law enforcement duties. (Van Allen 2007)

Prior to Confederation, when the province of Ontario was known as Upper Canada, there were no police forces and most of Ontario's diminutive population lived in small towns and rural farming areas. When Canada became a Dominion in 1867, only the largest cities had their own police forces. The North West Mounted Police (NWMP) was formed in 1873 to provide law and order in Western Canada.

In 1875, the Government of Ontario hired Detective John Wilson Murray to conduct serious criminal investigations throughout Ontario. Several additional Constables were hired throughout Ontario until 1909, when the Ontario Provincial Police (OPP) was formed to provide law enforcement services for Ontario towns without their own police force, as well as patrol traffic on provincial highways. (Higley 1984)

The Royal Canadian Mounted Police (RCMP) was formed in 1920 with the merging of the North West Mounted Police and the Dominion Police. The RCMP continues to be Canada's federal police force and shares responsibility for provincial policing duties in Canada with two provincial police forces (OPP and Sûreté du Québec [SQ]). (Walma & West 2002)

Throughout the years, policing in Ontario has continued to evolve as numerous smaller services amalgamated to minimize duplication of services and achieve operational efficiencies. Currently, Ontario is policed by fifty-nine various municipal and regional police services, and the Ontario Provincial Police. Since 1991, various tripartite agreements between First Nations, the federal government and provincial/territorial governments now provide independent policing services for nine First Nations territories, including:

Akwesasne Mohawk Police Service

Anishinabek Police Service

Lac Seul Police Service

Nishnawbe-Aski Police Service

Six Nations Regional Police Service

Treaty Three Police Service

Tyendinaga Mohawk Police Service

United Chiefs and Councils of Manitoulin Anishinaabe Police

Wikwemikong Tribal Police

Numerous other law enforcement agencies provide specialized enforcement duties throughout Ontario including Canadian National Railway Police, Canadian Pacific Railway Police, Department of National Defence Military Police and Niagara Parks Police. Numerous provincial ministries and federal departments provide specialized regulatory and criminal enforcement in areas such as taxation, natural resources, transportation, the environment, etc.[6]

1.3   THE ROLE OF THE POLICE IN CANADA

"No society can exist without a police force. History has shown that the more dominant and totalitarian the state, the greater the need of that state for a large and powerful police presence. Yet it is equally true that no democratic society can exist without the police."[7]

Honourable Mr. Justice Peter deC. Cory, The Inquiry Regarding Thomas Sophonow.

Enforcement *n.* enforce + ment (*L. fortis* = strong) 1. an instance of compelling observance (of a law, etc.) 2. the imposition of an action, conduct or one's will [by force, if necessary].

The Concise Oxford Dictionary (9th edition)

Laws are bodies of rules which exist to govern the behaviour of members of any society. Laws are both recognized and enforced by the government, in most cases by an array of regulatory and investigative agencies that comprise the enforcement branches of the various levels of government. Governments also recognize the validity of laws by establishing courts to conduct hearings into alleged violations of the law and to penalize offenders convicted of offences.

If people in a small group, such as students in a classroom, established a set of rules to govern their own behaviour, the validity of such rules would not be recognized by the government, nor would they be enforced by the government. Organizations pass rules and bylaws to govern their own conduct, but such rules do not constitute law.

Some laws are created by elected legislative bodies (**statute law**) while others are established as the result of previous court decisions (**case law**). Still other law is based on unwritten traditions and practices which have become so entrenched in our legal system as to become deemed to be law (**common law**).

Laws are intended to represent the collective will of the majority of members of a particular society at any given point in time. What might be illegal behaviour in a specific jurisdiction might be perfectly legal in another – such as so-called public order offences including drug use, prostitution and gambling, which are legal in certain jurisdictions. In addition to not being universal in their nature and extent, laws are always changing.

New laws are continually being passed while outmoded laws are repealed (cancelled) to better reflect the will of society as beliefs and values regarding acceptable behaviour change with the times. Modernized laws are passed to effectively deal with emerging crime trends – such as organized crime, cyber-crime and terrorist offences. Obsolete laws are repealed or diminished to adjust contemporary beliefs and values regarding relations between spouses, sexual offences, de-criminalization of drugs, etc.

---

[6]Ministry of Community Safety and Correctional Services 2006 Police Services Directory.

[7]The Inquiry Regarding Thomas Sophonow www.gov.mb.ca/justice/publications/sophonow/intro/therole.html. Retrieved: March 17, 2007.

For a law to be of any value to the society that created it, any breach of that law must also be enforceable. There would be no purpose served by passing a law if the society that did so was not prepared to hold individuals accountable for violating it. Therefore, not only should the laws of a society clearly communicate limits of unacceptable behaviour to its members, but the law must also prescribe standardized penalties for any violation of a particular law.

While the purpose of laws is to communicate acceptable standards of behaviour to members of society, Canada and most other nations impose an onus (responsibility) on individuals to be familiar with the laws of the respective jurisdiction. In Canada, the *Criminal Code* states that, "Ignorance of the law by a person who commits an offence is not an excuse for committing that offence."[8] This liability applies not only to all Canadian citizens but also to every individual, regardless of nationality, who is subject to Canadian law while in Canada, in the same way that Canadian citizens are subject to the laws of every jurisdiction they visit.

The law enforcement duties carried out by police officers are vital to the very survival of society. For law and order to exist, those who are responsible for the enforcement of society's laws must be provided with the necessary tools to impose society's will in situations in which voluntary compliance cannot otherwise be achieved. Laws must be enforced in a fair and equitable manner for all persons.

The main objective of law enforcement is to ensure voluntary compliance with the laws of a particular society through effective **deterrence** – the discouraging of unlawful behaviour by punishing offenders. Police powers – namely, powers of arrest, use of force and search and seizure – exist because of the reality that police work is often challenging, potentially dangerous and frequently unpopular with certain segments of the population who are inclined to break society's laws. We will focus our examination of police powers within the context of society's need to maintain effective law enforcement, including the preservation of order and crime control.

The police don't make laws – they uphold them. It isn't the responsibility of the police to establish boundaries or to determine the balance of order within Canadian society – it is their job only to maintain such boundaries and balance. "They do not decide who deserves punishment, nor do they decide what punishment to mete out." (Bjorkquist 2002 p. 11)

Many civil libertarians believe that current Canadian police powers are already too wide-reaching and excessive, claiming that they infringe on individual rights. To provide safety and security for its citizens, any free and democratic society must strike an appropriate balance between the rights of individuals and the fundamental rights of society as a whole. One of society's basic rights is that of effective law enforcement to ensure order and crime control.

Without the broad powers granted to them under Canadian law, peace officers would be ill-equipped to uphold the law or to control or prevent crime. Without powers of arrest, police officers would be powerless to apprehend individuals observed committing crimes, or to restrict an individual from committing a crime. In the absence of a statutory authority to legally use physical force – proportional (equivalent) to, and reasonable under the circumstances of any given situation – to effect the arrest of an individual, the use of such force would constitute an assault by the police officer upon the individual being arrested.

---

[8]*Criminal Code*, R.S. 1985 c. C-46, s. 19.

Without the broad powers of search and seizure granted by statute and common law, the ability of the police to gather evidence in support of investigations and prosecutions would be greatly reduced. In exchange for granting these wide-ranging powers, society demands that police discharge their duties lawfully – and with integrity, fairness, and honesty.

To accept the responsibility for a career in law enforcement involving the prevention, detection and investigation of crime and the preservation of public order requires that – in all instances – these extraordinary powers be used diligently and ethically.

1.4 THE ROLE OF THE POLICE IN ONTARIO

As we have seen, the police have no innate (natural) authority and must rely on the provisions of statute and common law for their law enforcement powers. It is one thing for a statute to create an offence for a violation of prohibited behaviour – but police officers must be familiar with the source of their powers that mandate them to perform an enforcement action in a given situation.

As municipal, regional and provincial police officers in Canada are sworn to enforce the laws only within their province of appointment, their powers as police officers may be exercised only within the province's borders for which they are appointed. The core responsibilities for police services in Ontario are mandated by the *Police Services Act* (*PSA*), which sets out the following minimum standards for adequate and effective delivery of policing services, including:

1. "Crime prevention.

2. Law enforcement.

3. Assistance to victims of crime.

4. Public order maintenance.

5. Emergency response."[9]

The *Police Services Act* (*PSA*) is therefore the statute that creates the authority for the province and municipalities to create police services and to appoint police officers. The *PSA* also establishes the duties and responsibilities of individual police officers to exercise the powers of peace officers, set out in other statutes, to prevent crime, enforce laws and maintain public order. Much more information surrounding police oversight and the use of force provisions of the *Police Services Act* will be discussed in Chapters 2 and 4 of this textbook.

1.5 ETHICAL ISSUES

It is vital for police officers to always strive to ensure that they conduct their duties and exercise their powers of arrest, use of force and search and seizure within the strict "letter of the law". While strict observance of the lawfulness of executing police powers is vital, there are additional requirements that also need to be satisfied. The responsible

---

[9]*Police Services Act*, R.S.O. 1990, c. P-15, s. 4(2).

use of police powers also requires that they be utilized in an ethical manner. Simply stated, this means that the police must enforce the law lawfully and fairly in relation to all individuals. The police are themselves subject to the law and must never act or appear to be "above the law".

According to the International Association of Chiefs of Police (IACP) Code of Conduct (1989), "A police officer shall perform all duties impartially, without favour or affection or ill will and without regard to status, sex, race, religion, political belief or aspiration. All citizens will be treated equally with courtesy, consideration and dignity."[10]

It is possible for police officers to execute their powers in a lawful manner and still be unethical in their duties. If **reasonable grounds** exist to arrest an individual for an offence under statute law, such an arrest would, in all likelihood, be considered to be lawful. If an officer arrests – or fails to arrest an individual for an offence only because they were of a certain race, gender or religion, the officer's exercise of his or her powers of arrest, while lawful, would be unethical by reason of racial or gender bias.

While the powers granted to Canadian police officers are extraordinary, they are by no means absolute. Police officers must be aware of the source and intent of the laws that grant them their powers, as well as any limitations governing their use. The IACP published Canons of Police Ethics, Article 2 of which states:

> "The first duty of law enforcement officers, as upholders of the law, is to know its bounds upon them in enforcing it. Because they represent the legal will of the community, be it local, provincial or federal, they must be aware of the limitations which the people, through law, have placed upon them. They must recognize the genius of the Canadian system of government which gives to no individual, groups of people, or institutions, absolute power, and they must insure that they, as prime defenders of that system, do not pervert its character."[11]

A police officer who resorts to illegal methods to achieve a "lawful" objective, such as fabricating evidence to convict an innocent person, is liable to the same legal sanctions for their actions that any citizen would be. Should an officer fall short of actually breaking the law but be revealed to have resorted to unethical methods to achieve what they believe is a "moral" purpose, the officer risks not only potentially negative consequences from the legal system, but also possible disciplinary action from their police service and the loss of public confidence.

Public approval requires that the police carry out their duties not only in a lawful fashion, but also in a fair and ethical manner. Even though the penalties for breaking the law are the same, society's expectations that police officers will abide by the law while enforcing it are far higher than societal expectations of behaviour on the part of average citizens.

Public opinion once held the criminal justice system to be infallible. The actions of the police and the findings of criminal courts were implicitly trusted by the public at large (Sher 2002). Public confidence in the police and support for their efforts, however, is never unconditional.

Public support for policing is diminished any time the police are seen to resort to illegal or unfair tactics – regardless of the demands or circumstances of the situation that

---

[10]IACP Code of Conduct (1989) quoted from Bjorkquist p. 248.

[11]IACP Canons of Police Ethics (1957 & 1991) quoted from Bjorkquist p. 245.

prompted the abuse (Schmalleger et al. 2004). With each allegation of abuse of police powers, public confidence in the integrity of the criminal justice system becomes weaker. The result has been unprecedented media and judicial scrutiny of police investigations and investigative practices (Van Allen 2007).

Police service is one of the highest forms of expression of public trust. Society's sense of fair play is offended when police officers – "the good guys" – who are supposed to represent and defend society's moral code, act as if they were somehow above the law themselves. Courts are quick to exclude evidence obtained as the result of flagrant breaches of individual rights if to admit the evidence would bring the administration of justice into disrepute – regardless of the nature or severity of the charge.[12]

1.6 WHERE DO POLICE POWERS ORIGINATE?

The term "peace officer" is defined in section 2 of the *Criminal Code*. This classification, among several elected and appointed positions, includes police officers. While peace officers share a great many powers, for the remainder of this textbook I intend to concentrate primarily on the legal arrest, search, seizure and use of force situations that are generally encountered by police officers.[13]

Police officers derive their legal authorities from a combination of statute law, case law, common law and even municipal bylaws. It is imperative that police officers be intimately familiar with the origins, extent and limitations of their legal authorities in order to stay within the bounds of their powers. Police officers require a clear understanding in order to be able to justify and defend their actions.

Statute Law: Statutes are codified (written) laws that have been enacted by a legislative body such as the Parliament of Canada in Ottawa or the Legislative Assembly of a province, such as Queen's Park in Toronto, Ontario. All statutes must receive **Royal Assent** (approval by the appropriate vice-regal representative, such as the Governor General of Canada or the Lieutenant Governor of a province) prior to coming into force of law. Depending on the jurisdiction of the legislative body that passes the law, the statute will be either a federal or provincial statute.

To summarize, a statute must meet three basic criteria:

1. It must be codified (written).

2. It must have been enacted by a legislative body.

3. It must have received Royal Assent prior to coming into force in law.

Statute law contains offences (prohibited acts or omissions) that are enforced in order to administer the law. Such law is referred to as **substantive law**. Statute law also creates rules which govern legal procedures and are referred to as **adjective law**.

Case Law: Case law is law that has been established by previous court decisions and is based upon the **rule of precedent**. Case law originated in the Middle Ages in England

---

[12]*Charter of Rights and Freedoms*, Being Part I of the *Constitution Act*, 1982, Enacted by the *Canada Act* 1982 (U.K.) c. 11; proclaimed in force April 17, 1982 as amended, c. S.24(2).

[13]*Criminal Code*, R.S. 1985, c. C-46, s. 2.

when travelling judges began recording decisions, which were then circulated to other judges and trial lawyers. These decisions served as the basis in subsequent legal proceedings involving cases of a similar nature.

Case law is a fundamental part of western law as lower courts are bound by the decisions of higher courts. Courts of equal or higher status than the court that issued the decision may and often do take the decisions of lower courts into consideration when adjudicating similar issues, but aren't bound by decisions of lower courts. Throughout this textbook we will examine several case law decisions that have resulted in changes in the way police function in Canada.

Compare the following characteristics of case law and statute law:

1. Case law is published in written form in a variety of case law publications, such as *Canadian Criminal Cases* (*C.C.C.*), *Supreme Court Reports* (*S.C.R.*), *Dominion Law Reports* (*D.L.R.*) and numerous others. Only a portion of court decisions – those which deal with noteworthy issues – are reported in case law publications.

2. Case law originates in the court system and is therefore not enacted by a legislative body.

3. Case law does not receive Royal Assent prior to coming into force in law.

Common Law: Common law refers to unwritten laws which are based upon custom, tradition and practice, rather than originating from court decisions or statute law. Practices such as the legal authority for the search of a person at the time of their arrest (search incident to arrest) have become so entrenched in our legal system that all practitioners of the law know of it and accept its existence as law.

Photo 1.1 - The Supreme Court of Canada may grant leave to appeal decisions in criminal matters. Supreme Court decisions comprise the highest form of case law in Canada and are binding on all courts.

TABLE 1.1	Characteristics of Laws		
	Statute	Case Law	Common Law
Written or Codified	Yes	Reported in case law publications	Unwritten, although frequently referenced in case law decisions
Source	Enacted by a legislative body (such as Parliament or the legislative assembly of a province or territory)	Established by previous court decisions	Based on custom, tradition and practice
Royal Assent	Yes	No	No

[handwritten note: Look at it as precedent. Such as you have the right to defend yourself. Trudeau said "We don't have any right to look in the bedroom" passed on from generation to generation]

Although common law is frequently referenced in case law decisions, it is largely unwritten and is not laid down in written form as statutes or reported case law decisions are. Neither is common law passed or enacted as legislation by any government, nor does it receive Royal Assent. Common law is different from statute law and case law in all of these respects, yet shares the same weight in law. See Table 1.1.

1.7   FEDERAL STATUTES

The majority of our current police powers, including arrest, search, seizure and use of force, originate from federally-enacted statutes that have been passed by the Parliament of Canada and that have received Royal Assent by the Governor General, Her Majesty Queen Elizabeth's representative in Canada. This is, for a large part, on account of the division of legislative responsibilities created by the *Constitution Act* of 1867. The *Constitution Act*, passed in the United Kingdom, created Canada as a Dominion under the British Commonwealth and granted the government of Canada the exclusive right to create **criminal law** to deal with more serious offences. Fortunately, this resulted in a single class of legislation that is in force throughout Canada, rather than each province having its own law respecting criminal matters.[14]

There are literally hundreds of **federal statutes** that deal with various areas of federal responsibility, such as income tax, aeronautics administration, fisheries, international treaties, etc. The more commonly-encountered federal statutes we will be dealing with throughout this textbook include the *Criminal Code*, the *Controlled Drugs and Substances Act*, the *Youth and Criminal Justice Act*, the *Charter of Rights and Freedoms* and the *Canada Evidence Act*.

The *Criminal Code* is only one example of a federal statute. It is codified legislation enacted by the Parliament of Canada that has received Royal Assent. The *Criminal Code* contains many of the police powers that we will examine throughout this textbook. Because it was enacted by the federal government, it is considered criminal law, as is the case with every other federal statute, such as the *Controlled Drugs and*

---

[14]*Constitution Act*, 1867 (formerly the *British North America Act*, 1867), 30 & 31 Victoria, c. 3. s. 91-9.

Photo 1.2 - The Parliament of Canada passes all federal legislation. Federally enacted laws are criminal laws that have force and effect throughout all of Canada.

Substances Act, Income Tax Act, Firearms Act and *Youth Criminal Justice Act*, etc. Also, because they were enacted by the federal government, federal or criminal statutes apply across Canada.

> ***Federally enacted law = criminal statute = nation-wide jurisdiction***

1.8   PROVINCIAL STATUTES

Provincial statutes refer to legislation that has been passed by a legislative assembly, such as in Queen's Park, Toronto and which has received Royal Assent by the Lieutenant Governor, Her Majesty's provincial representative. As with federal legislation, the authority for provinces to pass law relating to less-serious matters, including education, transportation, and minor offences, was created by the *Constitution Act, 1867.*[15]

Although federal legislation takes precedence over provincial legislation, provincial statutes still grant a number of police powers in areas of provincial governance that aren't covered by federal statute. Throughout this textbook, we will examine a number of legal authorities authorizing arrest, apprehension, and search and seizure that are found in provincial statutes in Ontario.

The *Liquor Licence Act* is an example of a provincial statute enacted by the Legislative Assembly of Ontario. The *Liquor Licence Act* (*LLA*) is in written form and also received Royal Assent prior to coming into force in law. Because it was enacted by a

Smoke free Ontario Act

---

[15]*Constitution Act*, 1867, supra, s. 92.

provincial legislature, the *LLA* applies only within the province in which it was enacted. Every province in Canada has some form of equivalent provincial legislation that regulates the sale, possession and consumption of alcohol. Certain provincial statutes, such as the *LLA*, contain powers of arrest, search and seizure for police officers engaged in the enforcement of those statutes.

Provincially enacted law = provincial statute = province-wide jurisdiction

A more in-depth examination of the specific provisions of federal and provincial statutes, as they relate to arrest, use of force, and search and seizure, will be covered in those respective chapters of this textbook.

1.9   WHAT IS AN OFFENCE?

Canadian law includes federal, provincial and municipal (bylaw) legislation. Statute law consists entirely of federal and provincial legislation, as only these forms of enacted laws receive Royal Assent. Laws prescribe acts or omissions (things that a person must do or failure to do something they are required to do) of unlawful or prohibited behaviour that range from the operation of motor vehicles and the possession and consumption of alcohol (regulatory provincial offences) to incidents involving personal violence, property and public order offences (**criminal offences**). Therefore, an **offence** is considered to be any breach or violation of statute law.

Of course, not all infractions of the law come to the attention of law enforcement authorities. For example, if an individual drives a motor vehicle on a highway at an

Photo 1.3 - Provinces are authorized to pass provincial laws in certain matters. Provincial laws are in force only within the province that enacted them. Provincial laws in Ontario are enacted at the Legislative Building, Queen's Park, Toronto.

excessive rate of speed, enforcement action is possible only where the violation of the *Highway Traffic Act* comes to the attention of the police. Offences can become known to the police as the result of being witnessed by a police officer or by being reported to the police by a member of the public.

Where a violation of the law comes to the attention of the police, enforcement action can take the form either of the laying of a charge, if sufficient evidence to support a prosecution exists, or by issuing the offender a warning, if **discretion** is warranted. If, however, a speeding driver successfully avoids coming to the attention of the police, even though an actual offence has occurred, no enforcement action will result. The same lack of enforcement would result for an infraction of a municipal bylaw (e.g., expired parking meter where the operator moves the vehicle before being noticed), or the theft of property that is never reported to the police.

Canadian law contains certain overlaps between federal and provincial legislation. A driver operating a motor vehicle at excessively high speed is liable to penalties prescribed by the *Highway Traffic Act* or its equivalent in any province outside of Ontario. The same individual driving the motor vehicle while his or her ability to operate it is impaired by alcohol or a drug, is liable to penalties prescribed by the *Criminal Code*, reflecting the increased severity of the prohibited behaviour. Because federal (criminal) legislation is in force across Canada, more serious prohibited behaviour, such as impaired driving, is considered to be an offence under a single law that is in force nation-wide.

The powers and authorities for the police to take enforcement action are found within the statutes that create the offences – otherwise, no enforcement action would ever be possible. Statutes may even prescribe situations in which citizens and police officers may arrest individuals to prevent or interfere with a **breach of the peace** – even if an offence has not yet been committed.[16]

1.10   FACTS IN ISSUE

The **facts in issue** of an offence are those essential elements of the specific offence that must be proven to form the basis for a finding of guilt in court. This is referred to as *prima facie* evidence, which establishes sufficient proof that, if not contradicted, will prove one or more facts in issue or could result in a conviction (finding of guilt). In addition to the facts in issue, it is always necessary to prove the following fundamental elements in any offence:

- Identity of the accused
- Date of the alleged offence
- Location of the alleged offence (municipality and judicial district)
- *Mens Rea* [L. = guilty mind, or required degree of criminal intent]
- *Actus Reus* [L. = guilty act, an act prohibited by law]

In proving ***mens rea*** or criminal intent, it should be pointed out that specific offences differ in the degree of intent that is required to be proven. An offence such as speeding requires only the identity of the accused, date and location, plus evidence of the operation

---

[16]*Criminal Code*, S.C. 1985, c. C-46, ss. 27, 27.1, 30, 31.

of a motor vehicle upon a highway at a speed greater than the legally-posted speed limit for there to be a finding of guilt. It need not be proven that the accused intended to speed, making this offence one of absolute liability. If the commission of the offence itself is proven, the accused may be convicted without the necessity of proving that the accused deliberately intended to commit the offence.

Serious criminal offences, such as Unlawfully Causing Bodily Harm (s. 269 *CC*) require that the bodily harm caused to a person be unlawful, (i.e., a deliberate act prohibited by federal or provincial statute). It must be proven that the accused intended to commit a deliberate act which caused an injury, whether or not they intended to cause the bodily harm. The level of intent required to be proven in such cases is referred to as general intent. Before an accused can be convicted of such an offence, it must be proven that the occurrence involved some deliberate action as opposed to an accident the accused did not deliberately intend.

Among others, offences such as Assault [s. 265(1) *CC*], Theft [s. 322(1) *CC*], Possession of Property Obtained by Crime [s. 354(1) *CC*], and Murder [s. 229 *CC*] all require that it be proven that the accused possessed the specific intent to commit the offence charged. These sections will all contain the words or phrases "knowingly" or "with intent", making intent part of the facts in issue that are required to be proven.

Mens rea other than deliberate intention on the part of the accused may be proven through establishing other elements of behaviour such as recklessness, wilful blindness and penal negligence. Recklessness is where the behaviour of the accused is such that they knew or reasonably ought to have known that risk to someone or something would be a likely outcome of their actions. The intentional discharge of a firearm through a wall of an apartment building into an adjoining apartment would be reckless. The accused could not use the defence that he or she did not intend to hurt someone who was struck by their bullet on the other side of the wall.

Wilful blindness occurs when the accused deliberately suppresses a suspicion of risk that might occur as the result of their actions. If you purchase a new stereo, still in the box, out of the back of a van parked in a parking lot of a bar for less than half of the normal retail price, you might not ask any questions about the legality of the property you purchase, if only due to the considerable savings involved. If the circumstances would cause a reasonable person to fear that the stereo might be stolen property, but the accused suppressed that suspicion merely because they didn't want to know, the element of knowingly being in possession of property obtained by crime can be established through their wilful blindness.

Penal negligence involves a marked departure from the standard of care expected of a reasonable person under the circumstances. If a driver of a motor vehicle drives up onto the sidewalk to avoid a traffic jam and travels the length of a city block, sending many pedestrians scurrying out of the way but striking several of them, the driver's negligence would be sufficient evidence of *mens rea*. The driver could be held accountable without having had the specific or deliberate intention to run down or injure the pedestrians.

In proving the ***actus reus,*** it is always necessary to refer to the relevant offence under investigation to determine the individual facts in issue of the section of the statute. Take, for example, the offence of Pointing a Firearm. The facts in issue of this offence include:

- everyone who, without lawful excuse,
- points a firearm (whether loaded or unloaded)
- at another person[17]

These are the facts in issue – the specific facts that must be proven before a person can be convicted of this offence. If any one of the facts in issue is missing, such as, "without lawful excuse", no offence would be committed. A police officer or other individual who points a loaded or unloaded firearm at another person in self-defence is therefore not committing this offence. If the object pointed is anything other than a firearm as defined in section 2 of the *Criminal* Code, another offence might be committed, but not the offence of Pointing a Firearm. If the object the firearm is pointed at is anything other than "another person", again, the offence of Pointing a Firearm will not have been committed. (Van Allen 2007)

1.11   CLASSIFICATION OF OFFENCES

All offences created by criminal legislation (federally enacted laws) fall into one of three classifications (See Figure 1.1):

1. **indictable offences**, (pronounced in-DITE-a-bul)
2. **summary conviction offences**, and
3. **dual procedure offences** – also referred to as **hybrid offences**

Indictable offences include the more serious offences, including thefts, frauds, drug offences, assaults, sexual offences, arsons, manslaughter, murder, etc. Summary conviction offences consist of less serious offences, including causing a disturbance, trespassing at night, towing a water-skier behind a vessel without a lookout or after one hour past sunset, etc. An explanation of dual procedure offences will be covered in section 1.12.1.

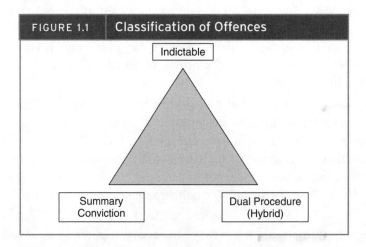

| FIGURE 1.1 | Classification of Offences |

Indictable

Summary Conviction

Dual Procedure (Hybrid)

---

[17]*Criminal Code*, S.C. 1985 c. C-46, s. 87(1).

Some offence sections contain their own punishments. The offence of Trespassing at Night states:

"Every one who, without lawful excuse, the proof of which lies on him, loiters or prowls at night on the property of another person near a dwelling-house situated on that property is guilty of an offence punishable on summary conviction."[18]

Similarly, the offence of Causing Bodily Harm by Criminal Negligence states:

"Every one who by criminal negligence causes bodily harm to another person is guilty of an indictable offence and liable to imprisonment for a term not exceeding ten years."[19]

Certain offences only define the offence but do not contain the punishment for that offence. The penalty for such sections is found in a subsequent (following) penalty (or punishment) section. For example, section 233 of the *Criminal Code* contains the offence of Infanticide, which states:

"A female person commits infanticide when by a wilful act or omission she causes the death of her newly-born child, if at the time of the act or omission she is not fully recovered from the effects of giving birth to the child and by reason thereof or of the effect of lactation consequent on the birth of the child her mind is then disturbed."[20]

Notice that section 233 defines how the offence of infanticide may be committed but does not provide any penalty for this offence. The penalty for Infanticide is found in section 237 of the *Criminal* Code and reads:

"Every female person who commits infanticide is guilty of an indictable offence and liable to imprisonment for a term not exceeding five years."[21]

Therefore, to identify whether a specific offence is classified as indictable, summary conviction or dual procedure, we must examine the offence itself if the section contains its own penalty, or look to its penalty or punishment section if it is located in a different section of the statute.

When an offence is classified as a dual procedure (or hybrid) offence, the penalty section will contain different punishments depending on whether it is proceeded with in court as either an indictable offence or as a summary conviction offence.

For example, the offence of Escaping from Custody states:

"Every one who escapes from lawful custody,... is guilty of an indictable offence and liable to imprisonment for a term not exceeding two years or is guilty of an offence punishable on summary conviction."[22]

Note that section 145(1)(a) contains the definition of the offence, but also contains punishments that provide separate and distinct penalties depending on whether the charge is proceeded with in court as an indictable offence or as a summary conviction offence. It

[18]*Criminal Code*, R.S. 1985, c. C-46, s. 177.

[19]*Criminal Code*, R.S. 1985, c. C-46, s. 221.

[20]*Criminal Code*, R.S. 1985, c. C-46, s. 233.

[21]*Criminal Code*, R.S. 1985, c. C-46, s. 237.

[22]*Criminal Code*, R.S. 1985, c. C-46, s. 237.

is because of this option of proceeding with the charge in either of two methods that it is deemed to be dual procedure or hybrid in nature. An explanation of how, when, why and by whom this decision is made will be discussed in upcoming section 1.12.1.

1.12   DIFFERENCES BETWEEN INDICTABLE AND SUMMARY CONVICTION OFFENCES

To review, we have discussed that indictable offences are the more serious types of criminal offences and that summary conviction offences are the less serious types. We have also seen that dual procedure offences or hybrid offences contain punishments both if the charge is proceeded with by indictment or by summary conviction. Finally, we learned that to identify the classification of an offence, we must look to the penalty provided for that offence, whether it be contained in the definition section or in a following penalty section.

It is important for police officers to understand the differences between indictable, summary conviction and dual procedure offences due to the differences in powers of arrest and release of prisoners from custody (judicial interim release). See Table 1.2.

TABLE 1.2	Differences Between Indictable and Summary Conviction Offences	
	Indictable	Summary Conviction
Level of Court	Begin in lower courts but can be tried in higher courts (*)	Remain in lower courts
Preliminary Hearing	Accused is entitled to a preliminary hearing	No preliminary hearing
Maximum Penalty	Life Imprisonment	$2000 fine or 6 months imprisonment, or both (**)
Statute of Limitations	No limitation period	Six months limitation
Appearance of Accused	Accused must appear in court in person (***)	Accused may appear in court by agent
Powers of Arrest	Reasonable grounds must exist to believe that accused committed the offence	Must find the accused committing the offence to arrest, but may still lay appropriate charge

*   The *Canadian Charter of Rights and Freedoms* guarantees any person charged with an (indictable) offence punishable by a maximum of five years imprisonment or more the option to be tried by a jury. An accused who wishes to be tried by a judge and jury must elect their trial in the Superior Court of Justice.[1]

**   Certain summary conviction offences contain section-specific penalties that provide a term of imprisonment of eighteen months (e.g., Level II assault, Disarming a Peace Officer, Sexual Assault, etc.)[2]

*** The *Criminal Code* provides three exceptions for an accused charged with an indictable offence not appearing personally:

1)   if the accused is a corporation, it may appear by attorney or agent[3]

2)   the accused appears by closed-circuit television or other means of simultaneous visual and oral communication (for portions of proceedings that do not involve the giving of evidence by a witness[4]

3)   the accused may apply to have legal counsel designated as their agent and with the approval of the court, be represented by agent for portions of the proceedings except the giving of evidence by a witness, jury selection or sentencing, etc.[5]

[1] *Canadian Charter of Rights and Freedoms*, Being Part I of the *Constitution Act*, 1982, Enacted by the *Canada Act* 1982, (U.K) c.11 proclaimed in force April 17, 1982, s. 11(f)

[2] *Criminal Code* R.S. 1985, c. C–46 s. 787(1)

[3] *Criminal Code* R.S. 1985, c. C–46 s. 620

[4] *Criminal Code* R.S. 1985, c. C–46 s. 650(1)

[5] *Criminal Code* R.S. 1985, c. C–46 ss. 650.01(1) & (3)

Additional information on the differences between indictable offences and summary conviction criminal offences will be provided in later sections. All provincial offences are classified as summary conviction offences to set limits on maximum penalties. This designation also results in trials for minor offences remaining within the jurisdiction of lower Provincial Offences courts.

1.12.1 Dual Procedure (Hybrid) Offences – Crown Election

Many offences are classified as dual procedure offences. We have seen that dual procedure means that the offence is one that is designated as being either indictable or summary conviction – depending on how it is proceeded with in court. The offence section or the penalty section, where different than the definition section, will prescribe different penalties for trial by indictment or by summary conviction.

Why is it that some offences are purely indictable while others are straight summary conviction and yet others are dual procedure or hybrid (mixed designation)? The simple and easy answer is that indictable offences such as robbery, murder, kidnapping, and arson are deemed the most serious and carry the most severe penalties.

Most indictable offences (except those designated as being the absolute [exclusive] jurisdiction of a provincial division court or the superior division court) allow the accused to elect the court in which they wish to be tried. If the accused elects trial by superior division judge or jury, a preliminary inquiry will usually be held in provincial division court to determine whether there is sufficient evidence to bind the accused over for trial in the higher court.

Conversely, summary conviction criminal offences such as Trespassing at Night, Injuring Animals, and Causing a Disturbance are deemed to be relatively minor compared to indictable offences and carry lower penalties. Summary conviction offences are limited to being tried in the provincial division courts, preventing the accused from electing to be tried in a higher court. This is done so as to keep relatively minor charges within the jurisdiction of the more numerous lower courts and to save the higher courts' caseload for the most serious charges.

Certain offences are designated as dual procedure or hybrid offences in recognition that the circumstances of two similar charges can vary widely in terms of the nature of the criminality involved in the crimes. Two assaults might differ in terms of the injuries suffered by the victim, while two thefts may differ substantially in terms of the amount of property stolen.

Crimes that are otherwise similar in many respects may be analyzed quite differently depending on whether the accused is a first offender or someone with a lengthy list of previous criminal convictions. For these reasons, certain offences are designated as dual procedure (hybrid) to allow for flexibility in prosecuting crimes of differing severity and in dealing with offenders of various levels of criminality.

For police officers, the main distinctions in the classification of offences include the effect on their powers of arrest and the statute of limitations for laying a particular charge. It is necessary for the police officer to witness a summary conviction offence being committed to justify arresting the offender. Indictable offences, on the other hand, require only that the police officer have reasonable grounds to believe that the offence was committed or is about to be committed. These distinctions will be examined more in-depth in future sections dealing with arrest.

When an offence is designated as dual procedure, police officers are to treat the offence as indictable for the purposes of powers of arrest and for statute of limitations. This is to the advantage of the police officer as it allows a suspect to be arrested on reasonable grounds (rather than found committing) and to lay charges for offences that occurred more than six months previously (as opposed to the six month limitation for straight summary conviction offences). It is the prosecutor who will decide how the charge will be dealt with in court at the time of **arraignment** of the accused person.

When an accused charged with a criminal offence appears in court, the charge(s) against them will be read to them, usually by a court clerk. The official reading of the charge to the accused in court is referred to as the arraignment. Prior to the accused being asked to indicate their plea to the charge, if the charge is a dual procedure offence, the court clerk or the judge will ask the Crown Attorney how they elect to proceed on the charge, either by indictment or by summary conviction.

The Crown election is conducted first to allow the accused to appreciate the severity of the possible punishment they are facing before being expected to enter any plea to the charge. An accused might be willing to plead guilty to an offence if they know the maximum punishment they face on summary conviction is a $2 000 fine or six months imprisonment or both. The same accused may plead not guilty and request a trial if they realize that they potentially face a term of several years imprisonment if the Crown elects to proceed by indictment.

If we sat in a courtroom, the actual proceedings would sound something like this:

John Smith answers to his name and stands before the court when his name is called from the docket.

Court: "Are you John Smith?"

Accused: "Yes, I am."

Court: "John Smith stands charged that he, on or about the 10th day of May, 2007, at the City of Orillia in the Central East Region, did unlawfully break and enter a certain place, to wit: a building situated at 800 West Street, with intent to commit an indictable offence contrary to paragraph 348(1)(e) of the Criminal Code of Canada.

Do you understand the charge against you?"

Accused: "Yes, I do."

As the offence of breaking and entering with intent to commit an indictable offence in relation to a building, other than a dwelling house, is a dual procedure (or hybrid) offence, the court must now seek the Crown Attorney's election as to whether or not to proceed on the charge by indictment or by summary conviction.

Court: "How does the Crown elect to proceed in this matter?"

Prosecutor: "By summary conviction, please Your Honour (or Your Worship)."

Summary conviction offences or dual procedure offences, where the Crown elects to proceed by summary conviction, will be tried in Provincial Court and will not have a preliminary hearing. If the offence is an indictable offence that is designated as being the absolute jurisdiction of the Provincial Court under s. 553 of the *Criminal Code*, the trial will still be conducted in the Provincial Court, but the accused will be liable to the greater penalty provided by way of trial by indictment.[23]

---

[23]*Criminal Code*, R.S. 1985, c. C-46, s. 536(1).

Once the accused is aware of the Crown's election, the accused will be asked how they plead to the charge, "Guilty" or "Not guilty". Where the accused does not answer or refuses to enter a plea, the court will enter a plea of "Not guilty" and proceed as if the accused had requested a trial.[24] The only time an accused is allowed to enter a different plea is if they plead "Not guilty" to the offence charged, but guilty to another offence, with the prior consent of the prosecutor.[25]

Court: "Mr. Smith, how do you plead to this charge?"

Accused: "Not Guilty."

In any case where the charge is an indictable offence punishable by five years imprisonment or more, other than an offence listed in s. 469 *Criminal Code* (absolute jurisdiction of Superior Court Judge) or a dual procedure offence where the Crown elects to proceed by indictment, the accused would then be asked in which court they elect to be tried. As the charge against John Smith is neither a s. 469 nor a s. 553 *Criminal Code* offence, had the Crown elected to proceed by way of indictment, the following words would be read to the accused by the judge:

Court: "You have the option to elect to be tried by a judge without a jury and without having had a preliminary inquiry; or you may elect to have a preliminary inquiry and to be tried by a judge without a jury; or you may elect to have a preliminary inquiry and to be tried by a court composed of a judge and jury. If you do not elect now, you shall be deemed to have elected to have a preliminary inquiry and to be tried by a court composed of a judge and jury. How do you elect to be tried?"[26]

Accused: "By judge and jury."

If the accused refuses to elect a court in which to be tried, their trial will be conducted by a superior court composed of a judge and jury.[27] Dual procedure offences recognize that it is in the public interest that certain offences be tried in different courts and be subject to different punishments, depending on the circumstances of the facts of the crime and the nature of the accused.

1.13   *CANADIAN CHARTER OF RIGHTS AND FREEDOMS*

The *Constitution Act, 1982* which contains the *Canadian Charter of Rights and Freedoms*[28] "is the supreme law of Canada, and any law that is inconsistent with the provisions of the *Constitution* is, to the extent of the inconsistency of no force or effect."[29] The *Charter of Rights and Freedoms* is a fundamental part of the supreme law of Canada, and contains

---

[24]*Criminal Code*, R.S. 1985, c. C-46, s. 606(2).

[25]*Criminal Code*, R.S. 1985, c. C-46, s. 606(4).

[26]*Criminal Code*, R.S. 1985, c. C-46, s. 536(2).

[27]*Criminal Code*, R.S. 1985, c. C-46, s. 471.

[28]*Canadian Charter of Rights and Freedoms*, Being Part I of the *Constitution Act*, 1982, Enacted by the *Canada Act* 1982, (U.K.) c.11, proclaimed in force April 17, 1982.

[29]Ibid, Part VII General, s. 52(1).

several rights that are guaranteed to all individuals in Canada and that "guide the relationship between individuals and the state, and between various parts of the state." [30]

Police officers are considered to be agents of the state for the purpose of enforcing the law and there are many instances during the day-to-day investigation and prevention of crimes where the actions of the police often conflict with the rights of individuals. It is vital for police officers to have at least a basic understanding of the rights guaranteed to individuals under the *Charter of Rights and Freedoms* and how the exercise of police powers can impact on individual rights.

Many of the rights contained in the *Charter*, while vital to our everyday quality of Canadian life, generally have little impact on law enforcement, such as the right to equality before the law and the freedoms of religion, expression and association, etc. We will confine our examination of the *Charter* to those specific areas which have the greatest influence on policing and court proceedings.

Section 7 of the *Charter* states, "Everyone has the right to life, liberty and security of the person and the right not to be deprived thereof except in accordance with the principles of fundamental justice."

Among other things, section 7 protects an individual's right to remain silent when interrogated by the police. If the police use trickery by using an undercover police officer or an **agent provocateur** to elicit a statement from a detained prisoner after he or she had indicated they did not wish to make a statement, the suspect's section 7 rights would be violated.[31] The right to remain silent guaranteed by section 7 does not apply to suspects who are not under arrest.[32]

Another example of a right guaranteed by section 7 would be that of an individual to make full answer and defence to any charges against him or her. If the police or the prosecution were to intentionally fail to disclose evidence in their possession that might tend to prove the innocence of the accused, the accused's right to make full answer and defence would be violated by hiding the evidence from the defence.

Section 8 of the *Charter* states, "Everyone has the right to be secure against unreasonable search or seizure."

This guaranteed right protects everyone's reasonable expectation of privacy against police evidence gathering techniques that range from searches for property and information with and without a search warrant, seizure of biological samples, interception of private communications, etc. "The purpose in this section of protecting individuals from unjustified state intrusions upon their privacy requires a means of preventing unjustified searches before they happen, not simply of determining, after the fact, whether they ought to have occurred in the first place... Accordingly, where it is feasible to obtain prior authorization such authorization is a pre-condition for a valid search and seizure."[33] More will be covered on section 8 in later sections dealing with search and seizure authorities.

Section 9 of the *Charter* states, "Everyone has the right not to be arbitrarily detained or imprisoned."

---

[30]Quoted from McKenna (2002) at p. 3.

[31]R. v. Hebert, [1990] 2 S.C.R. 151, 57 C.C.C. (3d) 1, 77 C.R. (3d) 145, and R. v. Broyles, [1991] 3 S.C.R. 595, 68 C.C.C. (3d) 308, [1992] 1 W.W.R. 289 (7:0).

[32]R. v. Hicks, [1990] 1 S.C.R. 120, 54 C.C.C. (3d) 575, 73 C.R. (3d) 204 (7:0) affg 42 C.C.C. (3d) 394, 64 C.R. (3d) 68 (Ont. C.A.).

[33]Hunter v. Southam Inc., [1984] 2 S.C.R. 145, 14 C.C.C. (3d) 97, 11 D.L.R. (4th) 641, quoted from 2006 Martin's Annual Criminal Code at p. CH/23.

In our free and democratic society, we prize the freedom to not have our liberty taken away from us without a just and sufficient cause. When an individual who is under investigation is being questioned by the police, in or outside of a police station, the issue arises of whether or not they are being detained. If detention is found to exist, at what point does the detention commence and is it a lawful detention or an arbitrary detention that could violate the rights of the individual?

If a person who is in police custody has an honest belief that they were not free to leave, they may believe that they were being detained, whether or not they had been lawfully arrested. A police officer does have limited rights to detain an individual for investigative purposes where an objective reasonable suspicion exists that links the person detained to the criminal activity being investigated.[34] These issues and more will be dealt with at greater length in later sections dealing with police officers' powers of arrest.

Section 10 of the *Charter* states, "Everyone has the right on arrest or detention

(a) to be informed promptly of the reasons therefore;

(b) to retain and instruct counsel without delay and to be informed of that right; and

(c) to have the validity of the detention determined by way of habeas corpus and to be released if the detention is not lawful."

This section guarantees four separate rights that are all related to arrest or detention. Section 10(a) of the *Charter* applies to individuals who have been lawfully arrested and those individuals not under arrest who are physically constrained by the police to the point that their liberty has been taken from them. Individuals in either situation have the right to be informed as to the specific reasons for their arrest or detention.

For example, someone arrested for driving on a highway while intoxicated by alcohol has the right to be informed that they are under arrest either for driving a motor vehicle while their ability to operate the vehicle is impaired by alcohol or having the care or control of a motor vehicle while impaired by alcohol.[35]

Section 10(b) of the *Charter* contains two guarantees for every detained or arrested individual. First, persons under arrest or detention are guaranteed the right to retain and instruct (speak with – consult) legal counsel. Second, the individual under arrest has the right to be informed (by the police) that they have the right to retain and instruct counsel. While this second right may appear to be redundant in light of the actual right to retain and instruct counsel, this is the only guaranteed right of which the individual must be informed by the police.

An individual does not have the right to be informed that they are guaranteed freedom against unreasonable search or seizure or to be free from arbitrary detention or imprisonment. Persons who find themselves suddenly and, in most cases unexpectedly, in police custody have a most urgent need to avail themselves of the advice of a lawyer – if they choose to do so. More will be said on this issue in later sections dealing with arrest.

The final right guaranteed by section 10(c) of the *Charter* is referred to as a right to **habeas corpus** (L. = you have the body). *Habeas corpus* provides a mechanism by which a prisoner, or someone on their behalf, can challenge the lawfulness of their

---

[34]R. v. Mann, [2004] 3 S.C.R. 59, 185 C.C.C. (3d) 308, 21 C.R. (6th) 1.

[35]*Criminal Code*, R.S. 1985 c. C-46, s. 253(a).

detention. A writ of *habeas corpus* issued by a judge requires the keeper of a prisoner to produce the prisoner to appear before the court for a hearing to determine the legality of the detention or whether the prisoner should be released.

Section 11 of the *Charter* states, "Any person charged with an offence has the right

(a)   to be informed without unreasonable delay of the specific offence;

(b)   to be tried within a reasonable time;

(c)   not to be compelled to be a witness in proceedings against that person in respect of the offence;

(d)   to be presumed innocent until proven guilty according to law in a fair and public hearing by an independent and impartial tribunal;

(e)   not to be denied reasonable bail without just cause;

(f)   except in the case of an offence under military law tried before a military tribunal, to the benefit of trial by jury where the maximum punishment for the offence is imprisonment for five years or a more severe punishment;

(g)   not to be found guilty on account of any act or omission unless, at the time of the act or omission, it constituted an offence under Canadian or international law or was criminal according to the general principles of law recognized by the community of nations;

(h)   if finally acquitted of the offence, not to be tried for it again and, if finally found guilty and punished for the offence, not to be tried or punished for it again; and

(i)   if found guilty of the offence and if the punishment for the offence has been varied between the time of the commission and the time of sentencing, to the benefit of the lesser punishment."

Section 11 contains no fewer than nine separate rights dealing with notification of charges against the accused, and trial procedures and sentencing. The rights guaranteed by this section include the right to be informed of the precise basis of any charges against the accused, to entitle him or her to make full answer and defence to those charges.[36]

Also guaranteed is the right to trial without unjust delay[37] and the irrebuttable presumption of innocence until the accused is proven guilty beyond a reasonable doubt. Section 11 also guarantees the right to opt for a jury trial for indictable offences punishable by five years imprisonment or more,[38] the right not to be tried twice for the same offence[39] and the right to receive the lowest punishment for an offence if the prescribed punishment was varied between the crime and sentencing for the offence.[40]

Section 12 of the *Charter* states, "Everyone has the right not to be subjected to any cruel and unusual treatment or punishment."

---

[36]R. v. Lucas, (1983), 6 C.C.C. (3d) 147, 150 D.L.R. (3d) 118, 21 M.V.R. 293 (C.A.).

[37]R. v. Askov, [1990] 2 S.C.R. 1199, 59 C.C.C. (3d) 449, 79 C.R. (3d) 273.

[38]R. v. Turpin, [1989] 1 S.C.R. 1296, 48 C.C.C. (3d) 8, 69 C.R. (3d) 97.

[39]R. v. Shubley, [1990] 1 S.C.R. 3, 52 C.C.C. (3d) 481, 74 C.R. (3d) 1.

[40]R. v. Dunn, [1995] 1 S.C.R. 226, 95 C.C.C. (3d) 289, 35 C.R. (4th) 247.

This purpose of this section of the *Charter* is to ensure that any punishment to which an accused person is sentenced in court is both proportional to (appropriate to) the offence and in accordance with recognized sentencing principles.[41]

Section 13 of the *Charter* states, "A witness who testifies in any proceedings has the right not to have any incriminating evidence so given used to incriminate that witness in any other proceedings, except in a prosecution for perjury or for the giving of contradictory evidence."

Section 13 is intended to prevent testimony given by a witness at any prior trial being used to incriminate them in any subsequent judicial proceedings. An accused may be cross-examined to challenge the credibility of the witness if it contradicts later testimony by the same witness. The testimony cannot be used to prove their guilt, but can be used only to demonstrate that their present testimony contradicts something they testified to previously. This section does not protect an accused from being incriminated for perjury by testimony which was knowingly false when given under oath by as witness.

We will fully examine the issues of how individuals challenge evidence that violates their *Charter* rights and how the admissibility of evidence obtained as the result of *Charter* violations is affected in Chapter 10.

SUMMARY

- Peace officers possess extraordinary powers of arrest, use of force and search and seizure that are entrusted to no other professions within our society.

- Police officers are publicly and judicially accountable for their use of powers and may be subject to criminal liability or civil liability for any damage, loss or injury that results from an abuse of their mandated powers.

- Police officers must rely on the provisions of statute and common law for their law enforcement powers and must be aware of the source, scope and limitations of each.

- The responsible use of police powers also requires that they must be exercised in an ethical manner. All individuals must be treated equally and fairly before the law. The police themselves should never be seen to be acting above the law while executing their duties.

- The facts in issue of an offence are those essential elements of the specific offence that must be proven to form the basis for a finding of guilt in court.

- To determine whether a specific offence is classified as indictable, summary conviction or dual procedure, we must look to the offence itself if the section contains its own penalty, or look to its penalty or punishment section if it is located in a different section than the definition section.

- It is vital for police officers to have at least a basic understanding of the rights guaranteed to individuals by the *Charter of Rights and Freedoms* and of how the exercise of police powers can conflict with individual rights.

---

[41]R. v. Smith, [1987] 1 S.C.R. 1045, 34 C.C.C. (3d) 97, 58 C.R. (3d) 193.

DISCUSSION QUESTIONS

1. What factors might be involved in an otherwise lawful arrest by a police officer that could constitute an unethical use of police powers?

2. Police officers derive many of their powers from statute law. What are the three criteria of a statute? How do these criteria differ from other sources of law?

3. What are the three classifications of criminal offences? What are the main differences between them as they affect police powers? How do you determine the correct classification of a criminal offence?

WEBLINKS

www.canlii.org

Canadian Legal Information Institute website. Searchable case law database and links to provincial and federal statutes and regulations, courts, appeal courts and various tribunals, boards and committees.

www.lexum.umontreal.ca/index_en.html

University of Montreal, Faculty of Law website. Searchable Supreme Court of Canada decision database, with links to federal and provincial legislation, periodicals and law libraries. Site features a wide variety of national and international legal resources.

http://www.e-laws.gov.on.ca/index.html

Government of Ontario. Provincial statutes and associated regulations

http://laws.justice.gc.ca/en/index.html

Department of Justice, Government of Canada. Selected federal statutes and links to sites of case law databanks.

Chapter 2

Police Services Act, R.S.O. 1990, c. P-15

"Civilian oversight ensures that public servants are accountable to the public. Civilian oversight ensures that the balance between human rights and national security, endorsed by Parliament and enshrined in legislation, is respected... Because prevention, not prosecution, is the new watchword."[1]

Shirley Heafey, Former Chair Commission for Public Complaints Against the RCMP,
Speech delivered to the University of Ottawa, Faculty of Law, October 17, 2003.

Learning Outcomes

After reading this chapter, students should be able to:

- Explain the rationale for civilian governance and oversight of police services.
- Describe the various duties and responsibilities of respective civilian agencies that provide oversight of police services.
- Summarize the basic principles and core responsibilities of providing adequate and effective policing services in Ontario, as set out in the *Police Services Act*.
- Describe the limitations on activities with respect to involvement in political activities and secondary full-time and part-time employment.
- Distinguish between the offences of Discreditable Conduct and Neglect of Duty as part of the Code of Offences for which a police officer may be disciplined.

2.1 INTRODUCTION

Every democracy that is governed by the rule of law must provide adequate and effective law enforcement services for the protection and security of all persons within that society. In addition to being adequate and effective, the provision of policing services must be conducted fairly and in a manner that is both open and accountable to the public.

Because societies create laws which authorize the existence and set out responsibilities of police organizations, such law enforcement agencies are ultimately accountable to the members of the society that appoint them.

---

[1]Quoted from: www.cpc-cpp.gc.ca/DefaultSite/Archive/index_e.aspx?articleid=474.

The Ontario *Police Services Act* (*PSA*) is a provincial statute that is made up of nine parts, including:

Part I	– Responsibility for Police Services
Part II	– Ontario Civilian Commission on Police Services
Part III	– Municipal Police Services Boards
Part IV	– Police Officers and Other Police Staff
Part V	– Complaints
Part VI	– Repealed (1997)
Part VII	– Special Investigations
Part VIII	– Labour Relations
Part IX	– Regulations and Miscellaneous
Part X	– Court Security[2]

The *PSA* contains the legislative authorities for the creation, administration and oversight of police services, including the responsibilities of such agencies and of individual police officers, and even rules governing their conduct.

2.2   CIVILIAN GOVERNANCE AND OVERSIGHT

In every civil society, civilian governance or control over the policing function is viewed as essential to ensure that policing services are provided in accordance with that society's expectations. Civilian governance also safeguards against potential abuses of the powers with which police agencies are invested.

The terms "governance" and "oversight" are often used interchangeably in the context of the relationship between society and the police. While there is, of necessity, an overlap between governance and oversight, there are some perhaps not-so-subtle differences. Governance implies the exercise of authority or control, while oversight sometimes involves only a lesser degree of supervision or management.

By definition, civilian governance of policing cannot be accomplished without oversight, while the converse of that statement is not always true. Nor does all civilian oversight and governance involve the exercise of authority or control over every possible aspect of a police agency.

Civilian oversight is intended to provide a framework of checks and balances within which police services operate that is consistent with the overall values of society. Civilian governance has a responsibility in broad matters of policy and procedure without interfering with the traditional responsibility of the police to direct day-to-day operational activities. (McKenna 2003)

Professor Kent Roach of the Faculty of Law, University of Toronto, and an advisory committee member to the Ipperwash Inquiry into the killing of Dudley George, states the following in his paper, entitled "Four Models of Government/Police Relationships": "[T]he idea that the police are directed by the government of the day raises concerns about improper partisan concerns influencing or appearing to influence the machinery of justice. There is a need to respect and balance both principles of independence and

---

[2]*Police Services Act*, R.S.O. 1990, c. P-15.

accountability and to do so in a manner that advances our aspirations to be a democratic nation that is governed by law."[3]

The necessary balance between the principles of independence and accountability referred to by Professor Roach has to do with "...the often-difficult distinction between policy matters that fall within the responsibility of the [Police Services] board, and of operational matters which fall within the responsibility of the [C]hief of police."[4]

Maintaining a distinction between civilian oversight and operational **constabulary independence** of the police strikes a necessary balance between the need to establish accountability and to prevent any political group from controlling or interfering with the police in order to further their own self-interests. "...specific police operations are not subject to Cabinet-level direction"[5]

Both terms, "governance" and "oversight", refer primarily to the accountability of police agencies to civilian bodies and agencies to ensure police conduct that is in accordance with legislation, policy matters and societal expectations.

As with the duties and responsibilities of police officers, the duties and responsibilities of Ontario civilian oversight agencies are also laid out in the *PSA*.

2.2.1   Ministry of Community Safety and Correctional Services

The **Ministry of Community Safety and Correctional Services** (formerly the Solicitor General) is responsible for the overall governance of Ontario's police services. The ministry advises and audits Ontario municipal police services and the OPP to ensure that adequate and effective services are provided and minimum policing standards are maintained.[6]

The **Community Safety Division** ([CSD], formerly known as **Policing Services Division**) of the Ministry is responsible for the ongoing provision of certain training, both *ad hoc* and through the Ontario Police College (OPC) Aylmer. Staff from the various sections of this division work with police services and stakeholder agencies to develop professional standards and policies. Systematic inspections of police services are conducted and advisory support is also available. Additionally, members of CSD collaborate with police services to develop community safety and crime prevention initiatives.

2.2.2   Ontario Civilian Commission on Police Services

The **Ontario Civilian Commission on Police Services** (OCCPS) is an independent quasi-judicial civilian agency that operates under the Ministry of Community Safety and Correctional Services with a mandate to investigate matters related to the provision of policing services. Any police officer found guilty of an offence under the *PSA* Code of

---

[3]Report on the Police Complaints System in Ontario (2005) The Honourable Patrick J. Lesage, Q.C. quoted from: www.attorneygeneral.jus.gov.on.ca/english/about/pubs/LeSage/ at p.7.

[4]Ibid, at p.53.

[5]Ibid, at p.6.

[6]*Police Services Act*, R.S.O. 1990 c. P-15, s. 3(2).

Photo 2.1 - The Ministry of Community Safety and Correctional Services provides overall goverance of Ontario police services, ensuring that adequate and effective services are provided and minimum policing standards are maintained.

Conduct by a police disciplinary tribunal may appeal the disciplinary hearing decision to OCCPS The commission also provides oversight to municipal police services boards.[7]

OCCPS has the statutory authority under Part II of the *PSA* to investigate and hold hearings into allegations that a municipal police service or police services board repeatedly fails to provide prescribed standards of policing. OCCPS may, in extreme circumstances, convene hearings to suspend a Chief of Police or member(s) of the police services board, either with or without pay, remove such person from office for reasons of misconduct, or to even disband a police service.[8]

As a regulatory (non-criminal) lay tribunal (non-judicial), decisions of OCCPS are subject to appeal to the Ontario Court of Justice (Superior Division). Ultimately, Chiefs of police, members of police services and police services boards themselves are accountable to the public through OCCPS.

2.2.3 Police Services Boards

Every municipality and regional municipality that maintains a police service is required under Part III of the *PSA* to have a **police services board** to provide oversight and general management and to develop policy for the police service.[9] The composition of the board depends on the population of the community, with smaller communities having

---

[7]*Police Services Act*, R.S.O. 1990 c. P-15, s. 22(1).

[8]*Police Services Act*, R.S.O. 1990 c. P-15, s. 23(1).

[9]*Police Services Act*, R.S.O. 1990, c. P-15. s. 27(1).

TABLE 2.1	Composition of Police Services Boards	
Population	Number of Members	Composition
< 25 000	3	the head of the municipal council, or another member of the council appointed by council resolution; one person appointed by council resolution who is neither a member of the council nor an employee of the municipality; and one person appointed by the Lieutenant Governor in Council
< 25 000	5 (may be increased by council resolution under the authority of s. 22(6) *Police Services* Act R.S.O. 1990, c. P-15)	as above, plus a member of council appointed by council resolution; and a second person appointed by the Lieutenant Governor in Council
+ 25 000	5	the head of the municipal council or another member of the council appointed by council resolution; one member of council appointed by council resolution; one person appointed by resolution of the council who is neither a member of the council nor an employee of the municipality; and two persons appointed by the Lieutenant Governor in Council
+ 300 000	7 (municipal council may apply to the Lieutenant Governor in Council for approval to increase size of board from five to seven members)	the head of the municipal council, or another member of the council appointed by resolution of the council; two members of the council appointed by resolution of the council; one person appointed by resolution of the council who is neither a member of the council nor an employee of the municipality; and three persons appointed by the Lieutenant Governor in Council

a population of 25 000 or less being required to have a minimum of three members.[10] The council of a municipality of less than 25 000 may, however, decide to increase that number to five members by passing a council resolution. See Table 2.1.

Communities having a population of 25 000 or more people are required to maintain a police services board of no less than five members.[11] Municipalities having a population in excess of 300 000 may apply to the Lieutenant Governor in Council to increase the size of their police services board from five to seven members.[12]

---

[10]*Police Services Act*, R.S.O. 1990, c. P-15, s. 27(4).

[11]*Police Services Act*, R.S.O. 1990, c. P-15, s. 27(5).

[12]*Police Services Act*, R.S.O. 1990, c. P-15, s. 27(9).

In addition to establishing policies for the effective management of the police service, municipal police services boards appoint all members of the police service, up to and including the Chief of Police. A police services board is further responsible for monitoring the Chief's work performance. Police services boards also establish guidelines for and review of the administration of public complaints and applications by police officers for secondary employment.

Police services boards are forbidden to direct the Chief of Police on specific operational decisions or with respect to the day-to-day operations of the police service. While a police services board may issue direction to a Chief of Police, no individual member of a board is permitted to give orders or direction to any member of a police service.[13]

In further recognition of the need to maintain a division of responsibility in the administration of justice and police oversight, the *PSA* prohibits serving judges, justices of the peace, police officers and persons who practice criminal law as defence counsel from membership on a police services board.[14]

2.2.4   Special Investigations Unit (SIU)

The **Special Investigations Unit** (SIU) is a civilian law enforcement agency that reports to the Ontario Ministry of the Attorney General. The Director of SIU, who may not be a former police officer, is authorized under Part VII of the *PSA* to authorize criminal investigations into circumstances of incidents involving police and civilians that have resulted in serious injury, including sexual assault, or death to members of the public.[15]

Most, if not all SIU investigators are former police officers who conduct investigations utilizing methods similar methods to those police investigators use while investigating personal injury occurrences. Current police officers may not be SIU investigators and former police officers are prohibited from investigating cases involving members of their former police service.[16] SIU members are peace officers[17] and lay charges in cases where reasonable grounds exist to believe criminal wrong-doing on the part of the police.

Incidents involving injury or death to the public resulting from police actions were formerly investigated by the involved police service; however, in an effort to enhance public confidence in the investigative integrity of such cases, the SIU was created in 1990 to independently conduct investigations into incidents that result in physical harm to the public.

It is the responsibility of the involved police service to report any incidents of death or serious injury to the public to the SIU that may reasonably fall within their mandate. Once notified, the SIU becomes the lead agency involved and has priority over any police agency even though the involved police service conducts a parallel investigation into the incident. The scene of an incident falling within the jurisdiction of the SIU and any physical evidence must be secured by the involved police agency in accordance with their established policies and procedures until the arrival of SIU investigators.[18]

---

[13]*Police Services Act*, R.S.O. 1990, c. P-15, s. 31(1)-(4).

[14]*Police Services Act*, R.S.O. 1990, c. P-15, s. 27(13).

[15]*Police Services Act*, R.S.O. 1990, c. P-15, s. 113(1).

[16]Ibid, s. 113(6).

[17]Ibid, s. 113(4).

[18]*Police Services Act*, O. Reg 673/98, s. 3-5.

Police officers involved in SIU criteria cases are either designated as **subject officers** or **witness officers**. Subject officer means a police officer whose conduct appears, in the opinion of the SIU director, to have caused the death or serious injury of a member of the public, which is under investigation by the SIU.

Witness officer means a police officer who, in the opinion of the SIU director, is involved in an incident under investigation but is not a subject officer.[19] Any time that a police officer's status is changed from subject officer to witness officer or vice-versa, the SIU is required to notifiy the Chief of Police in writing of such a change in status.[20]

Subject officers are required to complete full investigative notes regarding any incident they are involved with in accordance with their duty, but no member of the police force shall provide copies of the notes of the subject officer at the request of the SIU.[21] Any SIU request for officer's notes must clearly specify, at the time of the request, whether the officer is deemed to be a subject officer or a witness officer.

Witness officers are subject to being interviewed by SIU investigators and must provide copies of their investigative notes to the Chief of Police within 24 hours following

Photo 2.2 - S.I.U. investigators examine the scene of a traffic collision involving injuries to a member of the public which occurred during a police action.

[19] Ibid, s. 1(1).

[20] Ibid, s. 10(2).

[21] Ibid, s. 9(3).

the request unless there are appropriate grounds for delay or unless the time limit is extended by the SIU.[22]

Police officers involved in an SIU case are not to discuss the case with other police officers until the SIU has completed its interviews. Unless it would cause undue delay to an SIU investigation, every police officer is entitled to consult with legal counsel or a representative of their police association and to have legal counsel or a representative of the association present during his or her interview with the SIU.[23]

2.3   *PSA* BASIC PRINCIPLES

Section 1 of the *PSA* establishes the central principles by which all Ontario police services are expected to provide policing:

> "Police services shall be provided throughout Ontario in accordance with the following principles:
>
> 1. The need to ensure the safety and security of all persons and property in Ontario.
> 2. The importance of safeguarding the fundamental rights guaranteed by the *Canadian Charter of Rights and Freedoms* and the *Human Rights Code*.
> 3. The need for co-operation between the providers of police services and the communities they serve.
> 4. The importance of respect for victims of crime and understanding of their needs.
> 5. The need for sensitivity to the pluralistic, multiracial and multicultural character of Ontario society.
> 6. The need to ensure that police forces are representative of the communities they serve."[24]

The first principle embodies the philosophy of preservation of life. Police are charged with the responsibility for protecting citizens from physical harm and for protecting personal property. This basic requirement underscores the law enforcement responsibilities of the police to prevent crime and to investigate offences, as well as apprehend and prosecute offenders.

The second principle refers to the duty of the police to respect and protect individual rights as guaranteed to every person under the *Charter of Rights and Freedoms* and the *Human Rights Code*. This duty applies equally to persons regardless of the capacity of their involvement with the police, (e.g., victim, witness, bystander, suspect or accused) or their citizenship.

Principle number three recognizes the obvious need to maintain a close working relationship between the police and the community. The involvement of the civilian community extends beyond the participation of civilians on police services boards and OCCPS. "Police outreach and involvement with schools, businesses, and other community groups is encouraged by the Act and its regulations to enhance public safety, co-operation and citizen involvement." (Walma & West 2002)

---

[22]Ibid, s. 8(1).

[23]Ibid, s. 6-7.

[24]*Police Services Act*, R.S.O. 1990, c. P-15, s. 1.

Photo 2.3 - OPP Constable Kara Huffman pays a scheduled visit to Schreiber-Terrace Bay Public School to familiarize elementary students with the role of police officers in their community.

When Sir Robert Peel proposed the Metropolitan Police Act resulting in the creation of the police force in the City of London, England in 1829, he did so with the recognition that "[T]he power of the police to fulfill their functions and duties is dependent on public approval of their existence, actions and behaviour and on their ability to secure and maintain public interest." In fact, Peel's most enduring and widely-quoted assertion established that "the police are the public and the public are the police".[25]

The fourth basic principle reflects the spirit of Ontario's *Victims' Bill of Rights*[26] and society's recognition of the role of the victim in the investigation and prosecution of criminal offences. The *Victims' Bill of Rights* encourages Ontario police services to keep victims of crime informed at all stages of the investigation and prosecution, as well as to provide for their safety and security.

The act also provides for civil remedies for victims and the creation of the Victim Justice Fund, which is used to pay the cost of victims' programs. While the *Police Services Act* is reflective of the nature and intent of the *Victims' Bill of Rights*, regrettably, neither the *PSA* nor the *Victims' Bill of Rights* provide for any sanctions against any police officer or their police service for failing to comply with the recommended guidelines set out in the acts.

The fifth basic principle set out in Section 1 of the *PSA* reflects the need to respect the beliefs and practices of various cultures. The need for cultural sensitivity is just as important in rural and remote areas of Ontario as it is in large urban centres and the need for cultural sensitivity will continue to grow with the ever-changing demographics of our province.

[25]Peel's Principles of Policing quoted from www.edmontonpolicecommission.com Accessed: Sept 15, 2006.

[26]*Victims' Bill of Rights*, S.O. 1995, c. C-6.

According to 2001 census statistics, Ontario's nearly 11.3 million people are made up of approximately 19.4% of people who are members of visible minority groups.[27] Add to that number the difference in religions and it is clear that the population of Ontario comprises a wide variety of peoples from a range of backgrounds and values. No one culture holds the balance of power in a pluralistic civil society and every culture is free to practice their beliefs as long as those practices do not interfere with the rule of law or with the individual rights of others. (Bjorkquist 2002)

The sixth basic principle asserts "[T]he need to ensure that police forces are representative of the communities they serve." If, as Sir Robert Peel said, "The police are the people and the people are the police," a police service should, at least theoretically, mirror the cultural diversity of society as a whole. Most police services utilize affirmative action programs that are intended to recruit members of identified target groups of visible minorities, women and persons of First Nations ancestry.

While target figures evidently remain somewhat elusive, the intended purpose of affirmative action is to assimilate members of the target groups into policing to broaden and allow police services to become more representative of the community. The provision of policing services, in accordance with the expectations of the community at large, can best result when the values and beliefs of the police service are matched to those of the community it serves.

2.4   CORE POLICE SERVICES

In addition to the basic principles set out in Section 1 of the *PSA*, the act further states that every municipal police service must provide the following standardized minimum core police services to be considered adequate and effective:

"1. Crime prevention

2. Law enforcement

3. Assistance to victims of crime

4. Public order maintenance

5. Emergency response"[28]

Ontario Regulation 3/99 sets out in greater detail the level of services that every police service must provide to be considered adequate and effective. The regulation also requires that members of a police service who are designated to provide specialized services, such as criminal investigation, have adequate training to conduct the duties to which they are assigned.

The Adequacy and Effectiveness Regulation requires every Chief of Police to establish procedures and processes for his or her police service in specialized key areas, including:

- 24-hour supervision,

- criminal investigation,

- multiple officer calls for assistance,

---

[27] 2001 Community Profile Quoted from: www.12statcan.ca Accessed: September 15, 2006.

[28] *Police Services Act*, R.S.O. 1990, c. P-15, s. 4(2).

- patrol procedures,

- access and utilization of investigative support services,

- policing services in respect of navigable bodies of water within their respective community,

- victims' assistance,

- public order units,

- preliminary perimeter control and containment,

- ground searches, and

- counter-terrorism.

The Adequacy and Effectiveness Regulation recognizes the burden that maintaining highly specialized services imposes on medium-sized and small police services. The regulation allows police services, in specified instances, to contract the services of another police service or to provide certain services on a combined or regional or other co-operatively owned basis. Services which may be provided by way of alternative arrangement include such functions as:

- 24-hour communications dispatching,

- crime and public order analysis,

- criminal intelligence,

- investigative support,
  (e.g., forensic identification, breath analysis, technical collision investigation, surveillance, canine tracking, etc.),

- criminal investigation and

- emergency response services[29]

A copy of the Adequacy and Effectiveness Regulation (O. Reg. 3/99) may be viewed, or downloaded, free of charge, at the Government of Ontario Consolidated Law website at www.e-laws.gov.on.ca.

- select "Search or Browse Current Consolidated Law"

- select "Statutes and Associated Regulations",

- select the letter "P" from the alphabetized list,

- scroll to "*Police Services Act*, R.S.O. 1990 c. P-15"

- click on the + symbol in the left margin to access associated regulations

- select "Adequacy and Effectiveness of Police Services O. Reg. 3/99"

2.5   RESPONSIBILITIES OF THE OPP

The Government of Ontario created the Ontario Provincial Police Force (OPP) by order-in-council on October 13, 1909. At the time of its inception, the OPP comprised only fifty-one uniformed members, but it has since grown to an organization of approximately

---

[29] O. Reg.3/99, s. 7.

5 500 uniformed members, 800 auxiliary members and 1 800 civilian employees. The OPP provides policing services to 400 communities across Ontario through 79 detachments and 87 satellite offices.[30]

The *Police Services Act* sets out the responsibilities of the OPP as follows:

"1. Providing police services in respect of the parts of Ontario that do not have municipal police forces other than municipal law enforcement officers.

2. Providing police services in respect of all navigable bodies and courses of water in Ontario, except those that lie within municipalities designated by the Solicitor General.

3. Maintaining a traffic patrol on the King's Highway, except the parts designated by the Solicitor General.

4. Maintaining a traffic patrol on the connecting links within the meaning of section 21 of the *Public Transportation and Highway Improvement Act* that are designated by the Solicitor General.

5. Maintaining investigative services to assist municipal police forces on the Solicitor General's direction or at the Crown Attorney's request."[31]

Specialized investigative services that are maintained by the OPP and are available to other police services, upon request, include criminal investigation, drug enforcement, surveillance, anti-rackets (fraud), intelligence, forensic identification, emergency response units and behavioural sciences. The OPP also houses various provincial services, staffed by OPP officers and seconded municipal police officers, including the Violent Crime Linkage Analysis System (ViCLAS), Ontario's Sex Offender Registry, Project "P" (specializing in child pornography) and the Special Squad (relating to investigations of outlaw motorcycle gangs).

The Chief Coroner for the province of Ontario may request that the Criminal Investigation Branch (CIB) of the OPP provide investigative assistance to a coroner in an investigation or inquest, in any case he or she considers appropriate.[32]

2.6 DUTIES OF POLICE OFFICERS

"I solemnly swear (or affirm) that I will be loyal to Her Majesty the Queen and to C that I will uphold the Constitution of Canada and that I will, to the best of my ability, preserve the peace, prevent offences and discharge my other duties as (insert name of office) faithfully, impartially and according to law. So help me God" (delete in the case of a solemn affirmation).

Oath or affirmation of office for police officers, special constables and First Nations Constables.[33]

---

[30]OPP statistics quoted from Ontario Provincial Police 2005 Provincial Business Plan www.opp.ca/Intranetdev/groups/public/documents/webpage/opp_000690.pdf.

[31]*Police Services Act*, R.S.O. 1990, c. P-15, s. 19(1).

[32]*Coroners Act*, R.S.O. 1990, c. C-37, s. 9(2).

[33]O. Regulation 144/91, amended to O. Reg. 499/95, s. 2.

Although every police officer is appointed by a particular police service, the *Police Services Act* grants all municpal, regional and provincial police officers the authority to act as peace officers throughout the entire province of Ontario.[34] Practically, this allows every Constable of a municipal police service to exercise his or her duties beyond of the geographic boundaries of the municipality that hired them and also allows for members of the OPP to function as police officers across Ontario, regardless of which detachment they may be posted to.

Province-wide authority allows police officers to continue investigations that originate in a different municipality, in any location in Ontario. Courtesy dictates, however, that any police officer intending to continue an investigation in a place other than their home location ought to contact the police agency in that jurisdiction to inform the police service of their presence and purpose. Above and beyond the simple matter of courtesy, valuable local background knowledge of related matters may be gained and assistance may be made available or at least anticipated should it be required or the visiting officer's safety become compromised in any way.

Province-wide peace officer authority also allows for police services to share resources and to temporarily second personnel to joint-forces operations, allowing their officers to function outside of their normal work locations. As police officers in border areas are aware, their authority to act as police officers, including their powers of arrest and their authority to possess and carry restricted weapons, ends at the provincial borders of Ontario except in cases of fresh pursuit.

Ontario police officers who are required to operate outside of their home province for any length of time must be temporarily sworn in as peace officers in the new province to enable them to perform the statutory and common law duties of peace officers. These limitations do not apply to members of the Royal Canadian Mounted Police (RCMP), as they are appointed under a federal statute that grants them peace officer status throughout Canada.[35]

The *PSA* differentiates between the duties of a Chief of Police and all other ranks within a police service. Section 41(1) *PSA* sets out the duties of a Chief of Police as follows:

"The duties of a chief of police include,

(a)   in the case of a municipal police force, administering the police force and overseeing its operation in accordance with the objectives, priorities and policies established by the board under (1); subsection 31

(b)   ensuring that members of the police force carry out their duties in accordance with this Act and the regulations and in a manner that reflects the needs of the community, and that discipline is maintained in the police force;

(c)   ensuring that the police force provides community-oriented police services;

(d)   administering the complaints system in accordance with Part V."

"The duties of a police officer, other than a chief of police, include:

(a)   preserving the peace;

(b)   preventing crimes and other offences and providing assistance and encouragement to other persons in their prevention;

---

[34]*Police Services Act*, R.S.O. 1990, c. P-15, s. 42(2).

[35]*Royal Canadian Mounted Police Act*, R.S. 1985, c. R-10, s. 9; R.S. 1985, c. 8 (2nd Supp.), s. 4.

(c)   assisting victims of crime;

(d)   apprehending criminals and other offenders and others who may lawfully be taken into custody;

(e)   laying charges and participating in prosecutions;

(f)   executing warrants that are to be executed by police officers and performing related duties;

(g)   performing the lawful duties that the chief of police assigns;

(h)   in the case of a municipal police force (and in the case of an agreement under section 10 for provision of police services by OPP), enforcing municipal by-laws;

(i)   completing the prescribed training."

2.7   CONSTABLE HIRING PROCESS

The entry level position for peace officers in all Ontario police services is the rank of Constable. The *Police Services Act* requires that every person appointed as a police officer must be:

"(a)   a Canadian citizen or a permanent resident of Canada;

(b)   at least eighteen years of age;

(c)   physically and mentally able to perform the duties of the position, having regard to his or her own safety and the safety of members of the public;

(d)   of good moral character and habits; and

(e)   has successfully completed at least four years of secondary school education or its equivalent."[36]

Although the *PSA* establishes the legal minimum age of a Constable as eighteen, police services generally prefer their officers to have more life experience than an average eighteen year old could reasonably be expected to possess. Applicants in their mid-twenties, thirties and older seem to be more widely favoured on the basis of added maturity, job skills and the enhanced life experience they bring with them.

Except for recruits who have previously completed a probationary period with another accredited Canadian police service, new recruits are required to serve a probationary period, usually until the twelve month anniversary of their appointment. Between their date of hire and their first anniversary, recruits usually attend standardized recruit training, prescribed by the ministry, at the Ontario Police College, Aylmer.

A recruit's employment may be terminated for cause by the police services board at any time during his or her probationary period after being provided with reasonable information in regards to the reasons for the termination. The police officer must also be given an opportunity to respond to their termination, orally or in writing, as decided by the terminating board.[37]

---

[36]*Police Services Act*, R.S.O. 1990, c. P-15, s. 43(1).

[37]*Police Services Act*, R.S.O. 1990, c. P-15, s. 44(1)-(3).

Photo 2.4 - In Ontario, all police recruits receive standardized training at the Ontario Police College (O.P.C.), Aylmer, ON.

Before performing the duties of a police officer, a recruit must take oaths or solemn affirmations of office and of secrecy in the form prescribed by *PSA* regulation. The oath of office for police officers may be found at the beginning of Section 2.6. The required oath of secrecy for police officers, Special Constables and First Nations Constables is as follows:

"I solemnly swear (or affirm) that I will not disclose any information obtained by me in the course of my duties as (*insert name of office*), except as I may be authorized or required by law. So help me God."
(Omit line in an affirmation)[38]

2.8 CADETS, AUXILIARY MEMBERS AND SPECIAL CONSTABLES

The *PSA* permits a Chief of Police to appoint persons as police cadets. Cadets are paid uniformed members but do not have peace officer status. A police services board and the Commissioner of the OPP, with the approval of OCCPS, may appoint auxiliary members of the police service. Auxiliary members may be authorized by a Chief of Police to exercise the powers of a police officer, including bearing arms, in special emergent situations where the resources of a police service are insufficient to deal with the emergency, and then only if they are accompanied and supervised by a police officer.[39]

Special Constables may be appointed by a police services board or by the Commissioner of the OPP with the approval of OCCPS to perform specific purposes for specified

---

[38]O. Regulation 144/91, amended to O. Reg. 499/95, s. 4.

[39]*Police Services Act*, R.S.O 1990, c. P-15, s. 51-52.

periods of time.[40] Special Constable status has been awarded to certain civilian forensic technicians and to uniformed court security staff to grant them peace officer status to allow them to perform their duties.

2.9 LIMITATIONS ON POLICE SERVICE

The *Police Services Act* places restrictions on members of municipal police services with respect to the degree to which they may participate in political activity. Municipal police officers may only run for elected office of municipal boards – other than police services boards or for boards in municipalities that do not receive police services from the officer's service. Municipal police officers must apply for a leave of absence to run for provincial or federal government positions and, if elected, must immediately resign their position as a police officer.[41] Members of the OPP are considered employees of the Crown and, as such, are governed by similar restrictions under the *Public Service Act*.[42]

The *PSA* also restricts the part-time and full-time employment activities of police officers over and above their regular policing duties. These restrictions are intended to minimize the possibility of conflicts of interest or situations that might otherwise interfere in the officer's execution of their duties.

"A member of a police force shall not engage in any activity,

(a) that interferes with or influences adversely the performance of his or her duties as a member of a police force, or is likely to do so;

(b) that places him or her in a position of conflict of interest, or is likely to do so;

(c) that would otherwise constitute full-time employment for another person; or

(d) in which he or she has an advantage derived from employment as a member of a police force."[43]

Officers can and do participate in a wide variety of activities for which they may be remunerated, but must seek prior approval from their Chief of Police, police services board or Commissioner. Many police officers have obtained permission for part-time employment in the retail and service sectors and as sports referees, etc. Employment as a security officer or private investigator, however, could be seen to create potential conflicts of interest and is generally prohibited.

The restrictions on secondary employment do not apply to private paid duty services that are arranged through the member's police service, which a police officer may provide. Such functions often include providing extra uniformed security for institutions and public events, traffic direction and escort duties, and such. Police officers are required to disclose any activity they propose to undertake or have undertaken.[44]

---

[40]*Police Services Act*, R.S.O 1990, c. P-15, s. 53(1)-(3).

[41]O. Regulation 544/91, amended to O. Reg. 89/98.

[42]*Public Service Act*, R.S.O. 1990, c. P-47.

[43]*Police Services Act*, R.S.O. 1990, c. P-15, s. 49(1).

[44]*Police Services Act*, R.S.O. 1990, c. P-15, s. 49(2)-(3).

2.10 LIABILITY FOR TORTS AND LEGAL INDEMNIFICATION

Due to the hazardous nature of police work, there is a heightened risk of a police officer committing a **tort**. A tort is any wrongful or injurious misconduct that occurs outside of the context of a contract, for which the person committing the tort may be held to be civilly liable for damages suffered by others. Police officers involved in motor vehicle accidents for which they are at fault, or in using excessive force in an arrest, may be held to be liable for damages suffered by others.

The *PSA* specifies that police services boards or the Crown in right of Ontario, in the case of OPP officers, are civilly liable for any torts committed by police officers in the execution of their duties.[45] Police officers who incur legal expenses as the result of defending themselves in civil actions or criminal prosecutions may be reimbursed for reasonable legal expenses by their police services board or the Minister of Finance, in the case of an OPP officer, where the officer is found to have acted in good faith and is adjudicated as not liable or found not guilty, depending on the nature of the proceedings.[46]

2.11 RELEASE OF PERSONAL INFORMATION - SUSPECTS

A Chief of Police, or their designate, is authorized under the *PSA* to release personal information to any person about any (adult) individual who is charged with, convicted or found guilty of any federal or provincial act, whom they reasonably believe poses a significant risk of harm to other persons or property; on reasonable belief that the disclosure of the personal information would reduce that risk.[47] The Chief of Police is also authorized to release personal information to any victim of a crime or in the event of death, a spouse, child, or parent (providing they are not implicated in the crime in any way) concerning information about the progress of the investigation, charges laid, court proceedings, or escape/parole, etc.[48]

It must be noted that the authority to release personal information about suspects and accused persons applies only to adult offenders who have been formally charged (including arrested and released in accordance with Part XVI *Criminal* Code or served with a Part III summons in accordance with the *Provincial Offences Act*)[49] or convicted of an offence under any federal or provincial statute. Otherwise, an information must be laid charging the person about whom personal information is to be released prior to the release of the information.

This practice is commonly used to warn citizens, via the media, about escapees and suspects at large who represent a danger to the public. Information is commonly released about paroled sexual offenders, especially **paedophiles**, who are re-entering the community after having served custodial sentences. Public debate continues as to

---

[45]*Police Services Act*, R.S.O. 1990, c. P-15, s. 50(1).

[46]*Police Services Act*, R.S.O. 1990, c. P-15, s. 50(2)-(4).

[47]O. Regulation 265/98, amended to O. Reg. 297/05, s. 2-3.

[48]O. Regulation 265/98, amended to O. Reg. 297/05, s. 4(1)-(2).

[49]O. Regulation 265/98, amended to O. Reg. 297/05, s. 1.

whether or not this practice constitutes a form of double jeopardy, imposing a secondary punishment on offenders who have already served their court ordered sentences. Others feel the practice is justified as the rights of the public to be aware of potential risk and to protect oneself and one's family outweigh the rights of the individual in question.

A similar authority to release personal information relating to young persons (under the age of eighteen) exists within federal legislation that supercedes the *PSA*. The *Youth Criminal Justice Act* (*YCJA*) authorizes all peace officers to publish personal information that would identify a young person who has committed or allegedly committed an indictable offence in certain circumstances. Where a Youth Court judge is satisfied on *ex parte* application that the young person is a danger to others and that publishing personal information is necessary to assist in apprehending the young person, they may issue a court order that authorizes the publication of the information. Such an order is only in effect for a five day period from the date it is made.[50]

2.12   CODE OF CONDUCT – *PSA*

The Code of Conduct contained in the regulations made pursuant to the *PSA* contain a professional code of ethics for both municipal and provincial police officers in Ontario. The Code of Conduct governs relations between police officers and the public and between police officers themselves. Code of Conduct offences generally apply only to on-duty behaviour unless there is a connection between the prohibited conduct and the operational requirements for a police officer or the reputation of their police service.[51]

In addition to establishing standards of appropriate behaviour for members of the policing profession, the Code of Conduct creates offences for which police officers who are found guilty of misconduct may be disciplined. Prohibited behaviour is set out that defines the various ways that the offences of discreditable conduct, insubordination, neglect of duty, deceit, breach of confidence, corrupt practice, unnecessary or unlawful exercise of authority, damage to clothing or equipment and consuming drugs or alchohol in a manner prejudicial to duty can be committed.

Code Of Conduct

"1.   In this code of conduct,

"marital status" means the status of being married, single, widowed, divorced or separated and includes the status of living with a person in a conjugal relationship outside marriage;
"record" means any record of information, however recorded, whether in printed form, on film, by electronic means or otherwise, and includes correspondence, a memorandum, a book, a plan, a map, a drawing, a diagram, a pictorial or graphic work, a photograph, a film, a microfilm, a sound recording, a videotape, a machine readable record, any other documentary material, regardless of physical form or characteristics, and any copy thereof.

---

[50]*Youth Criminal Justice Act*, 2002 c.1, s. 110(1)-(5).

[51]*Police Services Act*, R.S.O. 1990, c. P-15, s. 74(2).

2. (1) Any chief of police or other police officer commits misconduct if he or she engages in,

    (a) Discreditable Conduct, in that he or she,

        (i) fails to treat or protect a person equally without discrimination with respect to police services because of that person's race, ancestry, place of origin, colour, ethnic origin, citizenship, creed, sex, sexual orientation, age, marital status, family status or handicap,

        (ii) uses profane, abusive or insulting language that relates to a person's race, ancestry, place of origin, colour, ethnic origin, citizenship, creed, sex, sexual orientation, age, marital status, family status or handicap,

       (iii) is guilty of oppressive or tyrannical conduct towards an inferior in rank,

       (iv) uses profane, abusive or insulting language to any other member of a police force,

        (v) uses profane, abusive or insulting language or is otherwise uncivil to a member of the public,

       (vi) wilfully or negligently makes any false complaint or statement against any member of a police force,

      (vii) assaults any other member of a police force,

     (viii) withholds or suppresses a complaint or report against a member of a police force or about the policies of or services provided by the police force,

       (ix) is guilty of an indictable criminal offence or a criminal offence punishable upon summary conviction,

        (x) contravenes any provision of the Act or the regulations, or

       (xi) acts in a disorderly manner or in a manner prejudicial to discipline or likely to bring discredit upon the reputation of the police force;

    (b) Insubordination, in that he or she,

        (i) is insubordinate by word, act or demeanour, or

        (ii) without lawful excuse, disobeys, omits or neglects to carry out any lawful order;

    (c) Neglect of Duty, in that he or she,

        (i) without lawful excuse, neglects or omits promptly and diligently to perform a duty as a member of the police force,

      (i.1) fails to comply with any provision of Ontario Regulation 673/98 (Conduct and Duties of Police Officers Respecting Investigations by the Special Investigations Unit),

        (ii) fails to work in accordance with orders, or leaves an area, detachment, detail or other place of duty, without due permission or sufficient cause,

       (iii) by carelessness or neglect permits a prisoner to escape,

       (iv) fails, when knowing where an offender is to be found, to report him or her or to make due exertions for bringing the offender to justice,

    (v) fails to report a matter that it is his or her duty to report,

    (vi) fails to report anything that he or she knows concerning a criminal or other charge, or fails to disclose any evidence that he or she, or any person within his or her knowledge, can give for or against any prisoner or defendant,

    (vii) omits to make any necessary entry in a record,

    (viii)feigns or exaggerates sickness or injury to evade duty,

    (ix) is absent without leave from or late for any duty, without reasonable excuse, or

    (x) is improperly dressed, dirty or untidy in person, clothing or equipment while on duty;

(d) Deceit, in that he or she,

    (i) knowingly makes or signs a false statement in a record,

    (ii) wilfully or negligently makes a false, misleading or inaccurate statement pertaining to official duties, or

    (iii) without lawful excuse, destroys or mutilates a record or alters or erases an entry therein;

(e) Breach of Confidence, in that he or she,

    (i) divulges any matter which it is his or her duty to keep secret,

    (ii) gives notice, directly or indirectly, to any person against whom any warrant or summons has been or is about to be issued, except in the lawful execution of the warrant or service of the summons,

    (iii) without proper authority, communicates to the media or to any unauthorized person any matter connected with the police force,

    (iv) without proper authority, shows to any person not a member of the police force or to any unauthorized member of the force any record that is the property of the police force;

(f) Corrupt Practice, in that he or she,

    (i) offers or takes a bribe,

    (ii) fails to account for or to make a prompt, true return of money or property received in an official capacity,

    (iii) directly or indirectly solicits or receives a gratuity or present without the consent of the chief of police,

    (iv) places himself or herself under a pecuniary or other obligation to a licensee concerning the granting or refusing of whose licence a member of the police force may have to report or give evidence, or

    (v) improperly uses his or her character and position as a member of the police force for private advantage;

(g) Unlawful or Unnecessary Exercise of Authority, in that he or she,

    (i) without good and sufficient cause makes an unlawful or unnecessary arrest, or

      (ii) uses any unnecessary force against a prisoner or other person contacted in the execution of duty;

  (h) Damage to Clothing or Equipment, in that he or she,

      (i) wilfully or carelessly causes loss or damage to any article of clothing or equipment, or to any record or other property of the police force, or

      (ii) fails to report loss or damage, however caused, as soon as practicable; or

  (i) Consuming Drugs or Alcohol in a Manner Prejudicial to Duty, in that he or she,

      (i) is unfit for duty, while on duty, through consumption of drugs or alcohol,

      (ii) is unfit for duty when he or she reports for duty, through consumption of drugs or alcohol,

      (iii) except with the consent of a superior officer or in the discharge of duty, consumes or receives alcohol from any other person while on duty, or

      (iv) except in the discharge of duty, demands, persuades or attempts to persuade another person to give or purchase or obtain for a member of the police force any alcohol or illegal drugs while on duty.

  (2) A police officer does not commit misconduct under subclause (1) (e) (iii) if he or she engages in the described activity in his or her capacity as an authorized representative of an association, as defined in section 2 of the Act.

  (3) A police officer does not commit misconduct under subclause (1) (f) (iii) if he or she engages in the described activity in his or her capacity as an authorized representative of an association, as defined in section 2 of the Act, or of a work-related professional organization.

  3. Any chief of police or other police officer also commits misconduct if he or she conspires, abets or is knowingly an accessory to any misconduct described in section 2."[52]

A police officer who is charged under a law of Canada or is suspected of misconduct may be suspended from duty with pay pending the disposition of any proceedings against them. If convicted of a criminal offence and sentenced to a term of imprisonment, the officer may then be suspended without pay.[53]

A police officer convicted of misconduct at a *PSA* hearing may face penalties ranging from forfeiture of pay or of time off, suspension, demotion or even dismissal from the police service.[54] Dispositions of *PSA* hearings may be appealed to OCCPS and further to the Ontario Court of Justice (Superior Division).[55]

---

[52]Ontario Regulation 123/98, amended to O. Reg. 296/05.

[53]*Police Services Act*, R.S.O. 1990, c. P-15, s. 67.

[54]*Police Services Act*, R.S.O. 1990, c. P-15, s. 68(1).

[55]*Police Services Act*, R.S.O. 1990, c. P-15, s.s. 70-71.

2.13 PUBLIC COMPLAINTS

Part V of the *PSA* contains the procedure for a member of the public to complain either about the conduct of an individual police officer or about the policies or services provided by a particular police service.[56] The 2004 Annual Report of OCCPS recorded a total of 3110 public complaints submitted in relation to the 21 835 police officers employed in Ontario at that time. 26.65 per cent of the 3110 complaints related to excessive use of force and excessive use of authority (450 and 379, respectively).[57]

Whenever a complaint is received from a member of the public, the Chief of Police evaluates whether or not to take any additional action regarding the complaint. The Chief of Police may decide not to take any action regarding any complaint that he or she considers to be frivolous (not serious), vexatious (a petty annoyance), made in bad faith, or that is made more than six months after the incident to which it relates.

Public complaints may also not be dealt with if the complainant was not directly affected by the incident that is the subject of the complaint.[58] In all such cases, the Chief of Police must notify the complainant of the reasons for deciding not to take action regarding their complaint.

Where the Chief of Police decides to continue with the complaint, notice of the complaint must be given to the subject officer unless giving notice to the officer might prejudice the investigation.[59]

Complaints of a non-serious nature may be resolved informally through mutual agreement of the complainant and the police officer.[60] Serious complaints are investigated and depending on the results of the investigation, if the complaint is found to be unsubstantiated, no further action is taken. If the complaint substantiates a claim of officer misconduct, a hearing will be held.[61]

On Tuesday, May 15, 2007, the Ontario legislature unanimously passed the *Independent Police Review Act* on third and final reading. This Act re-establishes an independent civilian agency to oversee public complaints against municipal and provincial police officers in Ontario. A former civilian body previously existed in Ontario until 1997, when it was terminated by a previous provincial government.

It is anticipated that the Director of the proposed agency will have the authority to investigate a public complaint, or to refer it to the involved police agency for investigation or request that an independent police service undertake an objective investigation. No additional information was available at the time of this printing, however, the new agency is expected to be operational sometime in 2008.[62]

---

[56]*Police Services Act*, R.S.O. 1990, c. P-15, s. 56(1).

[57]2004 Annual Report - Ontario Civilian Commission on Police Services, at pp. 40-46.

[58]*Police Services Act*, R.S.O. 1990, c. P-15, s. 59.

[59]*Police Services Act*, R.S.O. 1990, c. P-15, s. 56(7).

[60]*Police Services Act*, R.S.O. 1990, c. P-15, s. 58(1).

[61]*Police Services Act*, R.S.O. 1990, c. P-15, s. 64(6)-(7).

[62]News Release - Ministry of the Attorney General - May 15, 2007, "New System Means Increased Confidence and Respect of Public and Police".

2.14 LABOUR RELATIONS

Part VIII of the *PSA* deals exclusively with labour relations, including collective bargaining for municipal police officers (excluding Chiefs and Deputy Chiefs of Police) and memberships in trade unions. The part covers collective bargaining for remuneration, pensions, sick leave credit gratuities and working conditions. This part also provides for arbitration processes to settle disputes and greivances.

2.15 PROCEDURES RELATING TO FOUND AND SEIZED PROPERTY

Part IX of the *PSA* deals with the storage and retention of found property that comes into the possession of the police service from a member of the public or is recovered or seized by members of the police service in the course of their duties. Specific procedures are also set out dealing specifically with found and recovered money and firearms.

2.15.1 Property Other Than Money or Firearms

If property other than money or firearms is turned in to the police service, or is either recovered or seized by a police officer under circumstances that do not involve subsequent legal proceedings and its owner is determined, the property is returned to the lawful owner. Where the property is required as evidence in a legal proceedings, it is retained until the expiration of all court proceedings, including any appeals. If the court directs how the property is to be disposed of, the court order must be complied with.

If the property is not required for evidence in court and if its lawful owner cannot be established, "the Chief of Police may cause the property to be sold [by public auction or by public tender], and the board may use the proceeds for any purpose that it considers in the public interest."[63] Motor vehicles and bicycles may be sold after a retention period of one month, but any other non-perishable property must be retained for no less than three months. Perishable property that cannot be traced to an owner may be sold at any time.[64]

Where the lawful owner of any property makes a claim of ownership of an item that was sold before the three month time period expired, the owner is entitled to receive the proceeds, minus storage and advertising costs that were incurred by the police service.

Police services are required to maintain a register of found, recovered and seized property that contains the following information:

"1. The description and location of every item of property shall be recorded.

2. If the property is sold, full particulars shall be recorded.

3. If the property is returned to its owner, his or her name, address and telephone number shall be recorded."[65]

---

[63]*Police Services Act*, R.S.O. 1990, c. P-15, s. 132(2).

[64]*Police Services Act*, R.S.O. 1990, c. P-15, s. 133(3)-(4).

[65]*Police Services Act*, R.S.O. 1990, c. P-15, s. 133(6).

2.15.2 Procedures Relating to Money and Firearms

Money that is found or turned in to a police service must be accounted for and retained for a period of three months. If the retention period has elapsed and the owner has not claimed it, the money may be used by the police services board for any purpose it considers in the public interest. This policy also applies to money seized by a police service that is not ordered disposed of upon finalization of court proceedings.[66]

Firearms that are found or turned in to a police service or are seized must be securely stored and either returned to their lawful owner, disposed of in any other way directed by a court if proceedings are held, or destroyed after three months. If a found or seized firearm is not ordered destroyed at the finalization of any court proceedings and is deemed to be an antique or of special educational or historical value, the Chief of Police may offer it to the Director of the Centre of Forensic Sciences for inclusion in the collection maintained there. A firearm may be disposed of by any alternative method with the prior approval of the Solicitor General (Minister of Community Safety and Correctional Services).[67]

Every police service must maintain a register of found, recovered and seized firearms that includes the following information:

"1. Every firearm's description and location shall be recorded.

2. When a firearm ceases to be in the possession of the board or of a member of the police force, full particulars shall be recorded, including the name of the person who disposed of it and the date and method of disposal.

3. If the firearm is returned to its owner, his or her name, address and telephone number shall also be recorded.

4. On or before the 31st day of January in each year, a statement shall be filed with the Solicitor General listing the firearms that have come into the possession of the police force during the preceding calendar year, indicating which firearms are still being retained and which have been disposed of, and giving the particulars of disposition."[68]

SUMMARY

- The *Police Services Act* contains the legislative authorities for the creation, administration and oversight of police services including the responsibilities of such agencies and of individual police officers, and rules governing their conduct.

- The Ministry of Community Safety and Correctional Services (formerly the Solicitor General) is responsible for the overall governance of Ontario's police services.

- Ontario Civilian Commission on Policing Services is an independent quasi-judicial civilian agency that operates under the Ministry with a mandate to investigate all matters related to the provision of policing services.

[66]*Police Services Act*, R.S.O. 1990, c. P-15, s. 133(1)-(3).

[67]*Police Services Act*, R.S.O. 1990, c. P-15, s. 134.

[68]*Police Services Act*, R.S.O. 1990, c. P-15, s. 134(8).

- Every municipality that maintains a police service is required under the *PSA* to have a police services board to provide oversight and general management and to develop policy for the police service.

- The *PSA* grants all municipal, regional and provincial police officers the authority to act as peace officers throughout the entire province of Ontario.

- The *PSA* places restrictions on members of municipal police services with respect to the degree to which they may participate in political activity as well as full-time and part-time employment activities.

- The Code of Conduct contained in the regulations made pursuant to the *PSA* contains a professional code of ethics for both on-duty and off-duty municipal and provincial police officers in Ontario.

- The *PSA* contains policies and procedures for the storage and disposal of found, recovered and seized property, including money, vehicles and firearms, both where the owner of the property is known and if ownership cannot be established.

- Part V of the *PSA* contains the procedure for a member of the public to complain either about the conduct of an individual police officer or about the policies or services provided by a particular police service.

- A police officer convicted of misconduct at a *PSA* hearing may face penalties ranging from forfeiture of pay or of time off, to suspension, demotion or even dismissal from the police service.

- The Special Investigations Unit is a civilian law enforcement agency that reports to the Ontario Ministry of the Attorney General. SIU conducts criminal investigations into circumstances of incidents involving police and civilians that have resulted in serious injury, including sexual assault, or death to members of the public.

DISCUSSION QUESTIONS

1. Explain the principles that justify the need to maintain civilian oversight of law enforcement while maintaining constabulary independence in the day to day operations of a police service.

2. Describe the restrictions on full-time and part-time employment placed on police officers by the PSA. Under what circumstances may a police officer engage in secondary employment duties and what, if any, approvals are required to do so?

3. A member of the public finds a suitcase full of money on the street near his residence and delivers it to the front desk of your police station. There are no distinguishing marks on the baggage that would assist in identifying the owner of the money. What procedure will you explain to the citizen that will be followed in the retention of the money? Can the finder claim the money if the lawful owner does not come forward to do so or is not found?

 WEBLINKS

www.occps.ca

The Ontario Civilian Commission on Police Services is an independent, civilian, quasi-judicial agency within the Ministry of Community Safety and Correctional Services. OCCPS is responsible for ensuring the adequacy and effectiveness of policing services, hearing appeals from police disciplinary tribunals, and adjudicating disputes between municipal councils and police services boards.

www.oapsb.ca/

The Ontario Association of Police Services Boards (OAPSB) is a non-profit association of municipal police services boards providing a wide variety of services designed to assist member agencies in discharging their duties of governance and oversight of police services with the highest degree of integrity and with all the knowledge required.

www.cacole.ca

Canadian Association for Civilian Oversight of Law Enforcement (CACOLE) is a national agency dedicated to advancing the concept, principles and application of civilian oversight of law enforcement throughout Canada.

www.siu.on.ca/home.asp

Special Investigations Unit is a civilian investigative agency committed to promoting and maintaining community confidence in Ontario's police services through independent investigations of circumstances involving police and civilians that have resulted in serious injury, including sexual assault, or death.

www.oacp.on.ca/content/programs/constable_selection.html

Ontario Association of Chiefs of Police (OACP) administers the Constable Selection Program for Ontario police services under licence from the Ministry of Community Safety and Correctional Services. This OACP website provides a breakdown of the minimum requirements, application and testing processes for applicants for the position of Police Constable.

Chapter 3

Arrest Procedures

"The liberties of none are safe unless the liberties of all are protected."

William O. Douglas (1898-1980),
Former U.S. Supreme Court Justice.

Learning Outcomes

After reading this chapter, students should be able to:

- Explain the meaning and purpose of a lawful arrest.
- Describe the factors that might render an arrest arbitrary.
- Describe the necessary steps in making a proper arrest.
- Compare a citizen's powers of arrest with those of a peace officer.
- Identify three things a police officer may search a prisoner for "incident to arrest."

3.1   WHAT DOES ARREST MEAN?

Arrest

> ### *n. L. ad + restare (to + keep)*
>
> *The detention of a person, or restriction of their liberty, whether or not by physical force, by a person acting under lawful authority either for investigative purposes, including the need to prevent the commission of an alleged offence, or to compel a person's attendance in court.*

Next to a police officer's legal authority to use force, the power to arrest members of the public is undoubtedly the most commanding in terms of both enormity and potential for impact upon the person being arrested. Picture yourself, walking down the main street of your hometown, going about your normal daily routine. Suddenly, a uniformed police officer involuntarily takes you into their physical control, placing you under arrest for an offence that you may or may not have committed.

In one brief instant, you lose the very freedom to come and go as you please that you enjoyed just a moment before. Your freedom to make the simplest of choices that we all take for granted has been effectively stripped away from you. At least for a while, those choices will now be made by strangers, without your consent. When you place yourself in the starring role of this hypothetical scenario, you can see that the power to deprive a person of their freedom is a very serious matter that carries with it a great responsibility.

Police officers must be able to recognize offences, either through the verbal description provided by a witness or complainant, or when actually witnessing an offence occurring. As we learned in Chapter 1, offences are classified differently (indictable, summary conviction and dual procedure), carry different penalties and involve different powers of arrest. A police officer must instinctively know when they may arrest and when they must not arrest to guard against infringing on the person's individual rights and to avoid incurring possible civil liability for themselves and their police service. Unlawful arrests may also create bad case law that can result in additional restrictions being placed on the future powers of arrest for every police officer in Canada.

The opening definition of arrest fairly adequately explains the basic concept of arrest. This definition assumes, however, that such an arrest was, in fact, a lawful arrest. To be considered lawful, every arrest must satisfy the following criteria:

1. the arrest is intentionally made

2. the person making the arrest is, in fact, acting under lawful authority (one prescribed by statute law or common law)

3. the arrest is conducted in a reasonable manner

4. the arrest resulted in at least a subjective belief on the part of the person being detained that their liberty was restricted to the point that they were not free to leave the custody of the person effecting the arrest

How could an arrest still be considered to be an arrest if it wasn't made intentionally?

How could an arrest still be considered to be an arrest if the person making the arrest wasn't acting under lawful authority?

What if the person being detained was only informed that they were under arrest but weren't provided with any other information regarding their arrest?

What if the person being detained had a subjective (in their own mind) belief that their liberty was restricted to the point that they were not free to leave the custody of a **person in authority**? How could such a singular belief on the part of the person being detained be considered to be an arrest?

There is one fairly simple answer to all the above questions – even unlawful arrests are still considered to be arrests.

Question:	For an arrest to be lawful, does it mean that the person actually committed the offence for which they were arrested?
Answer:	Providing that the person making the arrest had sufficient legal authority as a basis for their actions, the arrest of an innocent person may still be considered a lawful arrest.
Question:	If a person is arrested, do they have to be charged with an offence?
Answer:	The terms arrest and charge are mutually exclusive, yet are often related. An arrested person may be released uncharged if subsequent investigation proves that they did not commit the offence they were suspected of, or if reasonable grounds do not exist upon which

to lay a charge. Many people who are arrested are charged with an offence, however, a person may be arrested – and released without being charged or they may be charged without having been arrested. We will discuss these issues further in this textbook but appreciate for now that there is a distinction between being arrested and being charged.

Arrests may be conducted either with or without the legal authority of a court order in the form of an arrest warrant or committal warrant. Throughout this chapter, we will examine the various situations and authorities for which police officers may arrest individuals.

3.2   ARBITRARY ARREST

"Everyone has the right not to be arbitrarily detained or imprisoned."

Charter of Rights and Freedoms, Section 9 [1].

Arbitrary: adj. "based on or derived from uninformed opinion or random choice..."

The Concise Oxford Dictionary, (9th edition).

This section's opening quotation is to remind us that everyone in Canada is guaranteed the right to be free from **arbitrary arrest**, detention or imprisonment. To ensure that we never intentionally infringe upon anyone's right to be free from arbitrary arrest, let's spend some time to fully grasp the meaning of arbitrary arrest.

An arbitrary arrest is the exact opposite of a lawful or proper arrest. In determining whether or not an arrest was or was not arbitrary, a court will examine three main factors, including:

- Whether there was **articulable cause** for making the arrest;

    Every lawful arrest must be based on reasonable grounds that establish a nexus (a connection or link) between the detained person and the alleged offence. The person making the arrest must have reasonable grounds, exceeding mere suspicion, to justify detaining any person who is arrested and must be able to articulate (state) the reason(s) for their belief that the arrest was necessary. If no grounds or insufficient grounds existed to justify the arrest, it could be deemed to be arbitrary.

    Police officers must develop the ability to express, verbally and in writing, their observations, conclusions and justification for their actions, including arrests and searches in terms of the legal requirements of their action. It is not sufficient to merely state, in a report or while testifying in court, that you believed that a particular action was necessary. A skilled police officer must also be able to articulate why they believed that their action was necessary and justify that belief in terms of the specific facts, information or circumstances of the event or investigation.

- The extent and duration of the arrest;

    The nature and extent of the circumstances of the arrest itself will be examined. For example, paragraph 503(1)(a) *Criminal Code* requires that a person arrested without a warrant must be brought before a justice within 24 hours of

---

[1] *Canadian Charter of Rights and Freedoms*, Being Part I of the Constitution Act, 1982, enacted by the *Canada Act 1982* (U.K.) c. 11; Proclaimed in force April 17, 1982, s. 9.

being arrested.[2] This allows the police to hold a prisoner up to a maximum of 24 hours, at which time either a charge must be laid and the person brought before a justice, or at least as soon as possible if no justice is available,[3] or the accused must be released unconditionally. If a prisoner was held for longer than the prescribed time limitation, the arrest could be deemed to be arbitrary.

- The conduct of the police

    The behaviour of the police before, during and after the arrest will be scrutinized for evidence of tyrannical or oppressive and even unlawful behaviour toward the person arrested. If an arrested person was physically abused, or was either not informed of the reason for their detention or was denied their right to retain and instruct legal counsel, the arrest will likely be held to be an arbitrary arrest. (Rock et al. 2006)

3.3   WHY DO WE ARREST?

Police officers are authorized to arrest members of the public for any of several reasons in order to satisfy the public interest of effective law enforcement. A person may be arrested for committing, resuming or joining any breach of the peace. A person may be arrested to prevent them from committing an offence. If an offence has been committed a suspect may be taken into custody for investigative purposes including:

1. to satisfactorily establish their identity

2. to determine whether or not their involvement, if any, in an alleged offence establishes criminal liability

3. to search them for evidence of a crime, or weapons with which they might injure an investigating police officer

4. to compel the person's attendance in court

5. to take a person into custody on the authority of a Warrant for Committal in Form 8 *Criminal Code* to enforce a sentence in default of (refusal to pay) a monetary fine imposed by a court

3.4   REASONABLE GROUNDS

The legal standard for many actions by police officers, including lawful arrests, use of force and search, is one of objective, reasonably based probability – referred to as **reasonable grounds**. It is vital that police officers have an understanding of the meaning of reasonable grounds. (See Box 3.1.)

Reasonable grounds are defined as:

"A set of facts or circumstances, which if true, would give an ordinary, prudent (sensible), cautious (vigilant) individual a strong belief that exceeds mere suspicion."

---

[2]*Criminal Code*, R.S. 1985, c. C-46, s. 503(1)(a).

[3]*Criminal Code*, R.S. 1985, c. C-46, s. 503(1)(b).

BOX 3.1	Investigative Hypothesis

(Subjective belief + Objective belief) > mere suspicion = reasonable grounds

Reasonable grounds refers to a legal threshold that constitutes a strong belief in a fact, such as that a certain person has committed a particular offence. Below the required threshold of reasonable grounds, a person has only a suspicion that a particular suspect may have committed the offence under investigation. As we will soon see, mere suspicion may be sufficient to temporarily justify detaining a person for investigative purposes, but is not sufficient cause to justify a formal arrest of the individual.

Reasonable grounds may be derived from bits and pieces of information received from other persons, either by word or in writing, or developed as the result of an inquiry, or by an observation made by the officer. Reasonable grounds may even be formulated as the result of a conclusion or belief formed by assessing information from one or more sources, including the evaluation of either physical (real) or circumstantial evidence, or both. *find a murder case*

Reasonable grounds must first be considered to be reliable before they are acted upon and must always be more than just suspicion. The concept of reasonable grounds is a far lower threshold than proof **beyond a reasonable doubt**, which is the legal standard that is used by Canadian courts of law to determine guilt or innocence.

The police officer must have the subjective belief that it is necessary to arrest an individual in relation to an offence, or for the purpose of preventing an offence, or that a valid arrest warrant exists for the person in that particular jurisdiction. The officer's subjective belief will also be weighed against the concept of the reasonable person. Would an ordinary cautious, prudent, reasonable person agree with the officer's belief that the arrest of the individual was necessary? If so, it could be said that reasonable grounds existed to justify an arrest.

3.5   INVESTIGATIVE DETENTION

Often in the early stages of an investigation, the police may encounter individuals whom they need to question or investigate to determine whether or not they have been involved in an alleged crime. The existence of sufficient reasonable grounds to make a formal arrest is often not possible when officers first arrive on the scene of an occurrence.

Imagine, for example, that you are a police officer assigned to uniform patrol duties between 7:00 p.m. and 7:00 a.m. (1900 – 0700 hrs) in your town or city. At 3:45 a.m. (0345 hrs), you are dispatched in response to a burglar alarm at the Discount Drugs Pharmacy, just up the street from where you happen to be patrolling. You arrive momentarily and observe a newer sport utility vehicle with two male passengers drive from behind the pharmacy into the parking lot. You activate your cruiser overhead lights and, as you pull alongside the vehicle and lower your cruiser window, you engage in the following conversation with the driver:

Officer: "A burglar alarm just went off at the drug store."

Driver: "Don't know anything about it officer. Have a good night!"

Officer:	"Did you see anyone or anything suspicious?"
Driver:	"We didn't see a thing officer. So long, now!"
Officer:	"What were you doing behind the drug store?"
Driver:	"We're the night cleaners at the dry cleaners next door. We're off to our next stop. So if there's nothing else officer, we'll be going."

Let's carefully and methodically analyze the situation and answer the following questions:

Q: First, do we even have a crime?

A: At this point, we have not yet confirmed that a crime has been committed. Burglar alarms frequently go off for little or sometimes no reason at all. This may be one of those false alarms activated by noise, vibration or inclement weather.

Q: How can the officer arrest anyone if there is no confirmed crime?

A: The officer has not arrested the men but is clearly detaining them if he or she prevents them from driving away. The first officer remains with the suspects from the vehicle and requests that arriving backup officer(s) check the pharmacy. Within seconds the backup officers arrive and report that the rear door of the pharmacy has been forced open and the floor of the pharmacy is littered with pill containers and other merchandise. Now we have a confirmed crime.

Q: The men in the car have given a plausible excuse for their presence. There are no known witnesses to the break-in and there is no physical evidence to implicate them in the crime. The men are now starting to become agitated and are demanding to be allowed to proceed to clean their next business. Do reasonable grounds exist to arrest the two men? What should the officer do next? By detaining the men – that is what the officer is doing by preventing them from freely leaving the location – is he or she committing an arbitrary detention?

A: The officer has a common law authority to investigate crime and apprehend persons responsible for committing crime. Without making a formal arrest, the officer is still within their authority to detain the men in the car. As it is 3:45 a.m., the appearance of the men in the car from behind the scene of a break and enter is somewhat suspicious. While speaking to the driver, the officer notices that there aren't any cleaning supplies visible inside the men's car.

The two men should be instructed – not requested – not asked – instructed to step from the vehicle and should be separated prior to being questioned. For reasons relating to the officers' safety, both men should be subjected to a cursory "pat-down" or "frisk" search for weapons or possible tools of escape. In this instance, the passenger is found to have a large screwdriver and a Vise-grip® tool concealed in the waistband of his pants. While these items were not designed to be weapons, nor were they intended to be used as weapons, they easily could be used as weapons. I personally would not want to be struck by either of them and would seize them.[4] The tools do not exactly fit with his explanation of being a cleaner and legitimate tradespersons don't (as a rule) carry tools in their waistbands, especially at 3:45 a.m.

When questioned separately, neither man admits to ownership of the vehicle that they were in. Neither man is able to provide the name or address of the cleaning company they claimed to be employed by. A query of the Canadian Police Information Centre (CPIC) reveals their vehicle was reported stolen from Toronto two days before. You find identification on both men and upon querying them on CPIC, you learn that the driver is the subject of an outstanding arrest warrant from Kingston for armed robbery. Both the driver and the passenger have lengthy criminal convictions for thefts, and for breaking and entering several commercial businesses.

Question: Now does the officer now have reasonable grounds to arrest either or both men for the break-in at the pharmacy?

Answer: Although the initial investigation is proceeding quite favourably, I suggest that the officer, acting out of an abundance of caution, is still at the level of suspicion, but is very close to reasonable grounds. The good news is, it is now time to formally arrest both men – but not for the pharmacy break in.

The officer has reasonable grounds to arrest the passenger for Possession of Break In Instruments.[5] He can arrest the driver on reasonable grounds that an arrest warrant exists for him in the jurisdiction (province) in which he was found,[6] and can arrest both the passenger and driver for Possession of Property Obtained by Crime – the stolen motor vehicle from Toronto.[7] Both men must be advised they are under arrest, the reason for their arrest and be advised of their rights to obtain and instruct legal counsel.[8]

With both suspects securely in custody, the officer is free to continue his or her investigation of the pharmacy break in. Interrogation, fingerprint impressions, footwear impressions, executing a search warrant on the stolen vehicle and reviewing videotapes from security surveillance cameras, if present, may well provide additional reasonable grounds to link the suspects to the pharmacy break in.

In a 2004 decision, the Supreme Court of Canada ruled that while there is no statutory authority to detain anyone for investigative purposes, the police are entitled to briefly "...detain an individual if there are reasonable grounds to suspect in all the circumstances that the individual is connected to a particular crime and that the detention is reasonably necessary." The court also ruled that police officers who reasonably believe their safety may be at risk are entitled to conduct a pat-down search to ensure their safety – not to search the detained person for evidence of the crime. The Supreme Court drew a distinction between **investigative detention** and protective search and formal

---

[4]Weapon defined: *Criminal Code*, R.S. 1985, c. C-46, s. 2.

[5]*Criminal Code*, R.S. 1985, c. C-46, s. 351(1).

[6]*Criminal Code*, R.S. 1985, c. C-46, s. 495(1)(c).

[7]*Criminal Code*, R.S. 1985, c. C-46, s. 355(a).

[8]*Criminal Code*, R.S. 1985, c. C-46, s. 29(2) and *Canadian Charter of Rights and Freedoms*, being Part I of the *Constitution Act*, 1982, s. 10.

arrest authorities with the incidental power to search prisoners after arrest.[9] (Arcaro 2003) (See Chapter 7, Search Incident to Arrest.)

The only difference between being under arrest and being under detention is that an individual who is arrested should be informed of the officer's intention to take him or her into custody. This is accomplished using the formal pronouncement, "You are under arrest for [state the appropriate offence or reason]". A formal arrest involves physical control, even a symbolic touching of the person being arrested. See section 3.12 How To Make a Proper Arrest for more on this topic.

An individual who is being detained is also deprived of their liberty, but no formal pronouncement of arrest has been made. The detention may only consist of a belief in the mind of the person detained, if they believe they are not at liberty to leave the officer's custody. Detention, investigative or otherwise, never involves a formal declaration of arrest. In the case of an individual with an honest but mistaken belief that they were detained, the psychological effects of arrest and detention are identical to those of a person actually under arrest. (Arcaro 2003)

3.6   VOLUNTARY ACCOMPANIMENT

Another method of securing the attendance of a person for investigative purposes is when they voluntarily consent to accompany an officer for investigative purposes or to attend at a specified location, either by appointment or by invitation. Such an invitation may range from the simple privacy of a nearby police vehicle, to a police station for questioning, fingerprinting, to participate in an identification lineup or for polygraph testing, etc. This method of securing the attendance of persons can be used for victims, witnesses, non-witnesses, suspects and accused persons who are not in police custody, but in this case applies to **persons of interest** and **suspects**.

Usually, voluntary accompaniment will occur at the earlier stages of an investigation when, in the case of a person of interest, any belief of their involvement in the case under investigation is limited to suspicion only. An officer may wish to interview an individual outside of their normal comfort zone in the more formal environment of a police station.

Voluntary accompaniment is just what it indicates it is, voluntary – nothing more – nothing less. Voluntary accompaniment does not involve arrest, nor does it involve detention of any kind. The main distinction is the intention of the police officer to deprive an individual of their liberty and the ability of the individual to make an informed choice to voluntarily accompany the officer.

To be able to render a truly **informed consent**, an individual should be aware of the following information:

1. The nature of the incident under investigation that resulted in the request for their accompaniment

2. The nature of the police action that requires their attendance, meaning what it is they have been asked to consent to, such as an interview or for photographing or polygraph examination, etc.

---

[9]*R. v. Mann*, [2004] 3 S.C.R. 59, 2004 SCC 52 (CanLII).

3. That the results of the procedure form part of an official police investigation to determine the person responsible for a crime under investigation and may form evidence in future criminal proceedings

4. That the nature of the individual's attendance is consensual and that they are under no obligation to consent to any police procedure, unless they choose to

5. That their consent may be withdrawn or revoked at any time (Arcaro 2003)

There should be absolutely no ambiguity (uncertainty) whatsoever, either in the mind of the officer or the individual, regarding the person's freedom to choose to leave the officer's presence for any reason. The officer should be clear that if the individual were to invoke closure in the procedure and request to leave they would be allowed to so. The individual should also be aware that all they have to do to end the procedure and leave is to withdraw their consent. There are different methods to ensure that an individual knows that they are not being detained and the simplest of those is to verbally inform them of that fact.

Whether the officer has requested the person accompany them to a police vehicle or to a police station, they can simply inform the person, "You are aware that you are here voluntarily. Is that correct? You are not under arrest and you are free to leave whenever you wish. Is that right?" This method is particularly effective during a videotaped interview that captures the individual's responses and their demeanour that allow a court to assess the informed voluntary consent of the individual at a later time, if necessary.

Whether or not the exchange is video recorded, the officer should record such statements and responses in their investigative notebook. It doesn't hurt to repeat that the person is free to leave at several times during the meeting to refresh their memory and to demonstrate concern for their individual rights.

Some people tend to think that the individual's acceptance to being invited to a police station is in itself revealing of the lack of their involvement in an offence. Many times, however, guilty people will consent to accompany an investigator in an effort to persuade the officer of their innocence by appearing to cooperate with an investigation. Some guilty individuals may use the opportunity to try to gain more knowledge about the progress of the investigation and the strength of any evidence against them.

3.7 "FACTS IN ISSUE"

The **facts in issue** of an offence are those essential elements (or parts) of a specific offence that must be proven to form the basis for a finding of guilt in court. Proving all of the facts in issue is referred to as establishing a *prima facie* case. A *prima facie* case establishes sufficient proof that, if not contradicted, will result in a conviction or finding of guilt. In addition to the facts in issue, it is always necessary to prove the following fundamental elements in any criminal offence:

1. Identity of the accused.

2. Date of the alleged offence.

3. Location of the alleged offence (municipality and judicial district).

4. *Mens Rea* (Latin = guilty mind, or required degree of criminal intent)

5. *Actus Reus* (Latin = guilty act, an act prohibited by law)

In proving *mens rea* or criminal intent, it should be pointed out that specific offences differ in the degree of intent that is required to be proven. An offence such as Cause Disturbance requires only the identity of the accused, date and location, plus evidence of one of the acts prohibited by s. 175(1) *CC*, in order to obtain a finding of guilt. It need not be proven that the accused intended to cause a disturbance, making this offence one of absolute liability.

The offence of Unlawfully Causing Bodily Harm [s. 269 *CC*] requires that the bodily harm caused to a person only be unlawful, (i.e., a deliberate act prohibited by federal or provincial statute). It must only be proven that the accused committed a deliberate act whether or not they intended to cause the bodily harm, making this a general intent section.

Among others, offences such as Assault [s. 265(1) *CC*], Theft [s. 322(1) *CC*], Possession of Property Obtained by Crime [s. 354(1) *CC*], and Murder [s. 229 *CC*] all require that it be proven that the accused possessed the specific intent to commit the offence charged. An examination of these sections will contain the words or phrases, "knowingly" or "with intent", making them part of the facts in issue that are required to be proven.

In proving the facts in issue of the *actus reus*, it is always necessary to refer to the relevant offence under investigation to determine the individual the elements of the offence which need to be proven. Take, for example, the offence of Level II Sexual Assault [s. 272(1) *Criminal Code*] which reads:

272 (1) "Every person commits an offence who, in committing a sexual assault,

    (a) carries, uses or threatens to use a weapon or an imitation of a weapon;

    (b) threatens to cause bodily harm to a person other than the complainant;

    (c) causes bodily harm to the complainant; or

    (d) is a party to the offence with any other person

(2) Every person who commits an offence under subsection (1) is guilty of an indictable offence and liable

    (a) where a firearm is used in the commission of the offence, to imprisonment for a term not exceeding fourteen years and to a minimum punishment of imprisonment for a term of four years; and

    (b) in any other case, to imprisonment for a term not exceeding fourteen years."[10]

To identify the facts in issue of the substantive offence of Level II Sexual Assault, we must break down each component of the section. When we analyze the preceding section, we see that there are actually four different ways to commit this offence.

A person is guilty of Level II Sexual Assault if while committing a sexual assault, they either:

1. Carry, use or threaten to use a weapon or an imitation of a weapon, or they

2. Threaten to cause bodily harm to a person other than the complainant, or they

---

[10]*Criminal Code*, R.S. 1985 c. C-46, s. 272.

3. Actually cause bodily harm to the complainant, or they

4. Are a party to the offence (commit, aid or abet the offence) with any other person

Because the wording of the phrases which specify the various methods of committing this offence is separated by semi-colons (sometimes commas are used) or by the conjunction "or" these elements are separated (meaning this *or* this – one or the other but not both), rather than joined as in the use of "and" (meaning this *and* this – which require both elements to be present) we need only one of these elements before having a complete offence.

The significance of this is that the substantive offence of Level II Sexual assault can be committed in any of these four different ways. All four ways contain different "facts in issue". The number of facts in issue can vary from offence to offence. That is why it is necessary to break down each substantive offence to identify the facts in issue for each particular offence.

Let's say for demonstration purposes that a victim of a sexual assault receives a broken arm during the commission of the offence. We must be able to correctly identify the relevant offence and be able to recognize when the offence is complete. If all of the facts in issue have not been satisfied, we cannot arrest nor lay a particular charge; if the facts in issue are not there – we have no offence. For the offence of Sexual Assault causing Bodily Harm, we have only two facts in issue which need to be proven:

- Everyone (regardless of gender) who, in committing a sexual assault [assault is defined in s. 265(1) *CC* as the intentional application of force to another person, without their consent, directly or indirectly – the definition of sexual assault is found in the Supreme Court decision of *R. v. Chase* which states that an assault as described in s. 265(1) *CC* "in circumstances of a sexual nature such that the sexual integrity of the victim is violated" is a sexual assault]. [11]

- Causes bodily harm to the complainant (victim) [bodily harm is defined in s. 2 *CC* as "any hurt or injury to a person that interferes with the health or comfort of the person and that is more than merely transient or trifling in nature"].

We are not required to prove that the assailant used, carried or threatened to use a weapon while committing a sexual assault as that is a separate method of committing Level II Sexual Assault with different facts in issue that aren't relevant to our case.

We are not required to prove that the assailant obtained consent from the victim only by reason of threatening bodily harm to a person other than the complainant as again, that is its own separate method of committing the offence.

Nor are we required to prove that the assailant was a party to the offence of sexual assault with any other person, whether or not a weapon was used, or if bodily harm was caused to the complainant or threatened to a third party, as this is yet another different way of committing the offence.

Sexual Assault + Use or Threatened use of Weapon or imitation = Level II Sexual Assault [s. 272(1)(a) *CC*]

---

[11]*R. v. Chase*, [1987] 2 S.C.R. 293, 37 C.C.C. (3d) 97, 59 C.R. (3d) 193 6:0.

Sexual Assault + Threats of Bodily Harm to third person = Level II Sexual Assault [s. 272(1)(b) *CC*]

Sexual Assault + Bodily Harm = Level II Sexual Assault [s. 272(1)(c) *CC*]

Sexual Assault + Party to Offence with another person = Level II Sexual Assault [s. 272(1)(d) *CC*]

But what about the wording contained in subsection 272(2)? Do we need to be concerned with it? Is it part of the facts in issue for our offence?

"(2) Every person who commits an offence under subsection (1) is guilty of an indictable offence and liable

(a) where a firearm is used in the commission of the offence, to imprisonment for a term not exceeding fourteen years and to a minimum punishment of imprisonment for a term of four years; and

(b) in any other case, to imprisonment for a term not exceeding fourteen years."

Subsection 272(2) is an example of procedural or adjective law as opposed to substantive law. It affects how the charge will be dealt with in court and states minimum and maximum punishments for the four methods of committing Level II Sexual Assault. Subsection (2) is not part of the facts in issue of the offence and does not have to be present before the charge is complete nor does this subsection have to be proven before an offender can be convicted of the offence.

This is not to say that subsection (2) is unimportant, as it is this subsection that classifies the offence as an indictable offence and subsequently defines a police officer's powers of arrest for this offence, as we shall soon see. Just know for now that facts in issue and offence classification are two separate issues that are both important in their own right.

3.8   CLASSIFICATION OF OFFENCES

During our initial discussion of the different classification of criminal offences in section 1.11, we learned that criminal offences (federally enacted offences) can either be classified as summary conviction offences or as indictable offences. To distinguish between the two types of offences, we must look to the penalty (or punishment) section of the particular offence. The penalty section will state that any person who commits this offence is either guilty of an indictable offence or is guilty of an offence punishable upon summary conviction, depending on how the offence has been classified.

We previously learned that indictable offences are more serious offences, while summary conviction offences are considered to be less serious in nature. In section 1.12, we examined the differences between the two classifications. Being more serious, indictable offences carry a higher range of punishment, while summary conviction offences are punishable by a fine of up to $2 000 or up to six months imprisonment, or both. Some summary conviction offences, such as impaired driving and Level II assault, contain specific sections that exceed the general penalty for summary conviction offences.

We also learned in section 1.12.1 that if the penalty section of an offence contains punishments both by way of indictment and by summary conviction, the offence is classified as a dual procedure or hybrid offence. The main significance to police officers is that the classification of an offence [summary conviction, indictable or dual procedure] is what determines the officer's powers of arrest in relation to that offence.

3.9 WHO MAY BE ARRESTED?

Police officers must always refer to the relevant statute to ascertain what their powers of arrest are. Not all statutes contain arrest authorities and certain statutes specify different authorities for peace officers and for citizens. To be effective, police officers must be totally conversant with statute law and maintain a solid understanding of relevant definitions, facts in issue, classification of offences and powers of arrest.

Police officers must also be familiar with citizens' powers of arrest as a duty is imposed on citizens who arrest other citizens to turn such a person over to a police officer as soon as practicable. A police officer who receives such a prisoner into their custody must first be satisfied that the initial arrest was legal before making the decision to continue the arrest.

3.9.1 Citizens' Powers of Arrest

Let's examine the powers of arrest that citizens are afforded under the authority of the *Criminal Code*.

494 (1) "Any one may arrest without warrant

   (a) a person whom he finds committing an indictable offence

   (b) a person who, on reasonable grounds, he believes

   (i) has committed a criminal offence, and

   (ii) is escaping from and freshly pursued by persons who have lawful authority to arrest that person."

This authority allows citizens to arrest individuals without warrant for committing an indictable offence if the citizen actually witnessed the individual commit the offence. A citizen may also arrest a person if he or she did not actually witness the offence being committed but has a reasonable belief, exceeding mere suspicion, that the individual is escaping from and is "freshly pursued" by someone who does have the lawful right to arrest him or her. This is the classic scenario where an individual is being chased out of a store or down a street by a victim yelling, "Stop! Thief!," or is being chased by one or more police officers.

(2) "Any one who is

   (a) a the owner or a person in lawful possession of property, or

   (b) a person authorized by the owner or by a person in lawful possession of property, may arrest without warrant a person whom he finds committing a criminal offence on or in relation to that property."

Property owners and persons in lawful possession of property (or persons who are authorized by the owner or person in lawful possession of property) may arrest any person they witness committing any offence against a federal statute on or in relation to the property. This might include the owner or tenant of a house, or the owner of a business or his or her employees, family members or any person(s) designated by the owner to safeguard the property (such as a security officer or watchperson).

Additionally, citizens may also detain any person whom they witness either committing or about to join in, continue or renew a breach of the peace, and deliver that person to a peace officer.[12]

(3) "Any one other than a peace officer who arrests a person without warrant shall forthwith deliver the person to a peace officer."[13]

Police officers continuing an arrest made by a citizen must always be mindful of the requirements of sections 10(a) and 10(b) of the *Charter of Rights and Freedoms* relating to a peace officer's duties to promptly advise any person arrested of the reason for the arrest, and the duty to inform the arrested person of their legal right to retain and instruct counsel without delay and their right to silence.

3.9.2 Peace Officers' Powers of Arrest

A police officer's primary powers of arrest are found in the *Criminal Code*. Police officers must have expert knowledge of their arrest powers as they may be required to articulate what their grounds were for making an arrest in order to prove the arrest they made was lawful.

Subsection 495(1) *Criminal Code* reads:

"A peace officer may arrest without warrant;

(a) a person who has committed an indictable offence or who, on reasonable grounds, he [or she] believes has committed or is about to commit an indictable offence;"

For a police officer to arrest an individual for an indictable offence contained in any federal statute (or a dual procedure offence which, for the purposes of arrest is treated as indictable), the officer must have a reasonable belief, exceeding mere suspicion, that the suspect committed the offence. This authority also allows a police officer to arrest an individual for the purpose of preventing the commission of an offence when the officer has reasonable grounds to believe the person is about to commit an indictable offence.

(b) "a person whom he [or she] finds committing a criminal offence; or"

A police officer may arrest any individual he or she finds committing a summary conviction, dual procedure or indictable offence contained in any federal statute. Note the distinction between summary conviction offences and indictable offences. A police officer must find a person committing a summary conviction offence to be able to lawfully arrest them. A police officer may also arrest someone they find committing an indictable offence, but may also arrest on reasonable grounds a person who they believe has committed or is about to commit an indictable offence. A police officer may not arrest a person on reasonable grounds that they committed a summary conviction offence – they must find the person actually committing the offence.

---

[12]*Criminal Code*, R.S. 1985, c. C-46, s. 30.

[13]*Criminal Code*, R.S. 1985, c. C-46, s. 494(1)-(3).

(c) "a person in respect of whom he [or she] has reasonable grounds to believe that a warrant of arrest or committal, in any form set out in Part XXVIII in relation thereto, is in force within the territorial jurisdiction in which the person is found."[14]

The police officer may arrest the individual if the officer has reasonable grounds, such as a confirmed CPIC report or some other current and reliable information, that a warrant for the arrest or committal of a person exists within the territorial jurisdiction, meaning the region or province where the person is found.

You will remember the previous definition of "reasonable grounds" as a set of facts or circumstances, which if true, would lead an ordinary, prudent and cautious individual to have a strong belief that exceeds mere suspicion. The standard of reasonable grounds is a significantly lower standard than *prima facie* evidence and a far lower standard that proof beyond a reasonable doubt.

Police officers must often rely on the **hearsay evidence** of others and other available evidence for their reasonable grounds to arrest individuals. A police officer must remain objective when formulating reasonable grounds and must consider all available evidence. Police officers must never be selective in their determination of which evidence to rely upon and which evidence to disregard unless the discounted evidence is clearly unreliable.[15]

An officer may have reasonable grounds to effect a lawful arrest in a situation where a credible witness indicates that a certain person committed a specific crime. If sufficient reasonable grounds exist upon which to make the arrest, the arrest is lawful. The investigator must now make a decision as to whether or not to lay a charge against the prisoner.

3.9.3 Fresh Pursuit

Normally a municipal or provincial police officer can only exercise their peace officer status within the province in which they are appointed. This would include their powers of arrest, use of force and search and seizure. The Supreme Court of Canada has held that where a police officer has lawful authority to arrest a person in one province, they retain their peace officer status including all their powers if they freshly pursue the person from that province into an adjoining province.[16] This case law authority applies to arrest of a person both with or without warrant.

The terms **fresh pursuit** and **hot pursuit** mean virtually the same thing. The Honourable Mr. Justice R.E. Salhany, Q.C. provided the definition of fresh pursuit that has been relied upon by several courts, including the Supreme Court in the 1993 decision of *R. v. Macooh*.[17] In his book *Canadian Criminal Procedure*, Mr. Justice Salhany described a fresh pursuit as being a continuous pursuit that is conducted with reasonable diligence so that the commission of the offence, the pursuit and the capture all form one single transaction. This is an uninterrupted transaction, that involves no loss of sight or only reasonable and momentary loss of sight of the subject being pursued.

---

[14]*Criminal Code*, R.S. 1985, c. C-46, s. 495(1).

[15]*Chartier v. Quebec (Attorney General)* (1979), 2 S.C.R. 474, 48 C.C.C. (2d) 34, 9 C.R. (3d) 97.

[16]*R. v. Roberge*, [1983] 1 S.C.R. 312, 4 C.C.C. (3d) 304, 33 C.R. 289 (7:0).

[17]*R. v. Macooh*, supra.

As an example, an Ontario police officer has grounds to arrest an individual for impaired driving, or on an outstanding arrest warrant for robbery. The officer attempts to arrest the wanted individual but the person then flees by motor vehicle. The officer pursues the wanted person to the Manitoba border in the west or to the Quebec border in the east. The officer does not have to discontinue the pursuit and retains his or her peace officer status within the adjoining province.

Common sense and protocol would dictate contacting the police service having jurisdiction and requesting their assistance, but according to case law the original pursuing officer may fully exercise the powers of a peace officer in the adjoining province which the pursuit involved.

This authority is restricted to Canadian provinces and territories and does not extend to situations in which a wanted subject successfully flees across the border with the United States, nor to non-arrestable offences, such as speeding. See Section 7.13 dealing with warrantless entry of premises in relation to hot (fresh) pursuits.

3.10   STATUTE OF LIMITATIONS

The **statute of limitations** for an offence is the maximum time period following the commission of the offence during which a person may be arrested or a charge may be laid. In Canada, summary conviction offences have a statute of limitations of six months, while there is no statute of limitations for indictable offences.

3.11   BREACH OF THE PEACE

While the term **breach of the peace** is not defined in Canadian law, it applies to incidents of disorderly conduct that involve, or that are likely to result in, harm to persons, damage to property, or which may provoke such behaviour in others. There is no offence of breach of the peace – nobody is ever charged with committing a breach of the peace, nor can anyone be convicted of breach of the peace in court. It is primarily a legal procedure aimed at preserving the peace through intervention, by force, if necessary.

> 30   "Every one who witnesses a breach of the peace is justified in interfering to prevent the continuance or renewal thereof and may detain any person who commits or is about to join in or to renew the breach of the peace, for the purpose of giving him into the custody of a peace officer, if he uses no more force than is reasonable necessary to prevent the continuance or renewal of the breach of the peace or than is reasonably proportioned to the danger to be apprehended from the continuance or renewal of the breach of the peace."

A private citizen must actually witness a breach of the peace occur to be justified in detaining any person responsible for such behaviour. The wording of the authority to "detain" is different from the citizen's other authority to "arrest" for offences found in s. 494(1) *CC*. This distinction in wording may have been intended to reflect the reality that s. 30 *CC* does not create a substantive offence, however, s. 31 *CC* authorizes peace officers and citizens assisting peace officers to "arrest" individuals for the same circumstances. I suggest that for citizens, s. 30 draws no significant distinction between "arrest" and "detain", at least for this section of the *Criminal Code*.

31 "(1) Every peace officer who witnesses a breach of the peace and every one who lawfully assists the peace officer is justified in arresting any person whom he finds committing the breach of the peace or who, on reasonable grounds, he believes is about to join in or renew the breach of the peace.

(2) Every peace officer is justified in receiving into custody any person who is given into his charge as having been a party to a breach of the peace by one who has, or who on reasonable grounds the peace officer believes has, witnessed the breach of the peace."[18]

Section 31 authorizes peace officers and citizens assisting peace officers to arrest any person whom they actually witness committing a breach of the peace or to prevent them from joining or renewing a breach of the peace. The legal prerequisite of witnessing a breach of the peace occurring is identical to the requirement of "find committing" for summary conviction offences.

Subsection 31(2) authorizes peace officers to receive persons detained by citizens for involvement in a breach of the peace, but only if the citizen witnessed the breach of the peace occurring. It is the eye-witness evidence of the arresting citizen that gives the peace officer the reasonable grounds to continue the detention. In the event that a citizen arrested an individual without actually witnessing the breach of the peace, the peace officer would not be justified in continuing the unlawful arrest.

Incidents which may lead to criminal offences can and, if possible, should be prevented before escalating. I was taught at an early stage of my policing career that "any blow struck in anger" is an example of a breach of the peace.

3.12 HOW TO MAKE A PROPER ARREST

Although the procedure of placing someone under arrest sounds like a relatively simple act, a proper and legal arrest involves a surprising number of steps – six in all.

1. Identify yourself as a police officer.

An arrest made by a police officer is an official action by a law enforcement agent of the state. It is not sufficient that you be the only person involved in the action to know of your official status as a peace officer. The person being arrested should be informed that you have official legal status to deprive them of their liberty.

Don't assume that just because you are wearing a full or partial police uniform that everyone knows that you are, in fact, a police officer. Police officers in Ontario alone might wear either a khaki shirt (RCMP) or navy blue (OPP and many municipal services) or light blue (Peel Regional police). Tactical and special unit officers wear blue or grey fatigue uniforms.

Other professions such as security officers and delivery persons wear uniforms that could be confusing to some, especially considering recent relaxing of standards with police uniforms. While the shoulder flashes on your uniform may contain the crest of a police service, this also might not be familiar to the person you are arresting.

---

[18]*Criminal Code*, R.S. 1985, c. C-46, s. 30-31.

Identifying yourself as a police officer is even more important when you are wearing plain-clothes (casual or business attire) or are undercover. Proper identification should include at least the pronouncement of your name, rank and police service. "I am Sergeant Jane Smith, a police officer with the Belleville Police Service." Whether you are in uniform or not, the physical production and display of your police issued badge and warrant card, as proof of your contention that you are a police officer, is not unreasonable if the circumstances of the arrest permit you to do so.

The individual's comprehension of your identification as a police officer becomes very important in the event that they resist your efforts to place them under arrest, attempt to use force against you, or attempt to escape from your custody after being placed under arrest.

2. Inform the individual that they are under arrest.

This is accomplished by way of formally pronouncing to them, "You are under arrest for..." Alternatively, the officer may state, "I am placing you under arrest for..."

3a) Take physical control of the individual being arrested.

Proper arrest procedure requires the touching of the person to symbolize the taking of physical control of the individual. This is accomplished by placing the officer's hand on the subject or lightly grasping their arm. While the initial act is largely symbolic, it has various effects on people being arrested that range from passive acceptance to provoking defensiveness or hostility.

"It has also been accepted that if the accused submits or acquiesces [accepts or agrees without objection] because of words other than 'arrest' which bring home the loss of his or her liberty notwithstanding there is no physical contact, an arrest in law is acknowledged to have occurred."[19] The absence of a touch or taking of physical control of the individual does not necessarily nullify (invalidate or cancel) an arrest where the individual being arrested ran away from the officer after they were informed of the arrest and the reason for it.

3b) Appropriate use of force

As we learned in earlier sections of this chapter dealing with use of force, any force used by the officer to effect a legal purpose must be reasonable, minimal and proportional. Ideally, and as is often the case, no force will be required to be used. The use of force in relation to an arrest may range between no force whatsoever to empty-hand control techniques, handcuffing, intermediate weapons, hard control techniques or, in absolute worst case scenarios, lethal force.

3c) Search incident to arrest

Once an individual has been formally arrested, common law grants peace officers the legal authority to search prisoners and the area immediately surrounding them for:

(a) evidence;

(b) weapons; or

(c) tools of escape

---

[19]Groot at pp. 122-123.

Evidence of the offence the person is being arrested for, in any tangible form, would constitute proof that the person arrested is responsible for the commission of the offence under investigation. In the event that a person arrested for assault was found to be in possession of illegal drugs, the seizure would be legal if the original search incident to the arrest was legal. In such a case, the individual should also be placed under arrest for possession of the drugs under the appropriate offence.

Weapons, including anything that may be turned into a weapon against the officer should be confiscated to ensure the officer's safety and the safety of every person who may come into contact with the prisoner during the arrest and subsequent incarceration procedures.[20] (Van Allen 2007)

4. Inform the person of the reason for their arrest.

Informing the person of the legal reason for their arrest is usually done at the time of the arrest, such as, "You are under arrest for Break Enter and Theft". If the arrest is made on the authority of a legal arrest warrant, the officer should produce (not surrender) the warrant if it is in the officer's possession and if it is possible to do so.

The officer would then state, "I have (or there is) a warrant for your arrest on a charge of (state offence contained in warrant)" or "I have (or there is) a committal warrant for your arrest for unpaid fines". The duty to notify an arrested person of the reason for their arrest is found both within the *Criminal Code* and the *Charter of Rights and Freedoms.*

> "It is the duty of every one who executes a process or warrant to have it with him where it is feasible to do so, and to produce it when requested to do so."

> "It is the duty of every one who arrests a person, whether with or without a warrant to give notice to that person, where it is feasible to do so, of

> (a) the process or warrant under which he makes the arrest; or

> (b) the reason for the arrest."[21]

> "Everyone has the right on arrest or detention

> (a) to be informed promptly of the reasons therefor"[22]

5a) Inform prisoner of their rights to counsel and to legal aid.

This duty imposed on peace officers also originates from the legal rights guaranteed to individuals under *Charter of Rights and Freedoms*:

> "Everyone has the right on arrest or detention...

> (b) to retain and instruct counsel without delay and to be informed of that right."[23]

This legal duty actually imposes two requirements on police officer making an arrest. The first right is obviously that an arrested person has the right to retain (contact or hire) and instruct (consult with and authorize) legal counsel. In simple

---

[20]*Gottschalk vs. Hutton* (1921), 17 Alta. L.R. 347, 1 W.W.R. 59, 66 D.L.R. 499, 36 C.C.C. 298; *R. v. Storrey* (1990), 1 S.C.R.241; *Cloutier v. Langlois* (1990) 1 S.C.R. 158, 53 C.C.C. (3d) 257, 74 C.R. (3d) 316; *R. v. Caslake* (1998) 1 S.C.R. 51, 121 C.C.C. (3d) 97, 155 D.L.R. (4ᵗʰ) 19.

[21]*Criminal Code*, R.S. 1985, c. C-46, s. 29(1)-(2).

[22]*Charter of Rights and Freedoms*, Being Part I of the *Constitution Act* (1982), s. 10(a).

[23]*Charter of Rights and Freedoms*, Being Part I of the *Constitution Act* (1982), s. 10(b).

terms, a prisoner has the right to contact a lawyer and consult with and take advice from them regarding their arrest and legal rights. The second, and perhaps less obvious right is that of being informed of the first right. Not only does the person have a right to speak to a lawyer, they have the right to be informed of their right to speak to a lawyer.

The literal effect of s. 10(b) of the *Charter* is that only persons who have been arrested or detained are legally required to be advised of their rights to counsel.

In addition to being informed of their rights to counsel, the Supreme Court of Canada has ruled that arrested or detained persons must also be advised of the existence and availability of legal aid.[24]

In Ontario, an officer might use the following wording to discharge their responsibilities under s. 10(b) of the *Charter*:

"It is my duty to inform you that you have the right to retain and instruct counsel without delay. You have the right to telephone any lawyer you wish. You also have the right to free advice from a Legal Aid lawyer. If you are charged with an offence, you may apply to the Ontario Legal Aid Plan for legal assistance. 1-800-265-0451 is a toll free number that will put you in contact with a Legal Aid Duty Counsel lawyer for free legal advice right now. Do you understand? Do you wish to call a lawyer now?"

5b) Inform prisoner of their right to remain silent

The standard police caution is either read or recited to the prisoner by the arresting officer to inform them that they have the right to remain silent and not implicate themselves in connection with the offence under investigation. The officer might use the following words from their police issued caution card:

"You [are charged / will be charged / may be charged] with [the offence under investigation]. Do you wish to say anything in answer to the charge? You are not obliged to say anything unless you wish to do so, but whatever you say may be given in evidence. Do you understand?"

The purpose of administering the caution is first to inform the individual that he or she is being charged with or is at least considered a suspect responsible for the commission of an offence. Second, the caution informs the suspect or accused that they are not required to say anything but if they do voluntarily make any statement, whatever they say may be repeated in evidence in court. This is done in an attempt to ensure that any statement made by a prisoner is voluntary and that the voluntariness is the result of an informed decision on the part of the prisoner of the possible consequences of making such a statement.

If a suspect or accused was arrested or previously dealt with by another person in authority other than the officer who has a prisoner in custody, it is then necessary for the later police officer to administer what is referred to as the secondary caution to the prisoner to minimize the effect of any threat or inducement that

---

[24]*R. v. Brydges* (1990), 1 S.C.R. 190, 53 C.C.C. (3d) 330, (1990) 2 W.W.R. 220.

may have been made by any previous person in authority. The wording of the secondary caution is to the effect:

"If you have spoken to any police officer, or to anyone with authority, or if any such person has spoken to you in connection with this case, I want it clearly understood that I do not want it to influence you in making any statement. Do you understand?"

6. Ensure that the prisoner comprehends the reason for their detention and their rights to counsel

There is a professional, if not a legal obligation, on the part of an arresting officer to ensure, to the extent that is possible, that the arrested prisoner comprehends the reason for their arrest and their rights to counsel. There are many instances when a prisoner may not fully appreciate the nature and severity of the arrest.

The prisoner may be in a state of physical or emotional shock, or be suffering from a mental disorder. Intoxication by alcohol or drugs may affect the prisoner's rational thought. The elderly and the very young, or someone who is not fluent in the English language may not fully understand what is being said to them or may not fully grasp the ramifications of their detention or their rights attendant upon their arrest.

In such instances, an arresting officer owes a duty to safeguard the individual's rights by explaining them in a different way, by delaying the investigative process. The officer might encourage a confused prisoner to speak to a legal aid lawyer, or ensure that the prisoner detoxifies sufficiently to make informed decisions. In the event of a foreign speaking prisoner, the officer should take steps to secure the services of a translator to explain the situation and potential consequences.

A police officer who makes the effort to respect and safeguard the individual rights of a prisoner will be regarded only with respect in any subsequent court proceedings for their fairness and professionalism.

3.13   WHEN <u>NOT</u> TO ARREST - ABSOLUTE JURISDICTION OFFENCES

Certain limitations are placed on a police officer's warrantless powers of arrest. These limitations are set out in subsection 495(2) *Criminal Code* which states:

"A peace officer shall not arrest a person without warrant for (a) an indictable offence mentioned in section 553..."[25]

Section 553 sets out offences which are the exclusive or **absolute jurisdiction** of a provincial court judge to try. Even though these offences are dual procedure or hybrid offences, if the prosecutor were to elect to proceed by indictment, the accused may not elect to be tried in a higher court due to the designation of the offence as being the absolute jurisdiction of the provincial court.

The rationale for this absolute jurisdiction designation is to keep the lower-end offences at the provincial court level. Trials of this scope are numerous and are well within the capability of a Provincial Court judge to try without a jury. This list includes committing, counselling, conspiracies or attempts to commit the following offences:

---

[25]*Criminal Code*, R.S. 1985 c. C-46, s. 495(2).

- Theft under $5 000 (other than theft of cattle)

- False pretences under $5 000

- Possession of property under $5 000 obtained by the commission of an indictable offence

- Fraud under $5 000

- Mischief to property under $5 000, or with any of the following offences:

- Keeping a gaming or betting house

- Betting or bookmaking

- Placing bets

- Offences dealing with lotteries and games of chance

- Cheating at play

- Keeping a common bawdy-house

- Fraud in relation to fares (transportation fraud)

- Breach of recognizance

- Breach of probation order

- Possession of schedule II drugs in amounts less than the maximum amounts specified in schedule VIII of the *Controlled Drugs and Substances Act* (<30g of Cannabis [Marijuana] or <1g of Cannabis resin)

A peace officer shall not arrest, without warrant, for any of the following offences:

1. any designated section 553 *Criminal Code* offence listed above;

2. any dual procedure (hybrid) offence; or

3. any summary conviction offence

in situations where the public interest may be satisfied by not arresting the individual, especially if the following needs, described by the mnemonic "R.I.C.E." have been met, namely:

R   **R**easonable grounds – Court: No reasonable grounds exist which indicate that the accused, if not arrested, would fail to appear in court

I   **I**dentity: The identity of the individual has been satisfactorily established

C   **C**ontinuation or repetition of the offence: Prevention of the repetition of the offence, or another offence does not require the individual's arrest

E   **E**vidence: The arrest or continued detention of the person is not justified by the need to secure or preserve evidence of the offence[26]

A police officer may arrest a person without warrant for a section 553 *CC* (absolute jurisdiction) offence, a dual procedure (hybrid) offence, or a summary conviction offence where the public interest considerations of R.I.C.E. have not been satisfied. For example,

---

[26]*Criminal Code*, R.S. 1985, c. C-46, s. 495(2).

a person arrested for operating a motor vehicle while their ability to drive is impaired by alcohol contrary to section 253(a) *Criminal Code* may be returned to a police station for the purposes of administering breathalyzer tests.

The arrest of the allegedly impaired driver would be justified due to the public interest requirement to ensure that evidence of impairment could be established (secured or preserved). Once the breathalyzer tests are administered, however, the public interest requirement will have been met, and continued detention is no longer justified on the grounds of securing evidence.

Once the public interest considerations of R.I.C.E., plus the additional consideration of safety and security of any victim or any witness to the offence have been assured, any person arrested for a section 553 *CC* indictable offence, dual procedure offence or summary conviction offence must be released by way of appearance notice or be later issued with a summons as soon as practicable.[27]

3.14 ARREST WITHOUT WARRANT – OUT OF PROVINCE INDICTABLE OFFENCE

Peace officers may also arrest a person without a warrant for indictable offences that have been committed in Canada, outside of the territorial jurisdiction in which the person is found. If a valid arrest warrant exists in British Columbia for an armed robbery that occurred there and the person named in the warrant is subsequently found in Ontario, the person who is the subject of the warrant may be arrested without warrant in Ontario on the strength of the B.C. warrant. The arresting police service should only make such an arrest upon the expressed indication of the agency holding the arrest warrant of their intention to return the prisoner to the jurisdiction where the offence occurred.

In such a case, the arrested individual must be taken before a justice in the territorial jurisdiction in which the arrest took place, and be remanded into custody for a period of up to six days to allow the out of province police service to execute their warrant.[28] A warrant issued in one province must first be taken before a justice in the province where the arrest occurred and endorsed in Form 28 *Criminal Code* prior to execution in the new territorial jurisdiction.[29] (Van Allen 2007)

3.15 ENTRY OF DWELLING HOUSES TO EFFECT ARRESTS–FEENEY WARRANTS

In 1997, the Supreme Court of Canada declared that, except in exigent circumstances[30] (see Exigent Circumstances – Section 3.16) police officers could no longer enter dwelling houses without judicial pre-authorization to effect arrests.[31] An arrest warrant in Form 7.1 – known as a **Feeney Warrant** – may be issued to enter a dwelling house to arrest a person if:

---

[27]*Criminal Code*, R.S. 1985, c. C-46, s. 497(1).

[28]*Criminal Code*, R.S. 1985, c. C-46, s. 503(3)(b).

[29]*Criminal Code*, R.S. 1985, c. C-46, s. 528.

[30]*Criminal Code*, R.S. 1985, c. C-46, s. 529.1.

[31]*R. v. Feeney* (1997), 2 S.C.R. 13, 115 C.C.C. (3d) 129, 7 C.R. (5th) 101.

1. Reasonable grounds exist to arrest the person without warrant for a *Criminal Code* offence or the person has contravened or wilfully failed to comply or is about to fail to comply with a court disposition, or[32]

2. A warrant for a federal offence exists for the person anywhere in Canada, or

3. Grounds exist to arrest the person, without warrant, for any federal offence other than those contained in the *Criminal Code*.

A police officer executing such a warrant must make prior announcement of their entry unless, at the time of issuance, the justice is satisfied upon "information on oath" that entry without prior announcement is necessary to prevent the exposure of any person to imminent bodily harm or death or to prevent imminent loss or destruction of evidence.[33] Even after receiving such an authorization for entry without prior announcement, the officer may still not enter the dwelling house without announcing their presence and purpose unless reasonable grounds of the necessity to prevent exposure to imminent bodily harm or death or loss or destruction of evidence exist immediately before the entry.[34] (Van Allen 2007)

3.16 WARRANTLESS ENTRY OF DWELLING HOUSES TO ARREST IN EXIGENT CIRCUMSTANCES

Where reasonable grounds exist to obtain an arrest warrant but emergency conditions make it impracticable to obtain a warrant, a peace officer may in **exigent circumstances** enter a dwelling house for the purpose of arresting a person without a warrant. The only permissible reasons for not first obtaining a warrant would be the necessity to prevent imminent bodily harm or death or the imminent loss or destruction of evidence.[35]

Exigent circumstances that justify a warrantless entry to effect an arrest under s. 529.3(1) *Criminal Code* do not excuse the officer(s) of the requirement of prior announcement of their entry. Reasonable grounds must exist, immediately before the warrantless entry, to believe that to announce their presence would expose themselves or any person to imminent bodily harm or death or would result in the imminent loss or destruction of evidence, to justify not complying with the prior announcement requirement.[36]

Similar authorities exist for entering, searching and seizing evidence without a search warrant in exigent circumstances.[37] This issue will be addressed in detail in Chapter 8, dealing with search warrants.

3.17 OTHER ARREST POWERS

Powers of arrest exist within other statutes, including provincial statutes. Police officers regularly encounter such incidents and must be familiar with the arrest authorities and limitations contained within those respective statutes.

---

[32]*Criminal Code*, R.S. 1985, c. C-46, s. 495(1)(a) and 672.91.

[33]*Criminal Code*, R.S. 1985, c. C-46, s. 529.4(1).

[34]*Criminal Code*, R.S. 1985, c. C-46, s. 529.4(2).

[35]*Criminal Code*, R.S. 1985, c. C-46, s. 529.3(1).

[36]*Criminal Code*, R.S. 1985, c. C-46, s. 529.4(3).

[37]*Criminal Code*, R.S. 1985, c. C-46, s. 487.11.

3.17.1 *Liquor Licence Act*

The *Liquor Licence Act* of Ontario contains two separate arrest authorities for police officers to arrest individuals.

48 "If a police officer finds a person apparently in contravention of this Act or apparently in contravention of a prescribed provision of the regulations and the person refuses to give his or her name and address or there are reasonable grounds to believe that the name or address given is false, the police officer may arrest the person without warrant."[38]

Often while under the influence of alcohol, individuals will be inclined to refuse to identify themselves or to give a false name to avoid prosecution for liquor offences. Section 48 *LLA* permits police officers investigating liquor offences to arrest without warrant where an individual refuses to identify themselves or where reasonable grounds exist to believe that the name and address provided by such person is false.

Note that this does not apply to people who do not have proper government issued photo identification on them to produce to a police officer making such a demand. We have all at one time or another forgotten our identification at home. A person who is unable to produce documentary identification upon the demand of a police officer must, at a minimum, provide their correct name and address.

This is a useful section to rely on as it applies to all offences and regulations within the *Liquor Licence Act*. The not infrequent overlap between liquor offences and other enforcement matters allows this section to be utilized more often than one might expect.

31 (4) "No person shall be in an intoxicated condition,

(a) in a place to which the general public is invited or permitted access; or

(b) in any part of a residence that is used in common by persons occupying more than one dwelling in the residence."

31 (5) "A police officer may arrest without warrant any person whom he or she finds contravening subsection (4) if, in the opinion of the police officer, to do so is necessary for the safety of any person."[39]

Police officers may arrest anyone without warrant who is intoxicated by alcohol in a public place or within a common area of a dwelling house that contains multiple dwellings, such as a lobby, laundry room, hallways, exercise facilities, parking garages, etc., of an apartment building. An intoxicated person may only be arrested if in the opinion of the officer – a purely subjective standard lower than reasonable grounds – the arrest is necessary for the safety of any person – not just the safety of the intoxicated person.

36 (1) "A police officer who finds a person apparently in contravention of subsection 31 (4) may take the person into custody and, in lieu of laying an information in respect of the contravention, may escort the person to a hospital designated by the regulations."[40]

---

[38]*Liquor Licence Act*, R.S.O. 1990, c. L-19, s. 48.

[39]*Liquor Licence Act*, R.S.O. 1990, c. L-19, s. 31(4)-(5).

[40]*Liquor Licence Act*, R.S.O. 1990, c. L-19, s. 36(1).

Recognizing the social nature of alcohol abuse and that prosecution may not always be the best way of dealing with an intoxicated person, police officers may also take intoxicated persons into custody and instead of charging them, may escort them to a designated hospital with a detoxification unit.

3.17.2 *Trespass to Property Act*

Another provincial statute that police officers frequently enforce is the *Trespass to Property Act* (*TPA*). This act applies when individuals trespass on property which is not their own without the consent of the owner, engage in prohibited activity on another person's property, or if they refuse to leave another person's property when directed to do so by the owner or person authorized by the owner.

9(1) "A police officer, or the occupier of premises, or a person authorized by the occupier may arrest without warrant any person he or she believes on reasonable and probable grounds to be on the premises in contravention of section 2."

9(2) "Where the person who makes an arrest under subsection (1) is not a police officer, he or she shall promptly call for the assistance of a police officer and give the person arrested into the custody of the police officer."[41]

10 "Where a police officer believes on reasonable and probable grounds that a person has been in contravention of section 2 and has made fresh departure from the premises, and the person refuses to give his or her name and address, or there are reasonable and probable grounds to believe that the name or address given is false, the police officer may arrest the person without warrant."[42]

Subsection 9(1) *TPA* provides authority to arrest without warrant to both police officers and to owners and other authorized persons. Note that subsection 9(2) and section 10 do not require the police officer to actually witness the trespass occur, although it is common for officers to still find persons trespassing or refusing to leave premises while responding to trespassing complaints. As with other citizen's arrest authorities, anyone arrested by a private person must be promptly turned over to the custody of a police officer.

Section 10 allows a police officer on "reasonable and probable grounds" (a previous version of reasonable grounds that, for our purposes, means the same thing) to arrest a person who has made a fresh departure after committing a trespass and who refuses to identify themselves (at least verbally) or who there are reasonable and probable grounds to believe has given a name or address that is false.

3.17.3 *Highway Traffic Act*

Another useful provincial statute containing powers of arrest is the *Highway Traffic Act* (*HTA*). Like the rest of us, individuals who are inclined to break the law rely on transportation to get themselves around.

Subsection 217(2) *HTA* provides that a police officer or person appointed to enforce the Act may arrest without warrant any individual they have "reasonable and probable grounds" to believe has committed any of a list of designated offences. Subsection

---

[41]*Trespass to Property Act*, R.S.O. 1990, c. T-21, s. 9(1)-(2).

[42]*Trespass to Property Act*, R.S.O. 1990, c. T-21, s. 10.

217(3) provides that any one may arrest without warrant anyone whom they find committing any of the designated offences.[43]

Arrestable *Highway Traffic Act* offences include:

9(1)	False statement on application, affidavit or declaration
12(1)	Deface, alter or use or permit use of defaced number plates
13(1)	Use number plate other than issued number plate
33(3)	Refuse to identify
47(5)(6)(7)(8)	Offences relating to suspended or cancelled vehicle permits
51	Driving with suspended or cancelled vehicle permit
53	Driving while driver's licence under suspension
130	Careless Driving
172	Racing a motor vehicle upon a highway
184	Deface or remove highway notice or obstruction
185(3)	Pedestrian on highway in contravention of by-law
200(1)(a)	Fail to remain or immediately return to scene of accident
216(1)	Offences relating to examination of commercial motor vehicles

Additionally, subsection 217(3.1) authorizes police officers to arrest individuals for stopping or attempting to stop motor vehicles on a highway to solicit business contrary to subsection 177(2) *HTA*. This arrest authority may only be resorted to where a police officer has directed the individual not to engage in that activity and where the police officer has reasonable and probable grounds to believe that it is necessary to arrest the individual to establish their identity or to prevent the person from continuing or repeating the offence.[44]

3.17.4   Apprehension without Warrant – *Mental Health Act*

A very different authority is found in the *Mental Health Act* that allows police officers to take individuals into custody without warrant if they are apparently suffering from a mental disorder. This legal authority is very much different than arrest, as it does not involve an offence and its purpose is to ensure that people suffering from mental disorders are protected and receive appropriate medical treatment. I have included this authority in this section as it is an example of an authority found within statute law that authorizes police officers to interfere with the liberty of citizens under certain circumstances. The section contains strict limitations for its use.

17 "Where a police officer has reasonable and probable grounds to believe that a person is acting or has acted in a disorderly manner and has reasonable cause to believe that the person,

(a) has threatened or attempted or is threatening or attempting to cause bodily harm to himself or herself;

(b) has behaved or is behaving violently towards another person or has caused or is causing another person to fear bodily harm from him or her; or

(c) has shown or is showing a lack of competence to care for himself or herself,

---

[43]*Highway Traffic Act*, R.S.O. 1990, c. H-8, s. 217(2)-(3).

[44]*Highway Traffic Act*, R.S.O. 1990, c. H-8, s. 217(3.1).

and in addition the police officer is of the opinion that the person is apparently suffering from mental disorder of a nature or quality that likely will result in,

(d) serious bodily harm to the person;

(e) serious bodily harm to another person; or

(f) serious physical impairment of the person,

and that it would be dangerous to proceed under section 16, [obtaining an order from a Justice of the Peace] the police officer may take the person in custody to an appropriate place for examination by a physician." [45]

3.18 ARRESTING YOUNG OFFENDERS

The *Youth Criminal Justice* Act defines a **young person** as:

"A young person means a person who is or, in the absence of evidence to the contrary, appears to be twelve years old or older, but less than eighteen years old and, if the context requires, includes any person who is charged under this Act with having committed an offence while he or she was a young person or who is found guilty of an offence under this Act." [46]

When a police officer arrests a young person, virtually all of the same procedures and individual legal rights and rights to counsel apply as is the case with adult offenders. Police officers who arrest young offenders between the ages of 12 to 17 inclusive must also serve notice of the arrest to the child's parent or another adult.

26(1) "...if a young person is arrested and detained in custody pending his or her appearance in court, the officer in charge at the time the young person is detained shall, as soon as possible, give or cause to be given to a parent of the young person, orally or in writing, notice of the arrest stating the place of detention and the reason for the arrest."

26(4) "If the whereabouts of the parents of a young person are not known or it appears that no parent is available, a notice under this section may be given to an adult relative of the young person who is known to the young person and is likely to assist the young person or, if no such adult relative is available, to any other adult who is known to the young person and is likely to assist the young person and who the person giving the notice considers appropriate." [47]

3.19 APPREHENSION OF YOUNG PERSONS UNDER 12 YEARS

Section 13 *Criminal Code* fixes the age of responsibility for offences at 12 years of age. The *Youth Criminal Justice Act* defines a young person as being 12 years of age or more but under the age of 18 at the time of the commission of an offence. It is no longer

---

[45]*Mental Health Act,* 1990 R.S.O. c. M-7, s. 17.

[46]*Youth Criminal Justice Act,* S.C. 2002, s. 2(1).

[47]*Youth Criminal Justice Act,* S.C. 2002, s. 26(1) & (4).

uncommon, however, for a police officer to encounter persons under the age of legal responsibility who have committed an offence.

For example, a child under 12 years of age has thrown a brick through the plate glass window of a store or has committed a serious assault upon a classmate. You arrive at the scene and the involved child informs you that they are 10 years old and are well aware that they cannot be charged in relation to their actions.

In Ontario, the *Child and Family Services Act* authorizes peace officers to apprehend (not arrest) children under the age of 12 years who, on reasonable and probable grounds, have committed an offence for which a person over 12 could be convicted, and return them to their parent or a person having care of the child. If it is not possible to return the child to the parent or other person, the child may be taken to a place of safety, which does not include places of open or secure custody.[48]

This warrantless authority to apprehend children under 12 who have committed offences strikes a balance between the protection of children who are not legally responsible for their actions and the need to prevent continuation or recurrence of offences by returning the child to supervision. In certain cases, such as those involving the use or threatened or attempted use of violence or inappropriate sexual behaviour, ongoing care or treatment of the child may be indicated. If the circumstances of the case dictate, the police officer should notify the appropriate child protection agency of the incident so that they may work with the parent or person having care, or consider assuming responsibility for the child.

SUMMARY

- A person may be arrested for committing, resuming or joining any breach of the peace. A person may be arrested to prevent them from committing an offence.

- Arrests may be conducted either with or without the legal authority of a court order in the form of an arrest warrant or committal warrant.

- An arbitrary arrest is the opposite of a legal and proper arrest.

- A police officer's powers of arrest differ from those of a private citizen. A peace officer must find a person committing a summary conviction offence but may arrest on reasonable grounds in relation to indictable offences.

- Arrest authorities are located within each respective statute. Police officers must familiarize themselves with the scope and limitations of arrest powers for each statute.

- The statute of limitations is the maximum period following the commission of an offence for which a person may be arrested or charged.

- The only permissible reasons for not first obtaining a warrant to enter a dwelling house to arrest a person include the necessity to prevent imminent bodily harm or death or the imminent loss or destruction of evidence.

- Police officers must not arrest for summary conviction, dual procedure offences or indictable offences which are the absolute jurisdiction of provincial court judges to try if the public interest demands of R.I.C.E. have been met.

---

[48]*Child and Family Services Act*, R.S.O. 1990, c. C-11, s. 42(1).

DISCUSSION QUESTIONS

1. Can a person be charged and convicted of committing a breach of the peace? Why?

2. You are a uniformed police officer patrolling in your town or city. You observe an automobile with New Brunswick licence plates fail to stop at a stop sign. You pursue and stop the vehicle. Upon questioning the driver and running a CPIC check on his name, you determine that he is the subject of an outstanding arrest warrant from St. John, N.B. for Sexual Assault Level III.

   Part I – What procedure would you follow with regards to the New Brunswick arrest warrant? Can it be executed in Ontario? What will you do with the driver of the vehicle?

   Part II – What procedure would you follow with regards to this scenario if the warrant and driver originated from the state of Rhode Island?

3. You respond to a 9-1-1 hang up from a local residence. Upon arriving to check on the welfare of the people in the house, a man comes to the door and states that everything is fine and that nobody there contacted 9-1-1. He is dressed only in underwear and refuses your request to enter the residence. While standing at the door, a female voice from inside calls out, "Help me! He hurt me and he'll do it again if you leave. Help!"

   What will you do next? Do you have the right to enter the residence against the owner's instructions to stay out? If so, what are your legal authorities to act in this situation?

WEBLINKS

www.canlii.org

Canadian Legal Information Institute website. Searchable case law database and links to provincial and federal statutes and regulations, courts, appeal courts and various tribunals, boards and committees.

www.lexum.umontreal.ca/index_en.html

University of Montreal faculty of law website. Searchable Supreme Court of Canada decision database, with links to federal and provincial legislation, periodicals and law libraries. Site features a wide variety of national and international legal resources.

www.e-laws.gov.on.ca/home_E.asp?lang=en

Government of Ontario. Provincial statutes and associated regulations

http://laws.justice.gc.ca/en/index.html

Department of Justice, Government of Canada. Selected federal statutes and links to sites of case law databanks.

Chapter 4

Use of Force

"But without encountering evil at close quarters, the concept remains a mere abstraction."

Dr. Michael Stone, forensic psychiatrist,
"Quantifying Evil" - PAO - Police Association of Ontario,
Issue 27, Summer 2005 pp. 6-7.

Learning Outcomes

After reading this chapter, students should be able to:

- Differentiate between the terms reasonable, minimal and proportional in relation to the legal authorized use of force.
- Explain the meaning of the legal concept of reasonable grounds.
- Describe and analyze the factors that may assist in assessing the risk posed by a suspect to decide an appropriate level of force to respond to a situation.
- Describe the eight possible use of force response options available to Ontario police officers.
- Explain the mandate and purpose of the Special Investigations Unit (SIU).

4.1   INTRODUCTION

As we discussed in Chapter 1, the main objective of law enforcement is to ensure voluntary compliance with the laws of a particular society through the effective suppression of illegal activities and through deterrence – the discouragement that results from the prosecution and punishment of offenders. It would be naïve, however, for us to take for granted that everyone will always voluntarily comply with every request made to them by a police officer.

Police powers – including powers of arrest and use of force exist because of the reality that coercive (physical) force is sometimes necessary to apprehend offenders, to compel their attendance in a court of law, to further investigations or to prevent or stop harmful acts. Our society places a high value on effective law enforcement and recognizes that the use of force by law enforcement agents to uphold society's rights is sometimes necessary.

While the topics of arrest and use of force are often related, they are dealt with in separate chapters of this textbook. It must be remembered that while not every arrest involves the use of force, neither does every instance of police use of force necessarily involve an arrest.

For a variety of reasons, police officers are sometimes required to use force when people commit illegal acts or when a suspect either passively refuses to comply or actively resists the legal efforts of the police. During the course of their duties, police officers regularly encounter people at often emotionally charged episodes in their lives, including domestic disputes and other disturbances, to name but two. Emotions can easily cloud a normal person's judgement and can result in behaviour that is uncharacteristically inappropriate.

At other times, suspects may be under the influence of an intoxicating substance or a mental condition that impairs their rational judgement. Some people may resist the efforts of police officers out of fear, or resentment at being deprived of their liberty. Still others physically resist the actions of a police officer out of honest but mistaken beliefs that they are innocent, and dispute the justification for actions of the police.

The use of physical force is occasionally required to enable police officers to carry out a particular lawful purpose, to allow the officer to protect their safety or the safety of other persons, or to intervene to prevent or stop a breach of the peace. Regardless of the many reasons that may require police officers to use force to carry out their duties, Canadian laws provide police officers with a broad range of authority to utilize physical force where it is necessary to do so.

Powers that authorize the use of force carry with them a great responsibility to ensure that they are used in a judicious manner. Resorting to using physical force against a member of the public, for any reason, must be authorized by law and the degree of force used must be both **reasonable** and **proportional**, having regard to all the circumstances. Police officers who are expert in the both the scope and limitations of their powers to use force will be highly effective in carrying out their duties. Officers must be keep in their mind that they will always be accountable to the very public they serve for any use of force.

4.2   USE OF FORCE IN ADMINISTRATION AND ENFORCEMENT OF LAW

Under Canadian law, an assault is committed whenever one person intentionally applies force to another person, without their consent, either directly or indirectly. Assault may also be committed by threatening or attempting to apply force to another person, through an act or gesture, if the victim believes, on reasonable grounds, that their assailant has the present ability to carry out their purpose.[1]

Police officers are often required to use physical force while making arrests or when conducting searches during the course of their duties. The physical force used by police officers is intentional; it is applied directly to another person and is applied to the other person usually without their consent. We know that police officers are not above the law, so, what is it that prevents the force used by an officer in the execution of his or her duties from being considered a criminal assault?

---

[1]*Criminal Code*, R.S. 1985, c. C-46, s. 265(1).

One of the prime requirements in justifying the use of physical force by the police against citizens is that the use of force must be sanctioned (authorized) by law. The primary legal authority relied upon by law enforcement officers is found within Section 25 of the *Criminal Code*, which reads:

"Every one who is required or authorized by law to do anything in the administration or enforcement of the law

(a) as a private person,

(b) as a peace officer or public officer,

(c) in aid of a peace officer or public officer, or

(d) by virtue of his office,

is, if he acts on reasonable grounds, justified in doing what he is required or authorized to do and in using as much force as is necessary for that purpose."[2]

Paragraph 25(1)(b) *Criminal Code* is the principal source that authorizes peace officers (defined in section 2 *Criminal Code)* to use force. While seemingly straightforward, a careful analysis of this section reveals that this power not only authorizes the use of force by persons who are legally required to enforce the law, it also places strict limitations on its use.

First, in order to be justified in using force, the peace officer must be "required or authorized to do anything in the administration or enforcement of the law". This means that the peace officer must be actually engaged in the execution of their lawful duties at the particular time that the force was used, for example, while making a lawful arrest, search, seizure, etc.

Any officer who uses physical force in making an unlawful arrest or while conducting some other unlawful action is not afforded the protection from criminal liability offered by this section. Force that is used against a person during unlawful police actions constitutes a criminal assault.

A police officer who is sitting in a police cruiser on the side of the road operating radar is not authorized to use force, as the circumstances of operating the radar unit don't require any use of force. Let's suppose that the officer is called away from her radar duties and dispatched to a disturbance. If upon her arrival, she observes two males involved in a physical altercation which could not be ended by any less violent means, the appropriate use of force by the officer would be considered legal. In such a situation as this, the officer would be required by law to intervene to end the disturbance.

Second, the section requires that the officer must act on **reasonable grounds.** The concept of reasonable grounds will be referred to several times throughout this textbook, in relation to powers of arrest, search and seizure as well as the use of force, so let's take a moment to define exactly what it means. Reasonable grounds are defined as:

"A set of facts or circumstances which if true, would lead an ordinary, prudent, cautious individual to have a strong belief that exceeds mere suspicion."

Reasonable grounds refer to a legal threshold that constitutes a strong belief in a fact, such as that a certain person has committed a particular offence or that illegal property

---

[2]*Criminal Code*, R.S. 1985, c. C-46, s. 25(1).

is situated in a certain place. Reasonable grounds may be formed from bits and pieces of information received from other persons, either in word or in writing, or obtained as the result of an inquiry, or an observation made by the officer. Reasonable grounds may even be a conclusion or belief formed by assessing information from one or more sources, including both physical (real) or circumstantial evidence. See Box 4.1.

Reasonable grounds must first be considered to be reliable before they are acted upon and must be more than just suspicion. The concept of reasonable grounds is a far lower threshold than proof **beyond a reasonable doubt**, which is the legal standard that is used by Canadian courts of law to determine guilt or innocence.

For example, if we suspect that John Smith committed an armed robbery at a local bank two weeks ago, but as we have no reliable information or evidence, we are left with a mere suspicion of his guilt that lacks any basis of reliability. If, however, we are told by a confidential and reliable informant that John Smith admitted to him having committed the bank robbery, giving accurate details about the crime; and we find John Smith's fingerprints on the hold-up note recovered inside the bank; plus we recover a $50 bill (with the identical serial number to one stolen from the bank) that was spent by John Smith at a local bar, we will have now comfortably reached the threshold of reasonable grounds. We now have a strong subjective belief that John Smith is the robber.

However, based on the entirety of the information, it could be said that any prudent (sensible) and cautious (vigilant) individual would now have a strong belief that John Smith committed the armed robbery. This belief is now based on the reliable probability of the information, which did not exist when we merely suspected Smith of committing the robbery. We have also satisfied the objectivity test of reasonableness – that the "reasonable person" would agree with our subjective belief.

We can now use this information as reasonable grounds to charge John Smith with the offence, obtain a warrant for his arrest or search his residence for evidence of the armed robbery. We will discuss reasonable grounds in more depth later in this textbook.

Getting back to the example of the police officer responding to the disturbance, let's say that when she arrives at the scene, she finds two males wrestling with each other on the ground. The officer is clearly engaged in the lawful execution of her duties in that she is responding to the disturbance. Any officer responding to such a disturbance should by this time have notified their dispatcher of their arrival at the scene of this ongoing physical confrontation in the event that additional backup officers become needed.

Is the police officer in this scenario immediately justified under paragraph 25(1)(b) *Criminal Code* to use force against the combatants? Not so fast... It may not be necessary to use force unless the officer believes, on reasonable grounds, that it is necessary to do so. Our uniformed police officer should first announce her presence to the participants

BOX 4.1	Investigate Hypothesis
(Subjective belief + Objective belief) > mere suspicion = reasonable grounds	

in the physical altercation who may have been so pre-occupied with each other that perhaps they didn't notice her arrival. Just the mere presence of a uniformed officer can sometimes restore order to an unruly situation.

If the combatants, now being aware of the officer's presence, continue to struggle, the officer should firmly and authoritatively verbally command the fighters to discontinue the disturbance immediately in words to the effect of: "POLICE! – STOP FIGHTING! (and/or THAT'S ENOUGH) (or alternatively, BREAK IT UP!) – NOW!" It's possible that if the fighters don't speak English or they may be hearing impaired, they might not comprehend the officer's command to stop fighting. Regardless of the reason, if the males continue their struggle, the officer will have now formed a reasonable belief that some degree of force is necessary to allow her carry out her legal purpose of breaking up the disturbance.

Our officer is now legally authorized to use force and also has a reasonable belief that it is necessary to do so to break up the fight. Paragraph 25(1)(b) limits the officer to use, "as much force as is necessary for that purpose". The phrase "as much force as necessary" should be interpreted as meaning, "as little force as necessary" or the minimum or least amount of force that is reasonably necessary to carry out her lawful duty. "As much force as necessary", is not *carte blanche*, or licence to use unlimited physical force.

If, for example, the officer began repeatedly striking the combatants with her baton, or pulled her service revolver and threatened to shoot them if they refused to stop fighting, the degree of force resorted to would be neither reasonable nor proportional to the circumstances. The word reasonable is defined as being within the limits of objectively sound judgement.

Even if the officer subjectively (in her own mind) believed it was necessary to draw and fire her firearm to break up the fight, her actions will be judged against what an independent reasonable, clear-thinking **reasonable person** would objectively (unbiased and independent of the involved person) have done in the same situation. Drawing a firearm would constitute a level of force used that would not be proportional given what would be necessary under the circumstances. To be proportional is to be in a similar (not necessarily equal) or corresponding ratio or amount when compared to another measurable item, thing or concept.

Having been unsuccessful in ending the disturbance using only verbal commands, the officer is now legally authorized to use a minimal level of force, for example open-hand physical techniques or restraint holds to separate the fighters. Whatever force is used to separate the combatants, it must be no more than is necessary. Punching and kicking the fighters would not be considered to be proportional as lesser violent means to end the fight would, in all reasonable probability, suffice under these circumstances.

If a bystander were to happen by, prior to the arrival of additional officers, and volunteered to assist the officer in breaking up the disturbance, any use of force by that person – if reasonable and proportional – would also be considered lawful. We see that in paragraph 25(1)(c) *Criminal Code*, immunity from criminal liability is also extended to private citizens who use force to assist peace or public officers who are in the lawful execution of their duty. In such a case, the citizen would also be required to act on reasonable grounds and would similarly be limited to using no more force than was necessary for the peace or public officer to carry out their purpose.[3]

The *Provincial Offences Act* also provides police officers with legal justification in using as much (as little) force as is necessary to do what the officer is required or authorized to do in the enforcement of provincial statutes. The police officer must satisfy the standard of reasonable and probable grounds that the use of force is necessary. Reasonable and probable grounds is a formerly common, but slightly outdated expression of the term reasonable grounds that is now found throughout federal legislation – reasonable and probable grounds has virtually the identical meaning as reasonable grounds.

The Act also authorizes citizens who have been called upon to assist a police officer in using as much (as little) force as they believe on reasonable and probable grounds is necessary to render such assistance to the police officer.[4]

4.3   EXCESSIVE USE OF FORCE

No meaningful discussion of legally authorized use of force could take place without a thorough examination of the limitations on its use that are imposed by legal sanctions. We have looked at the requirements of minimal force, proportional force and the concept of reasonableness set by the Parliament of Canada. In light of the immunity from criminal liability conferred upon designated persons – including peace officers – what happens when a person who is authorized by law to use force uses force that exceeds the minimum amount of force necessary?

For the answer, we must turn to section 26 *Criminal Code*, and we see that Parliament, in granting the legal authority to use as much (as little) force as necessary to carry out a legal purpose, was quick to include sanctions for exceeding the boundaries of what is reasonably necessary. To ensure accountability for the use of force, the *Criminal Code* provides that if persons who are authorized to use force, including peace officers, use force excessively, they will be held accountable for that misuse:

> "Every one who is authorized by law to use force is criminally responsible for any excess thereof according to the nature and quality of the act that constitutes the excess."[5]

Section 26 applies to persons engaged in the administration of justice or enforcement of the law [Sec. 25(1) (a)-(d) *CC*]. This legal sanction for using excessive force also applies to everyone who uses force in self-defence, or to prevent the commission of an offence, or a breach of the peace, in defence of property and any other person authorized by law to use force.

In addition to the potential criminal liability for excessive use of force, police officers and their police services might also incur considerable civil liability in cases in which an individual suffers financial loss due to damage or injury due to the improper exercise of authority.

In effect what Parliament has said is, "We will excuse you from criminal liability if you use minimal, reasonable and proportional force in good faith to do those things

---

[3]*Criminal Code*, R.S. 1985, c. C-46, s. 25(1)(c).

[4]*Provincial Offences Act*, R.S.O. 1990, c. P-33, s. 146.

[5]*Criminal Code*, R.S. 1985, c. C-46, s. 26.

which you are legally authorized to do, but we cannot and will not condone unnecessary or excessive force – if you abuse this authority and use excessive force, you will be held criminally responsible."

4.4   USE OF LETHAL FORCE

Another limitation to the use of force authorized by subsection 25(1) is found in subsection 25(3) *Criminal Code*, which states:

> "Subject to subsections (4) and (5), a person is not justified for the purposes of subsection (1) in using force that is intended or is likely to cause death or grievous bodily harm unless the person believes on reasonable grounds that it is necessary for the self-preservation of the person or the preservation of any one under that person's protection from death or grievous bodily harm."[6]

This subsection authorizes the use of lethal force – force capable of taking the life of another human being – while limiting the protection from criminal liability for using force capable of causing death or grievous bodily harm (serious injury). To avoid criminal liability for the death of another person, the person who uses lethal force must reasonably believe it to be necessary to protect themselves or any other person from death or grievous bodily harm. Again, this limitation reflects the required proportionality of force used to overcome force and restricts the use of lethal force to only those cases where it is reasonably believed necessary to protect the life of the officer or the life of any other person.

The greater the force being used by the combatants, the higher degree of force the police can resort to for the purpose of carrying out the lawful purpose. Suppose now that one of the combatants pulls out a knife and threatens the officer with it. As the degree of threat involved has significantly escalated, so does the degree of proportional force that can be lawfully used to meet the threat. If the officer feared that her life was in danger, she would be justified in meeting the threat with a proportional level of force to protect herself from death or grievous bodily harm.

It is simply not possible to provide a checklist or precise level of force that can be applied in every situation. We cannot say that every punch deserves another punch or that a threat involving the use of a knife can only be met with another knife. Use of force is authorized on a continuum, or a sliding scale that authorizes reasonable and proportional force to be used to overcome the use of illegal force. The reasonableness of the force used will always be evaluated objectively by others.

The use of lethal force refers to the use of police issued firearms, restricted to those types of weapons prescribed by regulation. The *Police Services Act* restricts Ontario police officers from drawing or discharging a firearm "...unless he or she believes, on reasonable grounds, that to do so is necessary to protect against loss of life or serious bodily harm."

This limitation on the drawing and discharging of firearms does not apply to training, target practice, maintenance of the firearm, or to call for assistance in an emergency where there is no reasonable alternative. The regulations also allow a police officer to use their firearm to euthanize (destroy) a badly injured animal to end its suffering.[7]

---

[6]*Criminal Code*, R.S. 1985, c. C-46, s. 25(3).

[7]Ontario Regulation 926, R.R.O. 1990, Amended to O. Reg. 361/95, s.s. 9-10, *Police Services Act*, R.S.O. 1990 c. P.15.

4.5 USE OF LETHAL FORCE TO PREVENT ESCAPE

The *Criminal Code* authorizes peace officers and any persons assisting the peace officer to resort to lethal force in certain arrest situations. Where a peace officer is attempting to make a lawful arrest, with or without a warrant, for any offence for which the person could be arrested without warrant and, where they have a reasonable belief that it is necessary to use such force to prevent any person from "imminent or future" death or grievous bodily harm, the law provides that:

"A peace officer, and every person lawfully assisting the peace officer, is justified in using force that is intended or is likely to cause death or grievous bodily harm to a person to be arrested, if

(a) the peace officer is proceeding lawfully to arrest, with or without warrant, the person to be arrested;

(b) the offence for which the person is to be arrested is one for which that person may be arrested without warrant;

(c) the person to be arrested takes flight to avoid arrest;

(d) the peace officer or other person using the force believes on reasonable grounds that the force is necessary for the purpose of protecting the peace officer, the person lawfully assisting the peace officer or any other person from imminent or future death or grievous bodily harm; and

(e) the flight cannot be prevented by reasonable means in a less violent manner." [8]

It is difficult to conceive of many situations in which it might become necessary to rely upon this particular authority, other than perhaps armed hostage incidents or incidents of terrorist activity involving a high probability of death. If a situation of such gravity existed as to require killing a suspect to prevent them from escaping because of a belief that the protection of any person from "imminent or future" death or grievous bodily harm was reasonably probable, the use of lethal force authorized by this subsection could be warranted. As with any other use of force authority, the use of lethal force under these circumstances would only be justified when lesser violent means would be insufficient.

Factors that mitigate against (take a less serious approach to) using lethal force to prevent a "fleeing felon" from escaping lawful arrest for an offence for which they could be arrested without warrant would include the following:

1. the severity of the offence (e.g., break, enter with intent is an offence for which persons can be arrested without warrant – but is not likely to result in a set of facts that would involve the other criteria for using lethal force)

2. whether or not the identity of the offender was known

3. whether or not the apprehension of a known or unknown suspect could be carried out using other methods or at a later time or place

4. whether or not there was any other method of protecting the person whose life was considered to be in danger

---

[8]*Criminal Code*, R.S. 1985, c. C-46, s. 25(4) and Ontario Regulation. 926 R.R.O. 1990,, s. 9 Amended to O. Reg, 361/95, *Police Services Act*, R.S.O. 1990 c. P.15.

Police officers who are engaged in routine patrol duties would be well-advised to reserve this legal authority for only the very worst of possible arrest situations involving the worst possible offender, where the threat of death to the officer or to another person is imminently certain. In such rare occasions these circumstances are best managed by containing the situation, where possible, until the arrival of trained negotiators and/or tactical units.

Police officers were previously trained to shoot at a suspect's arms or legs to wound them. Modern police officers are trained to aim for a suspect's centre-mass where the vital organs of the body are located. Hits to the centre-mass area of the body are far more likely to neutralize the threat to human life caused by a violent suspect.

The use of lethal force should only be considered as an extreme power of last resort. It may be resorted to only when less violent means are not sufficient to save a life. Once a police officer fires a bullet – it can never be called back.

4.6 USE OF FORCE TO PREVENT COMMISSION OF AN OFFENCE

Law enforcement involves not just the investigation of offences or the apprehension and prosecution of offenders; it also involves the prevention of offences, where possible. As law enforcement in a civil society is everyone's business, we often see that legal authorization for the use of force is extended to private citizens as well as to persons employed in the administration of justice.

The *Criminal Code* authorizes every person – citizens and police officers alike – to use reasonable and proportional force, if necessary, to prevent the commission of an offence.

"Every one is justified in using as much force as is reasonably necessary

(a) to prevent the commission of an offence
  (i) for which, if it were committed, the person who committed it might be arrested without warrant, and
  (ii) that would be likely to cause immediate and serious injury to the person or property of anyone: or
(b) to prevent anything being done that, on reasonable grounds, he believes would, if it were done, be an offence mentioned in paragraph (a)."[9]

By breaking this legal authority down into its component parts, we note that the authorization to use force, while applying to both citizens and peace officers, is restricted to arrestable offences that would likely cause immediate injury to persons or property. Offences such as littering or simple speeding are neither arrestable, nor are they reasonably likely to cause immediate and serious injury to persons or to property. Muggings (robberies involving assault), serious assaults or arsons in relation to occupied buildings are some examples of offences for which offenders may be arrested without warrant and would be likely to cause serious injury to persons or damage to property.

---

[9]*Criminal Code*, R.S. 1985, c. C-46, s. 27.

This authority extends not only to offences being committed but extends to preventing anything that, if committed, would constitute offences that are arrestable without warrant and that would likely cause serious harm or property damage.

The legal use of force to prevent criminal offences is also authorized aboard any aircraft in flight – and only while actually in flight – within Canadian airspace or to any Canadian registered aircraft, also while in flight, outside Canadian airspace:

> "27.1 (1)   Every person on an aircraft in flight is justified in using as much force as is reasonably necessary to prevent the commission of an offence against this Act or another Act of Parliament that the person believes on reasonable grounds, if it were committed, would be likely to cause immediate and serious injury to the aircraft or to any person or property therein.
>
> (2)   This section applies in respect of any aircraft in flight in Canadian airspace and in respect of any aircraft registered in Canada in accordance with the regulations made under the Aeronautics Act in flight outside Canadian airspace."[10]

Therefore, Canadian law also protects all persons who use force to prevent criminal offences while flying on foreign aircraft within Canadian airspace. This could conceivably include an American aircraft departing from Los Angeles *en route* to a destination in Europe during any portion of its flight that occurs over Canada. Canadian law also applies to any aircraft registered in Canada wherever it may be in flight, for example, a Canadian charter aircraft in flight over the United States of America while returning vacationing passengers from a destination in the Caribbean.

4.7   USE OF FORCE TO PREVENT A BREACH OF THE PEACE

While the term breach of the peace is not defined in Canadian law, it applies to incidents of disorderly conduct that involve, or that are likely to result in, harm to persons or damage to property, or that may provoke such behaviour in others. There is no offence of breach of the peace – nobody is ever charged with committing a breach of the peace nor can anyone be convicted of breach of the peace in court. It is primarily a legal arrest procedure aimed at preserving the peace.

Incidents that may lead to criminal offences can and, if possible, should be prevented before escalating. I was taught at an early stage of my policing career that "any blow struck in anger" is an example of a breach of the peace.

> "Every one who witnesses a breach of the peace is justified in interfering to prevent the continuance or renewal thereof and may detain any person who commits or is about to join in or to renew the breach of the peace, for the purpose of giving him into the custody of a peace officer, if he uses no more force than is necessary to prevent the continuance or renewal of the breach of the peace or than is reasonably proportioned to the danger to be apprehended from the continuance or renewal of the breach of the peace."[11]

---

[10]*Criminal Code*, R.S. 1985, c. C-46, s. 27(1).

[11]*Criminal Code*, R.S. 1985, c. C-46, s. 30.

For example, two intoxicated patrons in a licenced premises watching a televised hockey game cannot come to agreement as to which of their favourite teams is the better of the two. They decide to settle their differences outside the bar in a physical fight – incredibly foolish behaviour, but it happens. As the fight is consensual, the **facts in issue** for the definition of assault have not been fulfilled – therefore, there is no assault. If nobody present in the area is disturbed by the fight, the facts in issue for the offence of cause disturbance have not been fulfilled – still no offence.

Now, are we just going to allow two fellow citizens to pummel each other senseless on the main streets of our towns and cities? Hopefully this situation would not be permitted to continue either in your town or in mine. If a citizen is inclined to – not legally required to – but inclined to, they may legally use as much force as is necessary for the purpose of interfering with or stopping (preventing the disturbance or preventing the continuation of an ongoing situation) the breach of the peace.

Having separated the two combatants, if they appear they are going to start fighting again, our citizen may once again use minimal, reasonable and proportional force to prevent the renewal of the breach of the peace. Should any friends of the two combatants indicate by word or actions their intention to join the disturbance, our citizen may legally use force to prevent them from joining in the breach of the peace. The citizen may also detain persons to prevent them from committing, joining or continuing a breach of the peace for the purpose of delivering them into the custody of a peace officer. See the chapter dealing with arrest for more on this issue.

Peace officers may also arrest persons committing, continuing or about to join in a breach of the peace and may rely upon their blanket authority to use reasonable and proportional force contained in section 25(1(b) *Criminal Code* to do so.

4.8   USE OF FORCE TO SUPPRESS A RIOT

A rarely used provision of the *Criminal Code* authorizes peace officers and military personnel to use force to suppress a riot. A riot may begin as an unlawful assembly, consisting of as few as three or more people who are unlawfully assembled to carry out common purpose and through whose conduct persons nearby fear, on reasonable grounds, they will disturb the peace tumultuously (irresponsibly or recklessly).[12]

The *Criminal Code* provides that everyone who is a member of an unlawful assembly is guilty of an offence punishable by summary conviction (a fine of up to $2 000 dollars and a term of imprisonment up to six months, or both).[13] If the same unlawful assembly (three or more people) begins to disturb the peace "tumultuously" it is now considered to be a riot.[14] The *Criminal Code* provides that: "Every person who takes part in a riot is guilty of an indictable offence and liable to imprisonment for a term not exceeding two years."[15]

When a riot involves twelve or more people, the *Criminal Code* imposes a duty on certain individuals, including justices, mayors, deputy mayors, sheriffs, deputy sheriffs,

---

[12]*Criminal Code*, R.S. 1985, c. C-46, s. 63(1).

[13]*Criminal Code*, R.S. 1985, c. C-46, s. 66.

[14]*Criminal Code*, R.S. 1985, c. C-46, s. 64.

[15]*Criminal Code*, R.S. 1985, c. C-46, s. 65.

wardens or deputy wardens of prisons and penitentiaries to proceed to the scene of the riot or as close as is safely practical, to command silence and to read the following Riot Proclamation in a loud voice:

> "Her Majesty the Queen charges and commands all persons being assembled immediately to disperse and peaceably to depart to their habitations or to their lawful business on the pain of being guilty of an offence for which, on conviction, they may be sentenced to imprisonment for life."[16]

Any person who intentionally and forcefully interferes with or prevents an official from delivering the riot proclamation is guilty of an offence. Everyone who fails to disperse within thirty minutes of the riot proclamation being read or within thirty minutes of when the proclamation would have been read had it not been prevented from being delivered, is guilty of an offence. All three offences in relation to the riot proclamation carry with them a punishment of life imprisonment.[17]

Police officers and private citizens are legally authorized to use as much force as necessary (reasonable and proportional) to suppress a riot where they believe on reasonable grounds that serious damage or injury may result from a riot before it is possible to secure the attendance of an authorized individual to read the Riot Proclamation.[18] Peace officers and anyone legally required (ordered to assist) by a peace officer to assist them to disperse or arrest persons involved in a riot after the Riot Proclamation has been read, is exempt from criminal or civil liability resulting from death or injury to persons who resist their attempts to disperse the riot.[19]

Fortunately, riots are a relatively rare occurrence in Canada. There have been approximately nineteen riots throughout Canada between 1832 and 2006, including politically motivated demonstrations and revolts, several involving unruly sports fans and one recent incident of alleged vigilantism.

4.9   USE OF FORCE IN SELF-DEFENCE

In earlier times, before police services were formed, citizens who faced hostile attacks had no choice but to resort to self-defence to protect themselves. Civilizations dating back to ancient times have always respected the right of their citizens to resort to force in self-defence against thieves and assorted law-breakers. Even with modern law enforcement capabilities and improved response times, Canadian law still authorizes private citizens to defend themselves against attack.

Subsection 34 of the *Criminal Code* states:

> 34 (1) "Every one who is unlawfully assaulted without having provoked the assault is justified in repelling force by force if the force he uses is not intended to cause death or grievous bodily harm and is no more than is necessary to enable him to defend himself."[20]

---

[16]*Criminal Code*, R.S. 1985, c. C-46, s. 67.

[17]*Criminal Code*, R.S. 1985, c. C-46, s. 68.

[18]*Criminal Code*, R.S. 1985, c. C-46, s. 32(4).

[19]*Criminal Code*, R.S. 1985, c. C-46, s. 33(2).

[20]*Criminal Code*, R.S. 1985, c. C-46, s. 34(1).

If a person is unlawfully assaulted without having done anything to provoke the assault committed upon them, they are entitled to use reasonable, minimal and proportional force to defend themselves. This section prohibits the use of force that could cause death or grievous bodily harm (serious physical injury) to the person who unlawfully assaulted them. This section allows the truly innocent victim to use no more force than is necessary to deal with unlawful and unprovoked assaults against them.

Subsection 34(2) *Criminal Code* addresses the use of lethal force by truly innocent assault victims in self-defence and states:

34(2) "Every one who is unlawfully assaulted and who causes death or grievous bodily harm in repelling assault is justified if

(a) he causes it under reasonable apprehension of death or grievous bodily harm from the violence with which the assault was originally made or with which the assailant pursues his purposes' and

(b) he believes, on reasonable grounds, that he cannot otherwise preserve himself from death or grievous bodily harm."[21]

This subsection still applies only to innocent assault victims who have not provoked or aggravated their assailant to attack them. Such a person is justified in using lethal force capable of causing death or life-threatening injury if they reasonably believe the force used against them is capable of causing their own death or extremely serious harm.

The last requirement imposed by paragraph 34(2)(b) *Criminal Code* is that the person must also believe that lesser force would not be sufficient to preserve themselves. We still see the elements of reasonable forseeability of death or grievous bodily harm and the reliance on lethal force only as a last resort imposed by this section on persons before the use of deadly force is legally justified.

What about the bully who originally provoked the unlawful assault? What should happen to him if, after initiating the unlawful assault on the innocent victim, our innocent victim flies into an uncontrollable rage and attempts to repel the initial assault with lethal force that is neither reasonable nor proportional under the circumstances?

Say, for discussion purposes, our bully slaps or punches our innocent victim who then chases the bully down the street with a knife screaming, "I'm going to kill you!" Do we write off the bully and say that he brought any resulting death or injury upon himself?

35 "Every one who has without justification assaulted another but did not commence the assault with intent to cause death or grievous bodily harm, or has without justification provoked an assault on himself by another, may justify the use of force subsequent to the assault if

(a) he uses the force

(i) under reasonable apprehension of death or grievous bodily harm from the violence of the person whom he has assaulted or provoked, and

(ii) in the belief, on reasonable grounds, that it is necessary in order to preserve himself from death or grievous bodily harm;

(b) he did not, at any time before the necessity of preserving himself from death or grievous bodily harm arose, endeavour to cause death or grievous bodily harm; and

---

[21]*Criminal Code*, R.S. 1985, c. C-46, s. 34(2).

(c) he declined further conflict and quitted or retreated from it as far as it was feasible to do so before the necessity of preserving himself from death or grievous bodily harm arose."[22]

So, here we have our bully, who clearly committed the initial unjustified assault. However, the initial assault was committed without any intention of causing the death of the innocent victim. Our bully is now being chased down the street by a knife-wielding, no-longer innocent victim, who is bent on killing or at least seriously wounding our bully. Our once-innocent victim can no longer rely on the protection of subsections 34(1) or (2), as he can no longer be said to be defending himself from the bully who is now running for his very life.

At some point, our bully believes that the only way to save himself from serious physical harm or death is to turn and face his former victim-turned-assailant. The bully meets the victim's threat of lethal force, in the form of the knife, with a handgun he had concealed in the waistband of his pants. He delivers two gunshots to our victim-turned-armed assailant, who falls to the ground, mortally wounded.

Certainly the bully will be charged with second degree murder for his role in the fatal shooting as the result of this victim-precipitated homicide. At his trial, however, he will resort to claiming self-defence on the basis that the initial assault, although unlawful, was not intended to cause death or grievous bodily harm.

He will also lead evidence that he was, while running away from the fight, under a reasonable belief that he would suffer death or serious injury and that resorting to lethal force was the only way to preserve his life. Our fictitious bully probably stands a very good chance of being acquitted on the charge of second degree murder even though he could still face related charges for the initial assault and for carrying a concealed weapon.

Canadian law protects not-so-innocent victims as well as truly innocent victims.

4.10 USE OF FORCE TO PREVENT ASSAULT

While both sections 34 and 35 *Criminal Code* deal with repelling actual force with force for the purpose of defending oneself, the law also authorizes the use of force to repel an assault against oneself, or against any one under the defender's protection.

37 (1) "Everyone is justified in using force to defend himself or any one under his protection from assault, if he uses no more force than is necessary to prevent the assault or the repetition of it.

(2) Nothing in this section shall be deemed to justify the wilful infliction of any hurt or mischief that is excessive, having regard to the nature of the assault that the force used was intended to prevent."[23]

While the term "any one under his protection" is not defined in the *Criminal Code,* it can be presumed to include spouses, children, and any person who is in a relationship involving dependency or one of authority with the defender. Therefore parents, caregivers,

---

[22]*Criminal Code*, R.S. 1985, c. C-46, s. 35.

[23]*Criminal Code*, R.S. 1985, c. C-46, s. 37.

teachers, etc., could all fall within the category of persons who would be legally justified in using force to prevent an assault against themselves or of one of their charges. The limitations of minimal and proportional force that are characteristic of other use of force sections are evident within this legal authority also.

4.11   USE OF FORCE IN DEFENCE OF PERSONAL PROPERTY

We have already seen that private citizens are authorized in using reasonable and proportional force in self-defence situations. The concept of self-defence extends also to the protection of a person's property and to their dwelling-house. The *Criminal Code* states:

38 (1) "Every one who is in peaceable possession of personal property, and every one lawfully assisting him, is justified

　　　(a) in preventing a trespasser from taking it, or
　　　(b) in taking it from a trespasser who has taken it

if he does not strike or cause bodily harm or cause bodily harm to the trespasser

　　　(2) Where a person who is in peaceable possession of personal property lays hands on it, a trespasser who persists in attempting to keep it or take it from him or from any one lawfully assisting him shall be deemed to commit an assault without justification or provocation."[24]

By reading the above section, we note that it is not just the owner of the property who may claim the protection of this legal authority. Any person in whose custody the property had been left for safekeeping would also be authorized to defend it. In addition, any person lawfully assisting either the owner or someone safeguarding the property would also be protected by this section of the *Criminal Code*.

Note that whoever is relying on the protection of this legal authority is covered, whether they are protecting the property from someone who is trying to take it, or are taking it back from someone who has already taken it from them. A stricter limitation is placed on people in peaceable or lawful possession in that they not allowed to strike or cause bodily harm to any person who is either trying to take the property or has already taken it.

Subsection 38(2) provides that once a person who is in peaceable possession of property lays their hands on it, continued efforts by anyone to take it or keep it from them without legal justification, constitutes an assault. Simple disputes over property that do not involve crimes are best dealt with by the competent civil authorities.

There are times, however, when the owner of a piece of property may not have peaceable possession and may not be entitled to their personal property. If, using the example of a motor vehicle, an illegally parked vehicle has been towed to an impound lot, the towing company has a legal right of claim to the vehicle. Or, if you take your motor vehicle to a garage for repairs and cannot pay the repair bill, the garage may register a lien on the vehicle to recover their repair bill.

---

[24]*Criminal Code*, R.S. 1985, c. C-46, s. 38.

Once such a person has a legal claim of right, the *Criminal Code* authorizes them to defend the property:

39 (1) "Every one who is in peaceable possession of personal property under a claim of right, and every one acting under his authority, is protected from criminal responsibility for defending that possession, even against a person entitled by law to possession of it, if he uses no more force than is necessary.

   (2) Every one who is in peaceable possession of personal property, but does not claim it as of right or does not act under the authority of a person who claims it as of right, is not justified or protected from criminal responsibility for defending his possession against a person who is entitled by law to possession of it."[25]

Examining the above section, we see that there are a number of persons other than the actual owner of the property to whom this section could conceivably apply. A person repossessing property as the result of a defaulted loan, or a tow truck driver or mechanic or anyone acting under their lawful authority may also claim this legal protection.

The principle requirement for this section to apply is the legal claim of right. For example, a landlord is not entitled to seize personal property for back rent owing and would not be entitled to use force against a tenant who was reclaiming property that had been illegally seized. A person in peaceable possession of the property who has a claim of right to it may defend the property against the owner of the property or against anyone else who may have a claim of right to it.

As with other use of force authorities, we once again recognize the limitations imposed by the phrase, " is protected from criminal responsibility... if he uses no more force than is necessary."

4.12 USE OF FORCE IN DEFENCE OF A DWELLING HOUSE

"The house of everyone is to him as his castle and fortress, as well for his defence against injury and violence as for his repose."[26]

Sir Edward Coke, English jurist (1552-1634).

The sanctity of a person's residence and the concept that "every man's home is his castle" extends back at least to early seventeenth century England, when it was formally stated by the judge during a trial that became known as *Semayne's Case*. Every person may defend their dwelling-house (defined in section 2 *Criminal Code*) against those who attempt to forcibly break and enter without lawful authority.

"Every one who is in peaceable possession of a dwelling-house, and every one lawfully assisting him or acting under his authority, is justified in using as much force as is necessary to prevent any person from forcibly breaking into or forcibly entering the dwelling-house without lawful authority."[27]

---

[25]*Criminal Code*, R.S. 1985, c. C-46, s. 39.

[26]*Semayne's Case (Semayne v. Gresham)* 5 Co. Rep 91a, 93a, 77 Eng. Rep. 194, 198 [K.B. 1604].

[27]*Criminal Code*, R.S. 1985, c. C-46, s. 40.

Whether or not a person feels that their life is endangered by a person breaking into their home, they are justified in using force to prevent their residence from being unlawfully entered. Note that not all forcible entries can be legally defended against. If a police officer is executing a legal search warrant or Feeney warrant to enter a residence to arrest a person, they would be entering with legal justification.

If, however, an illegal and warrantless police search – not all warrantless searches are illegal – were to be made, a property owner or person in peaceable possession or anyone lawfully assisting them would be protected by law for defending the dwelling-house against such an illegal search.

While section 40 *Criminal Code*, above, justifies a person in committing an assault against an unjustified trespasser, this applies only for dwelling houses – not businesses and not real property where there is no dwelling house. We again note that the amount of force that can be used is not unlimited. The by now-familiar phrase, "... as much [as little] force as is necessary" imposes the limitations of minimal force, reasonableness and proportionality.

What this means is that a property owner or other person in peaceable possession, and any person lawfully assisting them, is not authorized by this section to use lethal force just to prevent a break in of their house. The justification for using lethal force in such a situation would be restricted to the existence of reasonable grounds to believe that using lethal force was necessary to preserve themselves or someone else from death or grievous bodily harm as anticipated by subsection 34(2) *Criminal Code*.

So, if section 40 *Criminal Code* authorizes people to use force to prevent unlawful breaking and entering in relation to dwelling houses, what if an unlawful break and enter has already occurred? What if the property broken into is something other than a dwelling house?

Evidently, we aren't the first ones to raise those questions, as Parliament anticipated those very scenarios when it enacted section 41 *Criminal Code*, which states:

41 (1) "Every one who is in peaceable possession of a dwelling house or real property, and every one lawfully assisting him or acting under his authority, is justified in using force to prevent any person from trespassing on the dwelling-house or real property, or to remove a trespasser therefrom, if he uses no more force than is necessary.

(2) A trespasser who resists an attempt by a person who is in peaceable possession of a dwelling-house or real property, or a person lawfully assisting him or acting under his authority to prevent his entry or to remove him, shall be deemed to commit an assault without justification or provocation." [28]

A person in peaceable possession of real property could be a tenant of a commercial business or their employee who is not the actual owner of the property. A person acting under the owner's authority might even include a security guard, hired to protect the property. The degree of force they are legally entitled to use is minimal, reasonable and proportional and any resistance by the trespasser constitutes an assault. This section applies both to prevention and dealing with trespassers who have actually broken in or have entered.

---

[28] *Criminal Code*, R.S. 1985, c. C-46, s. 41.

4.13 ONTARIO USE OF FORCE MODEL (2004)

There has always been a question of just exactly what is the correct amount of force to use in a given situation. Is every punch equal to a punch? Perhaps not, if an 86-year-old woman punches a 25-year-old male police officer weighing 90 kilograms who decides to retaliate. Punch for punch in this fight might be proportional – only in number – but such force would not be considered reasonable by any objective standard.

Yet, the force required to apprehend a suspect who is resisting arrest must be at least marginally greater than the force of resistance or the arresting officer would not be able to accomplish their purpose. The difficulty facing persons who must use force to defend themselves or to carry out lawful purposes, such as an arrest, is how much force can reasonably and objectively be applied in this situation?

There are factors that, if known to the officer at the time of the incident, may assist in assessing the risk posed by a suspect and in deciding the appropriate level of force with which to respond. They might include:

1. the number of suspects, their gender, age and any differential in size and physique between the involved individual(s) and the officer(s)

2. the suspect's demeanour and the degree of aggression, if any, displayed or any intention of aggression expressed by them (e.g., verbal threats or apparent combativeness) or that has been committed toward other persons

3. whether or not a suspect is armed with a weapon (defined in section 2 *CC*)

4. the suspect's apparent emotional and psychological condition (e.g., delusional behaviour, incoherent speech, yelling, swearing, screaming, etc.)

5. the level of force used by a suspect to resist the efforts of the police

6. past criminal history of assaultive behaviour toward authorities on the part of a suspect, if any

7. evidence of suspect's intoxication by alcohol or drugs, if any

8. the severity of the offence(s), if any, allegedly committed by the suspect

9. imminent or potential danger to other members of the public or to the officer(s) that may result due to the suspect's actions

10. the availability of additional backup or alternative methods of subduing the suspect (Walma & West 2002)

In Ontario, police officers are instructed regarding use of force response options using an assessment tool in the form of a wheel-shaped continuum that graphically illustrates proportional responses to various suspect behaviours. It is intended as a learning tool to complement, not replace departmental policy or statutory requirements. (Aveni). For your convenience, a colour version of the Ontario Use of Force Model (2004) has been re-printed with permission on the inside rear cover of this textbook.

The centre of the wheel-shaped model depicts the situation in which the officer's decision must occur and reflects the reality that various bits of information may become known to the officer at various times throughout the situation. As new or additional information becomes known, or as the situation changes, the officer(s) are encouraged to continually assess, plan and act in response to the changing situation.

4.13.1 Suspect Behaviour Profile

The inner wheel surrounding the situation comprises five different sectors that represent the suspect/offender's behaviour profile. Each sector indicates a progressive level of resistance to which the officer's alternative response options correspond.

Cooperative: This is the desired state of suspect behaviour. The suspect voluntarily follows the officer's requests – the situation requires only the officer's presence

Passive Resistant: The suspect passively resists the officer by sitting, standing or lying down, but makes no deliberate attempt or gesture to injure the officer

Active Resistant: The suspect verbally threatens or refuses to comply with the officer's requests or pulls away from the officer but still makes no deliberate attempt or gesture to injure the officer

Assaultive: The suspect intentionally and deliberately directs physical force, in the form of wrestling, biting, punching, or kicking against the officer

Serious Bodily Harm Or Death: Using either physical force or a weapon, the suspect attempts to cause serious injury or death to the officer

Photo 4.1 - A cooperative suspect voluntarily follows the officer's instructions.

Photo 4.2 - The passive-resistant suspect passively resists the officer by refusing to exit his vehicle.

Photo 4.3 - The active-resistant suspect verbally threatens or refuses to comply with the officer's requests or pulls away from the officer without deliberately attempting to injure the officer.

Photo 4.4 - The assaultive suspect intentionally and deliberately directs physical force against the officer.

Photo 4.5 - The suspect causes or attempts or threatens to cause imminent serious injury or death to the officer using either physical force or a weapon.

4.13.2 Officer Response Options

The outer wheel of the Ontario Use of Force Model (2004) represents the officer's possible response options that correspond to the various levels of suspect behaviour. You will note that the officer has a range of potential options, some of which overlap the different suspect behaviour categories.

This overlap demonstrates the flexibility of the model and the realization that changing factors in the situations require officers to continually reassess, plan and react with appropriate options available to them under the circumstances. For example, as a response option, communication is depicted as an option for all stages of possible suspect behaviour.

The Ontario Use of Force Model (2004) does not propose that an officer must exhaust every lesser alternative prior to selecting the correct option. Nor is the model intended to be used as a quick-reference guide for an officer in the field who is facing an imminent violent threat from an assaultive suspect. The purpose of the model is merely to visually illustrate and give perspective to the various options an officer has at their disposal.

Officers of different gender, physical strength, ability and experience may well perceive the situation differently and may choose different options based on those perceptions. The officer must also assess a variety of tactical considerations that are available to them throughout an encounter, including the availability of backup or special units such as canine or tactical units to provide containment.

Disengagement is where the officer breaks off the confrontation, if appropriate, to avoid a life-threatening situation either to the suspect or to the officer. In reality, disengagement is always an option available to the officer and may be selected to provide additional time until containment or backup becomes available. (Aveni)

Officer Presence: The officer's mere presence and verbal direction results in compliance with expectations of desired suspect behaviour.

Communication: A standardized and professional approach to dealing with members of the public with the objective of resolving or de-escalating conflict. Notice that communication is a response option to all possible behaviours exhibited by a suspect.

Physical Control (Soft): Control-oriented strength and restraint techniques including wrist-locks, joint locks, pressure points and non-resistant handcuffing. This option includes methods that do not involve the use of weapons but include the use of the officer's baton as a lever to apply pressure to points of the body such as with an arm bar to gain compliance.

Physical Control (Hard): Hard techniques involve the direct application of force where there is a higher probability of injury to the suspect. Hard techniques involve empty hand techniques such as the officer delivering strikes, punches and kicks to the suspect.

Intermediate Weapons: Use of less-lethal weapons to strike blows to overcome resistance or the use of a TASER™ or similar approved conducted energy weapon (CEW) to incapacitate a suspect without further injury. This option includes Oleoresin capsicum (pepper spray) or other approved chemical agents to overcome resistance or to render the suspect incapable of assaultive behaviour. Intermediate weapons are those which are not intended to cause bodily harm or death to a suspect.

Lethal Force: Use of authorized lethal force in the form of firearms or other techniques capable of causing bodily harm or death. When disengagement is no longer an option, the selection of any other option than lethal force in response to offender behaviour in the category of serious bodily harm or death, in my opinion, places the officer at an unacceptably high level of risk.

Whenever there is a real threat to an officer's life or the life of another person, I believe that resorting to the lethal force option – after issuing the appropriate Police Challenge – is the only appropriate option. The Police Challenge comprises the command, "Police! – Don't Move!", which in reality is part of the ongoing communications option. The Police Challenge, if feasible, is the final requirement of cautioning a suspect before resorting to the use of lethal force.

Photo 4.6 - The officer achieves the suspect's compliance through their mere presence and use of verbal directions.

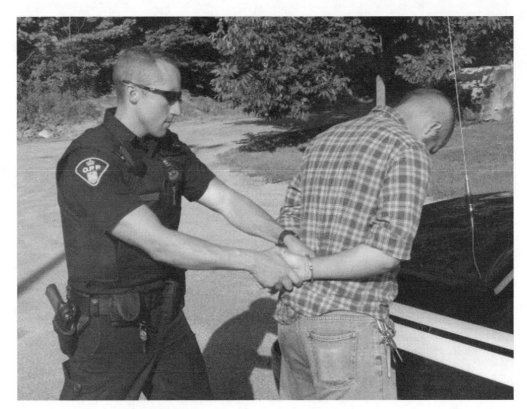

Photo 4.7 - An officer demonstrates proper handcuffing technique on a passive prisoner.

Photo 4.8 - An officer demonstrates proper handcuffing technique on a prisoner who is resisting arrest.

Photo 4.9 - An officer achieves compliance by exerting physical restraint techniques that are not intended to injure the resisting subject.

Photo 4.10 - An officer applies reasonable but proportional force to an assaultive suspect through the use of hand strikes or kicks.

Photo 4.11 - An officer prepares to strike an assaultive suspect with a telescoping metal baton.

Photo 4.12 - An officer prepares to overcome an assaultive suspect using aerosol oleoresin capsicum (pepper) spray.

Photo 4.13 - An officer prepares to incapacitate an assaultive suspect through the use of conducted electrical energy using a Taser device.

Photo 4.14 - An officer who fears for their own life or safety or the life or safety of another person is authorized to resort to lethal force, including firearms.

4.14   USE OF FORCE REPORTS

The *PSA* requires members of police services to complete and submit a report to their Chief of Police or Commissioner, as the case may be, in any of the following instances:

14.5 (1)   "A member of a police force shall submit a report to the Chief of police or Commissioner whenever the member,

(a) draws a handgun in the presence of a member of the public, excluding a member of the police force while on duty, or discharges a firearm;

(b) uses a weapon other than a firearm on another person; or

(c) uses physical force on another person that results in an injury requiring medical attention."[29]

Accidental and intentional discharges of police weapons, except those that occur on a target range, and any incident in which a person is killed or injured by the discharge of a firearm by an on-duty police officer are required to be investigated immediately.[30]

The **Special Investigations Unit** (SIU) is a civilian law enforcement and oversight agency that reports to the Ontario Ministry of the Attorney General. The Director of SIU, who may not be a former police officer, is authorized under Part VII of the *PSA* to authorize criminal investigations into circumstances of incidents involving police and civilians that have resulted in serious injury, including sexual assault, or death to members of the public.[31]

Most, if not all SIU investigators are former police officers who conduct investigations utilizing methods similar to those police investigators use while investigating personal injury occurrences. Current police officers may not be SIU investigators and former police officers are prohibited from investigating cases involving members of their former police service.[32] SIU members are peace officers[33] and lay charges in cases where reasonable grounds exist to believe criminal wrong-doing on the part of the police. (See Special Investigations Unit [SIU] Section 2.2.4.)

SUMMARY

- Police powers – including powers of arrest and use of force, exist because of the reality that coercive (physical) force is sometimes necessary to apprehend offenders, to compel their attendance in a court of law, to further investigations or to prevent or stop harmful acts.

---

[29]Ontario Regulation 926, R.R.O. 1990, Amended to O. Reg. 361/95, *Police Services Act*, R.S.O 1990, c. P-15, s. 14.5(1).

[30]Ibid. ss. 12-13.

[31]*Police Services Act*, R.S.O. 1990, c. P-15, s. 113(1).

[32]Ibid, s. 113(6).

[33]Ibid, s. 113(4).

- Resorting to use of physical force against a member of the public, for any reason, must be authorized by law and the degree of force used must be both reasonable and proportional, having regard to all the circumstances.

- Section 25 *Criminal Code* authorizes everyone who is required or authorized by law to do anything in the administration or enforcement of the law who acts on reasonable grounds to use as much (little) force as is necessary to effect their legal purpose.

- Section 26 *Criminal Code* states that everyone who is authorized by law to use force is criminally responsible for any excess thereof according to the nature and quality of the act that constitutes the excess.

- Citizens may also legally use force to prevent or stop a breach of the peace, to prevent an offence, in self-defence of themselves or others, in defence of personal or real property and in defence of a dwelling house. The force authorized must also be no more than is what is reasonable and necessary under the circumstances.

- In Ontario, police officers are instructed regarding use of force response options using an assessment tool called the Use of Force Model in the form of a wheel-shaped continuum that graphically illustrates proportional responses to various suspect behaviours.

- The Special Investigations Unit (SIU) is a civilian law enforcement agency that reports to the Ontario Ministry of the Attorney General. The SIU conducts criminal investigations into circumstances of incidents involving police and civilians which have resulted in serious injury, including sexual assault, or death to members of the public.

DISCUSSION QUESTIONS

1. Define the legal standard of reasonable grounds and explain its relationship to a police officer's decision whether or not to resort to the use of force in carrying out their lawful duties. What is the difference between the officer's subjective belief and the objective standard of the reasonable person?

2. What is a breach of the peace? What are the three ways in which a citizen might be legally justified in using force in relation to witnessing a breach of the peace?

3. Under which two conditions may a person who has been unlawfully assaulted and who did not do anything to provoke the assault against them, be legally authorized to use lethal force in self-defence?

4. What factors, if known to the officer at the time of an incident, may assist them in assessing the risk posed by a suspect and in deciding the appropriate level of force with which to respond?

5. Name and explain the use of force response options for police officers as set out in the Ontario Use of Force Model.

 WEBLINKS

www.siu.on.ca/home.asp

Special Investigations Unit (SIU) is a civilian investigative agency committed to promoting and maintaining community confidence in Ontario's police services through independent investigations of circumstances involving police and civilians that have resulted in serious injury, including sexual assault, or death.

www.e-laws.gov.on.ca/DBLaws/Regs/English/900926_e.htm

Government of Ontario website for Ontario Regulation 926 – Guidelines for Ontario police officers relating to approved equipment, including firearms, and Use of Force.

Chapter 5

Charging Suspects
and Judicial Interim Release

"The foundation of justice is good faith."[1]

Marcus Tullius Cicero (106-43 B.C.),
Ancient Roman lawyer, writer and scholar.

Learning Outcomes

After reading this chapter, students should be able to:

- Describe the legal requirement for laying a charge against an offender.
- Describe the details that must be contained in a charging document known as an information.
- Summarize the public interest considerations which justify detention of arrested persons.
- Describe the methods for compelling the attendance of an accused to court.
- Interpret the mandatory situations for which police must release people from custody.

5.1 INTRODUCTION

If topics are said to be mutually exclusive, each subject must be considered independently of the other, or it may also mean that they do not depend on each for their existence. During our examination of the issue of arrest in Chapter 3, we briefly touched upon the fact that the topics of arresting and charging a suspect are often related but are mutually exclusive. As we will soon see, a person may be arrested in relation to an offence but not be formally charged and prosecuted. And often in law enforcement a person is charged with an offence without having been arrested.

A police officer might lay a charge against an offender who has committed an offence but has not been arrested if the offender's whereabouts are not known. A police officer may also charge an offender when the requirements of the public interest

---

[1]Opening quotation retrieved Dec 5/06 from www.quotationsbook.com.

(R.I.C.E.) have been met without necessarily requiring the arrest of the suspect. Let's turn our minds to how a police officer lays one or more charges against a suspected offender and initiates the court process.

5.2   LAYING AN INFORMATION

An **information** is the name given to the formal charging document upon which the identity of the informant–the person laying the charge–the identity of the **accused** and the alleged charge(s) are stated. A *Criminal Code* information must be in Form 2 (See Part XXVIII *Criminal Code*).[2] The information must be laid before a justice (a provincial court judge or justice of the peace) in writing and on oath or solemn affirmation of the informant. The laying (affirming or swearing) of an information marks, "...the commencement of criminal proceedings".[3]

The laying of the information is conducted as an *ex parte* hearing before the justice, meaning the procedure occurs outside the presence of one of the involved parties – in this case, the accused is not present when the charge(s) are laid against them. The accused has no right to object to the procedure and has no right to cross-examine the informant.

While the information contains the offences(s) alleged to have been committed by an accused person, once it is laid it constitutes one or more charges. The information creates the charge but does not compel the attendance of the accused to court. There must also be some form of **compelling document** that commands the accused to appear in court at a designated time, date and location.

The compelling document might be in the form of an appearance notice, promise to appear or a recognizance before an officer in charge. These forms are used by police officers to release suspects from custody before charges are formally laid. A compelling document may also be in the form of a summons or an arrest warrant that is issued by the justice once the information has been laid.

5.3   TIME LIMITATIONS FOR LAYING
AN INFORMATION

If a police officer arrests an individual without a warrant for an indictable, dual procedure or summary conviction offence (where R.I.C.E. is not satisfied), or continues the lawful arrest of a citizen, the accused must be charged within a maximum period of twenty-four hours or they must be released from custody.[4] This allows the police to hold the prisoner for up to 24 hours, at which time, a charge must either be laid, or the accused must be released unconditionally – without charge or any restrictions on them.

For example, if an accused is arrested for an offence but insufficient reasonable grounds exist to charge the offender within the 24-hour period, the suspect must be released. The fact that the suspect is released does not mean that further investigation

---

[2]*Criminal Code*, R.S. 1985, c. C-46, s. 504, 505, 506, 788.

[3]*R. v. Southwick, ex p. Gilbert Steel Ltd.*, [1968] 1 C.C.C. 356, 2 C.R.N.S. 46 (Ont. C.A.).

[4]*Criminal Code*, R.S. 1985, c. C-46, s. 503(1)(a).

into the offence cannot continue. If, subsequent to the release of a suspect, evidence of a charge is developed, a charge may be laid at any time, within the statute of limitations of the offence, whether or not the suspect was previously arrested and released.

The statute of limitations is the time limit following an offence during which a charge must be laid. To determine the statute of limitations for any offence, you must look to the classification of the respective offence. There is no statute of limitations for indictable offences, while a charge for a summary conviction offence must be laid within six months after the offence, unless both the prosecutor and the accused consent to an extension.[5] Charges for dual procedure (hybrid) offences may be laid more than six months following the offence as they are treated as indictable offences for the purposes of determining the statute of limitations.

For example, a charge of breaking and entering of a dwelling house[6] is an indictable offence which is punishable by life imprisonment. Indictable offences have no statute of limitations. If reasonable grounds are developed five or ten years – or even longer – after the actual offence, a charge may still be laid. A charge of causing a disturbance[7] is an offence punishable on summary conviction. If the identity of a suspect is established seven months after the actual disturbance, no charge can be laid as the six month statute of limitations will have expired.

Whether an individual is issued an appearance notice in lieu (instead) of arrest, requiring them to appear in court, or if they were released conditionally, or were held pending a bail hearing, judicial proceedings commence with the swearing or affirmation of an information. Where a suspect is issued with an appearance notice under section 496 *Criminal Code* or is released from custody in accordance with sections 497 or 498;

> "...[A]n information relating to the offence alleged to have been committed by the accused or relating to an included or other offence alleged to have been committed by him shall be laid before a justice as soon as practicable thereafter and in any event before the time stated in the appearance notice, promise to appear or recognizance issued to or given or entered into by the accused for his attendance in court."[8]

For example, if an individual is arrested for driving a motor vehicle having consumed alcohol in excess of 80 milligrams of alcohol in 100 millilitres of blood,[9] once the public interest has been satisfied, the accused may be released by the arresting officer and issued with an appearance notice. The accused may alternatively be released on a promise to appear or by way of a recognizance entered into before an officer in charge. At the time of the individual's release from custody, a court date and location are specified to compel the attendance of the accused in court. Section 505 *Criminal Code* requires that an information must be laid before the court date and time specified in the release document. We will examine the issues surrounding the release of individuals in more detail in section 5.8 dealing with Judicial Interim Release.

---

[5]*Criminal Code*, R.S. 1985, c. C-46, s. 786(2).

[6]*Criminal Code*, R.S. 1985, c. C-46, s. 348(1)(d).

[7]*Criminal Code*, R.S. 1985, c. C-46, s. 175(1).

[8]*Criminal Code*, R.S. 1985, c. C-46, s. 505.

[9]*Criminal Code*, R.S. 1985, c. C-46, s. 253(b).

Failure to lay a charge prior to the designated time and date in an appearance notice, promise to appear or recognizance before an officer in charge does not cancel the charge but does nullify (invalidate) the release document. In such circumstances, the charge could be laid and the attendance of the accused in court could be compelled by way of a summons.

5.4 CONTENTS OF AN INFORMATION

Every information alleging a criminal offence should contain the following details:

1. The province and judicial region in which the charge is laid

2. The name and signature of the informant (the person who is laying the information)

3. The identity of the accused person(s)

4. A statement of the circumstances of each **count** (offence) that is alleged to have been committed in sufficient description to give the accused notice of the charges against them.[10] The description of the charge should also specify the statute that enacted the offence and should be laid contrary to the punishment section of the statute, if it is different than the definition section.

5. The signature of the justice who accepts the information and the date and municipality where the information was laid.

The following form (Figure 5.1A and 5.1B) depicts what a completed information might look like at the time it is presented to a justice. The information should be signed by the informant in front of the justice.

This particular form is used for a single accused and is limited to no more than two counts. Where there are more than one accused or where there are more than two counts against an offender, a long form information (not shown) must be used (See section 5.7 on Joinder of Accused and Joinder of Counts).

Certain blank areas of the information are for administrative purposes and are filled in by court officials and should be left blank by the police officer informant. Such areas include the assignment of a file number to the information, Crown election in the event the charge is a dual procedure or hybrid offence, taking the plea of the accused and recording any court appearances and final court disposition. All sections of the information that relate to the investigating officer, the informant (if different than the investigating officer) and the charge should be completed prior to presenting the information before a justice.

Students may consult *Martin's Annual Criminal Code*[11] for suggested wordings for *Criminal Code* charges. The coloured section at the back of the book is a very useful feature for police officers as it breaks down the suggested wordings for the facts in issue of various charges.

---

[10]*Criminal Code*, R.S. 1985, c. C-46, s. 581.

[11]*Martin's Annual Criminal Code*, Edward L. Greenspan & Marc Rosenberg, Canada Law Book Inc.

FIGURE 5.1A   Criminal Code Information Form

CANADA
PROVINCE OF ONTARIO
PROVINCE DE L'ONTARIO

Information of   Detective Inspector William Murray Van Allen
Dénonciation de:
of/*de:*   Ontario Provincial Police - Criminal Investigation Branch

Central East   Peace Officer   The informant says
(Region/*Région*)   (occupation/*profession*)   *Le dénonciateur*

that he/she believes on reasonable grounds that
déclare qu'il a des motifs raisonnables de croire que

John Doe   of   417 Smith Street West, Barrie, ON
    de

(1) on or about the   5th   day of   December,   2006   at the   City   of   Orillia
le ou vers le   *jour de*   *à*   *de*
in the said region.
dans ladite région.
Did unlawfully endanger the life of Jane Doe, thereby committing an aggravated assault contrary to subsection 268(2) of the Criminal Code of Canada

Sworn before me at the   City   of   Orillia
Déclaré sous serment devant moi   *de*
in the said region this   5th
dans ladit région le
day of   December, 2006
jour de

A Justice of the Peace in and for the Province of Ontario/*Juge de paix dans et pour la province de l'Ontario*   Informant/*Dénonciateur*

☐ Appearance Notice   ☐ Promise to Appear   ☐ Recognizance for   Confirme on
Citation à comparaître   *Promesse de comparaître*   *Engagement pour le*   *Confirmé(e) le*   J.P.

Date			
	Crown Elects to Proceed/ *Choix du poursuivant*		
	☐ Summarily *Procédure sommaire*	☐ By Indictment *Acte d'accusation*	☐ Summary Conviction Offence(s) *Infraction(s) punissable(s) sur déclaration de culpabilité par procédure sommaire*
	Accused Elects Trial by/ *Choix de prévenu*		
	☐ Justice (Superior Court) *Juge seul (Cour supérieur)*	☐ Justice and Jury *Juge et jury*	☐ Discharged/*Libéré(e)*
	☐ Ordered to Stand Trial *Astreint en jugement*	☐ With Consent of Accused and Prosecutor *Avec le consentement du prévnue et du poursuivant*	
	Without Taking or Recording /*Sans recueillir ou consigner*		
	☐ Any Evident (or) *de preuve (ou)*	☐ Further Evidence *de preuve supplémentaire*	Bail $ *Cautionnement* $
	Accused Elects Trial by/*Choix du prévenu*		
	☐ Justice (Ontario Court) *Juge (Cour de l'Ontario)*	☐ Absolute Jurisdiction *Juridiction absolue*	
	Pleads/*Plaidoyer*		
	☐ Guilty/*Coupable*	☐ Not Guilty/*Non coupable*	☐ Withdrawn/*Accusation(s) retirée(s)*
	Found/*Décision*		
	☐ Guilty *Coupable* ☐ Not Guilty *Non coupable* ☐ In Absentia *Défaut de comparution*	☐ Absolute Discharge *Absolution inconditionnelle*	☐ Conditional Discharge *Absolution sous condition*

Fined $ & $ costs. Time to Pay ....
Amende de $ et   *$pour les dépens. Délai de paiement*

	Day/Jour	Mo./Mois	Yr./Année

or   Date of Birth
ou   *Date de naissance*   17-Jul-1985

Probation for
Période de probation de

Sentenced to
Peine de

(Single Accused - Not More Than Two Charges)   Justice/*Juge*
(*un seul accusé - maximum deux accusations*)

FOR INFORMATION ON ACCESS   POUR PLUS DE RENSEIGNEMENTS SUR L'ACCÈS
TO ONTARIO COURTS   DES PERSONNES HANDICAPÉES
FOR PERSONS WITH DISABILITIES, CALL   AUX TRIBUNAUX DE L'ONTARIO, COMPOSEZ LE
1-800-387-4456   **1-800-387-4456**
TORONTO AREA 326-0111   RÉGION DE TORONTO 326-0111

CC 0924 (rev. 05/97)

Charge wordings are listed sequentially, by definition section number. Note, however, that on the sample information provided, alleging a fictitious charge of Aggravated Assault, I have alleged the facts in issue that are contained in the definition section which is subsection 268(1) *Criminal Code*. Note also that in the wording of the charge on the face of the information, I have alleged that the aggravated assault was committed, "contrary to subsection 268(2) of the *Criminal Code*". All charges should be laid contrary to the penalty or punishment section rather than the definition section, which defines the wording for the charge.

| FIGURE 5.1B | Criminal Code Information Form |

Top table header:
Date / Date	Defendant Appears Adjournment / Prévenu Comparaît Ajournement	Parties Consent / Consentement des parties	Bail and/or other action / Cautionnement et/ou autre mesure	Fails to Appe / Omet de comparaître	Bench Warrant / Mandat du tribunal	Certificate of Default / Certificat de défaut

Center of form (rotated text):

No. of Information/N°. de la dénonciation

Return Date of summons/Sommation rapportée le
6 December, 2006

INFORMATION Against/DÉNONCIATION visant

Address/Adresse

John Doe,
417 Smith Street, West
Barrie ON

CHARGE/ACCUSATION
Aggravated Assault (Level III) S. 268(2) C.C.

☐ Summons / Sommation ☐ Warrant / Mandat ☒ Arrest / Arrestation

☐ Offence M.V. / Infraction V.M. (Code de la route 184) ☐ Reportable M.V. / Rapport V.M. (Code de la route 184) ☐ C.V.O.R. No. (Commercial Vehicles Only) / Numéro I.V.U.O. (véhicules utilitaires seulement)

Was defendant owner? / Le défendeur était-il propriétaire? ☐ Yes ☐ No

☐ Involves an Accident / Infraction reliée à un accident

Plate No./Numéro de plaque

Driver's Licence Number/Numéro du permis de conduire

Sex / Sexe M

Birth Date/Date de naissance 17-Jul-1985

Informant / Dénonciateur D/Insp. Wm M. Van Allen

Date Sworn / Date d'assermentation

Officer / Agent de police W.M. Van Allen

Div. / Div. No. / N°. 5073

Div. / Div. Dist. / Dist.

Courtroom/Salle d'audience Ontario Court of Justice (Provincial Division)
745 Memorial Avenue, Courtroom "C"

CC 924

AVA

Bottom table header:
Date / Date	Clerk / Greffier	Reporter / Sténographe	Prosecutor / Poursuivant	For Defendant / Pour le prévenu	Justice Initials/ Initiales du juge de paix

5.5 WHO MAY LAY AN INFORMATION

If, at any time, sufficient reasonable grounds exist upon which to lay a charge in relation to a summary conviction, dual procedure or an indictable offence, anyone including citizens and peace officers may lay an information before a justice. The greatest number of informations are laid by criminal justice professionals, with the majority of those being laid by police officers.

As is frequently the case, peace officers are not always able to lay their own charges because of workload, scheduling or for reasons of departmental policy.

If a police officer is working night shift and has a prisoner in lock-up waiting to appear in court the next morning, or if the officer investigates an offence but is leaving on vacation prior to the laying of the charge, the investigating or arresting officer does not have to be the informant on their own charge. Depending on the size and policies of their police service, the investigating officer may either prepare the necessary paperwork or dictate the details of the case to allow clerical support staff to prepare the necessary court documents.

The informant for a charge does not have to be the officer who dealt with the case in the first instance. Another police officer would be able to swear to the information providing they have reasonable grounds to believe that the accused committed the alleged offence.

I was once the informant on a charge of impaired driving which had been investigated by another police officer. I was quite surprised when, without any prior notice, I was called to the witness stand to testify on a motion by the defence to quash (reject or cancel) the information on the grounds that the informant, in this case myself, had insufficient reasonable grounds at the time the information had been sworn.

I testified that as the designated court officer at the detachment where I was stationed at that time, it was one of my responsibilities to lay informations for other police officers at my detachment and for those of a neighbouring detachment. As such, I regularly acquired reasonable grounds from a variety of sources, including:

1. Personal conversations with or written instructions received from other police officers regarding the nature and circumstances of their cases

2. Familiarizing myself with the overnight occurrences, including traffic reports, and arrest reports

3. Reviewing the prisoner log of arrested persons, if any, and often fingerprinting them and serving documents to them, as required, prior to releasing them from custody

4. Receiving and reading packages of documents prepared by arresting officers, including Crown briefs, prepared informations, breathalyzer documents, and various release forms and bail documents

5. If clarification was required on any point, I also had access to the officers' investigative notebooks, which were stored at the detachment when they were off duty.

Due to the passage of time since the particular charge before the court had been laid, I was not able to accurately recall what had actually transpired to give me the reasonable grounds to believe that the particular accused had committed the particular offence. The provincial court judge listened attentively as I related my regular duties and described the number of various methods by which reasonable grounds were regularly transferred from the arresting officer to the informant.

The judge ruled that the routine practices within the detachment were sufficiently diligent and of adequate quantity to conclude that, at least on a balance of probabilities, at the time the information was laid I had sufficient reasonable grounds. The informant on a charge is required only to have reasonable grounds, which we have seen is an objective and reliable belief that the alleged offence was committed by the accused. "The informant does not have to be a witness or a victim to the alleged offence."[12] The trial judge dismissed the defence motion to quash the information, the trial continued and the accused was subsequently convicted.

---

[12]Groot at p. 417.

5.6   JUSTICE TO RECEIVE THE INFORMATION

An information laid by a police officer or other justice professional is referred to as a public prosecution, while an information laid by a private investigator, security officer or private individual is referred to as a private prosecution. The *Criminal Code* requires the justice to receive any information where it is alleged the accused committed an indictable offence[13] or a summary conviction offence[14] for which they may be tried within the territorial jurisdiction of the justice.

Where an accused has been released on an appearance notice, promise to appear or recognizance issued or entered into before an officer in charge, and an information is brought before a justice charging the accused, the justice must accept the information and cancel or confirm the releasing document. In cancelling a releasing document, the justice may either issue a summons or a warrant for the accused. Where the justice does not confirm the releasing document and does not consider it in the public interest to issue a summons or warrant, the justice shall notify the accused of the cancellation of the releasing document.[15]

Where an accused named in an information for a public prosecution was not previously arrested, the justice may hear the contentions of the informant and may even hear the evidence of other witnesses relating to the offence(s) contained in the information. Where a justice considers it appropriate in the public interest to do so in a public prosecution, they may issue a summons or a warrant to compel the attendance of the accused to court to answer to the charge.[16]

Where an information relating to a private prosecution is brought before a justice, the justice shall accept the information but must refer the information to a provincial court judge or designated justice to consider whether or not it is in the public interest to issue a summons or a warrant. A summons or warrant in a private prosecution may only be issued where the issuing justice has heard *ex parte* and considered the allegations of the informant and the sworn evidence of relevant witnesses, if any.[17]

A summons issued by a justice for an indictable offence may also require the accused to appear at a time and date for the purposes of fingerprinting and photographing under the *Identification of Criminals Act*.[18]

Once judicial proceedings have been commenced in a public or in a private prosecution and before judgement in the case, the Attorney General for the province has the power to intervene and direct the court to enter a **stay of proceedings**. Where a stay of proceedings has been entered, the trial is postponed for a period of up to one year. Where proceedings are not recommenced, the proceedings shall be deemed to never have been commenced.[19]

The purpose of a justice receiving the information is not to determine guilt or innocence but to commence judicial proceedings into the matter.[20]

---

[13]*Criminal Code*, R.S. 1985, c. C-46, s. 504.

[14]*Criminal Code*, R.S. 1985, c. C-46, s. 788(1).

[15]*Criminal Code*, R.S. 1985, c. C-46, s. 508(1).

[16]*Criminal Code*, R.S. 1985, c. C-46, s. 507.

[17]*Criminal Code*, R.S. 1985, c. C-46, s. 507.1

[18]*Identification of Criminals Act*, R.S. 1985, c. I-1.

[19]*Criminal Code*, R.S. 1985, c. C-46, s. 579.

[20]*R. v. Jean Talon Fashion Centre Inc.* (1975), 22 C.C.C. (2d) 223, 56 D.L.R. (3d) 296 (Que. Q.B.).

5.7 JOINDER OF ACCUSED-JOINDER OF COUNTS

If more than one accused are charged with the same offence, they may be charged jointly on the same information in Form 4 *Criminal Code*. The main benefit to charging multiple accused jointly is to limit the number of preliminary inquiries and trials. An adult accused must never be joined on the same information as an accomplice who is a young offender.

One or more accused persons may be charged with multiple charges on the same information if all of the counts apply jointly to them all. The exception to this rule prohibits a charge of murder being joined to any other indictable offence except where it arises out of the same circumstances as the charge of murder, or with the accused's consent.[21]

If a court believes that it is in the public interest to do so, it may order that where more than one accused is charged with the same offence, that one or more of the accused be tried separately. Likewise, where an accused is charged with more than one offence, the court may order that the accused be tried separately on one or more of the counts.[22]

5.8 JUDICIAL INTERIM RELEASE

"Justice without force is powerless; force without justice is tyrannical."

Blaise Pascal (1623-1662),
French mathematician and physicist.

Bail, or **judicial interim release**, is any form of conditional release into the community of an accused charged with an offence, prior to trial or sentencing. If each and every person arrested and charged with an offence were held in custody until the end of their trial, our lock-ups, jails and prisons would quickly be filled beyond capacity. Unnecessary detention of charged persons causes undue hardship on families and employers and the overall economy.

Society recognizes distinctions between the severity of different offences and the potential threat imposed to society by various offenders. It is simply not in the **public interest** to detain every accused person for a lengthy period of time to await the finalization of court proceedings against them.

Although the term public interest is widely used in both federal and provincial legislation, and in our previous examination of R.I.C.E., nowhere is public interest clearly defined, resulting in the term being somewhat vague at times. If the public interest is not defined, who then decides what the public interest is and how it should be best protected?

According to case law, public interest "must be interpreted in light of the legislative history of the particular provision in which it appears and the legislative and social context in which it is used."[23] Public interest can be thought of as anything that concerns the general welfare of the public at large and where the interests of the wider society come before the interests of an individual person.

---

[21]*Criminal Code*, R.S. 1985, c. C-46, s. 589.

[22]*Criminal Code*, R.S. 1985, c. C-46, s. 591(3).

[23]*R. v. Zundel*, [1992] 2 S.C.R. 731, 1992 CanLII 75 S.C.C.

Within the general context of law enforcement, the public interest involves the efficient detection and investigation of crime and the apprehension of offenders. Within the specific context of judicial interim release, the public interest focuses on the prevention of additional offences, protection of citizens from harm, and effective prosecution of offenders.

The public interest is met when offenders who pose no serious threat to society are released to pursue their lives until the charges against them may be dealt with, while dangerous offenders who pose a threat are detained either until the finalization of the trial process or until assurances are received that any probability of threat is diminished.

The release of an accused person may occur at three main stages throughout an investigation: at the time of the offence, after arrest but before a charge is laid, and following the laying of a charge during court proceedings. In some cases, it is the nature of the offence that requires the release of the suspect, while in others it is the circumstances of the suspect. With very few exceptions, it is expected that an arrested individual will be released from custody rather than be detained, unless there are compelling reasons to justify their continued detention.

A person who has been arrested but not yet charged with an offence must be released by a police officer at the scene of the occurrence, once the public interest has been met. The police officer may choose to release a suspect unconditionally, that is without laying a charge, or by serving the accused an Appearance Notice or Promise to Appear informing them that they will be charged or by proceeding at a later date to lay a charge and serve the accused with a summons.

If a person is arrested with or without warrant and is not released by the arresting officer, or by the officer in charge of a police station, the arrested person must be released from custody or taken before a justice within twenty-four hours.[24] The justice is required to release the individual on their undertaking to appear in court unless the prosecutor "shows cause" why the continued detention of the individual is necessary or why the accused should be made to comply with certain conditions, known as conditional release.[25] An accused arrested with or without warrant for a section 469 *CC* offence [absolute jurisdiction of a superior division court] must also appear before a justice within twenty-four hours but will be remanded in custody to be dealt with by a superior court judge.

At any time before or during an interim release or "show cause" hearing, a justice may, on the application of the prosecutor or the accused, remand the accused into custody for a period of up to three "clear" days. "Clear days" is a term meaning excluding the first day and the last day. An accused person remanded on Monday for three clear days would have to appear again on or before Friday of the same week as the Monday and the Friday were not included in the three day remand. An accused may be remanded for longer than three clear days if they consent to the remand.[26]

Let's now examine the various circumstances and methods by which persons accused of offences are released pending trial.

---

[24]*Criminal Code*, R.S. 1985, c. C-46, s. 497(1).

[25]*Criminal Code*, R.S. 1985, c. C-46, s. 515.

[26]*Criminal Code*, R.S. 1985, c. C-46, s. 516(1).

5.8.1   Release by Peace Officers of Accused Arrested With and Without Warrant

Arrest is not the only way to compel the attendance of the accused to court. A police officer may issue an Appearance Notice in Form 9 *Criminal Code* instead of arresting a person who has not yet been charged for a section 553 *CC* (absolute jurisdiction) offence, a dual procedure (hybrid) or summary conviction, where R.I.C.E. has been satisfied.[27] Offences that are the absolute jurisdiction of the provincial court and R.I.C.E. were previously addressed in Chapter 3.

A police officer may arrest a person without warrant for a section 553 *CC* (absolute jurisdiction) offence, a dual procedure (hybrid) offence, or a summary conviction offence where the public interest considerations of R.I.C.E have not been satisfied. For example, a person arrested for operating a motor vehicle while their ability to drive was impaired by alcohol contrary to section 253(a) *CC* may be returned to a police station for the purposes of administering breathalyzer tests. The arrest of the allegedly impaired driver would be justified due to the public interest requirement to ensure that evidence of their impairment could be established (secured or preserved), to establish the identity of the accused and to prevent a continuation of the offence.

Once the breathalyzer tests are administered, however, that particular public interest requirement will have been met and continued detention is no longer justified on the grounds of securing evidence. In the event that reasonable grounds exist to lay the appropriate charge, the public interest also requires that the accused be identified and be compelled to answer to the charge in court. Providing that the offence will not be continued or repeated or another offence be committed, the public interest no longer requires the continued detention of a suspect.

Once the public interest considerations of R.I.C.E. plus the additional consideration of safety and security of the victim or any witness to the offence have been assured, any person arrested for a section 553 *CC* indictable offence (absolute jurisdiction–provincial court), dual procedure offence or summary conviction must be released by way of appearance notice.[28]

The *Criminal Code* places additional responsibility upon the officer in charge of a police station or detachment to release persons arrested without warrant for section 553 indictable (absolute jurisdiction–provincial court), dual procedure (hybrid) offences, summary conviction offences and any other offence punishable by a term of imprisonment not exceeding five years, as soon as practicable.

Interim release options available to an officer in charge include a summons (Form 6 *CC*), Promise to Appear (Form 10 *CC*), or a Recognizance entered into before an officer in charge (Form 11 *CC*). The officer in charge may also require that the person in custody pledge money or other valuable security in an amount not exceeding $500 without deposit and without **sureties**. Without deposit means that the person being released doesn't deposit the money in cash with the police but can be ordered to forfeit that amount if they do not appear in court as required. Without surety means that nobody else is allowed to pledge the money or valuable security on behalf of the arrested person.[29]

---

[27]*Criminal Code*, R.S. 1985, c. C-46, s. 496.

[28]*Criminal Code*, R.S. 1985, c. C-46, s. 496.

[29]*Criminal Code*, R.S. 1985, c. C-46, s. 498(1).

The *Criminal Code* also allows for additional release methods if the person who has been arrested without warrant, but not yet charged, is either not ordinarily resident within 200 km of the place they are in custody or are a resident of a different province. In these instances, once the public interest has been met, the officer in charge may release such person on a recognizance in an amount not exceeding $500 with deposit but without sureties.

Out of province or beyond 200 kilometre residents are required to deposit the $500 with the police. No sureties are allowed to deposit money on behalf of an arrested person with an officer in charge – only the arrested person can do so. The money or valuable security is forwarded to the Ontario Court of Justice with the other relevant court documents.[30]

An officer in charge may also release a person arrested under the authority of a warrant for any offence (except as mentioned in section 522 *CC*, which are the absolute jurisdiction of the Superior Court), if the warrant has been endorsed for release by a justice under subsection 507(6) *CC*. In effect, the justice's endorsement pre-approves the release for offences for which the officer in charge would not otherwise be entitled to release.

If the warrant has been previously endorsed, the officer in charge may release the accused by Promise to Appear or Recognizance in an amount of money or valuable security not to exceed $500 without deposit and without sureties. If the person arrested by the endorsed warrant is a resident of a different province or beyond 200 kilometres of the location of the arrest, the officer in charge may release the accused on deposit of money or valuable security in an amount not to exceed $500 without sureties.

If the person has been arrested on a previously endorsed warrant, the officer in charge may also require that the accused enter into an undertaking with conditions in Form 11.1 *Criminal Code*. The possible conditions are listed in paragraphs 499(2)(a)-(h) and include:

(a) "to remain within a territorial jurisdiction specified in the undertaking;

(b) to notify a peace officer or another person mentioned in the undertaking of any change in his or her address, employment or occupation;

(c) to abstain from communicating, directly or indirectly, with any victim, witness or other person identified in the undertaking, or from going to a place specified in the undertaking, except in accordance with the conditions specified in the undertaking;

(d) to deposit the person's passport with the peace officer or other person mentioned in the undertaking;

(e) to abstain from possessing a firearm and to surrender any firearm in the possession of the person and any authorization, licence or registration certificate or other document enabling that person to acquire or possess a firearm;

(f) to report at the times specified in the undertaking to a peace officer or other person designated in the undertaking;

---

[30]*Criminal Code*, R.S. 1985, c. C-46, s. 498(1)(d).

(g) to abstain from
   (i) the consumption of alcohol or other intoxicating substances, or
   (ii) the consumption of drugs except in accordance with a medical pre-scription; and

(h) to comply with any other condition specified in the undertaking that the offi-cerin charge considers necessary to ensure the safety and security of any victim of or witness to the offence."[31]

When a person who is not yet charged with an offence has been issued an Appear-ance Notice or was released from custody on a Promise To Appear or a Recognizance entered into before an officer in charge, an information (Form 2) charging the alleged offence should be laid as soon as practicable, or at least before the returnable court date set on the release form. Otherwise, the method of release will be invalidated and the accused must be summoned to court.[32]

When a police officer or officer in charge releases a young person from custody, by way of Summons, Promise to Appear, recognizance or undertaking, the officer in charge must give or require another police officer to give a written notice of the release form to a parent of the young person. If no parent is available, the notice may be given to an adult relative, if available, or some other appropriate adult who is known to the young person and who is likely to assist them.[33]

A police officer or an officer in charge must release unconditionally any person arrested without warrant on reasonable grounds they were about to commit an indictable offence once they are satisfied the continued detention of the person is no longer necessary to pre-vent the commission of the indictable offence.[34] If a person is arrested with or without war-rant and is not released by the arresting officer, or by the officer in charge, the arrested person must be released from custody or taken before a justice within twenty-four hours.[35]

If the person responsible for the commission of an offence cannot conveniently be located or is avoiding service of a summons or has absconded (fled from) the jurisdiction of the court, a warrant to arrest the person may be issued by a justice in Form 7, if a justice considers it in the public interest to do so. (See Table 5.1, Arrest and Release Matrix.)

5.8.2 Show Cause Hearings

Where the prosecutor feels that the continued detention of an arrested accused person is necessary, they may attempt to **show cause** why the accused should not be released for one or more of the following reasons:

1. detention is necessary to ensure the person will attend court

2. detention is necessary to ensure the protection or safety of the public (including any victim or witness) having regard to the likelihood the accused, if released, would commit a criminal offence or interfere with the administration of justice

---

[31]*Criminal Code*, R.S. 1985, c. C-46, s. 499(2)(a)-(h).

[32]*Criminal Code*, R.S. 1985, c. C-46, s. 505.

[33]*Youth Criminal Justice Act*, S.C. 2002, c. 1, s. 26(2).

[34]*Criminal Code*, R.S. 1985, c. C-46, s. 503(4).

[35]*Criminal Code*, R.S. 1985, c. C-46, s. 497(1).

TABLE 5.1	**Arrest and Release Matrix**			
Arrest By	*Offence*	*Release by*	*Section*	*Release Method*
Citizen	Breach of Peace	Peace Officer	30 CC	Unconditional once public interest satisfied
Peace Officer	Breach of Peace	Peace Officer or Officer in charge	31 CC	Unconditional once public interest satisfied
Citizen	Found committing Indictable offence or criminal offence and accused fleeing lawful arrest	Same as if arrested by Peace Officer depending on nature of offence	494(3) CC 497 CC 503(1) CC 503(2) CC	Unconditional, or Appearance Notice, Promise to Appear, summons if public interest satisfied
Peace Officer (arrest without warrant)	Sec 553 CC indictable offence, dual procedure or summary conviction	Peace Officer	496 CC 497(1) CC	Appearance Notice once public interest satisfied or proceed by summons
Peace Officer (arrest without warrant)	Sec 553 CC indictable offence, dual procedure, summary conviction or offence punishable by less than 5 years	Officer in charge if not released by Peace Officer, or Out-of-province resident or resides more than 200 km of place where in custody	498(1) CC 498(1)(c) CC 498(1)(d) CC	Promise to Appear or Recognizance entered into or given to Officer in charge without sureties – once public interest satisfied – or proceed by summons
Peace Officer (arrest without warrant)	Indictable offence other than s. 553 except murder, etc	Officer in charge or by Justice	498(1) CC 498(1.1) CC 515(1) CC	Summons, Promise to Appear or undertaking given to a Justice with conditions
Peace Officer (arrest without warrant)	469 CC Indictable offences	Absolute jurisdiction of Superior Division judge	522(1) CC	Recognizance before a Justice with or without sureties
Peace Officer (arrest with warrant)	Other than 469 CC indictable offence	Release by Justice unless endorsed by Justice under 507(6) CC	499(1) CC 503 CC 515 CC	Promise to Appear, Recognizance, undertaking given to a Justice with conditions
Peace Officer 495(1)(a) CC	Arrest warrant for out-of-province indictable offence	Remand by Justice for up to six days	503(3) CC 528 CC	Release to out-of-province authorities once warrant backed

3. detention is justified in order to maintain public confidence in the administration of justice due to the severity and circumstances of the offence, the probability of conviction, and the potential for a lengthy term of imprisonment if convicted

While the *Criminal Code* places the onus on the prosecutor to "show cause" why the accused should not be released from custody, it is still the responsibility of the police to gather the evidence that will be relied upon to show cause and provide it to the prosecutor, who will introduce it in court.

The *Criminal Code* describes the types of admissible evidence that may be introduced by a prosecutor during a show cause hearing and includes the following:

"(i) ...that the accused has previously been convicted of a criminal offence,

(ii) ...that the accused has been charged with and is awaiting trial for another criminal offence,

(iii) ...that the accused has previously committed an offence under section 145, [Escape Lawful Custody, Fail to Attend Court, Fail to Appear for the Purposes of the Identification of Criminals Act, or Fail to Comply with the Conditions of an Undertaking] or

(iv) to show the circumstances of the alleged offence, particularly as they relate to the probability of conviction of the accused;"

and also:

"(d) the justice shall take into consideration any evidence submitted regarding the need to ensure the safety or security of any victim of or witness to an offence and

(e) the justice may receive and base his [or her] decision on evidence considered credible or trustworthy by him [or her] in the circumstances of each case"[36]

Evidence that demonstrates the probability that the accused, if released, might fail to attend court might include evidence regarding their lack of stability or attachment to family and to the community. Investigators should gather all information relating to an accused that would assist the court to make a finding as to an order for release or detention, including:

1. Criminal record: If convicted for the offence charged, is there a strong likelihood of conviction and punishment in the form of a period of imprisonment? Does the accused have a history of failing to appear in court or breaching the conditions of previous releases?

2. Residence: Does the accused have a fixed residence where they have lived for any length of time, or do they relocate frequently from place to place or depend on others for housing?

3. Employment: Does the accused have an occupation and were they employed at the time of the offence? What is the accused's previous employment history?

4. Family Status: Does the accused have family or relatives in the area that would be able – and willing – to provide support (financial, moral or emotional), or be responsible for them if released from custody? If so, are they trustworthy?

5. Personal history: Is the accused suffering from any known disorders or addictions which, if left untreated, might tend to place them at risk of re-offending if released? Does the accused have a stable environment to return to, if released from custody?

6. Offence: Is there evidence of planning and premeditation in the offence charged?

---

[36]*Criminal Code*, R.S. 1985, c. C-46, s. 518(1).

7. Victims/Witnesses: Is there evidence of any threats of violence or previous violence or threats of violence toward any victim or witness in this case?

8. Investigation: Is there any evidence that the accused, if released, could destroy or tamper with evidence in the case or otherwise interfere with the investigation or the administration of justice?

Witnesses may be called to give sworn evidence at a show cause hearing and may include hearsay evidence, "provided it is credible and trustworthy."[37] As an investigator I often testified at show cause hearings, to summarize the findings of an investigation, including the events of the case, the findings of other investigators and the anticipated evidence of civilian witnesses.

Where the prosecutor successfully shows cause why an individual should not be released from custody, the justice will order that the accused be detained in custody until they are dealt with according to law.[38] Where an accused is charged with a Superior Court absolute jurisdiction (s. 469 *CC*) offence, the justice must remand the accused in custody for one week at a time until they are dealt with by a Superior Court Judge.[39]

If a prosecutor does not show cause justifying the individual's continued detention, the individual must be released on their undertaking before the justice and may be required to comply with appropriate conditions that include:

1. reporting to police or other persons at stated intervals

2. remaining within the jurisdiction of the court or other jurisdiction

3. notification to police of change of address or employment

4. abstention of communication with victims or witnesses or refraining from attending at designated locations

5. deposit of their passport, if any

6. any other condition considered necessary to ensure the safety and security of victims or witnesses

7. prohibition of possession of weapons, ammunition or explosive substances if the offence involved personal, threatened or attempted violence, terrorism, criminal harassment, or designated *Controlled Drugs and Substances Act* offences

Accused persons who are remanded in custody or who are ordered detained in custody until dealt with by law may also be required to abstain from communicating with victims or witnesses or other designated persons, as the justice deems appropriate.[40]

5.8.3 Reverse Onus – Show Cause Hearing

There are instances where the law places the onus (responsibility) on the accused to show cause why their continued detention is not necessary. Among others, some of the more common **reverse onus** situations include those where an accused is charged with:

---

[37]*R. v. Powers* (1972), 20 C.R.N.S. 23, 9 C.C.C. (2d) 533 (Ont. H.C.).

[38]*Criminal Code*, R.S. 1985, c. C-46, s. 515(5).

[39]*Criminal Code*, R.S. 1985, c. C-46, s. 515(11).

[40]*Criminal Code*, R.S. 1985, c. C-46, s. 516(1).

1. an indictable offence other than s. 469 *CC* offence (Superior Court absolute jurisdiction) while at large awaiting appeal [see s. 679, 680 *CC*],

2. designated offences involving criminal organizations,

3. a designated terrorism offence,

4. an indictable offence other than s. 469 *CC* offence (Superior Court absolute jurisdiction), while not ordinarily a resident of Canada,

5. failing to attend court or to comply with the conditions of a summons, Appearance Notice, Promise to Appear, recognizance before an officer in charge or a recognizance or an undertaking given to a justice while at large for another offence, or

6. an offence punishable by life imprisonment under sections 5–7 of the *Controlled Drugs and Substances Act*[41]

As the onus usually lies with the Crown to show why an individual's continued detention is necessary, it is this reversal of the legal burden of proof to the accused that results in the term reverse onus. Even though the onus is placed on the accused to establish why they should not be further detained, an investigator must still gather relevant evidence, if any, as for a normal show cause hearing to assist the prosecutor to rebut evidence introduced by the defence.

5.8.4 Superior Criminal Court – Absolute Jurisdiction Offences

Only a judge of a Superior Court may release an accused from custody or try an accused charged with committing, attempting or conspiring to commit one of the following offences as set out in section 469 *Criminal Code*:

1. Section 47 *CC* Treason,

2. Section 49 *CC* Alarming Her Majesty,

3. Section 51 *CC* Intimidating parliament or a legislature,

4. Section 53 *CC* Inciting to mutiny,

5. Section 61 *CC* Seditious offences (illegal acts to overthrow a government),

6. Section 74 *CC* Piracy,

7. Section 75 *CC* Piratical acts, or committing or conspiring to commit the offence of Murder, Sec. 235 CC, or committing any of the following offences:

8. accessory after the fact to murder or treason,

9. bribery by the holder of a judicial office, or an offence under sections 4–7, *Crimes Against Humanity and War Crimes Act*

The most commonly encountered offences that are the absolute jurisdiction of Superior Court of criminal jurisdiction are the offences of murder, conspiracy to commit murder and accessory after the fact to murder. The offence of attempted murder is not in

---

[41]*Criminal Code*, R.S. 1985, c. C-46, s. 515(6).

this class of offences and consequently an accused charged with this offence also has the option to elect to be tried by Provincial Court Judge.[42]

5.9 STRUCTURE OF CRIMINAL PROCEEDINGS

Our court system is based on the adversarial system involving a prosecution pitted against one or more accused, who are usually, but may not always be, represented by defence counsel. If the accused pleads guilty to the offence(s) charged, the court will hear evidence, which has been stipulated (agreed to) by the accused, as read by a prosecutor. The accused may be convicted on that evidence without the necessity of calling any witnesses or the production of any exhibits.

If an accused has been arraigned and has entered a plea of not guilty, a trial date will be set. If the offence charged is one for which the accused may elect trial by a superior court judge, sitting without a jury, the trial will be presided over by a judge as the "trier of fact". If the accused elects trial by judge and jury, a judge will still preside over the trial but the jury becomes the "trier of fact".

In a jury trial, both parties to the proceedings will make opening arguments prior to the calling of evidence to highlight their positions regarding the case for the members of a jury. Opening arguments are not considered evidence and differ significantly on crucial points such as identity of the accused or the facts in issue of the charge(s).

As all charges are prosecuted by the Crown, the Crown bears the onus of proving the case in every trial and will put forth the case for a conviction. The Crown introduces evidence first by way of oral testimony of witnesses and through the production of physical and circumstantial evidence. If the prosecution evidence does not establish a *prima facie* case, the judge may direct a verdict of not guilty.

When a witness is called to testify in a judicial proceeding, they will be asked questions by counsel for whichever party called them in what is referred to as "examination-in-chief". Following the examination-in-chief, the witness will be asked questions by the opposing party in a procedure known as "cross-examination".

When the Crown has introduced all of their evidence to prove the facts in issue, the prosecution will rest their case. Following the case for the prosecution, the accused is then permitted to make full answer and defence to the charge(s), either personally or by way of counsel for the defence.[43]

In a jury trial, following the introduction of all of the evidence, each party will offer a summation to the jury in the form of a verbal address to summarize their interpretation of the evidence as it relates to the guilt or innocence of the accused. If, following the case for the prosecution, the defence elects not to call any evidence, the prosecution will proceed with their summation, followed by summation for the defence.[44] If the defence does call evidence on behalf of the accused, the defence will offer their summation to the jury and the prosecution will deliver their summation last.[45]

---

[42]*Criminal Code*, R.S. 1985, c. C-46, s. 554(1).

[43]*Criminal Code*, R.S. 1985, c. C-46, s. 650(3) and 802(1).

[44]*Criminal Code*, R.S. 1985, c. C-46, s. 651(1).

[45]*Criminal Code*, R.S. 1985, c. C-46, s. 651(3).

5.10 ARRAIGNMENT, CROWN ELECTION, PLEA AND ELECTION BY ACCUSED

When an accused charged with a criminal offence appears in court, the charge(s) against them will be read to them, usually by a court clerk. The reading of the charge to the accused in court is referred to as the arraignment. Prior to the accused being asked to indicate their plea to the charge, if the charge is a dual procedure offence, the court clerk or the judge will ask the Crown Attorney how they elect to proceed on the charge, either by indictment or by summary conviction.

If we sat in a courtroom, the actual proceedings would sound something like this:

John Smith answers to his name and stands before the court when his name is called from the docket.

Court:	"Are you John Smith?"
Accused:	"Yes, I am."
Court:	"John Smith stands charged that he, on or about the 25th day of December, 2006, at the City of Orillia in the Central East Region, did unlawfully break and enter a certain place, to wit: a building situated at 25 Godfrey Drive, with intent to commit an indictable offence contrary to paragraph 348(1)(e) of the *Criminal Code* of Canada. Do you understand the charge against you?"
Accused:	"Yes, I do."

As the offence of breaking and entering with intent to commit an indictable offence in relation to a building, other than a dwelling house, is a dual procedure offence, the court must now seek the Crown Attorney's election as to whether or not to proceed on the charge by indictment or by summary conviction.

Court:	"How does the Crown elect to proceed in this matter?"
Prosecutor:	"By summary conviction, please Your Honour."

Summary conviction offences or dual procedure offences, where the Crown elects to proceed by summary conviction, will be tried in Provincial Court. If the offence is an indictable offence that is designated as being the absolute jurisdiction of the Provincial Court under s. 553 *Criminal Code*, the trial will still be conducted in the Provincial Court, but the accused will be liable to the greater penalty provided by way of trial by indictment.[46]

Once the accused is aware of the Crown's election, the accused will be asked how they plead to the charge, "Guilty" or "Not guilty". Where the accused does not answer or refuses to enter a plea, the court will enter a plea of "Not guilty" and proceed as if the accused had requested a trial.[47] The only time an accused is allowed to enter a different plea is if they plead "Not guilty" to the offence charged, but guilty to another offence, with the prior consent of the prosecutor.[48]

Court:	"Mr. Smith, how do you plead to this charge?"
Accused:	"Not Guilty."

---

[46]*Criminal Code*, R.S. 1985, c. C-46, s. 536(1).

[47]*Criminal Code*, R.S. 1985, c. C-46, s. 606(2).

[48]*Criminal Code*, R.S. 1985, c. C-46, s. 606(4).

In any case where the charge is an indictable offence other than an offence listed in section 469 *Criminal Code* [absolute jurisdiction of Superior Court Judge] or a dual procedure offence where the Crown elects to proceed by indictment, the accused would then be asked in which court they elect to be tried. As the charge against John Smith is neither a section 469 nor a section 553 *Criminal Code* offence, if the Crown elects to proceed by way of indictment, the following words would be read to the accused by a justice of the peace or by the judge:

Court: "You have the option to elect to be tried by a judge without a jury and without having had a preliminary inquiry; or you may elect to have a preliminary inquiry and to be tried by a judge without a jury; or you may elect to have a preliminary inquiry and to be tried by a court composed of a judge and jury. If you do not elect now, you shall be deemed to have elected to have a preliminary inquiry and to be tried by a court composed of a judge and jury. How do you elect to be tried?" [49]

Accused: "By judge and jury."

If the accused refuses to elect a court in which to be tried, the trial will be conducted by a Superior Court composed of a judge and jury.[50]

5.11   ADJOURNMENTS

When an accused initially appears on a charge, it may take several court appearances for the judicial proceedings to be finalized. Various motions may be brought before the court by either party to the proceedings, such as dealing with matters of custody, or the mental competency of the accused to stand trial. Once the plea of the accused is taken, and the preliminary inquiry or trial commences, it may still take several sittings of the court before the charge(s) are finally dealt with. These breaks in the trial are referred to as adjournments.

On occasion, one party may request that a scheduled appearance be adjourned due to the non-availability of a witness or to grant additional time to prepare for a hearing. The other party may consent or object to the adjournment. The justice or judge will then determine whether or not the proceedings or any party to the proceedings are unfairly prejudiced and whether or not, having regard to all the circumstances, it is in the public interest to grant the adjournment.[51]

5.12   APPEARANCE BY THE ACCUSED

In criminal proceedings against individuals charged with summary conviction offences, the accused may appear personally, or if represented, by counsel or by agent (person acting on behalf of the accused). An accused may be ordered to appear personally by the court and a warrant may be issued for the arrest of the accused. Where an organization

---

[49]*Criminal Code*, R.S. 1985, c. C-46, s. 536(2).

[50]*Criminal Code*, R.S. 1985, c. C-46, s. 471.

[51]*Criminal Code*, R.S. 1985, c. C-46, s. 571.

is charged with a summary conviction offence, the organization must appear represented by counsel or by an agent. A court, once satisfied that a summons was served upon an organization charged with a summary conviction offence, that is not represented, may proceed with the trial *ex parte* (in the absence of the accused).[52]

In proceedings involving indictable offences, the accused may file with the court an appointment of a designated counsel to appear on their behalf during any part of the proceedings, except when the oral evidence of a witness is taken, or during jury selection. An accused charged with an indictable offence must also be present for the purposes of entering a plea of guilt and the passing of sentence, unless the court orders otherwise. A court may at any time order the accused to be personally present by issuing a summons or a warrant for the arrest of the accused.[53]

Where an organization is charged with an indictable offence, they must appear and plead to the charge by counsel or by agent.[54] The notice of an indictment that is served upon an organization must advise that if the organization fails to appear and enter a plea, a plea of not guilty will be entered by the court and the trial will proceed *ex parte*.[55]

Except when the evidence of a witness is being taken, for both summary conviction and indictable offences, where the accused is in custody, they may appear in court by means of closed-circuit television or by any means that allows for simultaneous visual and oral communication between the court and the accused.[56] A court may have an accused removed from the court for interrupting the proceedings during any part of the trial, if necessary.

5.13 PRELIMINARY INQUIRY

If the accused elects trial by a Provincial Court Judge, the court will set a date for trial or may proceed directly if both parties are ready to proceed with the trial. If the accused elects to be tried by a Superior Court Judge sitting alone or sitting with a jury, the court will set a date for a preliminary inquiry. If the accused refuses to make an election, they will be deemed to have elected trial by judge and jury and a preliminary inquiry will be scheduled.

Unlike a trial, the purpose of a preliminary inquiry is not to determine the guilt or innocence of the accused. The purpose of a preliminary inquiry is to determine whether or not there is sufficient evidence to warrant the trial proceeding to a judge and jury. Preliminary inquiries are held at the Provincial Court level. A prosecutor may use a preliminary inquiry to test the strength of the witnesses and evidence of a case while the defence may use a preliminary inquiry to obtain a better sense of disclosure regarding the Crown's case.

If the judge finds as the result of the preliminary inquiry that there is enough evidence for a properly instructed jury to convict upon, the accused will be committed to stand trial before a court of competent jurisdiction. If, in the opinion of the judge, there is insufficient evidence to convict, the accused will be discharged.

---

[52]*Criminal Code*, R.S. 1985, c. C-46, s. 800.

[53]*Criminal Code*, R.S. 1985, c. C-46, s. 650.01.

[54]*Criminal Code*, R.S. 1985, c. C-46, s. 620.

[55]*Criminal Code*, R.S. 1985, c. C-46, s. 621.

[56]*Criminal Code*, R.S. 1985, c. C-46, s. 650 and s. 800(2.1).

The accused may be sent directly to trial without a preliminary inquiry if the prosecutor prefers a "direct indictment", but this procedure may be done only with the consent in writing of the Attorney General or Deputy Attorney General.[57]

5.14 CHANGE OF VENUE

Prior to trial for an indictable offence, a prosecutor or the accused may request a change of venue (location) to a different territorial jurisdiction in the same province where:

(a) it would be expedient to the ends of justice, or

(b) a jury cannot be convened at the location where the trial would normally have been held[58]

An example of a case where the venue was changed was the trial of convicted serial rapist and murderer, Paul Bernardo. Due to the scope and magnitude of the proceedings, the intense media scrutiny, security considerations and the anticipated duration of the trial, the murder and rape trials were held in Toronto, where the court facilities could support a trial of that complexity, although the events giving rise to the trial had taken place in St. Catharines.

Other grounds for requesting a change of venue would be the necessity of ensuring a fair and impartial trial,[59] or a jury that would be unable or reluctant to render a verdict due to fear of retaliation.[60]

The venue of a trial may also be changed to a different territorial jurisdiction in the same province if the court orders that the accused's trial be held in one of Canada's official languages and services for conducting the trial in the language best understood by the accused are not available in the jurisdiction where the trial would normally be held.[61]

5.15 PRODUCTION OF A PRISONER

Occasionally, it becomes necessary to have a prisoner removed from a jail or prison to testify in court or for investigative purposes, such as to conduct an interview. A judge of a Superior Court may order in writing that a prisoner be brought before the court. If the prisoner is being produced for investigative purposes, the prisoner must consent, in writing, to the transfer. A prosecutor may apply for an order for the production of a prisoner for a specified period of time where the judge is satisfied that the order is necessary. A Provincial Court judge may exercise the authority of a Superior Court judge for the purpose of this procedure where the person in custody is within the jurisdiction of the judge.[62]

---

[57]*Criminal Code*, R.S. 1985, c. C-46, s. 577.

[58]*Criminal Code*, R.S. 1985, c. C-46, s. 599(1).

[59]*R. v. Turvey* (1970), 1 C.C.C. (2d) 90, 12 C.R.N.S. 329 (N.S.S.C.).

[60]*R. v. Lafferty* (1977), 35 C.C.C. (2d) 183 (N.W.T.S.C.).

[61]*Criminal Code*, R.S. 1985, c. C-46, s. 531.

[62]*Criminal Code*, R.S. 1985, c. C-46, s. 527.

5.16 INCLUDED OFFENCES

Where an accused is charged with an offence and the full offence is not proved, but the evidence proves the accused attempted to commit the offence, the accused may be automatically convicted of the attempt to commit the offence without relaying the charge.[63] In certain other instances, where an accused is charged with an offence but the evidence fails to prove the full offence or an attempt to commit the full offence, the accused may still be convicted of an "included offence" or an attempt to commit an included offence without re-laying the charge.[64]

For example, the *Criminal Code* specifies that a person charged with murder may be acquitted of the charge of murder and convicted of the included offences of manslaughter or infanticide if the evidence proves the commission of those offences.[65] Included offences are also held to be any offence that the accused had to commit as part of the full offence that is charged but not proved. An example would be in a charge of Level I Sexual Assault, for which the facts in issue are:

- the application of force to another person
- intentionally
- without their consent
- directly or indirectly
- in sexual circumstances
- that violate the sexual integrity of the complainant.

If the evidence fails to prove the assault occurred under sexual circumstances that violated the sexual integrity of the complainant, but the remaining facts in issue were proved, the accused could still be convicted of the included offence of Assault Level I as that offence was committed in the commission of the offence that was charged.[66]

SUMMARY

- The terms "arrest" and "charge", while not synonymous, are often related. Not every person arrested is charged with an offence – not every person charged with an offence is arrested.

- An information is the charging document which contains, among other things, the alleged offences committed by an accused person.

- The information creates the charge but does not compel the attendance of the accused to court. There must also be some form of compelling document that commands the accused to appear in court at a designated time, date and location.

---

[63]*Criminal Code*, R.S. 1985, c. C-46, s. 660.

[64]*Criminal Code*, R.S. 1985, c. C-46, s. 662(1).

[65]*Criminal Code*, R.S. 1985, c. C-46, s. 662(3).

[66]*R. v. Foote* (1974), 16 C.C.C. (2d) 44, (N.B. S.C. App. Div.).

- An accused person who is arrested without a warrant for a criminal offence must be charged within a maximum period of twenty-four hours or be released from custody.

- The statute of limitations is the time limit following an offence during which a charge must be laid. There is no statute of limitations for indictable offences, while a charge for a summary conviction offence must be laid within six months after the offence.

- A joinder of accused means that more than one accused may be jointly charged with the same offence on a single information.

- A joinder of counts means that more than one offence may be charged against one, or jointly against one or more accused persons on a single information.

- The public interest is met when the identity of the accused has been established; there are no reasonable grounds to believe they would fail to attend court; if released the accused would not continue or repeat the offence or commit another offence; the accused, if released, could not destroy or tamper with evidence; and the accused will not interfere with the security of the victim or any witness.

- A justice is required to release arrested individuals on their undertaking to appear in court unless the prosecutor is able to "show cause" why the continued detention of the individual is necessary or why, if released, the accused should be made to comply with certain conditions.

- If a young person is released from custody and is issued a summons, appearance notice, promise to appear, recognizance or undertaking, the officer in charge or another police officer designated by them must serve written notice to a parent, if available, or adult relative, or appropriate adult known to the young offender.

- The trial or interim judicial release for offences listed in section 469 *Criminal Code* (murder, etc.) is the absolute jurisdiction of a Superior Division Court judge.

DISCUSSION QUESTIONS

1. You are a police officer and while on patrol you arrest two individuals without warrant for causing a disturbance by fighting, to prevent the continuation of the offence. Both persons are local residents who are well known to you. You have no reason to believe that, if released, they would not appear in court. Now that you have arrested them, are you legally authorized to release them? Do you have a choice as to whether or not to release them? If release is possible, what methods of release would be available to you?

2. A citizen stops you while on patrol and turns over a person they arrested to you because they strongly believe he is the person who caused property damage to their car, parked outside a restaurant in which they were having lunch, 30 minutes ago. The citizen did not observe the damage being done but received information from a witness who described the vandal and arrested the person matching the description that was given to them. They demand that you do your job and charge the person for

damaging their car. Will you continue this arrest? State the reasons for your decision, whether it is yes or no. Regardless of your answer, how will you release the arrested person from custody?

3. While on patrol, you conduct a traffic stop on a local resident of your town or city who has recently returned from an extended absence. Upon conducting a CPIC check, you learn that there is an outstanding warrant for this person from Saskatchewan on a charge of Attempted Murder. Do you have any legal authority to arrest the person based on the existence of an arrest warrant from a different province? If so, what bail provisions apply in this situation? How may you release this person from custody pending trial, if at all?

WEBLINKS

www.canlii.org/ca/sta/c-46/

Canadian Legal Information Institute On-line *Criminal Code*, R.S. 1985, c. C-46

www.owjn.org/archive/arlene2.htm

Ontario Women's Justice Network Website
Transcript of the 200 joint recommendations from the July 1998 inquest into the murder of Arlene Allison May and the death of Randall Joseph Iles. Many of the recommendations deal with matters of charging suspects and judicial interim release to improve the safety of victims in cases of domestic violence.

canada.justice.gc.ca/en/dept/pub/crim/crimd06e_pt7.html

Department of Justice Policy Paper regarding investigation, charging and judicial interim release in spousal assault prosecutions.

Chapter 6

Use of Discretion

"Perish discretion when it interferes with duty."

Hannah More (1745-1833),
English writer.

Learning Outcomes

After reading this chapter, students should be able to:

- Distinguish between personal and professional discretion.
- Give examples of situations in which police discretion is used.
- Summarize considerations for evaluating the appropriateness of discretion.
- Explain the different meanings of the term "zero tolerance" in relation to policing.
- Give examples of situations in which police discretion must not be used.

6.1   WHAT IS DISCRETION?

Discretion involves individuals exercising their own judgment and using free will, uninfluenced by external factors, to make responsible choices or to act within appropriate limits. We all exercise discretion in our everyday lives in the activities in which we choose to involve ourselves and with the people with whom we choose to associate. Discretion has more than one meaning in modern language.

To be discreet means to act in a prudent and reserved manner. If someone is told a secret in confidence by a friend, discretion requires the person who is told the secret to maintain that confidence and not tell the secret to others. Acting in a discreet manner might also involve exercising conservative behaviour within normal expectations or limits. Promiscuity and the abuse of intoxicating substances are both examples of behaviour that might be described as being less than discreet.

A discreet person is one who acts responsibly and makes responsible choices. A lack of discretion is indicated when, through one or a series of poor choices, a person engages in inappropriate activities that are likely to damage their reputation or raise criticism against them from others. A person in a committed relationship who cheats on their partner would be guilty of an indiscretion in betraying the trust of their partner.

The type of discretion that we will be examining is the discretion that a person exercises during the course of their professional life. Many professions routinely use discretion in the course of their employment in deciding when to act – or not to – and in selecting the correct course of action, having regard to all the circumstances of a given situation.

Parents, teachers and employers all have discretion over matters relating to the imposition of both rewards and discipline over their children, students and employees, respectively. A parent might choose to exercise discretion by allowing a child to stay up past their normal bed-time as a reward for an achievement or for exhibiting desirable behaviour.

A teacher might choose to exercise discretion by awarding bonus marks to a student who is struggling on the verge of passing or failing a course. Discretion is also demonstrated by making a choice not to impose discipline in certain circumstances, in favour of some other method of resolving a situation.

The use of discretion is also a well-accepted and long-standing feature of our criminal justice system. Crown attorneys have discretion to decide which charges are worthy of being prosecuted. During the course of a trial, prosecutors have discretion over which witnesses to call upon to testify and which evidence will be submitted before the court. Justices of the peace and judges have discretion over the issuance of legal processes such as search warrants and, during judicial proceedings, have discretion over the severity of legal sanctions, if any, to be imposed upon conviction.

In addition to discretion being a widespread part of our personal life, common law has long provided police officers with the authority to exercise discretion while carrying out their law enforcement duties. Overall, society recognizes that our laws cannot possibly take into account every possible situation a police officer might encounter and that the police have to be flexible in their application of the law to deal effectively with offenders.

6.2   PROFESSIONAL DISCRETION

Professional discretion is "[t]he freedom or authority to make reasonable [and fair] decisions while carrying out one's professional responsibilities."[1] The use of discretion by educators, legal and medical professionals, and by the police raises a number of moral issues which require that to be appropriate, the application of discretion must be responsible, lawful, consistent, ethical and accountable.

The controversy surrounding the use of professional discretion can be simply explained by analyzing its potential consequences. A lack of discretion in one's own personal life might only cause damage to an individual's own reputation or character, but the inappropriate use of professional discretion can result in the abuse of power, the violation of individual rights of others and a high potential for loss of public confidence.

Of all the examples of the types of discretion that are used during everyday life and by a wide variety of professions, it is police discretion which is sure to attract the most scrutiny and is most likely to separate those who support it from those who oppose its use.

[1]Bjorkquist at p. 147.

6.3   POLICE USE OF DISCRETION

Police officers exercise discretion every day in determining which law enforcement priorities to focus enforcement efforts upon and when dealing with individuals suspected of having broken the law. Police officers are granted with considerable freedom to use discretion in deciding when to invoke legal sanctions or when not to invoke legal sanctions, even when an offence has been obviously committed and the relevant law is clearly applicable.

The Law Enforcement Code of Conduct, published by the International Association of Chiefs of Police (IACP) in 1989, addresses the use of police discretion as follows:

> "A police officer will use responsibly the discretion vested in his position and exercise it within the law. The principle of reasonableness will guide the officer's determinations, and the officer will consider all surrounding circumstances in determining whether any legal action shall be taken.
>
> Consistent and wise use of discretion, based on professional competence, will do much to preserve good relationships and retain the confidence of the public. There can be difficulty choosing between different courses of action. It is important to remember that a timely word of advice rather than arrest – which may be correct in appropriate circumstances – can be a more effective means of achieving a desired end." [2]

As in previous chapters, we again see the concept of "reasonableness" – that is objective reasonableness – in the IACP Code's expectations of the use of police discretion. You will recall that the test of reasonableness is a two-part test that combines the subjective reasonableness in the officer's state of mind with an objective analysis of whether or not the "reasonable person" would have resorted to the same action or decision under similar circumstances.

What the IACP Code of Conduct doesn't do is provide police officers of any level of experience with any specific guidelines as to precisely when or how to properly exercise discretion in the discharge of their duties. Nor does the Code of Conduct address the issues surrounding the potential problems that can be caused by the inappropriate use of discretion.

While the *Police Services Act* of Ontario clearly sets out the duties of police officers, it is strangely silent on the specific issue of discretion. The *PSA* Code of Conduct, which governs Ontario police officers, does address certain circumstances that might include certain examples of unequal treatment of individuals that could include situations of abuse of discretion under the heading of Discreditable Conduct.[3] (See Section 6.3.3)

6.3.1   Letter of the Law vs. Latitude

While police work is often characterized as boring, routine and repetitive, in reality, it is anything but. Each and every event the police encounter is individually unique in terms of its circumstances, location, timing and the participants it involved. It cannot be said

---

[2]Bjorkquist at pp. 248-249.

[3]O. Reg. 123/98, Part V, s. 2(1)(a).

that every theft is the same as another or that if you've seen one traffic collision, property crime or crime involving personal violence that "you've seen them all".

The dynamics of each incident differ remarkably in terms of who was involved, what motivated the incident, what factors resulted in the people behaving in the manner they did and the consequences of the event for the various participants. Most importantly, each event can be said to differ substantially in terms of the best solution for dealing with the respective participants, assuming that multiple options are available to the responding officer(s), which there usually are. "Discretion is the power to decide which rules apply to a given situation and whether or not to apply them." (Ericson 1982)[4]

Every provincial legislature in Canada has enacted and enforces a provincial statute governing the operation of motor vehicles upon highways within their respective jurisdictions. The *Highway Traffic Act* of Ontario creates the offence of operating a motor vehicle on a highway at a speed greater than the posted speed limit.[5]

It is inconceivable to imagine that the Ontario legislature intended that everyone driving 81 km/h in a posted 80 km/h speed zone should be stopped and charged by the police. Nor is it possible for the police in every jurisdiction to take enforcement action against each and every person who commits a minor offence. (McKenna 2002)

Most police officers will exercise discretion by allowing drivers to exceed the posted speed limit within a certain range or may stop but not charge every driver for marginal infractions. Officers may elect to issue warnings for minor offences such as possession of required documentation or for forgetting to install a previously purchased current validation sticker on their vehicle licence plate.

A police officer who charges every violator for breaching every possible offence is unquestionably acting within the bounds of the law, but such a strict application of the law involves a lack of discretion that might not be the best possible approach in every case. A complete lack of discretion can reflect poorly, both on the individual officer and on the public image of their police service.

The strict "letter of the law", an approach to law enforcement that is both firm and inflexible, is a form of "cookie-cutter" justice – one that treats all incidents and all participants of the event in the same way regardless of individual circumstances. What works in one situation, however, is not always the best option for dealing with a similar incident involving different participants and circumstances. The public interest, which involves the principles of reasonableness, fairness and equality, consistency and accountability, is not always best served by laying a charge in every situation where a charge could be laid.

Individual police officers frequently work alone or in small units, often with little or no immediate supervision. Often an officer's actions will be based on their individual values and beliefs regarding what they feel is appropriate or inappropriate, rather than strict observance of policy that is dictated by their police service.

This freedom creates situations in which police officers often take widely differing approaches to the scope and magnitude of discretion they exercise. Critics point out, however, that leaving the power to decide who will charged and who won't be charged with frontline patrol officers creates an environment that allows for abuses of discretion to occur. (McKenna 2002)

---

[4]Ericson (1982) cited from McKenna (2002) at p.119.

[5]*Highway Traffic Act*, R.S.O. (1990) c. H-8, s. 128(1).

Police officers must decide if laying a specific charge – and the determination of the severity of the charge to be laid – or the making an arrest is the most appropriate course of action to take in a particular situation. For example, it may well be more effective under the circumstances to treat a first-time offender more leniently than one would in a similar situation involving a chronic, repeat offender.

An officer may decide that a first-time offender may benefit from receiving a "break" in the form of a warning or caution that might result in the offender voluntarily choosing to obey the law in the future. The same officer may view a repeat offender as not being deserving of a break, and choose to lay a charge on the basis that a court-imposed fine or other sanction is the appropriate method to deter such an offender from committing similar acts in the future.

In the case of a minor traffic collision, the use of discretion might involve merely issuing a traffic citation to a young driver who is at fault. In a similar situation involving an elderly driver, discretion may require taking steps to suspend the driver's licence of the at-fault driver for medical reasons to ensure their safety and the safety of others. As with most things in everyday life, police work is rarely clear-cut or simple.

Critics of the use of unfettered police discretion sometimes favour a more-or-less cookie-cutter approach to restrict the use of choice by a police officer to pre-determine the eventual outcome of an event. Removing the power of discretion from the police is seen by them as a way in which to reduce the potential for abuses by police officers.

Supporters of police discretion maintain that our criminal justice system benefits from police officers as first-responders being able to resort to using discretion to manage the manner in which people are dealt with by the courts. In fact, supporters contend that our criminal justice system would not function effectively without there being broad freedom on the part of the police to exercise discretion.

Both critics and supporters of the use of police discretion agree that in order to best serve the public interest, the exercise of discretion must be responsible, lawful, consistent and ethical. Given the enormous and lasting effects that the actions of the police can have on individuals, the power of discretion should be considered almost as potentially invasive as the powers of arrest, use of force and search and seizure.

There are certain instances involving exceptions including domestic violence, spousal abuse, or workplace sexual harassment where the use of police discretion is restricted by policy. Experience has shown that the use of discretion does not always best serve the participants of the event or the public interest. (See section 6.8 relating to issues of "Zero Tolerance" later in this chapter.)

6.3.2 Latitude – Not Licence

The controversy surrounding the use of police discretion is fuelled by the lack of statutory authority for it and by the lack of clear guidelines that provide limitations surrounding its use. The very lack of direction and limitations on the use of police discretion can contribute to both ambiguity and misunderstanding on the part of police officers as to whether or not the use of discretion is appropriate in a given situation. Unfortunately, it isn't reasonably practical to attempt to set out procedures to be rigidly followed that would apply to every possible situation.

There is a monumental difference between having latitude (recognized freedom from restrictions) to exercise discretion in certain situations and having licence (unlimited freedom from restrictions) to use discretion in all situations. To be considered appropriate, the use of discretion must be based on the principles of equality, fairness, consistency and accountability.

The freedom to exercise discretion does not translate into a licence to "turn a blind eye" to a certain offender or to a certain class of offender while targeting other offenders for unfair treatment. A member of a visible minority who receives a citation for a traffic offence when a Caucasian driver is given a warning is being treated unfairly even though the manner in which they are treated is still perfectly legal, within the letter of the law. (Bjorkquist 2002) (McKenna 2002)

Just as an officer must be able to articulate his or her legal grounds for arrest, search, seizure and use of force in court, an officer ought to be able to articulate their moral grounds for taking or not taking enforcement action against a certain individual. As a respected colleague relates to his ethics students, "If you can live with your friends and family seeing what you've done 'live' on the six o'clock news, your actions are in all probability ethical."[6]

It is important that if discretion, in any form, is used by an officer, it be within the officer's lawful authority. The use of discretion by a police officer to act or not act in any situation must never involve a breach of the policy or statute law on the officer's part. Nor must the use of discretion ever be used to disguise the compounding – the decision not to prosecute in exchange for some consideration – of an offence that was committed. If the officer's action requires that deceit or secrecy be used to hide or disguise it after the fact, such actions can hardly be said to be a responsible or ethical use of police discretion.

A police officer must be able to accurately record their motives for taking or not taking action in relation to an incident or an offender in their investigative notes, official report to superiors, Crown brief, or if called upon, to provide justification to some other authority.

6.3.3 Discretion vs. Abuse

Imagine yourself as a police officer on traffic patrol when you observe an oncoming car pass a school bus stopped on the roadway with its red lights flashing to warn motorists of disembarking passengers. As the vehicle passes you, you notice that the driver is a middle-aged white male, dressed in a business suit. You clearly observe that he is holding a cell phone and is speaking into it. A young child, about to cross the road in front of the school bus, sees the passing car at the last moment and jumps back in front of the bus to avoid being struck by the car.

There should be no question whatsoever in your mind as to whether or not to react in a situation such as this. Making no effort to pull over the driver of a vehicle after witnessing such an incident would not be an appropriate use of discretion. In fact, not taking enforcement action would be interpreted as neglect of duty. Public confidence requires every police officer to react if they witness a near tragedy involving a child.

---

[6]From personal conversation with Professor Tony Turner, Justice and Public Safety Institute, Georgian College of Applied Arts and Technology, Orillia Campus, Fall 2006.

You turn and pursue the vehicle at the posted speed limit, activating the overhead emergency lights on your police cruiser. You follow the vehicle for two kilometres while the driver appears to continue his cell phone conversation. Finally to attract his attention, you activate your siren. The driver sticks an arm out the window and tries to wave you past. After following for a short distance, with the continued use of your emergency lights and siren, the vehicle pulls to the right shoulder of the road.

Before you even speak with the offending driver, I suggest that you should already have some idea as to what your intention regarding taking further enforcement action will be. If the incident is serious enough for you to have pursued the offender and pulled them over, you might already be leaning strongly toward issuing the driver with a ticket, unless there is some compelling reason not to. If you have made a decision about what will happen next, what is it that you have decided? Will you charge the driver or not charge the driver?

Situation # 1:

The driver is a top executive for a manufacturing plant in your town. When you advise him that he passed a stopped school bus, narrowly missing striking a child, the driver becomes very emotional, admits to having been distracted, claims to have grandchildren the same age as the passengers on the bus and is very remorseful. Upon checking his driver's licence history, you learn that he has one previous conviction for speeding from three years prior. The driver is very polite and apologetic. While you are speaking to the driver, the school bus driver pulls up and asks whether or not you need to speak to him as a witness. He indicates that he is willing to testify in court, if required.

Do you think that in this situation you would issue the driver with a traffic citation? State your reasoning for doing so whether your answer is yes or no.

Situation # 2:

The driver is the same person as in situation # 1. When you advise him of the reason for stopping him, he claims to be in a hurry to get to an important meeting. He is gruff and impatient with you. He expresses his opinion that you are over-reacting to the situation and could be putting your time to far better use. When you ask him to produce his driver's licence, vehicle registration and insurance certificate, he inquires, "Don't you know who I am?" He makes further comments regarding being harassed and about this being a waste of tax-payers' money.

Based on your response to situation # 1, do you think that you would be inclined to treat the driver any differently based on this change of demeanour that is no longer polite and apologetic? State your reasoning whether your answer has changed from the first situation or not.

Situation # 3:

The driver of the vehicle is a member of a visible minority. He politely suggests that you are incorrect in your story about the school bus incident as he has no recollection of having observed one and he certainly would have stopped, as required by the law, had there been a bus there. The driver is polite but adamant that he did nothing wrong. He implies that you have singled him out to be stopped because he is not Caucasian, stating that police officers are always picking on him for fictitious infractions.

Do you think that you would issue this driver with a traffic citation? State your reasoning for doing so whether your answer is yes or no.

Situation # 4:

The driver of the vehicle is a plain-clothes police officer driving an unmarked police cruiser from a neighbouring city. When you ask him to produce his driver's licence and vehicle documents, he presents his police badge and warrant card to you instead. The driver implies that police officers "take care" of their brother and sister officers and that he would do the same for you if the situation were reversed.

Do you think that you would issue this driver, a fellow police officer, with a traffic citation? State your reasoning for doing so whether your answer is yes or no.

Follow up:

After clearing this occurrence, you receive a radio transmission to return to your police station and you find your supervisor meeting with the school bus driver and the school bus company owner. They compliment you for your response in pulling over the offending driver and inquire if charges were laid. What will you tell the bus company owner, the driver and your supervisor regarding your handling of the case?

Summary:

There should be absolutely no confusion as to the appropriateness of charging any driver in such a situation. I suggest that any experienced officer should have a clear intention, on a balance of probabilities, to would issue a ticket before they even begin speaking to the offending driver.

If you had decided, based on your best judgment, to warn Driver # 1 rather than issue a ticket, I trust that you at least arrived at that decision responsibly, consistently and ethically, giving the same consideration to the rude Driver # 2, Driver # 3, the member of a visible minority, and Driver # 4, the plain-clothes police officer.

If you came to a decision, prior to exiting your patrol vehicle, about what action you intended to take regarding charging the driver, did you follow through with your decision? Did your decision change, based on any change in the driver's demeanour between situation # 1 and # 2? If so, what was the change in your decision regarding whether or not to charge the driver and, if there was a change in the action you proposed, do you consider such a change to be justifiable? Why?

Was there any difference between your actions as to whether or not to lay a charge between Driver #1 and 2, and Driver #3 or Driver # 4? If so, what was that change and is it morally justifiable? If you did decide to treat any of the drivers differently, was the change in the manner in which you treated the drivers based on any difference in circumstances of the offence, or was the change, if any, based upon the circumstances of the offender?

Analysis – Driver # 1 and Driver # 2 (White male in business suit – polite/rude)

If you decided not to charge the polite and apologetic Driver # 1 because no "actual harm" was done, but decided to lay a charge against the same driver if they reacted rudely toward you, is their rudeness a justifiable basis upon which to change your decision? Is it the responsibility of police officers to enforce the law against people who commit infractions or is it only to charge those people who are rude to the officer? Should rudeness toward the police increase the probability that a person will be charged?

Any difference in the laying of charges between Driver # 1 and Driver # 2 would have to be on the basis of rudeness toward the officer as opposed to the identical infraction that was committed in both instances. I suggest that Driver # 2 initially did nothing differently than Driver # 1 and to charge Driver # 2 on the basis of his attitude toward the officer would be unfair – legal – but unfair. Drivers are required to stop for stopped school buses – but they are not legally required to be polite, apologetic or subservient.

The law should never to be used as a tool to punish offenders who are not as "nice" to us as we might want them to be. The existence of the offence of "Contempt of Cop" is a myth perpetuated by movie stereotypes and cynical street cops. Professional police officers do not subscribe to such a belief nor would they ever consider engaging in such behaviour.

Analysis – Driver # 3 (Member of visible minority)

The same holds for the treatment of Driver # 3, the member of a visible minority. If Driver # 3 was charged on the basis that Drivers # 1, # 2 and # 4 were also charged, no further analysis needs to be done. If, however, Driver # 3 was charged when the other drivers received warnings, the difference in the treatment between the drivers needs to be examined further. Was Driver # 3 was charged because he disagreed with the officer or because he is a member of a visible minority?

Disagreeing with a police officer about the circumstances of any infraction, or any other matter, is not an offence at law. Therefore, as with the case of Driver # 2, to punish Driver # 3 for arguing with the officer would also be unfair. The offence that prompted your original enforcement action was failure to stop for a school bus – not debating with you the merits of the case, or your perception of its merits.

The idea that any driver deserves to be charged merely for arguing with you suggests that a decision to charge is ego-driven rather than based on any underlying legal merit. An officer who explains that the driver "talked themselves into the ticket" has a flawed perspective of the role of the police in modern society. Law enforcement officers don't dispense justice and they don't decide who needs to be punished on the basis of their own insecurities or some need they may have to exert power over members of the public.

It is the role of the criminal justice system to adjudicate guilt and to dispense justice – that is not the role of the police officer. The requisite grounds to lay charges must be based solely on an accused's behaviour that resulted in a breach of statute law, but not on any suspect's post-offence behaviour toward the police officer – unless such behaviour also constitutes an actual breach of the law.

If the decision to lay a charge against Driver # 3 was made only because he was a member of a visible minority, such a decision would be indefensible on the basis of racial discrimination. Racial discrimination is the unequal treatment of someone purely on the basis of superficial qualities, such as gender, race, age or sexual orientation.

The *PSA* of Ontario's Code of Conduct defines discrimination as a serious misconduct and states:

2. (1) "Any chief of police or other police officer commits misconduct if he or she engages in,

    (a) Discreditable Conduct, in that he or she,

        (i) fails to treat or protect a person equally without discrimination with respect to police services because of that person's race, ancestry, place of origin, colour, ethnic origin, citizenship, creed, sex, sexual orientation, age, marital status, family status or handicap, . . . "[7]

---

[7] O. Reg. 123/98, Part V, Schedule, s. 2(1)(a)(i).

The province of Ontario is a pluralistic and diverse society comprised of a wide variety of social groups that are distinguished by numerous characteristics including, but not limited to race, creed, religion, age, gender and sexual orientation. Deciding to charge or not to charge someone as the result of discrimination on the basis any of the superficial characteristics mentioned in subparagraph 2(1)(a)(i) of the Code of Conduct simply cannot be tolerated in a society such as ours that places such high value on equal rights.

Analysis – Driver # 4 (Plain-clothes police officer)

There is an unwritten code which is supported by a certain segment of policing that considers it improper for one police officer to charge another. There is another segment of the policing profession which believes that it is improper to exercise favouritism – also a form of discrimination – when executing one's duties. It simply isn't possible to reconcile these two beliefs to the mutual satisfaction of all parties.

If you believe it is wrong to discriminate against persons on the basis of fairness, is it not equally wrong to discriminate on the basis of favouritism? In this scenario, if you charged Drivers # 1, # 2 and # 3, but let Driver # 4 off with a warning based on some skewed idea of loyalty, you would not have properly exercised your power of discretion.

While it is true that professional courtesies are granted and favours are repaid in the policing profession, is it not just plain wrong to treat people differently? Is there some justifiable basis for treating people differently other than for the offence that they committed? It would be difficult to explain to a victim or their surviving family that you elected not to charge an offender on account of their being a fellow police officer, especially when police officers are deemed to know the law and, because of their profession, are held to a higher standard of conduct than are ordinary citizens.

In closing, I can think of no good reason for treating any of these drivers differently.

6.4   INTEGRITY AND ETHICS

As we have seen in the previous scenarios regarding a relatively simple traffic violation, the use of integrity and ethics plays a central role in an officer's decision-making when exercising discretion. Integrity is all about honesty and involves the continuous practice of honesty in everything that a person says and in everything that they do to a high moral standard of behaviour. Being ethical involves the knowledge of what is right and wrong behaviour in any situation and choosing to do what is the right thing – for the right reason. (Bjorkquist 2002)

Every new recruit must swear an oath of office upon being appointed as a police officer. Ontario Regulation 144/91 made pursuant to the *PSA* sets out the wording for such an oath as follows:

> "I solemnly swear (affirm) that I will be loyal to Her Majesty the Queen and to Canada, and that I will uphold the Constitution of Canada and that I will, to the best of my ability, preserve the peace, prevent offences and discharge my other duties as (insert name of office) faithfully, impartially and according to law." [8]

To have integrity means to follow through on past promises to do what you said you would do. Integrity means everything to a police officer – without it, you will lose the

---
[8] O. Reg. 144/91, s. 2.

trust of your peers, family, superiors, the public and the judiciary and be left with nothing. A police officer cannot on one hand swear or affirm to discharge their duties "faithfully, impartially and according to law" and then create exceptions for visible minorities, or for people different than themselves or their friends, or for other police officers.

To treat people impartially means to treat everyone equally – without bias due to discrimination. Discrimination involves not only targeting someone for prosecution on the basis of race, creed, religion, gender or sexual orientation, it also involves not taking enforcement action on the basis of favouritism. A police officer who doesn't charge his or her friends, acquaintances, co-workers or relatives and treats them differently than strangers is guilty of discrimination as a result of favouritism.

Acting ethically does not require that you charge every person every time an offence is committed. When I was a serving police officer, there were numerous occasions when I did not lay a charge against a person with whom I was acquainted. Nor did I charge every stranger with every offence I had reason to believe they committed. What I attempted to do was to always treat persons equally, fairly and consistently. Later in this chapter we'll examine some of the considerations that an officer might use in deciding whether or not to charge or warn specific individuals.

6.5   EXAMPLES OF POLICE DISCRETION

Many of the previous examples of discretion have been limited to situations involving individual officers making decisions regarding charging single offenders. The use of discretion within policing is far more widespread than these few examples might suggest. Let's analyze a series of situations in which police services can and do exercise the power of discretion.

Like any other business or organization, police services are expected to function within the constraints of an annual budget allocated to them by their funding authority. The executive officers of a police service must therefore prioritize their activities for each fiscal period to ensure the financial means to cover incurred costs meet their operational needs. Achievable priorities are set while certain areas must be deferred to remain within those financial constraints.

In a world of competing demands, the provision of policing services is determined on a priority analysis of the needs of the community. There is always a potential for dissatisfaction when a particular group or neighbourhood believes they don't receive the policing services that they feel they should be entitled to.

Downtown merchants might want to see a more visible uniformed police presence in the form of foot patrols in the business core, while residents of a neighbourhood might expect more traffic patrols to curb speeding on residential streets. Many people want more investigative effort devoted to clearing up unsolved crime, while technological advances have resulted in new types of crime, such as internet crime, identify theft, and a proliferation of child pornography, that also demand the assignment of expert resources.

Police executives have the difficult job of determining which of these competing yet worthy demands they will dedicate finite police resources to. Discretion must be exercised in determining which deserving issue should potentially be overlooked in favour of another – not always as the result of choice, but of necessity.

Police services are sometimes forced to determine patrol priorities based on an assessment of risk of potential danger to the public. Selective initial response policies are drafted and implemented to determine the level of police response in certain situations such as minor thefts, property damage and vehicle thefts and incidents not involving a breach of the law.

In some jurisdictions, unless there is a high probability of solving minor property crimes, police services take information from complainants by telephone and report on the occurrence without conducting an actual investigation. Expensive and time-consuming investigative techniques are better spent on major crimes or at least those crimes with a higher probability of being solved. While this type of response would have been judged as less than adequate in earlier times, the sheer volume of cases and scarcity of resources today may require such a response to ensure that valuable resources are assigned to instances involving a higher risk to public safety.

Discretion in determining departmental patrol and investigative response priorities must also be based on the principles of fairness, equality and consistency as well as community interest. It would be discriminatory to dedicate more police patrols to wealthy upper-middle class neighbourhoods that experience a low crime rate at the expense of patrolling under-privileged "working-class" neighbourhoods.

It would be equally discriminatory to devote a higher level of investigative resources to the murder of a wealthy female business executive than a murder involving a sex trade worker with a history of substance abuse. If both victims are equally worthy – and unquestionably they are – how could any difference in the level of police response to these two crimes possibly be justified?

Individual police officers utilize discretion when determining items of evidence to be seized during an investigation, when to arrest an individual, when to charge suspects and in determining which charge is to be laid against them. Although our laws provide guidelines, individual officers also exercise discretion in matters of judicial interim release by making recommendations on whether to oppose release, or on the granting of bail conditions, in relation to arrested and charged individuals.

The use of discretion is also common when dealing with offenders who are mentally ill. Individuals who are known to be suffering from mental disorders at the time they commit offences cannot be held accountable for their actions if, at the time of the offence, they were "suffering from a mental disorder that rendered the person incapable of appreciating the nature and quality of the act . . . or of knowing that it was wrong."[9]

Although a person was suffering from a mental disorder at the time they committed an offence, if they understood the nature and quality of the act they committed and knew that it was wrong to do so, they may still be convicted in court. Often, however, an offender who is suffering from a mental disorder is treated as someone who is ill and in need of medical treatment, rather than as a law-breaker who deserves to be punished for a relatively minor offence.

Police officers might also use discretion in determining the appropriate level of use of force response during a confrontation. Because of differing physical characteristics, a physically strong officer may resort to soft physical control methods while a smaller or less physically capable officer may have to resort to intermediate weapons, such as O.C. spray.

---

[9]*Criminal Code*, R.S. 1985, c. C-46, s. 16(1).

What may cause one officer to subjectively fear for their life or the life of another and resort to lethal force may evoke a slightly lower response from a more physically able officer.

When dealing with youthful offenders, the police also have discretion to decide when to warn or attempt to employ alternative diversion programs to keep offenders out of the traditional justice system.

6.6 CONSIDERATIONS IN THE USE OF DISCRETION

Police officers may have prior knowledge of individuals whom they encounter during the course of their duties either as social acquaintances, business relations, neighbours, relatives or from previous professional dealings. Whether or not a particular offender is previously known to a police officer should be of little importance in determining whether to take enforcement action. What should drive the officer's decision are considerations such as departmental policy and the severity and nature of the incident under investigation.

If an incident does not involve a clear violation or a duty imposed by statute law, the officer is not legally required to take enforcement action beyond an initial response that is required by departmental policy. If an incident involves a breach of statute law, the officer must use discretion in deciding whether to take action and, if action is warranted, what level of action should be taken.

The officer may take into consideration any of the following relevant factors in making a decision on whether or not it is in the public interest to take enforcement action and, if any, in deciding the appropriate level of enforcement:

- Is the occurrence reactive in nature (initiated by a call for service from the public) or was it proactively initiated by the police?

- Does the incident involve a confirmed violation of statute law?
  - If an offence is involved is it of a minor or severe nature?

- Is the incident one of "zero tolerance"? (See section 6.8)

- If no offence is involved, is there some other statutory duty to investigate? (such as a sudden death,[10] or a motor vehicle collision involving personal injury or property damage in the amount of $1 000 or more)[11]

- If the situation involves an offence, is the situation still ongoing?

- Is there any possibility of an incident involving an offence recurring or other offences being committed if no enforcement action is taken?

- Was any person victimized during the incident?
  - Is the victim a child?
  - Is the victim another vulnerable member of society?
    - e.g., developmentally challenged, elderly

- Has a member of the public suffered physical harm or is physical harm to any person imminent?

---

[10]*Coroners Act*, R.S.O. 1990, c. C-37, s. 10(1).

[11]*Highway Traffic Act*, R.S.O. 1990, c. H-8, s. 199(1) and R.R.O. 1990, Reg. 596, s. 11.

- Is officer safety being compromised?

- Did the occurrence involve significant loss of property?

- Did the occurrence involve significant property damage?

- Is the offence, if any, one of organizational priority?

- Is the nature of the incident one of high community interest or perception?

- Would a lack of enforcement action bring potential disrepute upon you or your police service?

- Is the identity of the offender known?

  - Is the offender a first-time or a repeat offender?

- Is the offender in a minor case suffering from a mental disorder to such an extent that it could be considered a mitigating factor for their actions?

- Is the offender a young offender?

  - Is the incident one in which a young offender would be eligible for a diversion program?

- If enforcement action is indicated, is an arrest required?

- If an arrest is not required should a charge still be laid?

- If a charge is laid, would there be any probability of conviction?

- Would the laying of a charge impose a potential financial hardship on the offender?

- If a charge is not required, would a warning or caution benefit the offender?

- Could the exercise of discretion in a minor incident result in an opportunity to educate the offender and dissuade them from committing similar future offences?

- Could the use of discretion in a minor incident improve the offender's perception of or relationship with the police?

- If your decision is to exercise discretion, is your decision defensible or was it motivated by discrimination based on either bias or favouritism?

6.7   OFFENCE VS. THE OFFENDER

As a police officer, I exercised discretion on a regular basis in a wide variety of situations throughout my 29 years of experience. During that time, I issued warnings to people whom I knew and also to total strangers. In addition to the warnings I issued, the number of charges I laid was usually above the average for officers in the given location where I was stationed. Some critics of the use of police discretion believe that any decision by a police officer to exercise discretion should be based purely on an assessment of the severity of the offence and not affected by the circumstances of the offender. (Bjorkquist 2002)

Often my decision to use my power of discretion was motivated by the severity of the offence, such as the amount of injury, damage, or loss of property. Some of my decisions were affected, at least to some degree, by my view of the level of intent to commit the offence that was evident – being derived from the words and actions of the offender leading up to, during and following the commission of the incident under investigation.

Often my decision was affected by the circumstances of the offender themselves. A first-time offender for the offence of murder should be treated in the same manner as a repeat offender due to the severity of the offence and the demands of the public interest that precludes the use of discretion in such extreme crimes. I also viewed crimes of violence as deserving of charges where reasonable grounds existed to justify a charge. A sixty-seven year old female driver with no previous convictions for traffic violations who is stopped for speeding, however, does not necessarily warrant the same treatment as a twenty-two year old male with numerous traffic convictions.

If we warn the elderly female first-offender and issue a ticket to the young male repeat offender, is the decision to treat these two drivers differently an abuse of police discretion that is based on discrimination due to age and gender? I respectfully suggest that these two drivers can be treated differently, but still fairly, based on their individual merits, and that any such discrepancy in their treatment is still consistent with the public interest.

A joint study conducted by the University of Waterloo and the Canadian Centre for Justice Statistics compiled and analyzed the criminal activity of a cohort of 59 000 Canadians aged between 12 and 21 years of age between April 1991 and March 2003. The study found that " . . . only a small percentage of repeat offenders were responsible for the majority of court-related activity."

The findings of the study go on to state that " . . . chronic offenders, or those with five or more incidents accounted for only 16% of all offenders. But they were responsible for nearly 60% of all court referrals involving this specific group."[12] Police programs in certain jurisdictions that target certain offenders with a high risk of re-offending have been quite successful in reducing the number of crimes committed by them.

Parolees or prisoners released after having served their entire sentence, who are assessed by correctional services as representing a high risk to re-offend, are proactively targeted. Evidence of criminal activity is gathered under the watchful eyes of police surveillance officers who apprehend and charge targets whenever an offence is witnessed. The objective of such a proactive program is to devote investigative resources where they are likely to do the most good in terms of restricting the opportunity for chronic offenders to re-offend, minimizing the total number of crimes they commit.

Critics of such programs contend that specifically targeting "chronic offenders" for special enforcement attention is not equitable treatment as, because of their circumstances – in this case, their previous criminal history – they are being discriminated against. I'm not suggesting that anyone who commits a single offence is labelled for life as a chronic violator who deserves to be treated with the full force of the law at every encounter with the police.

Offenders most deserving of enforcement action are the chronic offenders – those with a demonstrated history of repeated law-breaking behaviour, indicating an unwillingness to comply with the law or to change their behaviour as the result of less formal dealings with the police. From my own experience, I firmly believe that all human beings are capable of making mistakes and errors in judgement. For some people, however, committing

---

[12]Statistics Canada – *The Daily*, Monday, November 21, 2005, "Study: Referrals and convictions in youth and criminal courts".

breaches of the law is uncharacteristic for them, while the same actions in others demonstrate an established course of conduct. I believe that a distinction between these types of offenders can be justified.

Research-based statistical probability provides a sound, logical, scientific justification for such enforcement action. Does the person who commits an uncharacteristic minor infraction of the law not deserve a warning in lieu of punishment, more so than a chronic offender for the same offence? If I encountered a neighbour or close friend committing a minor infraction, I would extend to them the same professional discretion I would give to a stranger in a similar situation. Alternatively, if one deserves to be charged – so does the other.

Consistency is the key to such a discretionary approach, providing that all chronic offenders matching pre-determined criteria are not discriminated against on the basis of any superficial characteristics such as age, religion, race, gender, colour or sexual orientation.

6.8   ZERO TOLERANCE

Zero tolerance – the opposite of discretion – involves incidents that require police officers to follow the "letter of the law" and take strict enforcement action. Such occurrences may be mandated either by legislation, by policing standards, by departmental policy or by community priority. Examples of incidents where zero tolerance has been implemented include domestic abuse, spousal assault, workplace sexual harassment, hate or bias motivated crime, child abuse in all of its forms, elder and vulnerable adult abuse, and impaired driving offences.

Not surprisingly, while public opinion is split on the issue of police discretion, the same is also true when the police have adopted a policy of zero tolerance to deal with various social issues. Some, for example, believe that families who break up as the result of zero tolerance enforcement in domestic abuse situations do not benefit when discretion for laying charges is taken away from the police.

Many others believe, however, that zero tolerance is necessary to curb the cycle of domestic violence by taking away the decision to lay charges from the victim, who might be reluctant to proceed with criminal charges out of fear of reprisal or economic hardship. In practice, a police officer should explain to a reluctant victim that they have no choice in laying charges and that only a Crown Attorney can withdraw a charge of domestic assault.[13]

In theory, taking the decision out of the hands of the victim and the police even for first-time offences is more likely to ensure that the situation that resulted in the domestic abuse will be improved. "From 1995 to 2001, the rate of incidents of spousal violence reported by police increased – and did so for both men and women. At the same time, victimization surveys suggest that victims may be more willing to report these experiences to police than they have been in the past."[14]

Changing social beliefs regarding drinking and driving offences has also led to stricter enforcement and established minimum legal sanctions for those convicted of first-time and subsequent offences for impaired driving and care or control of motor

---

[13]*Ontario Ministry of the Solicitor General Policing Standards Manual* (Feb 2000) LE-024 Domestic Violence Occurrences at p.7.

[14]Statistics Canada – *The Daily*, Monday, June 23, 2003, "Family Violence".

vehicles and vessels. According to Statistics Canada, Canadian police services reported a total of 75 613 incidents of impaired driving in 2005. This number reflected a decline of –7 percent from the previous year, 2004, and an overall decline of –33 percent for the period between 1995 and 2005.[15]

In Ontario, the Peterborough-Lakefield Community Police Service adopted a zero-tolerance policy in relation to public order crimes, including disturbances, public intoxication and vandalism committed in the downtown core of Peterborough and the nearby village of Lakefield. Crime rate statistics for the year 2002 dropped by 2.5 percent when compared with the previous year.[16]

Another zero tolerance situation deals with police pursuits. Guidelines have been established in most jurisdictions that take away discretion from police officers to choose to pursue unknown offenders for minor offences under dangerous conditions, such as bad weather, high speed or traffic volume in the area that would create a disproportionate risk to members of the public, the offender or the officer.[17]

Zero tolerance philosophy is also a fundamental principle of the "Broken Windows" theory of crime control that was developed in 1982 by James Wilson and George Kelling. The Broken Windows theory assumes that if a broken window in a building is left unattended, the person responsible for the unrepaired damage will conclude that nobody cares about the damage and will return and cause more damage. (Schmalleger & Volk 2005)

New York City implemented a zero tolerance policy on even minor offences such as jay-walking during the mid-1990s and reported an unprecedented decline of 65 percent in the overall crime rate and a 70 percent reduction in the rate of murders. (Giuliani 2002) A contradictory report published by The Center on Juvenile and Criminal Justice in San Francisco indicates that the decline in crime enjoyed by New York was surpassed by that in several urban centres in California. In fact, San Francisco's decrease in violent crime exceeded that of most major cities in America during similar periods.

What is significant in the findings of this report is that the California cities studied did not implement a Broken Windows style of enforcement in reaching their remarkable decline in crime rates. The California model opted for a so-called "soft on crime" approach involving selective incapacitation of felony offenders and alternative sentences and community involvement for convicted offenders. What can be concluded from the San Francisco experience is that different approaches to dealing with different classes of offenders is sometimes more effective than a "hard on crime" letter of the law approach for all offenders.[18]

6.9 ELIMINATING INVESTIGATOR BIAS

"[W]rongful conviction[s] have resulted from, . . . pressure on law enforcement officials to resolve the case either because it is high profile or because of resource or other institutional factors. That pressure in turn triggers and

---

[15]Statistics Canada – *The Daily*, Thursday, July 20, 2006 Impaired Driving.

[16]www.peacefulcommunities.ca/2003/February/feb10.htm Retrieved: March 19, 2007.

[17]O. Reg. 546/99 pursuant to the *Police Services Act*, R.S.O. 1990 c. P-15.

[18]Shattering "Broken Windows": An Analysis of San Francisco's Alternative Crime Policies.

justifies a bias known,... as 'tunnel vision',... that causes police investigators to select evidence to build a case for the conviction of their chosen suspect while suppressing or ignoring information and interpretations that point away from guilt."[19]

Dianne Lee Martin (1945–2004),
Professor of Criminal Law,
Osgoode Hall Law School, York University, Toronto, ON.

When the abuse of discretion involves the improper selection, suppression or ignoring of evidence during the course of a police investigation for any reason, it is also referred to as "investigator bias". In the preceding quotation, the late Professor Dianne Martin offered a plausible explanation for some unintentional causes of systemic (institutional) tunnel vision.

Undue public, media or internal pressure to solve a case can lead officers, consciously or unconsciously, to hastily develop theories regarding crimes for which no sound basis exists. This can lead investigators to ignore certain information, choosing not to follow up on certain leads and in worst cases, even to ignore evidence that tends to demonstrate a suspect's innocence.

During the investigation into the Scarborough rapes (1987–93) and the abduction, rape and murder of Leslie Erin Mahaffy, Paul Bernardo was simultaneously stalking young females in the City of St. Catharines. On the second of such incident involving the same woman, she was able to observe and write down the licence number of the car that had followed her on the two occasions. She reported the incident to a uniformed officer in St. Catharines at 3 a.m. August 9, 1991 and provided him the licence number of the car.

> "The officer recorded the licence number in his notebook, ran a C.P.I.C. vehicle check, and found that the car was registered to Paul Bernardo, 57 Bayview Drive, St. Catharines. The officer immediately drove to 57 Bayview Drive where he found the car, Gold Nissan 240 SX, licence number 660 HFH, parked in the driveway, with no one in or near it, and the house in darkness. The officer took no further action by way of follow up or inquiry or investigation or reporting. Although he indicated that he would normally file a general occurrence report for this kind of complaint, no report can be found on the Niagara Regional Police Service computerized ORACLE system. It is clear that he did not file a report." [20]

This is a clear example of a police officer making a conscious decision not to devote any further investigative efforts to what he presumably believed was a minor incident involving no clear breach – as the law existed at the time before the creation of the offence of criminal harassment which now exists.[21] We know now that Bernardo raped 18 women and killed three women between May 1987 and December 1992. Had the officer questioned Bernardo, or at least reported the incident, information concerning Bernardo's alleged stalking activities could have brought him to the attention of the Green Ribbon Task Force investigation at a far earlier stage in the investigation.

---

[19]The Canadian Review of Policing Research - Lessons About Justice from the "Laboratory" of Wrongful Convictions: Tunnel Vision, the Construction of Guilt and Informer Evidence.

[20]Bernardo Investigation Review – Report of Mr. Justice Archie Campbell, June 1996 at p. 114.

[21]*Criminal Code*, R.S. 1985, c. C-46, s. 264(1).

Tunnel vision also figured prominently during the judicial review into the wrongful conviction of Guy Paul Morin for the still-unsolved murder of Christine Jessop. Mr. Justice Fred Kaufman, in describing questionable practices of police, prosecutors and forensic scientists on the case defined tunnel vision as:

> "[A] single- minded and overly narrow focus on a particular investigative or prosecutorial theory, so as to unreasonably colour the evaluation of information received and one's conduct in response to that information."[22]

Mr. Justice Kaufman's succinct definition of tunnel vision, simply stated, warns investigators of the danger of making up one's mind before all of the facts of a case are known. Improper or inaccurate interpretation of evidence can result in investigators focusing on conclusions that are not supported by the evidence in a case. To form a "theory" that is not substantiated by the known facts of a case can often cause investigators to distort or misrepresent the facts and take inappropriate action due to their distortion of the facts.

These three quotes warn us of the improper use of discretion during an occurrence that could result in the development of tunnel vision. An investigation may fall victim to tunnel vision at any stage; during the initial response, while investigating a crime scene, during any lengthy investigation or even the prosecutorial phase. Awareness of the potential danger of falling victim to tunnel vision is crucial for police officers, as it invariably involves the improper use of discretion in conjunction with unhealthy doses of either faulty reasoning or investigator bias.

6.10 DISCLOSURE

"... Crown counsel is under a duty to disclose [to the defence] all information in his or her possession relevant to the guilt or innocence of the accused,... whether favourable or unfavourable to the accused... which is not clearly irrelevant."[23]

The Honourable G. Arthur Martin, O.C., O. Ont., Q.C., LL.D.,
The Martin Report (1993).

Once a criminal charge has been laid, evidence gathered during the course of an investigation doesn't belong exclusively to the police or to the Crown. If evidence can be said to be owned at all, it is the property of the effective administration of justice in a free and democratic society. Disclosure is an area of law where the police officer has no power of discretion to withhold evidence or information gathered during an investigation. The modern investigator must realize that while there may or may not be privilege in some of the findings of a criminal investigation, there is never any ownership in it.

Disclosure of evidence allows accused persons to make full answer and defence to charges against them by making all relevant evidence – inculpatory as well as exculpatory evidence – available to the defence prior to the commencement of trial. Benefits in disclosing evidence include:

---

[22]The Commission on Proceedings Involving Guy Paul Morin (Kaufman Report 1998) at p. 479.

[23]The Attorney General's Advisory Committee on Charge Screening, Disclosure and Resolution Discussions (The Martin Report) Recommendations and Opinions. Recommendation 41, at p. 7.

1. Helps to ensure against the possibility of wrongfully convicting persons by allowing accused persons the opportunity to investigate and rebut false or erroneous evidence.

2. Allows for the resolution of non-contentious issues of evidence that a well informed defence may stipulate (agree to).

3. Accused persons may elect to waive preliminary hearings or shorten the duration of their trial.

4. Accused persons may plead guilty to offence(s) when they are made aware of the strength of the evidence against them. (Martin Report 1993)

The 1993 Report of the Attorney General's Advisory Committee on Charge Screening, Disclosure and Resolution Discussions recommended that the responsibility of the Crown to disclose evidence to the accused extends even beyond the original police investigation. After initial disclosure of a case is made to the defence, the Crown is still required to disclose any evidence during or after a trial or appeal that would tend to demonstrate the innocence of the accused or reasonable doubt of their guilt. (Martin Report 1993)

An accused person who is unrepresented is entitled to disclosure in the same way as if they were represented by legal counsel but should be informed of their right to obtain disclosure by either the Crown or the court. Most, if not all, disclosure requests to the Crown are made in writing by counsel for the defence. Requests for disclosure must be made and responded to in a timely manner. (Martin Report 1993)

The 1993 Martin Report recommended that the defence is entitled to disclosure of the following types of evidence, including:

1. A copy of the charges contained in the information or indictment

2. A complete synopsis prepared by the investigating police agency setting out the circumstances of the alleged offences committed by the accused

3. Written statements or 'Will Say' statements of all persons, including statements of co-accused persons, interviewed during the police investigation, whether or not the Crown intends to call them as witnesses, and any police notes or reports from which they were prepared or in relation to interviews where no statements were taken

4. The defence shall be given an opportunity to view or listen to the original copy of electronically recorded statements in private. Copies or transcripts of such electronically recorded statements may be disclosed at the discretion of the Crown

5. The criminal record of the accused

6. A copy of any written statement of the accused, including transcripts, corresponding police reports or notes or the opportunity to view or listen to the original copy of an electronically recorded statement in private

7. Copies of any police occurrence report and supplementary report

8. Copies of forensic, medical or laboratory reports relating to the offence

9. Copies of documents, photographs, audio or video recordings of anything other than a statement of a person

10. Copies of search warrants and lists of seized items

11. Copies of judicial authorizations to intercept private communications

12. Upon request, copies of criminal records relating to proposed Crown or defence witnesses

13. All information relating to the visual identification of the accused where identity is an issue

14. Any material relevant to the credibility of any proposed Crown witness

The 1991 Supreme Court of Canada landmark ruling in the *Stinchcombe* decision set out similar guidelines for disclosure of relevant inculpatory or exculpatory evidence in the possession of the Crown.[24] The *Stinchcombe* decision and the recommendations of the Martin Report have since been entrenched in s. 603 *Criminal Code*.[25] As yet there is no statutory authority for the defence to disclose relevant defence evidence to the Crown.

As the investigating police agency is the source of the disclosable evidence, the obligation of the Crown to evaluate and disclose relevant evidence to the defence can only be met if the police fully disclose the findings of the case to the Crown in a timely fashion. Investigators must make full and timely disclosure of their case to the Crown Attorney and for greater certainty, should maintain detailed records of what evidence was disclosed to the Crown and when it was disclosed. (Van Allen 2007)

A police officer has no discretion to withhold information when the right of the accused to make full answer and defence to charges against them hangs in the balance.

SUMMARY

- Discretion involves individuals exercising their own judgment and using free will, uninfluenced by external factors, to make responsible choices or to act within appropriate limits.

- Police officers are granted considerable freedom to use discretion in deciding when to invoke legal sanctions or when not to invoke legal sanctions, even when an offence has obviously been committed and the relevant law is clearly applicable.

- The inappropriate use of professional discretion can result in the abuse of power, violation of individual rights of others and a high potential for loss of public confidence.

- The strict "letter of the law", an approach to law enforcement that is firm and inflexible, is a form of "cookie-cutter" justice that treats all incidents and all participants of the event in the same way regardless of individual circumstances.

- Police officers must decide if laying a specific charge (and determining the severity of the charge to be laid) or making an arrest is the most appropriate course of action to take in a particular situation.

- Critics of the use of unfettered police discretion sometimes favour a more-or-less cookie-cutter approach to restrict the use of choice by a police officer as a way of preventing possible abuses of discretion.

---

[24]*R. v. Stinchcombe*, [1991] 3 S.C.R. 326, 68 C.C.C. (3d) 1, 9 C.R. (4th) 277 (7 :0).

[25]*Criminal Code*, R.S. 1985 c. C-46, s. 603.

- Lack of direction and of limitations on the use of discretion can contribute to ambiguity and misunderstanding on the part of police officers as to whether or not the use of discretion is appropriate in a given situation.

- Freedom to exercise discretion does not translate into a licence to "turn a blind eye" to a certain offender or to a certain class of offender while targeting other offenders for unfair treatment.

- Zero tolerance – the opposite of discretion – involves incidents that require police officers to follow the "letter of the law" and take strict enforcement action.

- When the abuse of discretion involves the improper selection, suppression or ignoring of evidence during the course of a police investigation for any reason, it is also referred to as "investigator bias".

- Police discretion must be exercised lawfully and in accordance with the principles of responsibility, fairness, equality and accountability.

DISCUSSION QUESTIONS

1. Police in Canada have vast powers to exercise discretion during the course of their duties to decide whether or not to act in a given incident. Certain situations, such as domestic abuse complaints, have been designated as zero tolerance. Guidelines in such cases clearly set out what actions the officer is expected to take and any discretion to act or not to act are effectively removed. What are the considerations for having declared domestic abuse as a zero tolerance response? Given the wide powers of discretion police officers have in other situations, is the rationale for removing discretion in limited cases such as this proper? Whether your answer is yes or no, what are your reasons?

2. Do you feel that it is proper for a police officer to treat a member of the public in one way and to treat another member of the public differently? What considerations, if any, might justify them being treated differently? What considerations, if any, require members of the public to be treated the same?

3. You are on patrol late one evening and check out an automobile you find parked in a remote area that is commonly known as the local "lovers' lane". You observe two people inside the vehicle and approach it to investigate the possibility of underage drinking. You realize that the male in the vehicle is a married fellow police officer. You then become aware that the adult female in the vehicle is the wife of your best friend, another police officer. From the state of their attire, you have obviously found the man and woman in a compromising sexual liaison. There is no violation of the law and both parties plead with you not to reveal their affair. What will you do? Will you record the incident in your notebook? Will you inform your supervisor of your observations? Will you exercise discretion or will you inform your best friend of the actions of his wife?

 WEBLINKS

www.rcmp-learning.org/docs/ecdd1222.htm

Kevin M. Gilmartin, Ph.D.; John (Jack) J. Harris, M.Ed. Law Enforcement Ethics . . . The Continuum of Compromise Published in: *Police Chief* magazine January, 1998 Describes how the psychological effects of police work can lead some officers to compromise their personal ethics and rationalize acts of omission and acts of commission while carrying out their duties.

www.lfcc.on.ca/Handbook_for_Police.pdf

A Handbook for Police Responding to Domestic Violence: Promoting Safer Communities by Integrating Research and Practice (35 pages). Centre for Children and Families in the Justice System of the London Family Court Clinic, Inc., London, ON.

http://scholar.google.com/scholar%3Fq%3DUse+of+police+discretion%26hl%3Den%26cr%3DcountryCA%26oi%3Dscholart

Compilation of articles by a variety of authors dealing with the subject of the use of police discretion in a wide range of situations.

Chapter 7

Warrantless Search and Seizure

"The poorest man may in his cottage bid defiance to all the forces of the crown. It may be frail, its roof may shake, the wind may blow through it, the storm may enter, the rain may enter, but the King of England cannot enter; all his force dares not cross the threshold of the ruined tenement."

William Pitt, the elder (1708-1778),
British politician, during a speech to the House of Lords in 1763.[1]

Learning Outcomes

After reading this chapter, students should be able to:

- Distinguish between the terms "search" and "seizure."
- Explain the criteria for any search to be considered "reasonable."
- Describe the powers of a peace officer "incident to arrest."
- Explain the concept of warrantless search authorized by "exigent circumstances."
- Describe the six criteria of a legal "consent search."

7.1 WHAT IS A SEARCH?

The very mention of a police **search** conjures up images of one or more investigators in a house or some other building looking room-by-room for items of evidence. You might even imagine a uniformed police officer "frisking" a detained suspect for evidence or weapons. While both examples accurately describe types of searches that are routinely conducted by police officers, the term "search" has a far broader definition in law.

According to Canadian law, a search includes any type of official examination or carrying out of an investigative technique by agents of law enforcement for the purposes of:

1. gathering evidence of illegal activity, or

2. preventing the commission of an offence, or

3. for the purposes of ensuring public safety or officer safety under certain circumstances.

---

[1] William Pitt quotation from http://quotes.liberty-tree.ca/quote/william_pitt_quote_a246 Retrieved: February 25, 2007.

Searches are not restricted to visual searches and might include smelling for evidence.[2] For the purposes of this textbook on the subject of police powers, I have excluded other types of operational police searches, such as ground and building searches for missing persons or tactical purposes from this definition. Instead, I intend to focus only on search situations dealing with the legal issues of search and seizure as they relate to evidence gathering.

The terms search and seizure are commonly used together, but not all searches involve a **seizure**. (See section 7.2 What is a Seizure?) For example, the search of a prisoner following their arrest that does not result in the removal of anything from the prisoner's person would be an example of a search not involving a seizure. Trespassing upon a suspect's property, or looking over a fence into the property from an adjacent property to look for evidence of wrongdoing, without a search warrant, has also been held to constitute a search.[3] Electronic interception of private communications, video surveillance, and the use of tracking devices to secretly monitor peoples' movements are yet other forms of searches.[4]

To be considered a search, there must be some intrusion upon a person's **reasonable expectation of privacy** (see section 7.5 Reasonable Expectation of Privacy) that results from evidence gathering or investigative purposes. Some situations require that police officers first obtain a search warrant from a justice prior to commencing a search, while others authorize officers to proceed in the absence of a search warrant. (See section 7.3, Sources of Warrantless Search Authorities)

Specific warrantless search authorities will be covered in more detail throughout subsequent sections, including Search Incident to Arrest (section 7.7), Plain View Seizure Rule (section 7.12), Consent Searches (section 7.9), Abandoned Evidence (section 7.10), and Officer Safety Considerations (section 7.11).

Except for these examples, evidence may be seized without a warrant only where reasonable grounds exist to obtain a search warrant but due to urgent circumstances that require immediate attention, it is impracticable to obtain a warrant.[5] Such circumstances include situations of hot pursuit (see Hot Pursuit, section 7.13) where there is an imminent danger that evidence of an offence will be lost, destroyed or removed or where there is an imminent danger of death or bodily harm to a person.[6] (See Exigent Circumstances, section 7.14)

To be considered legal, every search must be reasonable. A reasonable search is defined as one that is:

1. authorized by statute, or covered by one of the warrantless search exceptions described in the previous paragraph, or

2. judicially pre-authorized by a justice of the peace or judge (search warrant), and

3. reasonable (necessary and appropriate under the circumstances), and carried out in a reasonable manner[7]

---

[2]*R. v. Evans* (1996), 104 C.C.C. (3d) 23 (S.C.C.).

[3]*R. v. Kokesch*, [1990] 3 S.C.R. 3, 61 C.C.C. (3d) 207, 1 C.R. (4th) 62.

[4]*R. v Duarte*, [1990] 1 S.C.R. 30, 53 C.C.C. (3d) 1, 65 D.L.R. (4th) 240, 71 O.D. (2d) 575n, also *R. v. Wong*, [1990] 3S.C.R. 36, 60 C.C.C. (3d) 460, 1 C.R. (4th) 1, also *R. v. Wise*, [1992] 1 S.C.R. 527, 70 C.C.C. (3d) 193, 11 C.R. (4th) 253.

[5]*R. v. Grant* (1993), 84 C.C.C. (3d) 173 (S.C.C).

[6]*Criminal Code*, R.S. 1985, c. C-46, s. 529.3(2)(a)-(b).

[7]*R. v. Collins* (1987), 33 C.C.C. (3d) 1 (S.C.C.).

In simple terms, if the search hasn't been authorized by a search warrant, the warrantless search must be specifically authorized by either statute (legislation) or some other recognized warrantless search authority, such as common law. The reasonableness of every search and seizure will be decided in court on a case-by-case basis, examining the individual circumstances of each case. A search begins the moment a police officer enters the premises to be searched. The entire search and any resulting seizure of evidence may be compromised if the initial entry itself is not conducted in a reasonable manner.

While there are many similarities between warrantless searches and those conducted under the authority of a search warrant, there are sufficient differences between them to justify their being separated into different chapters for discussion. Police officers' statutory and common law powers of search and seizure are undoubtedly the most powerful investigative tools that they have at their disposal. Search and seizure, either with or without warrant, is undoubtedly the most continuously evolving area of law dealing with police powers.

7.2   WHAT IS A SEIZURE?

A seizure involves the non-consensual taking of information or an article of evidence, where a suspect or accused has a reasonable expectation of privacy in that information or thing, for the purpose of proving illegal activity or for the purpose of furthering an investigation.[8] Seizures may involve tangible items such as real (physical) evidence or might involve information such as intercepted private communications, video images or remotely recorded numbers dialed on a suspect's telephone.

On occasion, seizures may be made by police without having conducted a search. The act of a police officer seizing a forged driver's licence from a driver who produces it upon the officer's request, would constitute a seizure that does not involve a search. Drivers are under a legal duty under provincial legislation to surrender their driver's licence for inspection upon demand to a police officer.[9] It has been held that the surrendering of a driver's licence does not constitute a search, as the act of surrendering the licence, in compliance with an existing legal requirement, does not intrude upon the driver's reasonable expectation of privacy.[10]

Difficulties arise when warrantless seizures, made under the authority of search or inspection provisions of provincial (regulatory) legislation, are used as evidence in criminal proceedings against the person from whom the seizure was made. Search or inspection authorities under certain provincial statutes are intended to assist officials in gathering information for purposes other than proving criminal offences. The purpose of such searches and inspections also includes special investigations such as coroner's investigations to determine the circumstances of a person's death, and to ensure compliance with the requirements of various acts of provincial legislation.

When the purpose of the seizing official changes from merely ensuring compliance with legislation to gathering evidence for the purpose of proving the guilt of a person for a serious offence, a search warrant must always be obtained, where practicable. Police

---

[8]*R. v. Dyment* (1988), 45 C.C.C. (3d) 244 (S.C.C.).

[9]*Highway Traffic Act*, R.S.O. 1990, c. H-8, s. 33(2).

[10]*R. v. Hufsky*, [1988] 1 S.C.R. 621, 40 C.C.C. (3d) 398, 63 C.R. (3d) 14.

officers and other investigative officials should not "piggy-back" one investigation on another. Evidence obtained through a warrantless inspection cannot serve to further a criminal investigation if it was obtained for a different purpose than determining a person's penal liability.[11]

Similar restrictions apply where samples of a person's blood are seized for medical purposes at a hospital and the blood or the results of blood alcohol analyses are seized, without a warrant, by the police as evidence for Impaired or Care or Control offences. The warrantless seizure of samples that are collected for medical purposes cannot be used to circumvent the necessity of obtaining a search warrant to collect evidence of criminal acts.[12]

7.3   SOURCES OF WARRANTLESS SEARCH AUTHORITIES

"Even where there is no arrest warrant, there is thus in a case of hot pursuit a right to enter residential premises to make an arrest both for provincial offences and for indictable offences, provided the circumstances justify an arrest without a warrant."

Honourable Mr. Justice Lamer, *C.J. R. v. Macooh*, [1993] 2 S.C.R. 802, 105 D.L.R. (4th) 96,
82 C.C.C. (3d) 481, 16 C.R.R. (2d) 1, 22 C.R. (4th) (7:0).[13]

During this chapter, we will examine a variety of common law search authorities as well as authorities granted to police officers by various federal and provincial statutes that permit searches to be conducted without the necessity of first obtaining a search warrant. Space constraints prevent us from examining every existing search authority, so we will concentrate on those authorities that are most likely to be resorted to by front line police officers during routine patrol duties.

We will examine search authorities such as those contained in the *Criminal Code, Controlled Drugs and Substances Act, Liquor Licence Act, Highway Traffic Act* and the *Fish and Wildlife Protection Act*. However, numerous other statutes such as the *Canada Shipping Act, Migratory Birds Act* and *Fisheries Act* also contain similar search and seizure powers. Where a warrantless search authority is provided by statute, it will be found within the statute itself. It is vital for police officers to be expert in the scope and limitations of their powers of search and seizure, both to effectively collect evidence of offences and to avoid violating the rights of private individuals.

7.4   *CHARTER OF RIGHTS AND FREEDOMS*

Many of the basic rights and freedoms afforded to persons in Canada under the *Charter of Rights and Freedoms* deal specifically with the rights of individuals in relation to fundamental justice and the rules of evidence. As such, police officers need to be familiar

---

[11]*R. v. Jarvis*, [2002] 3 S.C.R. 757, 2002 S.C.C. 73, also *R. v. Ling*, [2002] 3 S.C.R. 814, 2002 S.C.C. 74, also *R. v. Colarusso*, [1994] 1 S.C.R. 20, 87 C.C.C. (3d) 193, 26 C.R. (4th) 289.

[12]*R. v. Dyment*, [1988] 2 S.C.R. 417, 45 C.C.C. (3d) 244, 66 C.R. (3d) 348, also *R. v. Dersch*, [1993] 3 S.C.R. 768, 85 C.C.C. (3d) 1, 25 C.R. (4th) 88 (9:0).

[13]scc.lexum.umontreal.ca/en/1993/1993rcs2-802/1993rcs2-802.html Retrieved: April 6, 2007.

[handwritten margin note: officers need to be mindful of the Charter]

with the rights that are granted to individuals under the *Charter* when considering their conduct in selecting correct methods for gathering evidence during an investigation.

In addition to individual rights, such as the right to be informed of the reason for an arrest, the right to legal counsel, the right to remain silent, and the freedom against self-incrimination, one of the most common *Charter* rights (as guaranteed by section 8) is the "...right to be secure against unreasonable search and seizure."[14]

The 1984 Supreme Court decision of *Hunter v. Southam Inc.*[15] upheld the widespread and long-established common law search requirement of prior judicial authorization, in the form of a valid search warrant, in all cases where it is practicable and feasible. Warrantless searches have generally been held by the Supreme Court of Canada to be *prima facie* unreasonable. *Prima facie* is a term that describes a threshold of proof that once reached, establishes one or more facts – but can still be rebutted by the production of evidence to the contrary.

This means that evidence that is obtained during a warrantless search is initially considered to be inadmissible. The Crown has the opportunity to prove, on a balance of probabilities, that the warrantless search and seizure was either specifically authorized by law (statute law or common law) and was necessary. If no warrantless search authority exists in law, the Crown may also prove in instances where a search warrant would normally have been required that, due to the exigent circumstances (a sense of urgency requiring immediate action) of the case, obtaining a search warrant would have been impracticable. (See section 7.14 Exigent Circumstances)

Police officers should always abide by the following recommendations during the course of their duties:

1. Always utilize the most cautious (most reasonable and least intrusive) investigative strategy possible, under the circumstances.

2. To the extent possible, when engaging in any investigative action not involving prior judicial authorization, always follow the precise intent of any available legal authority for your actions.

3. Always ensure that a search warrant is obtained, if required and practicable.

Section 8 *Charter* violations will not always result in the exclusion of evidence, but they will be held to be *prima facie* unreasonable. If evidence is put before the court resulting from a warrantless search (not otherwise authorized by statute), the court will automatically hold the search to be "unreasonable" unless evidence to the contrary establishes the "reasonableness" of the search. Fortunately, the *prima facie* unreasonableness of warrantless searches does not apply to searches of suspects incident to (resulting from) an arrest.[16] (See section 7.7 Search Incident to Arrest and Chapter 10 Admissibility of Seized Evidence)

The Crown has the opportunity to lead further evidence that the investigator(s) acted in good faith and also to prove the circumstances, on a balance of probabilities, that made the search both necessary and "reasonable". Exigent, (emergency) circumstances may make it impracticable to obtain a search warrant where waiting for a warrant would have resulted in the loss, removal or destruction of evidence. Always thoroughly document all

---

[14]*Canadian Charter of Rights and Freedoms*, Being Part 1 of the *Constitution Act, 1982*, Enacted by the *Canada Act 1982* (U.K.) c. 11, proclaimed in force April 17, 1982, s.8.

[15]*Hunter v. Southam Inc.* (1984), 2 S.C.R. 45, 14 C.C.C. (3d) 97, 11 D.L.R. (4th) 641.

[16]*R. v. Golden* (2001), 3 S.C.R. 629.

circumstances that require the seizure of evidence that are not authorized by a search warrant. (See section 7.14 Exigent Circumstances.)

According to the (1987) Supreme Court decision of *R. v. Collins*, to be considered reasonable, a search must be:

1. Authorized by law (including warrantless search authorities)

2. The law itself must be reasonable, and

3. The manner in which the search was conducted must be reasonable[17]

Search Scenario:

A police officer is assigned to serve a summons at a private residence. As the observant officer knocks on the door of the residence, she smells the odour of marijuana emanating from inside. When the occupant of the residence opens the door, the officer observes a large piece of cannabis resin, weighing approximately one half a kilogram, on the kitchen table approximately three metres away.

Officer:	"What is that on the table?"
Occupant:	"You already know what it is. It's hash."
Officer:	"Who does it belong to?"
Occupant:	"I live here by myself. I guess it's mine."
Officer:	"I'm placing you under arrest for Possession of a Controlled Substance for the Purpose of Trafficking". (Also duly notifying the occupant of his right to remain silent and his rights to counsel under the *Charter of Rights and Freedoms*).

The officer then steps inside the residence, walks to the table and seizes the drugs on the table.

Occupant:	"Wait a minute, man. Don't you need some kind of search warrant or something to come into my house and take my stuff?"

As the search was made without a warrant – remember that warrantless searches are *prima facie* unreasonable – the officer's seizure of the drugs was *prima facie* unreasonable. At trial, the Crown need only prove that the officer had reasonable grounds to believe to believe that an offence was being committed – in this case, Possession of Controlled Drugs for the Purpose of Trafficking.

The officer developed her reasonable grounds through her observation of the illegal drugs on the table, which was corroborated by the admission of the occupant that the substance was, in fact, hashish. The officer was lawfully at the residence, the finding of the drugs was inadvertent, meaning that the officer didn't expect to find them, and the drugs afford evidence of a criminal offence.

The officer's search has now been proven to be one that was authorized by law (the common law doctrine of plain view seizure and statute law, in this case).[18] The authority for the seizure is reasonable under the circumstances and the seizure was carried out in a reasonable manner. The court may now find that the search was reasonable and that the seized evidence is admissible.

---

[17]*R. v. Collins* (1987), 1 S.C.R. 265, 33 C.C.C. (3d) 1, 56 C.R. (3d) 193.

[18]*Criminal Code*, R.S. 1985, c. C-46, s. 489(2).

When the officer observed the drugs, she clearly had reasonable grounds to obtain a search warrant. What would the probability have been of the drugs still being there had the officer left and returned four hours later, armed with a search warrant? I suggest that in the preceding scenario it would be extremely unlikely the evidence would not have been removed or destroyed had the officer attempted to obtain a warrant. The circumstances of this scenario would have rendered it impracticable for the officer to obtain a warrant prior to making the seizure.

Even though the evidence was seized without a warrant, the officer is still required to report the seizure to a Justice in accordance with sections 489.1(1) and 490 *Criminal Code,* as if the seizure had occurred under the authority of a search warrant. (See section 8.22 Report to a Justice.)

Even in situations where a statute does provide an authority to conduct warrantless searches, police officers should only resort "to its availability [in] situations in which exigent circumstances make it impracticable to obtain a warrant."[19] Unless the circumstances of a given situation require immediate action to preserve life or to prevent the imminent loss, removal or destruction of evidence, or where the opportunity exists to obtain a search warrant – always get a warrant!

7.5   REASONABLE EXPECTATION OF PRIVACY

The stakes are high when the success of your case depends on the evidence gathered during a search. We have seen that search is a term that is broadly defined and that is not confined solely to entry and search of a building or premises. A search may involve looking for evidence inside a motor vehicle, or obtaining documentary information regarding a suspect, or employing an investigative technique in any other situation where the suspect has, or could be held to have, a "reasonable expectation of privacy".

Reasonable expectation of privacy doesn't simply mean to be free from eavesdropping neighbours, or your co-workers reading your e-mail. Reasonable expectation of privacy means to be free from intrusion by the law enforcement agencies of the state. Reasonable expectation of privacy is a protective legal concept that is intended to prevent unreasonable intervention by the criminal justice system in the lives of citizens, rather than to merely provide a standard for determining after the fact whether such intrusion was warranted.

An individual may claim a reasonable expectation of privacy relating to any personal, territorial or informational matter affecting their confidentiality, integrity, dignity or autonomy. An individual's expectation of privacy is greatest within their own home and least when openly travelling in public places.

Where an accused alleges that their rights were infringed upon, a court will always apply the standard of "reasonable expectation of privacy" in determining whether or not a search is reasonable. For example, if an individual conceals stolen property in the basement of his house, he would be deemed to have a reasonable expectation of privacy that the evidence would not be discovered and used against him. The sanctity of the home as a person's "castle and fortress" has been entrenched in western law since *Semayne's Case* in 1604, and extends the same protection to individuals carrying on illegal activities within the privacy of their homes as to law-abiding citizens.

---

[19]*R. v. Grant* (1993), 3 S.C.R. 223.

Would an accused person have a reasonable expectation that their financial information would be kept confidential at the bank or financial institution where they conduct business? If you feel you should have that expectation regarding your financial affairs at your bank – so would an accused person. The court will determine whether the "reasonable person" would claim that the use of an investigative technique was so intrusive that it should have been pre-authorized by a justice.

Once, however, a person goes out in public, there is a greatly reduced expectation of privacy on their part due to their awareness that their actions are visible to others, including law enforcement officers. They would still be entitled to claim the expectation of privacy in regards to a conversation held inside a vehicle parked in a public place, as everyone would expect even normal conversations to be private and would not be used against them as evidence.

An individual cannot claim to have a reasonable expectation of privacy for incriminating information they put into an email and sent to numerous recipients. Once the "send" button is hit, the originator loses all control over what happens to their message, regardless of their original intention. Should an individual write something incriminating on a piece of paper that they then discard in a public place or throw out in the household garbage for pickup by a municipal sanitation system, they are deemed to have forfeited all expectations of privacy in any items that are so abandoned.[20]

7.6 REASONABLE GROUNDS

We previously discussed the legal requirement of reasonable grounds in our examination of arrest and use of force in chapters 3 and 4, respectively. Reasonable grounds is so absolutely vital in determining the justification for so many things that police officers are required to do that it bears repeating, especially in our discussion of search and seizure. I cannot overstress the importance of a sound understanding of the meaning of reasonable grounds as the basis for a police officer's actions.

Reasonable grounds are defined as:

"A set of facts or circumstances which, if true, would lead an ordinary, prudent, cautious individual to have a strong belief that exceeds mere suspicion."

Reasonable grounds refer to a legal threshold that constitutes a strong belief in a fact, such as that a certain person has committed a particular offence or that illegal property is situated in a certain place. A police officer is not allowed to randomly stop and search citizens walking down the street for drugs or weapons in their possession.

But where a police officer has a reasonable belief – exceeding simple suspicion – that a person is in possession of drugs or weapons, the threshold of reasonable grounds has been met. Suspicion may be sufficient to temporarily justify detaining a person for investigative purposes, but is not sufficient cause to justify a formal arrest or search of an individual.

Reasonable grounds may be formed from bits and pieces of information received from other persons – witnesses, victims and even other police officers, either verbally or in writing, or obtained as the result of an inquiry or an observation made by the officer. Reasonable grounds may even be derived from a conclusion or belief formed by assessing information from one or more sources, including both physical (real) or circumstantial evidence, or both.

---

[20]*R. v. Krist* (1995), 100 C.C.C. (3d) 58, 42 C.R. (4th) 159, 103 W.A.C. 133 (B.C.C.A.).

Reasonable grounds must first be considered to be reliable before they are acted upon, and must be more than just suspicion. The concept of reasonable grounds is a far lower threshold than that of proof beyond a reasonable doubt, which is the legal standard used by Canadian courts to determine guilt or innocence.

The police officer must have the subjective belief that it is necessary to conduct a search. The officer's subjective belief will also be weighed against the standard of the reasonable person. Would an ordinary cautious, prudent, reasonable person standing in the officer's shoes agree with the officer's belief that the particular search was reasonable and necessary? If so, only then it may be said that reasonable grounds existed to justify a search under the circumstances. See Box 7.2 for a Case Study example.

BOX 7.1	Investigative Hypothesis

(Subjective belief + Objective belief) > mere suspicion = reasonable grounds
Officer   Reasonable person

BOX 7.2	Case Study: Reasonable Grounds

You are dispatched to a complaint about a man armed with a handgun at a local licensed premises. The server at the bar reported that he observed a man sitting at a table with a handgun tucked inside the waistband of his pants. You and your partner arrive and approach a man, matching the description of the complainant, sitting alone at a table in the bar. No handgun is visible, but you detect a bulge in the man's clothing above his waistband that could be a concealed weapon.

Question: Do you have reasonable grounds to believe that the man is in possession of a handgun, or are you still at the stage of mere suspicion?

Considerations: You cannot see the gun yourself, nor can you reasonably question people inside the bar to determine if anyone else observed the weapon. What you do have is the unqualified statement of a single witness, of unknown reliability, concerning the presence of a handgun. You now also have your own observations of a patron matching the description given to your dispatcher by the server and your observation of a bulge under the patron's clothing which may – or may not – be a weapon.

Question: Do these facts constitute reasonable grounds – or mere suspicion?

First, you would by now have formed a strong subjective belief – that is, in your own mind – that the man at the table is in possession of a handgun. I suggest that while you do not have proof beyond a reasonable doubt, you could certainly have formed a strong belief at this stage. Next, would an independent, reasonable person standing in your shoes have formed a similar strong belief under these circumstances? I suggest that any reasonable, prudent cautious individual could have formed the same belief, given these facts.

At this point, I don't mean to suggest that a lengthy analysis of the situation is required every time an officer investigates an allegedly armed person. In fact, I suggest that immediately upon arriving at the bar, we would have quickly demanded identification from the patron – while taking precautions against his drawing a concealed weapon, and taken possession of the weapon – by force if necessary – failing the patron's immediate production of a police badge or permit to carry a restricted weapon.

Note that while we had reasonable grounds to believe the patron was in possession of a handgun, we did not necessarily have reasonable grounds to believe that a

BOX 7.2	*(Continued)*

crime was being committed. We had a suspicion that the patron might be committing a crime, but even if the patron had a lawful justification to have the handgun, our search could still have been justified, while a charge would not have been.

This very thing actually happened to me many years ago. While travelling for investigative purposes, I boarded an aircraft in Toronto bound for Winnipeg. I had already officially identified myself to the flight crew and had completed the necessary airline documentation in order to transport an unloaded weapon on the plane.

Prior to takeoff, I was requested by a flight attendant to change my seating assignment so that an elderly couple who had become separated might sit together during the long flight. As I was travelling alone on business, I agreed. Upon being shown to my new seat, and while placing my carry-on baggage into an overhead compartment, I accidentally exposed my shoulder holster beneath my suit jacket to my new seatmates.

My new travelling companions had apparently just been discussing recent aircraft high-jackings when they looked up and observed that their new seatmate was unexpectedly armed with a handgun. Their understandable distress prompted them to secretly report me to the flight crew – evidently to different flight crew that the ones who had previously been made aware that an armed plain-clothes police officer was onboard their aircraft. I was soon surrounded by numerous stern-looking airline officials who professionally – but firmly – demanded identification which, thankfully, I was able to produce to their satisfaction – honest mistake.

Did the airline officials have reasonable grounds to confront me and search me if necessary? – I believe they most certainly did.

Suppose that our patron back in the bar scenario produces a police badge and warrant card identifying himself as a police officer. No crime has been committed and no damage has been done. Although I suspect that I would question the officer's armed presence in a licenced premises – personally with them and also with their supervisor.

What if the patron had turned out to be an undercover police officer who was also legally justified to be armed and was legally justified to be in the bar while conducting an investigation? I would suggest that we should treat them as we would any other offender with a handgun, "arresting" them, publicly searching their person and "seizing" the handgun to protect their cover story.

I have never met an undercover officer who would not rather be arrested in a bar to protect their reputation and maintain the integrity of their investigation than be exposed as a police officer. The details of the "arrest" and "charges" would be worked out upon returning to your police station.

7.6.1   Reasonable Grounds Using Hearsay Information

Hearsay information that cannot be used as evidence in court is allowable in forming reasonable grounds but must be corroborated, or be otherwise shown to be reliable. Hearsay information may be obtained from a fellow police officer or from a witness or a confidential informer. In all cases, the information should be "sourced", meaning that every fact has to be attributed to the source from whom it was received and be clearly articulated as to how each particular source came to know the information that is attributed to them.

The confidential police informer who provides information should, of course, only be referred to as a confidential informer, or by an assigned informant number. An informer's reliability must also be "qualified" either on the basis of previous successful informant activity, or by way of independent corroboration of their information.

Where the information is known exclusively by the informer and as a result, if it was to become known to a suspect/accused, it would tend to identify the informer, the investigator should request that the issuing justice seal the search warrant information.

7.7 SEARCH INCIDENT TO ARREST

The warrantless search authority most frequently used by police officers is their common law right to search any person who has been lawfully arrested. To be arrested for committing an offence, the offence must be one that is, in fact, arrestable. A person who is detained at the side of the road for speeding is not under arrest and is therefore not subject to being searched. This common law authority applies equally to persons arrested for criminal offences as well as for provincial offences.

We have seen that arrest is sometimes necessary to establish the identity of a suspect or to prevent the commission, continuation or renewal of an offence. Common law grants peace officers the legal authority to search arrested prisoners and the area immediately surrounding them for:

1. evidence,

2. weapons, or

3. tools of escape.

All things for which a person may be searched incident to arrest provide some evidence that the prisoner is the person responsible for the commission of the offence under investigation, or might either injure or escape from the arresting peace officer(s).[21] Such searches are not restricted to a casual "pat-down" search, which is by its nature non-invasive.

Searches incident to arrest may involve the removal of articles of clothing, hats, belts, shoes, and other items of apparel if necessary. A strip-search is permitted where the officer has reasonable grounds to believe it is necessary, and takes precautions to protect the privacy and personal dignity of the prisoner. Strip-searches are obviously far more invasive than a "frisk" search and if they are resorted to at all, should only be conducted in the privacy of a police station. It is recommended that, where possible and where the prisoner cooperates, that they be allowed to remove their own clothing.[22]

Nothing in law requires that a prisoner be searched by a police officer of the same gender, although individual departmental policy may stipulate such orders for individual police services. Any subsequent evaluation of the reasonableness of the search will greatly depend on precautions taken by the searching officer to respect the dignity of the prisoner.

---

[21]*Gottschalk vs. Hutton* (1921), 17 Alta. L.R. 347, 1 W.W.R. 59, 66 D.L.R. 499, 36 C.C.C. 298; *R. v. Storrey* (1990), 1 S.C.R. 241; *Cloutier v. Langlois* (1990), 1 S.C.R. 158, 53 C.C.C. (3d) 257, 74 C.R. (3d) 316; *R. v. Caslake* (1998), 1 S.C.R. 51, 121 C.C.C. (3d) 97, 155 D.L.R. (4th) 19.

[22]*R. v. Golden*, [2001] 3 S.C.R. 679, 2001 S.C.C. 83.

It is obviously recommended that, where it is possible, an officer should search prisoners of their own gender. When circumstances are such that no officer of the same gender is available, there should at least be another witness officer present. In emergent situations when no officer of the same gender is available and officer-safety or the safety of any person is at risk, a searching officer must use their best judgment and take whatever precautions are possible, protecting the dignity of the prisoner to the best of their ability.

A searching officer of different gender might use the back of their hand or an object such as a ballpoint pen, baton or notebook to pass over the prisoner's person to detect possible concealed articles underneath their clothing. Under no circumstances should an officer ever participate in a strip-search of a prisoner of different gender. A lengthy but reasonable delay between the arrest and the strip-search would be permissible while arrangements were made for a same-sex officer to be summoned to a police station to conduct the search.

Searches incident to arrest, are not restricted to the prisoner's person. Common law also authorizes the search of the area immediately surrounding an arrested person in a public place, a residence or a motor vehicle.

Photo 7.1 - A student seizes a concealed knife during the search of a prisoner. Note the wide-spread stance of the prisoner's feet and the position of the searcher's right foot inside the prisoner's left foot to maintain physical control of the subject during the search.

7.8   SEARCHES OF MOTOR VEHICLES

Searches of motor vehicles typically present particular difficulty for police officers due to their inherent ability to be moved quickly. Although the reasonable expectation of privacy in relation to a motor vehicle is less than that of a dwelling house, the driver or owner of a motor vehicle still has an obvious expectation of privacy from intrusion resulting from police investigations.

This reasonable expectation of privacy does not extend to the passenger of a motor vehicle who is not the owner of it. If reasonable grounds exist to arrest the driver, and/or the owner, if they are a person other than the driver and are an occupant of the motor vehicle, the common law warrantless authority to search the prisoner incident to arrest also extends to the motor vehicle.[23]

The difficulty with searching motor vehicles is that by the time a search warrant is obtained, the vehicle may become mobile and may be far removed from where it was first observed. Exigent circumstances can be claimed where there are reasonable grounds to believe that evidence inside the motor vehicle may be removed, lost or destroyed[24] or in circumstances of a motor vehicle that is either mobile, or is about to move.[25] (Sherriff 1997)

I was once involved in a case in which a suspect transported bricks of cannabis resin by bus to a location where he had arranged for an accomplice to meet him and drive him by car to an unknown location. Surveillance was maintained at the location where the suspect was to disembark the bus. The accomplice arrived and the suspect was observed to get off the bus, place an overnight bag into the trunk of the vehicle and enter the front passenger seat.

Prior to that moment, while reasonable belief existed that illicit drugs would be in the accomplice's motor vehicle – that event was to occur in the future. Anticipatory or future grounds are not sufficient to conduct a search. When the suspect disembarked from the bus, carrying the package, believed to contain the drugs, he could have been arrested and searched incident to the arrest, however, he might have escaped on the busy thoroughfare or possibly disposed of the drugs during a foot chase.

The conditions for making an arrest were far more controllable after the suspect had entered the motor vehicle, however, it might then be said that he could have a reasonable expectation of privacy in his personal effects, now inside the vehicle – even though it was not his vehicle.

It was not practicable to obtain a warrant once reasonable grounds existed that the drugs were actually in the car, as the vehicle was about to become mobile. If we had then attempted to obtain a search warrant, who knows where the vehicle would have been by the time the warrant was issued?

Under legislation that existed at that time, both the driver and the passenger were arrested on reasonable grounds that they were in possession of narcotics for the purpose of trafficking. The trunk was opened, incident to the arrest, and the drugs were observed in the overnight bag. As a precaution, and in an effort to demonstrate good faith, the vehicle was towed to a nearby police station and kept under guard while a search warrant for the motor vehicle was obtained to seize the drugs.

---

[23]*R. v. Belnavis* (1989), 107 C.C.C. (3d) 195, 36 C.R.R. (2d) 32, 1996 C.R.R. Lexis 241.

[24]*R. v. Grant* (1993), 84 C.C.C. (3d) 97 (S.C.C.).

[25]*R. v. Rao* (1984), 40 C.R. (3d) 1, 12 C.C.C. (3d) 97 (Ont. C.A.).

Photo 7.2 - A student applies correct search techniques of a subject's motor vehicle during a simulated arrest scenario.

If an officer stops a motor vehicle routinely and wishes to examine the glove compartment or trunk for evidence of a crime, absent any reasonable grounds to arrest the driver/occupant that would justify a search incident to the arrest, the only lawful methods to search the motor vehicle are:

1. with the consent of the driver/owner, or

2. in exigent circumstances involving articulable reasonable grounds relating to the potential loss or destruction of evidence, or

3. on the authority of a search warrant.

7.9   CONSENT SEARCHES

There are many instances in which a person of interest, a suspect, or even an accused may **consent** to allow the police to conduct a search or examination that would otherwise require a search warrant. In the 1992 Ontario Court of Appeals decision of *R. v. Wills*,[26] Mr. Justice J. A. Doherty defined the six necessary conditions that, on a balance of probabilities, must exist to constitute a valid consent search:

1. The person giving the consent must have actually stated, or implied, (not verbally stated, but in some other way insinuated) their consent to the search or examination.

---

[26]*R. v. Wills* (1992), 70 C.C.C. (3d) 529 (Ont. C.A.).

2. The consent must be given by someone with the right to do so, (e.g., a guest in someone's house couldn't legally consent for the police to search the owner's house in their absence).

3. The consent must have been given voluntarily (not coerced or obtained by threat, etc.).

4. The person giving the consent must be aware of the nature of the police conduct they are being asked to consent to. Example – Mr. Smith, we would like you to provide samples of your hand-writing that will be compared to the forged document, to determine whether or not you are the person who wrote it.

5. The person giving the consent must be aware of their right to refuse to permit (or withdraw their consent for) the police to conduct the search or examination. Example – Mr. Smith, we would like to search your car for evidence of the bank robbery. As you are aware we would normally need a search warrant to do that but you have indicated that you want to cooperate with the investigation and let us examine your car without a warrant – is that correct? You are aware that you have the right to refuse to give us permission to search your car – is that correct?"[27]

6. The person giving the consent must be aware of the potential consequences of giving their consent. Example – Mr. Smith, you have indicated your intention to provide a voluntary DNA sample in regards to the sexual assault investigation we are conducting. You are aware that if the sample you provide identifies you as the person responsible for this offence that you will be charged with (Sexual Assault) and the sample you provide will be used as evidence against you in court – is that correct?

It is strongly recommended that, whenever possible, prior to conducting a "consent search" an investigator take the time to explain the elements of consent (as per the Wills decision – on a departmental form if your agency has such a pre-printed form) and obtain the consenter's signature. Investing a small amount of preparation can go a long way to proving to the court that, where charges are laid against the individual, the accused's consent was an "informed consent".

Where the person being requested to consent to a search or other police action is a "young person", they must also be advised of the special protection afforded to them under the *Youth Criminal Justice Act*[28] (their rights to counsel and to have a parent or another adult present). In serious cases, it would be unwise to proceed on the sole consent of a young person without also attempting to obtain a parent or guardian's consent in writing, if practicable to do so.[29]

A copy of a sample Consent to Search form may be found in the Appendices at the rear of this textbook.

7.10 ABANDONED EVIDENCE

There are times when a seizure by the police is not considered a search. One of those times includes when a suspect or accused provides a sample or thing voluntarily to the police. Another example is when a person abandons physical evidence that is then recovered by the police. Evidence such as a mucous or blood-stained tissue discarded by an individual

---

[27] *R. v. Lewis* (1998), 122 C.C.C. (3d) 481, 13 C.R. (5th) 34 (Ont. C.A.).

[28] *Youth Criminal Justice Act*, S.C. 2002, c. 1, ss. 1-165 and Schedule, in force April 1, 2003.

[29] *R. v. Stillman* (1997), 1 S.C.R. 607.

(even one who is in custody)[30] may be seized without warrant by the police for investigative purposes. The courts have held that when an individual discards property, they relinquish their privacy interest in that item and forfeit any reasonable expectation of privacy.

The same principle of abandonment holds true when investigators conduct a warrantless seizure of a person's trash left at the curb for pick-up. Courts have held that seizure of abandoned garbage does not breach an individual's privacy interest, as the individual can no longer claim any reasonable expectation of privacy.[31]

In sexual assault cases where suspect (questioned samples) DNA samples are needed to compare to samples from the crime scene (comparison samples) for the purpose of eliminating a person of interest or suspect from suspicion, a police officer might request the person to provide a voluntary (consent) sample. If there were no grounds to obtain a DNA search warrant and the subject refused to provide a sample voluntarily, or if such a request might jeopardize the investigation, the officer might try to collect an abandoned sample.

A not uncommon police practice is to place a suspect under physical surveillance and follow him from place to place until he discards a potential source of his DNA. A suspect's DNA can be deposited on a wide variety of material. If a suspect wipes his mouth with a napkin or drinks from a coffee cup or a bottle, nucleated epithelial cells from the mucous membranes of the suspect's mouth will yield his DNA profile. If the suspect is a smoker, a cigarette butt will yield the same biological material suitable for analysis.

Photo 7.3 - Case law authorizes police officers to seize abandoned evidence without a warrant as a subject forfeits any reasonable expectation of privacy in articles they abandon. This doctrine applies to garbage left out for pickup by a municipality or discarded items.

---

[30]*R. v. Stillman*, Supra.

[31]*R. v. Krist* (1995), 100 C.C.C. (3d) 58, 42 C.R. (4th) 159, 103 W.A.C. 133 (B.C.C.A), also: *Evans and Evans v. The Queen*, (1996), 104 C.C.C. (3d) 23 S.C.C., *Regina v. Joyce and Kennedy* (1997), 95 O.A.C. 321 (C.A.), *California v. Greenwood*, 486 U.S. 1625 (1988).

As the suspect discards the item into the trash, or leaves it behind in a public place, they abandon their reasonable expectation of privacy – in fact, they are expecting that someone will come along behind them and pick it up. They just don't anticipate what purpose it will be used for, but again, they have abandoned any privacy interest in the item, which may freely be seized without a warrant by an officer (wearing latex gloves to avoid contaminating the evidence).

7.11 OFFICER SAFETY CONSIDERATIONS

Experience and training is a must in developing an adequate understanding of all issues relating to the search and seizure of evidence. In this section, we are limited to a brief examination of some of the central issues dealing with crime scene examination.

Generally speaking, there are no legal search requirements to search a crime scene unless the offender is known to have some control over it or property interest in it. If a member of the public reports that their residence or business has been broken into, they are consenting to your entry onto their premises. The offender has no proprietary interest (right of ownership, etc.) in the property and therefore can have no reasonable expectation of privacy in the actions by the police that occur on the premises they have victimized.

Police officers have a common law (and to some extent statutory right under the *PSA*)[32] authority to investigate crime and enforce the law. Although crime scene examination is not specifically authorized by statute law, courts have consistently held that the investigation of crime scenes is one of the fundamental duties of the police in the investigation of crime. The Coroner's powers of entry, inspection and seizure[33] are discussed in section 7.20.4 dealing with provincial warrantless search authorities.

Common law also authorizes first responding police officers at violent crime scenes to enter without warrant to perform a cursory search for victims, offenders and weapons to ensure officer safety, where legitimate concerns exist. This unwritten authority does not authorize police officers to search the premises for evidence and expires as soon as officer safety concerns have been satisfied.

Additionally, section 487.11 of the *Criminal Code*[34] grants police officers the warrantless authority to enter buildings, premises or places to seize evidence in respect of offences against the *Criminal Code* (or to install, maintain, remove, monitor or have monitored a tracking device) under exigent circumstances (urgent circumstances requiring immediate action).[35] (See section 7.14 Exigent Circumstances.)

7.12 PLAIN VIEW SEIZURE RULE

In certain situations, incriminating evidence will be encountered inadvertently by the police in circumstances that make it absolutely impracticable to obtain a search warrant. A "common law" doctrine permits the warrantless seizure of inadvertently found evidence in circumstances that make it entirely impracticable to obtain a search warrant.

---

[32]*Police Services Act*, R.S.O. 1990, c. P.15 ss. 4(2).

[33]*Coroners Act*, R.S.O. 1990, c. C. 37 ss. 16(1)-(3).

[34]*Criminal Code*, R.S. 1985, c. C-46, s. 487.11.

[35]*Criminal Code*, R.S. 1985, c. C-46, s. 529.3(2).

Three conditions must exist for a "plain view" seizure to be considered valid:

1. The police officer must be lawfully positioned. The police must have a legal right to be where the viewing of the evidence occurs. An example of this was provided in the previous scenario involving a police officer serving a summons at a private residence. When the occupant opened the door, the officer observed a large quantity of cannabis resin on the kitchen table in plain view of the front door. The officer had a legal right to be at the residence.

2. The finding of the evidence must be inadvertent. Using the previous scenario, if the officer was not expecting to find the cannabis resin, and was not actively searching for it, the find would be held to be inadvertent.

3. The evidence must implicate the accused in some criminal activity. In this case, the cannabis resin would most certainly implicate the sole occupant of the residence who claimed actual possession of the controlled drug for the purpose of trafficking, and plain view seizure would be valid.[36]

Section 489(2) of the *Criminal Code* embodies the "Plain View Seizure Rule" in situations where a peace officer is lawfully positioned whether executing a search or not. It states that peace officers may seize, without warrant:

1. anything obtained by the commission of a criminal offence,

2. anything used in the commission of a criminal offence, or

3. anything that will afford evidence of a criminal offence.

Any such evidence seized is required to be treated in the same manner as if it had been seized under the authority of a search warrant.[37] (See section 8.22 Report to a Justice)

7.13 HOT PURSUIT (FRESH PURSUIT)

Common law allows peace officers to enter residential dwellings to arrest persons they are freshly pursuing from offences for which they may be arrested without warrant. The common law recognizes that it is impracticable for police engaged in a lawful pursuit to be forced to abandon the pursuit merely because the offender takes refuge in their home or the home of another person. Not only would the interests of law enforcement not be met, but evidence could also be lost and if the police gave up the pursuit and left, the suspect would be free to continue committing offences.

The terms **fresh pursuit** and **hot pursuit** mean virtually the same thing. The Honourable Mr. Justice R.E. Salhany, Q.C. provided the definition of fresh pursuit, which has been relied upon by several courts, including the Supreme Court in the 1993 decision of *R. v. Macooh*.[38] In his book *Canadian Criminal Procedure*, Mr. Justice Salhany described a fresh pursuit as being a continuous pursuit that is conducted with reasonable diligence so that the commission of the offence, the pursuit and the capture all form one single transaction.

---

[36]*Controlled Drugs and Substances Act 1996*, c. 19 s. 5(2).

[37]*Criminal Code*, R.S. 1985, c. C-46, s. 489.

[38]*R. v. Macooh*, supra.

For example, the driver of a motor vehicle, who is impaired by alcohol or a drug and who refuses to pull over for the police pulls into the driveway of a private residence, exits the vehicle and runs into the house. Whether or not the police know the identity of the suspect, they may immediately pursue the suspect into the house and make the arrest.

Three conditions must exist for a warrantless entry of a house in the case of hot pursuit:

1. the peace officer must have reasonable grounds to believe the person has committed a provincial offence or an indictable offence for which they may be arrested without a warrant, and

2. the peace officer must have reasonable grounds to believe the person being pursued may be found within the premises to be entered, and

3. the peace officer must announce his presence and the reason for the entry.[39]

7.14 WARRANTLESS ENTRY - EXIGENT CIRCUMSTANCES

Where reasonable grounds exist to obtain a search warrant but emergency conditions make it impracticable to obtain a warrant, a peace officer may, in such exigent circumstances, enter a building, receptacle or place and may seize evidence as if they were acting under a search warrant issued in accordance with s. 487(1) *Criminal Code* or a search warrant issued under subsection 11(1) *Controlled Drugs and Substances Act*.[40] The exigent circumstances anticipated by this section are the same type as described in section 529.3(2) *Criminal Code* and would include extreme situations involving imminent bodily harm, death or imminent loss, destruction or removal of evidence.[41]

A similar warrantless authority exists to enter a dwelling house for the purpose of arresting someone without a warrant where reasonable grounds for a warrant exist but it would be impracticable to obtain a warrant due to exigent circumstances and it is necessary to prevent imminent bodily harm, death or imminent loss or destruction of evidence.[42]

Exigent circumstances that justify a warrantless entry to effect an arrest under section 529.3(1) *Criminal Code* do not excuse the officer(s) of the requirement of prior announcement of their entry. Reasonable grounds must exist, immediately before the entry, to believe that to announce their presence would expose themselves or any person to imminent bodily harm or death or would result in the imminent loss or destruction of evidence, to justify not complying with the prior announcement requirement.[43]

---

[39]*R. v. Macooh*, supra., *Eccles v. Bourque*, [1975] 2 S.C.R. 739, *R. v. Landry*, [1986] 1 S.C.R. 145.

[40]*Criminal Code*, R.S. 1985, c. C-46, s. 487.11.

[41]*Criminal Code*, R.S. 1985, c. C-46, s. 529.3(2).

[42]*Criminal Code*, R.S. 1985, c. C-46, s. 529.3(1).

[43]*Criminal Code*, R.S. 1985, c. C-46, s. 529.4(3).

7.15   SEIZURE OF COUNTERFEIT MONEY OR TOKENS

The *Criminal Code* provides a warrantless seizure authority for counterfeit money, counterfeit tokens of value (defined in section 448 *CC*) and any machine or thing used or adapted for use in making them. All counterfeit money and tokens are deemed to belong to the Crown and may be used as evidence in proceedings or forwarded to the Minister of Finance for disposal.[44]

Although this statutory warrantless authority exists, it is strongly recommended that police officers intending to seize counterfeit money or tokens of value, utilize a regular section 487(1) or 487.1(1) search warrant to avoid the obvious invitation of a challenge under the *Charter of Rights and Freedoms*.

7.16   REPORT TO A JUSTICE – SECTIONS 489.1(1) AND 490 *CC*

A police officer who seizes anything under the authority of any of the search warrant provisions of the *Criminal Code*, or without a warrant either incident to arrest,[45] or under the "plain view seizure rule" embodied in section 489, or in exigent circumstances as authorized by sections 117.02(1) or 487.11 *Criminal Code*, must make a Report to a Justice reporting that they have done so.[46] Making a report involves either producing the article(s) seized, and/or making a written report in Form 5.2 *Criminal Code*.

The justice may order the seized item(s) be returned to the rightful owner, if known, unless the police or prosecutor shows that the item is required for the purposes of investigation, preliminary hearing, trial or other proceeding.[47] Such an order, if granted, is valid only for a period of not more than three months from the date of original seizure[48] and contains provisions that the person in whose custody the item is detained take "reasonable care to ensure that it is preserved."[49] A detention order may be extended for consecutive periods of three months unless in the meantime, proceedings are instituted in which the item is required as evidence.

A sample Report to a Justice dealing with items seized during a fictitious search may be found in the Appendices near the end of this textbook. A Report to a Justice for items seized without a warrant would be in the identical form but with the necessary changes made to indicate the warrantless nature of the seizure.

---

[44]*Criminal Code*, R.S. 1985, c. C-46, s. 462(1)(2).

[45]*R. v. Backhouse* (2005), 194 C.C.C. (3d) 1, 127 C.R.R. (2d) 1, 28 C.R. (6th) 31, 195 O.A.C. 80, CanLII 4937 (Ont. C.A.).

[46]*Criminal Code*, R.S. 1985, c. C-46, s. 489.1(1).

[47]*Criminal Code*, R.S. 1985, c. C-46, s. 490(1)(a).

[48]*Criminal Code*, R.S. 1985, c. C-46, s. 490(2).

[49]*Criminal Code*, R.S. 1985, c. C-46, s. 490(1)(b).

7.17 WEAPONS, AMMUNITION AND EXPLOSIVE SUBSTANCES

If it is impracticable to obtain a warrant due to exigent circumstances, and a police officer has reasonable grounds to believe that a weapon,[50] imitation firearm, prohibited device, ammunition, prohibited ammunition or explosive substance[51] has been used in an offence, or has reasonable grounds to believe that an offence is being committed or has been committed under the *Criminal Code* involving firearms, imitation firearms, cross-bows, prohibited weapons, restricted weapons, prohibited devices, ammunition, prohibited ammunition or explosive substances, they may search a person, vehicle or place other than a dwelling house without warrant, and seize that thing.[52]

If a peace officer has reasonable grounds to believe any person is in possession of a weapon, prohibited device, ammunition or explosive substance, and that such possession is not desirable in the interests of the safety of any person, a warrant may be obtained to search a dwelling house, building, receptacle or place to seize the thing.[53] If reasonable grounds exist to obtain a such a warrant to search any building, receptacle or place under section 117.04(1) *Criminal Code*, but due to exigent circumstances it is impracticable to obtain a warrant, a peace officer may enter a dwelling house, building, receptacle or place and seize weapons, prohibited devices, ammunition or explosive substances to prevent possible danger to the safety of any person.[54]

The warrantless exigent circumstances search provisions for weapons and ammunition contained in the *Criminal* Code are commonly resorted to in cases of persons threatening suicide, incidents involving persons suffering from mental disorder and often in cases of domestic disputes. A search of dwelling houses, buildings, receptacles or places for weapons, prohibited devices, ammunition or explosive substances conducted either with or without warrant also authorizes peace officers to seize any authorization, licence or registration certificate relating to the weapon, ammunition, explosive substance or prohibited device in the possession of the person.

7.18 APPLICATION TO JUSTICE FOR DISPOSITION - SEC. 117.05 *CC*

Where weapons, ammunition, prohibited devices or explosive substances are seized, with or without a warrant, a police officer must, within thirty days of the seizure, apply to a justice for an order of disposition with respect to the thing(s) seized. The justice will set a date for a hearing and direct that notices of the hearing be given to specified persons.[55]

---

[50]*Criminal Code*, R.S. 1985, c. C-46, s. 2.

[51]*Criminal Code*, R.S. 1985, c. C-46, s. 84(1).

[52]*Criminal Code*, R.S. 1985, c. C-46, s. 117.02(1).

[53]*Criminal Code*, R.S. 1985, c. C-46, s. 117.04(1).

[54]*Criminal Code*, R.S. 1985, c. C-46, s. 117.04(2).

[55]*Criminal Code*, R.S. 1985, c. C-46, s. 117.05(1).

At the hearing, which may be held *ex parte* (outside of the presence of the person who is the subject of the application), relevant evidence is heard and the justice may make an order prohibiting the person from possessing weapons, ammunition or explosive substances for a period not exceeding five years and order that items seized be forfeited to the Crown or otherwise disposed of in a manner directed by the court.[56]

7.19 *CONTROLLED DRUGS AND SUBSTANCES ACT*, S.C. 1996, C. C-19

Where a peace officer who executes a warrant issued under subsection 11(1) of the *Controlled Drugs and Substances Act* has reasonable grounds to believe that any person found in the place described in the warrant has on their person any controlled substance, precursor used in the manufacture of controlled substances, property or thing set out in the warrant, the peace officer may search the person for the controlled substance, precursor, property or thing and seize it.[57]

Even if a police officer is not executing a search warrant, the *CDSA* authorizes peace officers to exercise any of the search powers described in section 11 without a warrant if the conditions for obtaining a warrant exist but by reason of exigent circumstances it would be impracticable to obtain one.[58]

The same warrantless search requirements and case law apply to searches of motor vehicles and to searches incident to arrest for drugs as for any other criminal offence.

7.20 PROVINCIAL WARRANTLESS SEARCH AND SEIZURE

Many of the enforcement activities undertaken by Ontario police officers involve provincial legislation such as the *Highway Traffic Act* and the *Liquor Licence Act*. Police officers in rural areas outside the Greater Toronto Area may even encounter situations involving offences against the *Fish and Wildlife Conservation Act*. Even though search warrants may be obtained under the *Provincial Offences Act* to seize evidence of offences, these provincial statutes all contain their own sections granting limited powers of search or seizure without a warrant.

7.20.1 *Highway Traffic Act*, R.S.O 1990, c. H-8

Where a police officer has reason to believe that:

1. a number plate or

2. evidence of validation attached to a motor vehicle or trailer, or

3. a permit carried by the driver of a motor vehicle

---

[56]*Criminal Code*, R.S. 1985, c. C-46, s. 117.05.

[57]*Controlled Drugs and Substances Act*, S.C. 1996, C-19, s. 11(5).

[58]*Controlled Drugs and Substances Act*, S.C. 1996, C-19, s. 11(7).

was not furnished or authorized under the *HTA* for that motor vehicle, or was obtained by false pretences or has been defaced or altered in any way, they may take possession of it without a warrant and retain it until the facts have been determined.[59]

A police officer may also seize without warrant any driver's licence if they have reason to believe it has been altered, falsified, cancelled, revoked, suspended, loaned or is a duplicate driver's licence and forward it to the Registrar of Motor Vehicles upon finalization of any court proceedings.[60]

7.20.2 *Liquor Licence Act*, R.S.O. 1990, c. L-19

Some members of the public enjoy drinking alcoholic beverages. Many people also enjoying driving their cars and boats. Obvious problems arise when members of the public attempt to combine the two activities simultaneously. The *Liquor Licence Act* allows police officers who have reasonable grounds to believe that liquor is being unlawfully kept in a vehicle or boat (not equipped with permanent sleeping, sanitary and cooking facilities or any boat that is underway and not covered by a licence under the *LLA*) may, at any time, enter and search the vehicle or boat as well as search any person found in it.[61]

This fairly significant right of search of vehicles, vessels and persons recognizes the total impracticability surrounding obtaining search warrants to conduct liquor enforcement, especially when highly mobile conveyances are involved. The powers of search granted by the *LLA* are limited, however, to the search for liquor that is unlawfully possessed, and would therefore not permit a search for other things or of people found inside conveyances who are obviously not in possession of open containers (bottles – not packages) of liquor.

The *LLA* also allows police officers to seize without a warrant any thing, including but not limited to liquor, if,

    (a)   he or she reasonably believes that the thing will afford evidence of an offence under this Act;

    (b)   he or she reasonably believes that,

        (i) the thing was used or is being used in connection with the commission of an offence under this Act, and

        (ii) unless the thing is seized it is likely that it would continue to be used or would be used again in the commission of an offence under this Act; or

    (c)   he or she reasonably believes that the thing is proceeds from the commission of an offence under this Act.[62]

Also, if any offence appears to have been committed under the *Liquor Licence Act* and a police officer reasonably believes, in view of the offence apparently committed and the presence of liquor, that a further offence is likely to be committed, the police officer may seize the liquor and the packages – not just containers of liquor – in which it is kept.[63]

---

[59]*Highway Traffic Act*, R.S.O. 1990, c. H-8, s. 14(1).

[60]*Highway Traffic Act*, R.S.O. 1990, c. H-8, s. 35(3).

[61]*Liquor Licence Act*, R.S.O. 1990, c. L-19, s. 32(5).

[62]*Liquor Licence Act*, R.S.O. 1990, c. L-19, s. 47(1).

[63]*Liquor Licence Act*, R.S.O. 1990, c. L-19, s. 47(1.1).

Liquor Licence Act Case Study:

For example, you are patrolling a park within your municipality and you notice a group of six people who are acting in a disorderly manner. They are being loud and obnoxious and are obviously disturbing other people around them.

As you approach the group, you observe that two of them are holding open bottles (containers) of beer. Four empty beer bottles of the same brand are lying on the ground near the group. Two camping coolers full of ice and beer are also in their possession.

What are your powers of search and seizure, if any, in relation to the beer? Can any other items be seized without a search warrant?

7.20.3 *Fish and Wildlife Conservation Act,* S.O. 1997, c. C-41

For the purpose of the *Fish and Wildlife Conservation Act*, a conservation officer (all police officers and First Nations Constables are considered to be conservation officers)[64] may enter and inspect a building or other place, including,

"(a) a building or other place [other than a dwelling] where licences are issued;

(b) a building or other place [other than a dwelling] that relates to wildlife, invertebrates or fish; or

(c) a building or other place [other than a dwelling] that relates to hunting, trapping or fishing or to the transport, buying or selling of wildlife, invertebrates or fish." [65]

Note the difference in the legislation, which grants the right of "inspection" rather than search. Inspection differs from search as the intention of an inspection is to establish compliance with legislation rather than to gather evidence of an offence. Any official examination by a conservation officer, including police officers, should be restricted to the purpose of the original intent of the legislation.

Where a conservation officer, including a police officer, believes that an offence has been committed under the *Fish and Wildlife Conservation Act* or the regulations, they may obtain a search warrant in accordance with Part VIII of the *Provincial Offences Act*. The Act, however, provides for investigations in remote locations and exigent circumstances by providing warrantless search powers for any building or place other than a dwelling.

"If a conservation officer believes on reasonable grounds that there is in a building or other place [other than a dwelling] any thing that will afford evidence of an offence under this Act but that the time required to obtain a search warrant would lead to the loss, removal or destruction of the evidence, the conservation officer may, without a search warrant, enter and search the building or other place." [66]

---

[64] *Fish and Wildlife Conservation Act*, S.O. 1997, C-41, s. 87(2).

[65] *Fish and Wildlife Conservation Act*, S.O. 1997, C-41, s. 90(1).

[66] *Fish and Wildlife Conservation Act*, S.O. 1997, C-41, s. 91(2).

The *Fish and Wildlife Conservation Act* also embodies the concept of the Plain View Seizure Rule, which allows conservation officers to seize evidence without a warrant providing they are lawfully positioned. This section might apply when a conservation officer is executing a warrant or under circumstances that would render obtaining a warrant impracticable.

"A conservation officer who is lawfully in a building or other place may, without a warrant, seize any thing that he or she believes on reasonable grounds,

(a)   has been obtained by the commission of an offence under this Act;

(b)   has been used in the commission of an offence under this Act;

(c)   will afford evidence of the commission of an offence under this Act; or

(d)   is intermixed with a thing referred to in clause (a), (b) or (c)." [67]

7.20.4 *Coroners Act*, R.S.O. 1990, c. C-37

Police officers are often among the first to arrive at scenes of deaths, including motor vehicle accidents, industrial fatalities, accidents in and around the home, and sudden but unexpected deaths of medical cause. Deaths may either be homicides, suicides, accidental deaths or natural deaths. Most deaths occur with no involvement of foul play or criminal wrongdoing. Occasionally, however, an individual who is criminally responsible for the death of a person may attempt to make the death appear as a different type of death to avoid attracting suspicion for their actions.

In Ontario, the coroner has the legal authority to investigate certain types of deaths, in fact most deaths, except those that occur in hospital or while under a doctor's care. The coroner is a vital partner in the field of sudden deaths.

The statutory warrantless investigative powers under the *Coroners Act* granted to all coroners may also be delegated by the coroner to police officers or medical practitioners not designated as coroners, and authorizes these three classifications of persons to:

"View or take possession of any dead body"

"Enter and inspect [as opposed to enter, search and seize powers contained in s. 487(1) of the Criminal Code] any place where a dead body is found and any place from which the coroner has reasonable grounds to believe the body was removed from" [68]

"Inspect any place in which the deceased person was, or in which the coroner has reasonable grounds to believe was, before his or her death"

"Inspect and extract information from records or writings relating to the deceased, and

"Seize anything that there are reasonable grounds to believe is material to the investigation" [69]

---

[67]*Fish and Wildlife Conservation Act*, S.O. 1997, C-41, s. 92(1).

[68]*Coroners Act*, R.S.O. 1990, c. C.37, s. 16(1).

[69]*Coroners Act*, R.S.O. 1990, c. C.37, s. 16(2).

While there is no specific statutory authority for a coroner to issue a warrant to "enter", "inspect" or "seize" evidence, common practice (in Ontario) has been for the coroner to issue a warrant, in writing, notwithstanding the absence of documentation specifying the grounds for reasonable belief. Presumably, this practice began in an effort to formalize the delegation of the coroner's authority to police officers, as the grounds for believing that those actions are material and necessary must be the personal belief of the coroner – not of the police officer executing the coroner's delegated powers.

A police officer may not presume to be exercising the warrantless inspection powers of a coroner under the *Coroners Act* when the coroner has no knowledge of the case nor any personal belief of the necessity to enter, inspect or seize anything, material or otherwise, and where there has not been any directed delegation of the coroner's powers to the police officer(s).

A police criminal investigation must never "piggy-back" on the Coroner's investigation to circumvent the requirements of obtaining judicial pre-authorization for search and seizure. There must be a separation between the role of law enforcement to investigate crime and the role of the coroner to investigate certain classes of deaths.[70]

7.20.5 *Child and Family Services Act*, R.S.O. 1990, c. C-11

Another warrantless search authority deals primarily with the protection of children under 18 years of age, rather than enforcement in the traditional sense, that may or may not be encountered in circumstances that require investigation and possible laying of charges. The *Child and Family Services Act* (*CFSA*) of Ontario authorizes child protection workers to enter any premises without a warrant, by force if necessary, to search for and apprehend children under 18 years of age who are in need of protection, to take them to a place of safety. This warrantless search authority may only be resorted to if there are reasonable and probable grounds to believe there is substantial risk to the child's health or safety during the time it would take to obtain a necessary warrant.[71]

The CFSA defines a child in need of protection as any child under 18 years of age:

- who has suffered or is at risk of suffering physical harm due to inadequate care or neglect, or

- who has been or is at risk of being sexually molested or exploited, or

- who requires medical care that the person having charge of the child refuses to provide or is unavailable or is unable to consent to that care,

- who has suffered or is at risk of suffering emotional harm demonstrated by depression, anxiety, self-destructive or aggressive behaviour or delayed development,

- who has been abandoned,

---

[70]*R. v. Jarvis*, [2002] 3 S.C.R. 757, 2002 S.C.C. 73, also *R. v. Ling*, [2002] 3 S.C.R. 814, 2002 S.C.C. 74, also *R. v. Colarusso*, [1994] 1 S.C.R. 20, 87 C.C.C. (3d) 193, 26 C.R.(4th) 289.

[71]*Child and Family Services Act*, R.S.O. 1990, c. C-11, s. 40(11).

- who is a child under 12 that has killed or seriously injured a person or caused serious damage to another person's property where services or treatment is necessary to prevent a recurrence and that the person in charge of the child refuses to provide or is unable to provide or unable to consent to.[72]

The warrantless entry authority under this Act also applies to peace officers as if they were child protection workers.[73]

SUMMARY

- A search includes any type of official examination or carrying out of an investigative technique by agents of law enforcement for the purposes of:
  - gathering evidence of illegal activity, or
  - preventing the commission of an offence, or
  - for the purposes of ensuring public safety or officer safety under certain circumstances.

- A seizure involves the taking of information or articles of evidence for the purpose of proving illegal activity or for the purpose of furthering an investigation.

- A reasonable search is defined as one that is
  - authorized by law (statute law or common law), or
  - judicially pre-authorized by a justice (search warrant) and
  - carried out in a reasonable manner under a law that is reasonable.

- To be considered a search, there must be some intrusion upon a person's reasonable expectation of privacy that results from evidence gathering or investigative purposes.

- Evidence obtained through a warrantless inspection authorities contained in regulatory provincial offences cannot serve to further a criminal investigation if it was obtained for a different purpose than determining a person's penal liability.

- Warrantless searches have generally been held by the Supreme Court of Canada to be *prima facie* unreasonable. This means that evidence that is obtained during a warrantless search is initially considered to be inadmissible but may be rebutted by the Crown with evidence that a search was reasonable and authorized by statute or common law.

- Reasonable expectation of privacy is a protective legal concept that is intended to prevent unreasonable intervention by the criminal justice system in the lives of citizens, rather than to merely provide a standard for determining after the fact whether or not such intrusion was warranted.

- Reasonable grounds refer to a legal threshold that constitutes a strong belief in a fact, such as that a certain person has committed a particular offence or that illegal property is situated in a certain place.

---

[72]*Child and Family Services Act*, R.S.O. 1990, c. C-11, s. 37(2).

[73]*Child and Family Services Act*, R.S.O. 1990, c. C-11, s. 40(13).

- Common law authorizes peace officers to search arrested persons and the area immediately surrounding them for evidence, weapons and tools of escape.

- An individual may give informed consent for a search by the police if consent is implied or expressed, if they have the legal right to grant consent, if they know the nature of the police conduct, and if they are aware both of their right to refuse to consent and of the consequences of their granting consent.

- Abandoned evidence may be seized without a warrant as the person discarding an item forfeits their reasonable expectation of privacy in the discarded item.

- Common law authorizes first responding police officers at violent crime scenes to enter without warrant to perform a cursory search for victims, offenders and weapons to ensure officer safety, where legitimate concerns exist.

- Common law authorizes police officers to enter premises without a warrant if they are involved in the "hot pursuit" of a person for a provincial or indictable offence for which they may arrest without warrant, if the occurrence, reasonably diligent pursuit and arrest form one single transaction. Police officers must have the lawful authority to arrest, must have reasonable grounds to believe the person being pursued is within the premises to be entered and must announce their presence and entry.

- Police officers may seize evidence of a criminal offence without a warrant under the Plain View Seizure Rule if they are lawfully positioned, if the discovery is inadvertent and if the evidence found provides evidence with respect to the commission of a criminal offence.

- Warrantless search authority exists under the *Criminal Code* to seize evidence or to enter a dwelling for the purpose of making an arrest where the grounds to obtain a search warrant exist but due to the imminent potential for loss, removal or destruction of evidence or of risk of imminent bodily harm or death to any person it would be impracticable to obtain a search warrant.

- A police officer who seizes anything under the authority of any of the search warrant provisions of the *Criminal Code*, or without a warrant either incident to arrest, or under the Plain View Seizure Rule, or in exigent circumstances must make a Report to a Justice in Form 5 reporting that they have done so.

- If it is impracticable to obtain a warrant due to exigent circumstances, and a police officer has reasonable grounds to believe that a weapon, imitation firearm, ammunition, prohibited device or explosive substance has been used in an offence, or will afford evidence of an offence that has been committed under the *Criminal Code*, they may search a person, vehicle or place other than a dwelling house without warrant, and seize that thing.

- If a peace officer has reasonable grounds to believe any person is in possession of a weapon, prohibited device, ammunition or an explosive substance, and that such possession is not desirable in the interests of the safety of any person, but due to exigent circumstances it is impracticable to obtain a warrant under section 117.04(1) *Criminal Code*, a peace officer may enter a dwelling house, building, receptacle or place and seize weapons, prohibited devices, ammunition, or explosive substances to prevent possible danger to the safety of any person.

- Where weapons, ammunition, prohibited devices or explosive substances are seized, with or without a warrant, a police officer must, within thirty days of the seizure, apply to a justice for an order of disposition with respect to the thing(s) seized. The justice will set a date for a hearing and direct that notices of the hearing be given to specified persons.

DISCUSSION QUESTIONS

1. An offender breaks into a commercial business and steals a large quantity of money. During the investigation, the offender's fingerprints and traces of DNA are found in the crime scene. Other evidence is also discovered establishing reasonable grounds to charge the offender with Breaking, Entering and Committing an Indictable Offence. During his trial, the offender claims that his section 8 *Charter* rights were breached as his fingerprints and DNA were discovered during a warrantless search that violated his reasonable expectation of privacy. Does the offender have a valid challenge? Will the warrantless search of the crime scene be held to be unreasonable? State the reasoning for your answer.

2. You respond to the scene of a domestic homicide that has occurred in a private dwelling house. The husband reported to the dispatcher that he killed his wife as she was intending to separate and take the couple's children with her. The man and his children are waiting for you outside the house when you arrive. Paramedics have taken the wife to the hospital just prior to your arrival. You place him under arrest for the murder of his wife while other police officers attend to the children. The husband tells you the weapon he used was a firearm that is still inside the house. He further states that he set the house on fire when he saw the red emergency lights turn the corner to his street and that by the time you get a warrant, his house and all the evidence will have burned. Do you have any legal right to enter the house without a search warrant? State the reasoning for your answer.

3. You are investigating an armed robbery of a bank that occurred earlier in the day. You have no suspects. A woman telephones your police service and says that her brother was recently released on parole from prison after serving a five year sentence for armed robbery. She states that he has been living at a local boarding house since his release but that this afternoon he and a friend came to her house. Her brother asked her if she could keep some belongings for him in her garage and dropped off a large duffle bag. After they left, the woman looked in the bag and found ski masks, sawed-off shotguns and a bag of money. When she heard news reports of the bank robbery, she realized what her brother had done. You immediately drive to her residence and she gives you the items. You subsequently charge her brother and his accomplice with armed robbery. At his trial, he challenges the evidence, stating that his *Charter* rights were violated by the warrantless seizure of the evidence from his sister's garage. As warrantless searches are *prima facie* unreasonable, what grounds does the Crown have to justify your seizure? Explain the reasoning for your answer. Did the accused's sister have the legal authority to consent to surrendering the items to the police?

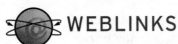
WEBLINKS

www.canlii.org/index_en.html

Canadian Legal Information Institute website. A searchable alphabetical database of federal statutes and associated regulations. Where a federal statute contains search authorities, they will be contained within the statute itself.

http://www.e-laws.gov.on.ca/index.html

Government of Ontario electronic law website. A searchable alphabetical database of Ontario provincial statutes and associated regulations. Where a provincial statute contains search authorities, they will be contained within the statute itself.

http://scc.lexum.umontreal.ca/en/index.html

University of Montreal Faculty of Law, searchable database of Supreme Court of Canada case law decisions.

C h a p t e r 8

Search Warrants

"A requirement of prior [search] authorization, usually in the form of a valid warrant, has been a consistent prerequisite for a valid search and seizure both at common law and under most statutes. Such a requirement puts the onus on the state to demonstrate the superiority of its interest to that of the individual."

Honourable Mr. Justice Dickson, C.J. Hunter v. Southam Inc.,
[1984] 2 S.C.R. 145, 11 D.L.R. (4th) 641, 14 C.C.C. (3d) 97, 1984 CanLII 33 (S.C.C.).[1]

Learning Outcomes

After reading this chapter, students should be able to:

- Compare the relationships between an individual's proprietary interest in various locations or things and the reasonable expectations of privacy respective to them.

- Explain the six warrantless search authorities that, if absent, require a police officer to obtain a warrant prior to conducting a search.

- Describe the process of setting out reasonable grounds for belief to obtain a search warrant and the permissibility of using hearsay information of third parties.

- List several common types of defects that, if contained on the face of a search warrant, could render the entire warrant invalid.

- Describe the different ways of proving the credibility (truth) and reliability (accuracy) of a confidential informant when drafting a search warrant.

- Explain the rationale for a police officer's duty to include facts in a search warrant information when those facts contradict the other known facts of a case.

---

[1] www.canlii.org/ca/cas/scc/1984/1984scc10017.html Retrieved: March 17, 2007.

191

8.1   SEARCH WARRANTS

A police officer's statutory and common law powers of search and seizure are some of the most powerful investigative tools that they have at their disposal. A properly obtained search warrant grants law enforcement officers and non-peace officers who might be required to assist them, the authority to enter onto private property and search for and seize specific items that will afford evidence with respect to the commission of offences.

In Chapter 7, we examined the various instances in which police officers are authorized to conduct searches for evidence without a search warrant. Unless a search is sanctioned by a certain warrantless common law or statute law authority, every search, to be considered lawful, must be pre-authorized by a justice (a justice of the peace or a judge) in the form of a search warrant. In this chapter, we will examine situations in which police officers commonly use search warrants to search for evidence of criminal activity or to prevent the commission of offences.

First though, imagine for a moment that you are at home, enjoying a peaceful evening in the company of friends or family. Without warning, a group of uniformed men and women arrives at your door. The officer in charge informs you that they are in possession of a court order that allows them to enter your home to search for a particular item or items in relation to a criminal act they are investigating.

Despite your objections, in the face of their legal authority you are powerless to refuse them entry. You watch in disbelief as they invade the very place where, until this point, you felt the safest. You helplessly look on as they systematically rummage through every room in your residence, examining your most personal belongings. As they continue searching, your liberty may be restricted – you are not free to come and go as you wish. You are virtually a prisoner in your own home.

Your children, fearful of the armed strangers who now control your family's home, are upset and crying. Your life-partner is enraged at whatever action, real or imagined, you have committed to bring this most unwelcome invasion of your family's normal evening routine.

When the intruders are finished their search, your house is in complete turmoil and disarray. The officer in charge informs you that a variety of your possessions have been seized as evidence. At best, you are permitted to remain in your house after they leave and are forced to deal with your irate family. At worst, you are placed under arrest, manacled, and led off to jail.

My point is this – whether or not the suspect is in fact guilty of any crime, having a group of strangers invade the privacy of their home is, short of being the victim of a violent crime, perhaps the most intrusive act that any private citizen might ever have to endure. The statutory authority granted to police officers to conduct warranted searches of private property is not treated lightly by the courts.

The authority to execute search warrants carries with it a heavy burden of responsibility on the part of those so entrusted, to ensure their actions are both justified and conducted in a reasonable manner. Every investigation leading up to the granting of a search warrant, including the content of the warrant itself, and the circumstances of the search methods used in the execution of the warrant, may be subjected to the highest degree of judicial scrutiny.

If your actions in relation to the execution of a search warrant are found to have been unjustified, you may be criticized, and your professional reputation damaged, perhaps irreparably, to say nothing of the potential for civil liability to you and your police service.

Your evidence could be excluded and your case may be lost. The accused might be acquitted and you will likely suffer some professional embarrassment.

Worse, you may create bad case law that could place further investigative limitations on how every police officer in Canada does their job in the future. Most importantly, you will be placed in the unenviable position of having to explain to the victim of the crime why their case was lost due to mistakes that could have been avoided.

8.2   DO I NEED A SEARCH WARRANT?

"The house of everyone is to him as his castle and fortress, as well for his defense against injury and violence as for his [relaxation]."[2]

Sir Edward Coke (1552–1634),
British jurist, Semayne's Case 1604.

Volumes have been written about this continuously evolving area of criminal law, dealing with police powers of search and seizure. Once again, space constraints preclude us from exhaustively examining every search authority granted to police officers by various statutes. We will focus our examination on situations that are most likely to be encountered during routine enforcement duties. (See Box 8.1.)

You will recall from section 1.13 in the chapter dealing with Sources of Police Powers, that the *Charter of Rights and Freedoms* guarantees every individual in Canada the freedom against unreasonable search and seizure.[3] The primary rule that every police officer must always remember is, that whenever it is practicable to obtain a search warrant, a warrant must be obtained, or the search will be held to be *prima facie* unreasonable (presumed so until contradicted by other evidence).[4]

Specific warrantless search authorities were covered in detail throughout previous sections, including: Search Incident to Arrest (section 7.7), Plain View Seizure Rule (section 7.12), Consent Searches (section 7.9), Abandoned Evidence (section 7.10), and Officer Safety Considerations (section 7.11). Except for these warrantless search authorities, real (physical) evidence may be seized without a warrant only where there is an imminent danger that evidence of an offence will be lost, destroyed or removed[5] (section 7.14, Exigent Circumstances). The reasonableness of a warrantless search conducted under exigent circumstances will be decided on a case-by-case basis depending on the individual circumstances of each case.

Therefore, to be considered lawful, a search must be "reasonable". A reasonable search is defined as one that is:

1. authorized by statute, is reasonable and is carried out in a reasonable manner, or

2. judicially pre-authorized by a justice of the peace or judge, or

3. is covered by one of the warrantless search exceptions described in the previous paragraph.[6]

---

[2]*Semayne v. Gresham*, 5 Co. Rep 91a, 93a, 77 Eng. Rep. 194, 198 (K.B. 1604).

[3]*Canadian Charter of Rights and Freedoms*, Being Part 1 of the *Constitution Act, 1982*, Enacted by the *Canada Act 1982* (U.K.), c. 11, proclaimed in force April 17, 1982, s.8.

[4]*Hunter v. Southam Inc.* (1984), 2 S.C.R. 45, 14 C.C.C. (3d) 97, 11 D.L.R. (4th) 641.

[5]*R. v. Grant* (1993), 84 C.C.C. (3d) 173 (S.C.C.).

[6]*R. v. Collins* (1987), 33 C.C.C. (3d) 1 (S.C.C.).

| BOX 8.1 | **Do I Need a Search Warrant?** |

When you are in a search and seizure situation in which a known or unknown suspect has a proprietary interest or could possibly have a reasonable expectation of privacy, and you are unsure of the legal search requirements, stop and ask yourself, "Do I need a search warrant?" It may be helpful to remember the mnemonic: S. E. P. I. C. O.

S – **Statute** – Is a warrantless search specifically authorized by statute law or by common law?

E – **Exigent circumstances** – Will evidence be lost, destroyed or removed unless you act immediately?

P – **Plain View** – Are you lawfully positioned (legally entitled to be there) when you inadvertently discover incriminating evidence?

I – **Incident to Arrest** – Is it a search incident to a lawful arrest?

C – **Consent** – Has a person having lawful authority to consent to the search done so?

O – **Officer Safety** – Do reasonable officer safety concerns exist? This temporary search authority is rescinded when any legitimate safety concerns end.

If your situation does not fall within one of these previous six exceptions, you most definitely require a warrant. To proceed further without obtaining a search warrant will certainly render any resulting seizure at risk of being excluded. (See Chapter 10, Admissibility of Seized Evidence.)

8.3   REASONABLE EXPECTATION OF PRIVACY

As we have seen, search is a term that is broadly defined and is not confined solely to entry and search of a building or premises – a search may involve looking for evidence inside a motor vehicle, or obtaining documentary information regarding a suspect, or employing an investigative technique in any other situation where the suspect has, or could be held to have a "reasonable expectation of privacy".

The court will apply the concept of "reasonable expectation of privacy" in determining whether or not a particular investigative action constituted a search. If, for example, an individual conceals stolen property in the basement of their house, they are deemed to have a reasonable expectation of privacy to be free from intrusion by the state.

The offender doesn't expect to have the illegal property discovered by the police and used as evidence against them without such an intrusion being pre-justified in the form of a search warrant. The sanctity of a person's home as their "castle and fortress" has been entrenched in western law since *Semayne's Case*, dating back to 1604, and extends the same protection to individuals who carry on illegal activities within the privacy of their homes as it does to law-abiding citizens.

If a reasonable expectation of privacy is deemed to exist, even when a police officer has reasonable grounds to believe that a criminal offence, such as counterfeiting or drug trafficking is occurring within a location, absent emergency circumstances that require immediate action, there is no legal authority to enter into the location to seize the evidence. To enter without a warrant would constitute a trespass and an unlawful search. (See also Box 8.2.)

Does an accused person have a similar reasonable expectation that their financial information will be kept confidential at the bank or financial institution where they conduct business? If you feel that you have that expectation regarding your financial affairs

---

BOX 8.2	**Investigative Relevance**

Reasonable expetation of privacy is closely associated with – but not restricted to – the proprietary interest that an individual has in a given location or thing. A person who owns their home has an obvious proprietary interest in it, due to their ownership of the premises. All members of a family would have a proprietary interest in their home, even though the actual title of the property might be in the name of a single individual. A tenant who rents an apartment or a room within a dwelling house has no less a reasonable expectation of privacy (in the portion of the structure or dwelling they rent) than does an owner in the property they own outright.

Proprietary interest, therefore, doesn't require official standing, in the form of actual proof of title or ownership, in the thing or the location. Even though a tenant doesn't own the premises they rent, the rent they pay to their landlord gives them certain rights at law, including a proprietary interest in the structure, or the portion(s) of it that they rent.

A suspect who conceals physical evidence of a break and enter inside a rented public storage facility will be held to have a reasonable expectation of privacy due to their temporary proprietary interest in that rental unit. The rental unit is theirs for the period of the rental agreement. An offender who commits a murder in the victim's residence, however, has no such expectation of privacy, unless the suspect also resides at that location, as in the case of a spouse, relative or tenant.

An offender who hides bloody clothing, or a weapon used in a violent crime at the residence of a relative, has no reasonable expectation of privacy if the relative consents to the seizure of the evidence by the police – providing that the offender does not also rent or live there. By the same reasoning, no offender can claim any reasonable expectation of privacy if they were to conceal evidence in a public place, such as a landfill site, a roadside ditch, a field or a city park, as the evidence could be discovered at any time by anyone, including the police.

An armed robber has no expectation of privacy in their electronically recorded image if they are recorded on video while committing a robbery of a convenience store. The preceding examples are all situations in which the suspect has no proprietary interest in the location and can therefore have no reasonable expectation of privacy.

Reasonable expectation of privacy extends to far more than just an individual's residence or rented locations and also includes an individual's personal property. The automotive garage that makes repairs to your car may place a lien on it until their services have been paid for. The mechanic's lien gives them a special proprietary interest at law even though they do not have title to the property in question.

An individual's reasonable expectation of privacy may be lower at some times than at others. A person may have a lesser expectation of privacy regarding a shed, their automobile, or their personal information than they have in relation to their residence. Once a reasonable expectation of privacy has been established, however, a search warrant of some sort will be deemed to be necessary, if it is feasible to obtain one.

There are many times, such as in unknown suspect cases, when the issues of proprietary interest and reasonable expectation of privacy are vague. If a suspect might possibly have a reasonable expectation of privacy in an item to be seized, or in the building, place or receptacle to be searched, or if the proprietary interest of the suspect isn't known or isn't clear to you at the time of your investigation, don't take any chances. When in doubt, always err on the side of caution and obtain a warrant, provided that it is practicable to do so.

at your bank – so would a suspect or an accused person have a similar expectation. The court will apply the objective standard to determine whether the "reasonable person" would claim that the use of any investigative technique was so intrusive that it should have been pre-authorized by a judicial official.

8.4 SEARCH WARRANTS – S. 487(1) *CRIMINAL CODE*

Our society places a high value on the rights of the individual and at the same time recognizes that there are occasions when the rights of society – including the right to effective law enforcement – sometimes supercede the rights of the individual. One of the ways in which societal rights are exerted over individual rights is in the granting of powers of search and seizure to the law enforcement agents of the state. To ensure that individual rights are protected, our criminal justice system oversees the actions of law enforcement agencies with a view to providing fairness and guarding against over-zealous law enforcement that might, intentionally or inadvertently, violate the rights of the individual.

The search warrant provisions of section 487(1) *Criminal Code* are the most commonly used by investigators for obtaining judicial authorization to enter and search any building, place or receptacle for evidence of crimes. Evidence may be seized in relation to an offence that has been committed or an offence that is suspected to have been committed. This section is can also be used to seize something that on reasonable grounds is intended to be used to commit an offence for which the person may be arrested without warrant. A section 487(1) search warrant may also authorize the seizure of offence-related property as defined in section 2 of the *Criminal Code*.[7]

The seizure of evidence authorized by section 487(1) *Criminal Code* is contemplated as real or physical evidence, meaning tangible objects, but may also include searching a computer system for data and seizing a print-out of the data.[8] Section 487 search warrants are issued in Form 5 *Criminal Code* and are directed either to an individual or to police officers within a judicial district or province.

A properly obtained search warrant grants law enforcement officers, and any person assisting them, the authority to enter onto private property and search for and seize specific items that will afford evidence with respect to acts or omissions that are prohibited by law.

The requirement of judicial pre-authorization recognizes that societal interests, including enforcement of laws and apprehension of offenders, on occasion outweigh the rights of the individual, but places the responsibility on the Crown to demonstrate that the need to enforce the law and to gather evidence does outweigh the individual's rights. Prior judicial authorization, in the form of a search warrant, will be granted only when credibly-based probability, (reasonable grounds) replaces suspicion.

At times a search warrant may be required for a building, receptacle or place in a different territorial division (province), outside the jurisdiction of the issuing justice. For example, a search warrant for a dwelling house in Winnipeg, Manitoba may be issued by

---

[7]*Criminal Code*, R.S. 1985 c. C-46, s. 487(1).

[8]*Criminal Code*, R.S. 1985 c. C-46, s. 487(2.1).

a justice in Ontario, Saskatchewan or Alberta. A justice in any province may issue a search warrant for a location in a different territorial division in Canada, but it must first be endorsed for execution by a justice (see Form 28 *Criminal Code*) in the territorial division where the building, receptacle or place is situated prior to being executed.[9]

Canadian police officers (other than members of the Royal Canadian Mounted Police) are peace officers only within the province for which they were appointed. As such, municipal and provincial police officers do not have peace officer status in any other province. Although they may be named in a search warrant to be executed in a different province, it is strongly recommended that they be accompanied by one or more peace officers, as required, from the jurisdiction where the search warrant is to be executed.

Not only does professional courtesy dictate the involvement of local police officers, it is only good sense, considering that resistance may be encountered and use of force may be required during the execution of the warrant. This is something persons without peace officer status would not be authorized to carry out, unless they are assisting an actual peace officer.

8.5 INFORMATION TO OBTAIN A SEARCH WARRANT

The first step in obtaining a search warrant is to complete an Information to Obtain a Search Warrant (information) in Form 1 *Criminal Code*. The information is a separate document that serves as a written application to support the issuance of the actual search warrant. The information identifies the person applying for the warrant, referred to as the informant or affiant, and specifies the building, receptacle or place to be searched, the things to be searched for, and the specific offences under investigation for which the things to be searched for will afford evidence.

The Information to Obtain should be organized in a structured format containing the following reasonable grounds for belief:

1. that an offence has been committed,

2. that the things to be seized will afford evidence of the offence,

3. that the things to be seized are at the place to be searched.

The information sets out the informant's reasonable grounds for belief that the issuance of a search warrant is justified by establishing the nexus (a link or a connection) between the things to be searched for, the place, and the offence(s) under investigation.[10] The facts contained in the information to obtain the search warrant are sworn under oath or are solemnly affirmed before a justice who, if satisfied that is in the public interest to do so, may then grant the search warrant. These issues will be explained in further detail in following sections. (See also Figure 8.1.)

The issuance of a search warrant takes place in an *ex parte* hearing that is conducted outside the presence of the suspect or accused. Neither the suspect, nor owner of the item to be seized, nor occupier of the building, place or receptacle to be searched, has

---

[9]*Criminal Code*, R.S. 1985 c. C-46, s. 487(2).

[10]*Criminal Code*, R.S. 1985 c. C-46, s. 487(1).

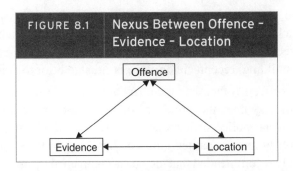

FIGURE 8.1 | Nexus Between Offence – Evidence – Location

any legal right to object to the procedure or to cross-examine the informant. The Canadian criminal justice system requires that a person who pre-authorizes a search be completely neutral and impartial in order to assess the sufficiency and reliability of the reasonable grounds upon which the application for the search is based.

The standard of reasonable grounds, which must be met by the informant, is only one of "reasonable probability". The grounds for belief must be credible and reasonable, and must exceed mere suspicion. As we have seen, reasonable grounds is a far lower standard than proof beyond a reasonable doubt, which is necessary to convict an accused person. As there is no universal definition of reasonable probability, each search warrant information will be judged in court on its individual merits, having regard to all the circumstances.

A search warrant information must be a stand alone document and must comply with the "four corners rule", meaning that all relevant information upon which the warrant may be issued must be contained within the four corners of the pages of the sworn document itself, including appendices. The search warrant affiant is not permitted to add oral facts to persuade a reluctant justice to issue a warrant. Nor is the issuing justice permitted to ask questions or cross-examine the affiant on the written information.[11] (Hill 1999)

8.6 PARTICULARS OF THE OFFENCE

As you will be searching for evidence of an offence, including anything obtained by or used in the commission of the offence, it is necessary to specify the offence(s) for which you believe the things to be seized will provide evidence. In the early stages of an investigation, all of the information needed to lay a charge against a suspect may not yet be known. A police officer drafting the search warrant information should include all available data alleging the time, date, and location of the offence, the victim's identity, if known, and at least a general statement of the offence, including the statute and section number.

For example, it is not sufficient merely to allege that the items to be seized will afford evidence with respect to the offence of break, enter and theft. The drafting police officer must provide all available facts about the offence under investigation, as in the following example:

". . . which there are reasonable grounds to believe will afford evidence with respect to the commission of an offence against the *Criminal Code*, namely, the offence of:

---

[11]Fairburn, Michal, "Litigating the Warranted Search: A Practical Overview" in *Search and Seizure: New Developments* (Law Society of Upper Canada, 1998), at pp. 9-10, cited from Hill, *Warranted Searches: A Practical Perspective* (1999) at p. 18.

That Harley MacDavidson, on or about the 24th day of March, 2007, at the City of Barrie, in the Central East Region, did unlawfully break and enter a certain place, to wit: Fly By Night Auto Sales, situated at 1313 Mulberry Lane, Barrie, Ontario and commit the indictable offence of theft, contrary to paragraph 348(1)(e) of the *Criminal Code of Canada*."

The offence(s) under investigation will also dictate the type of search warrant that is required to be obtained. Evidence of drug offences such as possession for the purpose of trafficking, trafficking or cultivation require the completion of a search warrant issued under the authority of the *Controlled Drugs and Substances Act*, while evidence in relation to a *Highway Traffic Act* or *Liquor Licence Act* investigation would require the completion of a *Provincial Offences Act* search warrant.

In more complex cases, when multiple offences are under investigation, it is only necessary to state one or two principal offences. It is not necessary to list all possible charges that could be laid in relation to the matter under investigation. A bank robbery involving the use of firearms would require identifying the substantive offence of armed robbery without the necessity of including each possible firearms offence or secondary offences relating to the use of disguises by the offenders. (Hill et al. 1999)

8.7   BUILDING, RECEPTACLE OR PLACE TO BE SEARCHED

When completing your Information to Obtain a Search Warrant, you must specify the precise address or location of the building, receptacle or place to be searched. The address must be as clear as possible so that an uninvolved fellow officer would know exactly which premises to search. This is especially crucial when dealing with rural addresses, multiple dwellings such as apartment buildings, or multiple structures/compartments within a single location, such as office buildings or rental storage units.[12]

I was once assigned to investigate a murder in a remote area that was unfamiliar to me. A local officer provided me with the lot, rural concession number and township of the address to be searched. Many hours later, we arrived at the location to execute the search warrant, only to discover that the address which I had been provided for the search location was incorrect. This resulted in a delay of several hours while a new search warrant was prepared for the correct address.

A serious error such as an incorrect address on a search warrant will render the entire warrant defective.[13] Had we proceeded further and executed the defective warrant, it would have been the same as conducting a warrantless search, and any evidence seized would have been excluded. The officer's error was an honest one – and we all make mistakes, but it could have been an extremely costly mistake.

My error, as the officer in charge of the investigation, was in relying on unproven information that came from a single source. Following that investigation, I always personally confirmed, to the extent possible, every last detail included in a search warrant before it was presented to a justice.

---

[12] *R. v. Royal American Shows Inc.*, [1975] 6 W.W.R. 571 (Alta. Q.B.).

[13] *R. v. Silvestrone* (1991), 66 C.C.C. (3d) 125 (B.C.C.A.).

The term building, receptacle or place applies to most locations you might ever expect to have to search, with the exception of seizing evidence from a person's body. The taking of bodily samples such as hair or impressions or seizing a bloody bandage worn by a suspect is not covered by s. 487(1) as "a person is not considered to be a 'building, receptacle or a place'."[14] (Hutchinson 1996)

The term "receptacle" refers to locations or things such as lockers in bus depots or airports, suitcases, briefcases, filing cabinets, etc. In addition to dwelling houses and other buildings, the term "place" includes, " . . . places of fixed location, such as offices, shops or gardens, as well as vehicles, vessels and aircraft. It does not include public streets or other public places."[15]

If detached outbuildings, such as garages, sheds, or workshops on a property are also to be searched, they must be separately described, both on the Information to Obtain a Search Warrant and on the face of the warrant itself. Numerous court decisions have held that the guaranteed right to be free from unreasonable search and seizure extends equally to dwelling houses and to structures other than dwelling houses.[16]

General warrants are now available to permit the seizure of bodily DNA samples[17] and for "handprints, fingerprints, footprint, foot impression, teeth impression or other print or impression of the body or any part of the body . . ."[18] as such seizures are not authorized by s. 487(1) and previous warrantless searches for impression evidence were held to constitute *Charter* violations. (See General Warrants – Chapter 9.)

8.8 DESCRIPTION OF THINGS TO BE SEIZED

When listing the things to be seized, they must be described in as much detail as possible. A fellow officer with no knowledge of the investigation should be able to identify all the listed items to be seized from their description on the search warrant, even if the investigating officer is not present. If applicable, every possible detail such as make, model, colour, size, serial number or other physical characteristics must be included to distinguish the items to be seized from similar items. If only class characteristics, such as make, colour and size are available, describe the item or class of items to be seized as precisely as possible.

Describing things to be seized can be a simple task when all of the details of the item are known, such as a stolen motor vehicle or television set, for which the owner can provide model numbers and serial numbers, etc. It can be somewhat more difficult, such as in the case of a homicide investigation, where investigators don't always know what it is they are searching for – sometimes until they find it – often before an autopsy has been conducted.(See also Box 8.3.)

An investigator must utilize common sense and include items that, from experience, are routinely encountered at a specific type of crime scene and allow "reasonable probability"

---

[14]*R. v. Mutch* (1986), 26 C.C.C. (3d) 477 (Sask. Q.B.); *R. v. Legere* (1988), 43 C.C.C. (3d) 502 (N.B.C.A.) *R. v. Miller* (1987), 38 C.C.C. (3d) 252 (Ont. C.A.); *Laporte v. R.* (1972) 8 C.C.C. (2d) 343 (Que. Mun. Ct.).

[15]*R. v. Rao* (1984), 40 C.R. (3d) 1, 46 O.R. (2d) 80, 12 C.C.C. (3d) 97, 4 O.A.C. 162, 9 D.L.R. (4th) 542, 10 C.R.R. 275, (Ont. C.A.).

[16]*R. v. Laplante* (1987), 48 D.L.R. (4th) 615, 40 C.C.C. (3d) 63, [1988] 33 C.R.R. 15, 59 Sask. R. 251, CanLII 209 (Sask. C.A.).

[17]*Criminal Code*, R.S. 1985 c. C-46, s. 487.05(1).

[18]*Criminal Code*, R.S. 1985 c. C-46, s. 487.092(1).

to be inferred that those items will also be located at the scene to be searched. Stating what investigative techniques, including videotaping as a form of electronic note taking, are anticipated to be employed in the search of a crime scene, if known, will also indicate good faith on the part of the investigators.

BOX 8.3	Proper Investigative Procedure

Always describe every possible item that can reasonably be included in your search warrant information. If you are investigating the theft of ten television sets in crates that were stolen from a warehouse, it would be reasonable to suspect that between the time of the theft and the time of the search, they might have been removed from their crates. If the television sets were described as "television sets in crates" the investigator will be restricted to searching spaces that are large enough to reasonably conceal a crate.

If, however, the investigator drafting the warrant includes descriptions of the remote controls and the owner's manuals that were also inside the crates, investigators assigned to execute the search warrant may then search much smaller areas that might conceal remote controls and paper manuals. If the stolen crates bore shipping labels at the time of the theft, I would also include them on the warrant in the event that the suspect(s) had removed them from the crates in order to prevent them from being identified.

The nature of the articles to be seized will also determine the type of the search warrant required. Section 487(1) *Criminal Code* search warrants only authorize the seizure of tangible things. Intangible items, such as printouts of data including billing information, and the authority to conduct investigative techniques that do not involve seizure of things, will require the issuance of a general search warrant under s. 487.01(1) *CC*, which will be examined in Chapter 9.

8.9 "BASKET CLAUSES" AND "FISHING EXPEDITIONS"

If evidence to be sought is in the form of documents, it may be necessary to include a descriptive clause to describe the groups or categories of documents that are targeted, to limit the discretion of searchers to seize unauthorized documents within the premises. For example, "advertising agreements, invoices, contracts, bank statements, cancelled cheques, billing statements and correspondence relating to the provision of general contracting and home renovation services by John Smith during the months of January to December 2006."

Police officers who draft search warrant applications must refrain, however, from using open-ended "basket clauses" that are vague and are designed to open the door to seize any possible items, incriminating or not. Clauses such as, "and any other evidence of any type", or "and any other documents",[19] if challenged, will be perceived as a "fishing expedition" indicating that the affiant really didn't have reasonable grounds to believe that form of evidence in relation to the offence could be found at the premises to be searched. (Hill 1999)

---

[19]*R. v. PSI Mind Development Limited et al.* (1977), 33 C.C.C. (2d) 263 (Ont H.C.).

8.10 REASONABLE GROUNDS FOR BELIEF

Drafting the search warrant information is a painstaking task if it is to be done well. This is especially true when it comes to setting out the informant's grounds for believing that the things to be seized are in the building, receptacle or place to be searched, and why they will afford evidence with respect to the offence(s) under investigation. Fastidious attention to detail is required to produce a search warrant that will withstand the test of the scrutiny it will undergo in court if it is challenged by the defence.

A search warrant information is a multi-page document that can reach several volumes in length in complex high-profile investigations. Through training and practice, a police officer will become experienced in recognizing the facts of a case that must be included in an Information to Obtain a Search Warrant. Search warrant preparation is an art, and the few police officers who make the effort to become proficient in the drafting of warrants and the supporting applications are valuable members of their police service who enjoy a certain status as the result of their expertise.

At the risk of appearing to be repetitive, we should review the definition of reasonable grounds. After all, it will be impossible to convince a court that you had reasonable grounds to obtain a search warrant if you can't articulate what reasonable grounds are or what your reasonable grounds for belief were. No legitimate discussion of search warrants would be complete without explaining the concept of reasonable grounds, which is:

> A set of facts or circumstances which, if true, would lead an ordinary, prudent, cautious person to have a strong belief, which exceeds mere suspicion.

When does suspicion become reasonable grounds? First and partly, when the fact(s) or circumstance(s) result in a strong subjective belief in the truth of the fact in the mind of the informant, such as, that the person committed the offence or that the stolen property is in a particular house. Second, and more importantly, would the facts or circumstances cause an independent, impartial, prudent, cautious individual, standing in the officer's shoes, to have a similar belief? If so, you now have reasonable grounds.

An informant's reasonable grounds for belief should set out the known history of the events of the investigation, including any that they may not have had direct involvement in. Reasonable grounds may be comprised of any or all of the following:

1. Direct evidence including witness interviews, or admissions or confessions of suspects, or evidence of confidential police informers;

2. Real (physical evidence) forensic analysis, previous searches; and

3. Circumstantial evidence, including a logical analysis of the circumstances of the case that tend to imply one or more facts and that are inconsistent with any other logical conclusion. Circumstantial evidence might include things such as fingerprints or other impression evidence, or the background of the suspect regarding previous similar criminal activity. Despite its bad reputation in the media, courts place the same weight on circumstantial evidence as on other types of evidence.

8.10.1 Sourcing Reasonable Grounds for Belief

A police officer who drafts a search warrant information must state precisely how and when they obtained their reasonable grounds to justify the search. It is not sufficient to merely state, "My investigation has revealed that a blue car was seen leaving the crime scene." The informant must state how they obtained this information in order to enable the justice who considers the application for the search warrant to assess the credibility of the information that forms the basis of the application.

In all cases, the facts that make up an officer's reasonable grounds for belief should be "sourced", meaning that every fact has to be attributed to the source from whom it was received. The information should be clearly articulated as to how and when each particular source came to know the information that is attributed to them and whether or not the information is deemed to be reliable.

While it may be implied that police officers had communication with other police officers, civilian witnesses, and informants, it is strongly recommended that each investigative source be identified, rather than to state the reasonable grounds in the form of an unsourced narrative. Failing to source each piece of information invites concerns regarding disclosure and the validity of the grounds. (Hill et al. 1999)

For example, "On Tuesday, February 08, 2007, the informant (or another police officer) personally interviewed Harry Johnson, Age 47, of 123 Smith Street, Podunck, Ontario. Mr. Johnson provided the informant with a signed statement indicating that at approximately 12:30 a.m., Feb. 8, 2007, he observed a late model blue car, make, model and licence number unknown, leaving the location of the offence at a high rate of speed in a southbound direction on Memorial Avenue." The witness' information, if accepted by the informant as credible (truthful) may now form part of the informant's reasonable grounds for belief.

All available grounds for belief must be truthfully and fairly disclosed in the information, not just those grounds that support the issuance of the search warrant. If information contained in the warrant is no longer current, it should be identified as such so that the justice may evaluate the information fairly. If a discrepancy exists between two facts, as is often the case during an investigation, both should be included in the information to obtain the warrant – not just those facts that favour the issuing of the search warrant.

In a 2005 Ontario Court of Appeals decision, Mr. Justice M. Rosenberg J.A. reinforced the Supreme Court of Canada's previous description of the responsibility of a police officer to include all reliable information when forming their reasonable grounds:

> "The appellant rightly relies upon what the Supreme Court said in Chartier v. Quebec (Attorney General) (1979), 48 C.C.C. (2d) 34 (S.C.C.) at 56, where the court explained the duty on a police officer in these terms:

> 'For a peace officer to have reasonable and probable grounds for believing in someone's guilt, his belief must take into account all the information available to him. He is entitled to disregard only what he has good reason for believing is not reliable.'"[20]

Evidence seized during a search may be subsequently declared inadmissible on account of any wilful non-disclosure or misrepresentation of the true facts of an investigation, unless there are sufficient remaining grounds upon which the warrant may survive

---

[20]*R. v. Backhouse* (2005), 194 C.C.C. (3d) 1, 127 C.R.R. (2d) 1, 28 C.R. (6th) 31, 195 O.A.C. 80, CanLII 4937 (Ont C.A.).

without it.[21] If incriminating evidence given by a witness is unreliable, or if their evidence disagrees with evidence of another source, you must include these details in your search warrant information.

Wilful non-disclosure of evidence has resulted in several high-profile miscarriages of justice, such as in the cases of David Milgaard, Guy Paul Morin, Thomas Sophonow and more recently, in the 2005 exoneration of James Driskell in relation to the 1990 murder of Perry Dean Harder. The public interest and your long-term credibility in the eyes of your local judiciary are far more valuable than the granting of a single search warrant. (Sherriff 1997)

8.10.2 Use of Hearsay Evidence in Reasonable Grounds

Hearsay evidence is the oral testimony of a witness that is not as the result of their direct knowledge. Hearsay is third person in nature, meaning that the witness hears something spoken by another person and then repeats it.

Hearsay evidence, with certain exceptions, is generally held to be inadmissible in court as the truthfulness (reliability) of the evidence cannot be assessed by the court. Neither does hearsay evidence present the accused with the opportunity to confront or cross-examine their accuser.

Hearsay information that cannot be used as evidence in court is allowable in a search warrant information but must be corroborated, or be otherwise shown to be reliable. Hearsay information may be obtained from a fellow police officer or from a witness or a confidential informer.

8.11   DISCLOSURE OF PREVIOUS APPLICATIONS

Both common law and the requirements of constitutional reasonableness oblige the informant (affiant) of a search warrant application to disclose any instances of previously refused applications for search warrants arising out of identical circumstances. This is a statutory requirement for obtaining telewarrants[22] (see Chapter 9), but is no less expected for any other type of search warrant application. The non-disclosure of previous search warrant applications could be fatal to the search if challenged in court. (Hill et al 1999)

Such a practice is intended to prevent "J.P. shopping" by police officers who, once refused a search warrant, attempt to find another justice who may be less stringent, or more forgiving. If you are refused a search warrant, it is highly recommended that where practicable, any successive applications for an identical warrant be made to the justice who refused the previous application. If that justice is unavailable, you must disclose the previous unsuccessful application and detail any new evidence which might now justify the issuance of the search warrant.

---

[21]*R. v. Bisson* (1994), 94 C.C.C. (3d) 94 S.C.C.

[22]*Criminal Code*, R.S. 1985, c. C-46, s. 487.1(4)(d).

8.12 USE OF CONFIDENTIAL POLICE INFORMANTS

Confidential police informants, alternatively called informers, are not always criminals or criminal associates, although they quite often are. An informant may be a person of any age, gender, walk of life or socio-economic standing. They can be upstanding members of the community – the spouses, intimate partners, sons, daughters, parents, relatives, associates, employers, employees, co-workers, business partners, landlords, or neighbours of the person(s) about whom they divulge their information.

In some cases, police officers are approached by someone with whom they have had past dealings, perhaps someone who was given a "break" on a traffic ticket, or someone who was charged with an offence but was treated fairly and with dignity. Either way, the officer will have made an impression upon this person and when they have information regarding criminal activity, the informant may seek out the officer in an attempt to repay the favour with information regarding criminal activity.

A confidential informer discloses information to the police on the condition of anonymity in order to protect their identity. The most important thing informants have in common is their need for confidentiality to ensure that those about whom they provide information never learn of their co-operation and seek revenge against them. Some informers do eventually elect to waive the Crown (police informer) privilege and become a witness and testify in subsequent judicial proceedings. That decision is their sole responsibility to make.

The confidential police informer who provides information should, of course, only be referred to in your investigative notes or an Information to Obtain a Search Warrant as an unnamed confidential informer, or by an assigned informant number. The informer's reliability must also be "qualified" either on the basis of previous successful informant activity, or by way of independent corroboration of their information.

When using information provided by a confidential informer, police officers should attempt to assess the motivation of the informer in supplying the information. Some informers divulge information to the police and do not seek consideration or compensation. The informer may be a law-abiding person acting out of a sense of civic duty. Confidential informers can be motivated by any of the following reasons:

- Self-Interest (For self or for others)
- Financial reward
- Pre-trial release from custody on bail or other form of conditional release
- Withdrawal or dismissal of outstanding criminal charge(s)
- Reduction of sentence or other criminal sanction, including probation conditions or parole
- Choice of location to serve an outstanding custodial sentence
- Elimination of rivals or unwanted criminal activities
- Revenge
- Self-Preservation
- Fear of harm from others

- Threat of arrest and/or criminal charges
- Threat of incarceration
- Witness protection program

Other Possible Motivational Factors

- Desire to go straight
- Guilty conscience
- Genuine desire to assist the police

8.12.1 Exclusivity of Information

If the information is exclusively known by the informant, so that to act on the information would identify the informant, it should be considered as intelligence information and not be used in an Information to Obtain a Search Warrant to avoid compromising the informant's identity. For example, an offender confesses to a close friend that he committed a theft. If the informant is the only person the offender confessed to, by acting on the exclusively known information, the offender will automatically know who was responsible for informing against them.

A cunning offender who suspects an individual of informing might even test the person by supplying them with exclusive (but false) information in order to see if the fabricated information becomes known to the authorities. In the case of Crime Stoppers© tipsters, who always remain anonymous, even the time and date of the call placed by the informant to the police might suggest to a criminal the identity of the informer.

The desire to use even exclusive information increases with the severity of the crime under investigation; however, any potential danger to the informant that might result from using the information must outweigh the benefit of using exclusively known information. An informant who remains adamant that they wish to remain confidential and not testify as a witness must be accorded the confidentiality they seek.

8.13 WITNESS/INFORMANT CREDIBILITY

If a witness or an informant relates third-party information, that is, information they obtained from someone else, they will have no way of knowing whether or not the information they are providing is, in fact, credible (true). The investigator must then assess the credibility of the witness or informant (was the individual, in fact, told the information?) and whether or not the information itself is reliable (is what the informant related accurate?).

Always be aware of any opportunities to independently corroborate what any witness or informant has told you. Some witnesses and informants are very good, while others are deceitful and manipulative. I once had an informant, who was an inmate in a jail, give me detailed information about being asked to arrange a contract murder for another inmate. The informant had an extensive history of informant activity on murders and conspiracies to commit murder and was fond of dropping the name of a now deceased, well-known senior investigator. It immediately struck me as odd that this person could be in the "right place" to become involved in so many similar cases – so many times.

I was never able to corroborate a single piece of information that the informant told me, and one day he said he had been visited at the jail by a female associate of the suspect who displayed a large "flash roll" of money. A cursory examination of the inmate visitor's register revealed the informant hadn't had any visitors on that date. I stopped accepting calls from that informant and, to this day, have serious reservations regarding the reliability of any previous information he provided to other investigators.

8.14   WITNESS/INFORMANT RELIABILITY

If information received from a witness or confidential informant is to be used as a basis for reasonable grounds for an arrest, criminal charge, search warrant, or application to intercept private communications, the witness or informant, as the case may be, must be qualified as to their reliability. One method of indicating a witness/informant's reliability is by confirming the accuracy of the information by corroborating information from another investigative source, meaning that the individual must be truthful because of independent corroboration identical to what the informant stated. If information supplied by a confidential informant cannot be independently corroborated, the only other way to qualify the informant's reliability is on the basis of previous successful informant activity, either for you, another officer within your police service, or for any other police service.

If you have used the same informant on a previous occasion(s), state in your report that "the informant has previously (state month and year) provided me (or another police officer) with information that successfully resulted in an arrest and prosecution for (state offence) or that resulted in the seizure of (state dollar amount) worth of stolen property/drugs, etc., and resulted in a successful prosecution (state name of accused) for (state offence and sentence)". Reliability of an anonymous repeat Crime Stoppers© informant, whose identity is known to you only as an informant code number, may be established in the same manner by relating the details of previous successes achieved as a result of information provided by them.

If the informant is not previously known to you, simply ask the informant for details of any past informant activity they may have had where information they previously provided was successfully acted upon. Obtain the investigating officer's name and police service and contact them for the details of the previous case, including an opinion as to the informant's reliability on any such previous occasions.

Credible information, that is, information that can be corroborated, that is received from an informant of unproven reliability, meaning that the informant has never previously provided information, may still be used because the corroboration establishes the credibility of the information. While an unproven informant is not necessarily qualified, corroborated information can still be acted upon and if successful, used as a basis to prove the reliability of the informant on future occasions.

8.15   CURRENCY OF THE INFORMATION

Another important consideration in acting on witness/informant information is the timeliness or currency of the information provided. If, for example, the witness or informant states that they observed stolen television sets in a suspect's garage six months previously, would it be reasonable to assume that the television sets are still there now? I suggest that it would be highly improbable and therefore not reasonable to act upon.

While the outdated nature of the information might keep it in the category of intelligence information, it might be possible to request the informant re-establish, through personal knowledge, whether or not the stolen appliances are still in the same location, if doing so and acting on the new information would not compromise them in any way. Taking an active role in a police investigation can have the effect of changing the status of a confidential informer to that of an **agent provocateur**. Agents do not enjoy the same Crown (police informer) privilege and may be identified in court even if they do not testify.

Always establish when and how the information first became known to the informant and accurately document when you first became aware of the information.

A sample of a seven-page Information to Obtain a Search Warrant and a four-page Search Warrant for a fictitious case has been included in the Appendices near the end of this textbook.

8.16   DECEPTIVE INFORMANTS

Informants have been known to provide horribly false information regarding crimes and suspects. Mild cases may result from an informant's honest but mistaken belief or mere speculation regarding certain facts. Once you are aware that an informant has lied, you must immediately attempt to ascertain if the false information was provided in error or if it was intentionally provided by the informant.

Informants have been known to exaggerate details for effect to make themselves appear more knowledgeable, or to exaggerate their status in the criminal community. Criminals and criminal-types may attempt to mislead and deceive a police officer to divert suspicion away from themselves, to avoid prosecution for offences, or in an attempt to improve their situation in jail, to receive bail or parole considerations, for monetary considerations, or even for the mere sport of "putting one over" on the police.

If you can prove than an informant has intentionally lied to you, you must consider terminating all dealings with the informant and, if justified, immediately conclude the police-informant relationship.

8.17   THE "IN-CUSTODY INFORMER" ("JAILHOUSE INFORMANTS")

The in-custody informer is, "someone who allegedly receives one or more statements from an accused, while both are in [police] custody [or in a correctional institution], and where the statement[s] relate to an offence(s) that occurred outside of the custodial institution. [The prosecution must intend to call the in-custody informer as a witness in a judicial proceeding.]"[23]

The concept of jailhouse informants is not new by any means, but In-Custody Informer is a recent designation in Ontario that is reserved solely for informants who,

---

[23]Ministry of Community Safety and Correctional Services Ontario Major Case Management (MCM) Manual, (Oct 1, 2004) p. 9, and Ministry of the Attorney General Crown Policy Manual 1-2 "In-Custody Informers", dated November 13, 1997, (Appendix "L") The Commission on Proceedings Involving Guy Paul Morin, Vol. II, pp. 1350-1355.

while in custody, including pre-trial custody or while under sentence, divulge information about crimes. Their information generally includes alleged admissions or confessions from other inmates relating to offences that occurred outside of the custodial institution. The in-custody informer is more than an ordinary informant as, to "earn" this status, the Crown Attorney must intend to call the in-custody informer as a witness to testify in a court proceeding. Therefore the in-custody informer is a witness who must waive the usual "Crown (police-informer) privilege" before being identified and giving testimony.

This official designation does not apply to incarcerated individuals who contact the police, or are recruited by the police to provide information regarding an accused who was not, at anytime, in custody with the informer regarding an offence that occurred outside of the custodial institution. Neither does the designation apply to an individual who, while in custody, provides information regarding an offence that occurred inside the custodial institution. Yet many of the same considerations and dangers apply as with in-custody informers when using their information to form reasonable grounds.

The danger with in-custody informers and jailhouse informants, such as a prisoner who informs on a suspect who is out of custody, for an offence that occurred either in or outside of jail, is that they are almost exclusively motivated by self-interest and are easily able to fabricate inculpatory evidence. Informants who are in custody can also be vulnerable to pressure, in the form of threats or other coercive methods, by unscrupulous investigators bent on solving a case – at any cost. Either scenario provides a recipe for a potential miscarriage of justice.

Many examples exist of persons being convicted and falsely imprisoned for crimes based on the false evidence of accomplices or cell-mates who were threatened either with additional charges or heavier sentences if they did not "cooperate". Other jailhouse informants willingly fabricate false evidence in an attempt to gain consideration such as having charges withdrawn, or receiving a lighter sentence, or early parole, etc.

Investigators must always remain vigilant about inadvertently divulging the facts of a case when dealing with in-custody informers and "jailhouse informants". A shrewd and manipulative inmate knows that their value as an informant or witness depends on their ability to match their story with the "official version" of the crime. Deceptive informants will be quick to pick up any fact available to them and incorporate it into their story.

For an informant's protection, whether the informant is an in-custody informer or merely an informant who is in custody, it may not be practicable to interview them inside the correctional facility, especially if the interview is to be videotaped. In such cases, it is necessary to remove a prisoner from the correctional facility and transport them to a secure location to conduct the interview.

It will first be necessary to obtain an order from a provincial court judge or a judge of a superior court for the release of the prisoner for the purpose of assisting a specified peace officer in the execution of their duty for a specified period of time. It must be noted that an application made by a prosecutor to a judge for an order for the release of a prisoner must include the written consent of the prisoner.[24] (See the following Case Study in Box 8.4.)

---

[24]*Criminal Code*, R.S. 1985, c. C-46, s. 527(7).

BOX 8.4	Case Study: Armed Robbery

You are assigned to investigate the armed robbery that occurred at a credit union on April 5, 2007. The robbery was committed by a lone male robber, wearing a black ski mask and armed with a black semi-automatic handgun. The robber handed a teller a hold-up note and received $5 000 in a white canvas deposit bag. The robber was seen to make his getaway in a black pickup truck. You are aware that a federal parolee, who has served time for armed robbery, took up residence in your city two weeks before the robbery.

The parolee fits the general physical characteristics provided by witnesses to the robbery. You might suspect that the parolee might be responsible for the armed robbery and your suspicion may be well-founded, however, your suspicion does not, at this time, amount to reasonable grounds.

You conduct inquiries with the subject's parole officer and learn that, since his release from custody, the parolee has resided with his brother. You query provincial vehicle registration records and learn that the suspect's brother owns a black pickup truck similar to the description of the get-away vehicle reported by witnesses. You and other officers conduct surveillance and observe the parolee leaving and returning to the brother's residence several times each day, driving the brother's black pickup truck.

You receive reliable information from a confidential informer who indicates that the parolee was talking about planning to commit an armed robbery at an unspecified location only two days prior to the credit union robbery. Your informer states that the suspect also inquired where he could obtain a handgun and ammunition. Following the robbery, the suspect was observed by the informer and others in a bar spending large amounts of money on food and liquor when only two days before, he was borrowing money.

You make inquiries with the police agency that convicted him of his previous robbery and learn that the wording of the hold-up note in the previous robbery was identical to the note passed in the credit union robbery. Handwriting comparison between the two notes cannot be completed for several weeks. Immersing the recent credit union hold-up note in a ninhydrin solution has, however, developed a latent fingerprint impression, which when submitted to AFIS (Automated Fingerprint Identification System) is positively identified as belonging to the parolee.

When viewed collectively, all of this information should be more than sufficient to meet the standard of "reasonable probability". A section 487(1) *Criminal Code* search warrant should be obtained to search the brother's/suspect's joint residence, including the pickup truck for:

1) the stolen money identified by amount, denomination and serial numbers if available

2) the white canvas bank deposit bag

3) the black ski mask and any other clothing similar to that which was described by the witnesses

4) the handgun and ammunition

5) any writing material including pens, note pads, etc., that may have been used to write the hold-up note or practice drafts of the hold-up note

What are the relevant facts of the case that would establish a nexus (a link or connection) between the items to be searched for and the locations to be searched?

What is the rationale that if the items to be searched for are located, they will provide evidence with respect to the commission of a criminal offence?

What specific information or documents might be included in the Information to Obtain the search warrant that might tend to establish the reasonable likelihood of the suspect having committed the offence under investigation?

BOX 8.4	(Continued)

Are there any other items to be searched for that might be listed in the Information to Obtain the search warrant?

What piece of information contained in the above scenario, which does not implicate the suspect, must be disclosed in the Information to Obtain the search warrant?

8.18 SEARCH WARRANT EXECUTION

The location of the building, receptacle or place to be searched and the items to be seized and offence(s) under investigation, which are identified in the Information to Obtain the warrant must also appear on the face of the warrant itself. The informant's reasonable grounds for belief are not replicated on the face of the warrant. The face of the search warrant should specify the times of execution, which should be limited, depending on the circumstances of the specific situation, but especially in situations involving searches of dwelling houses.

Unless authorized for execution by "night" a subsection 487(1) or 487.1 *Criminal Code* search warrant must be executed by "day", that is, between the hours of 6:00 a.m. and 9:00 p.m. local time. This does not mean that the search must conclude before 9:00 p.m., only that it must commence prior to 9:00 p.m.[25] If circumstances require that the warrant be executed after 9:00 p.m., reasonable grounds requiring execution by night must be included in the information to obtain the search warrant and the endorsement for execution after 9:00 p.m. must be completed on the face of the search warrant itself.[26]

Section 29(1) *Criminal Code* imposes the duty upon every one who executes a process or warrant to have it in their possession and to produce it when requested.[27] Failure to do so when executing a search warrant has been held to constitute a violation of the guaranteed right to be free from unreasonable search and seizure.[28]

Once raised at trial, any other issues surrounding the reasonableness of the execution of a search warrant may also be examined by the court. Police officers executing search warrants must first knock and announce their presence and purpose, unless reasonable grounds exist to believe that to do so could result in the loss or destruction of evidence, or unless reasonable officer safety concerns exist.

There is no standard announcement provided for police officers to announce their intention to search. Words to the effect of, "Police officers! We have a warrant to search your (specify nature of location to be searched)! Open the door!" Some expression of denial or some unreasonable delay by the occupant(s) to allow entry would then justify entering by the reasonable use of force. Exigent circumstances or officer safety concerns relied upon to avoid announcing entry and purpose must later be deemed sufficient by the court.

---

[25]*R. v. Woodall* [1993] O.J. No. 4001 (Ont. C.A.).

[26]*Criminal Code*, R.S. 1985, c. C-46, s. 488.

[27]*Criminal Code*, R.S. 1985, c. C-46, s. 29(1).

[28]*R. v. Bohn* (2000) 145 C.C.C. (3d) 320, 33 C.R. (5th) 265 (B.C.C.A.).

Unjustified force, at any time during the execution of a search warrant, could easily result in a search being ruled a section 8 *Charter* violation. The greater the amount of force used, the greater the responsibility of the police to justify such use of force.[29] It need hardly be mentioned that any use of force to search a dwelling house will be treated with far greater severity than the search of a place other than a dwelling house.

A search begins the moment a police officer enters upon the premises to be searched and may be compromised if the initial entry itself is not conducted in a reasonable manner. In a landmark decision, the Supreme Court of Canada held that the police cannot effect a warrantless entry to "freeze" a premises until a search warrant is obtained.[30] "Either you have the right to enter and search without warrant or you don't. An artificial [distinction] between entry and search won't work."[31]

Serious and obvious defects on the face of the search warrant, such as an incorrect address, failure to specify the things to be seized or omitting the times of execution will render the warrant invalid.[32] Where only a part of a warrant is found to be defective and there are still enough remaining grounds to justify the warrant, the defective parts may be severed during a trial, following an application to quash the warrant.[33]

Search warrants authorize the search of the specified building, receptacle or place but this authority does not extend to the search of persons found on the premises at the time of the search, although reasonable concerns for officer safety may require a search of all occupants for weapons in limited but extreme instances. The search of an occupant of a building being searched must be incident to their lawful arrest. If the principal owner, tenant or occupier of a premises being searched is arrested, their right to retain and instruct counsel under s. 10(b) *Charter of Rights* may still be exercised in privacy, but the police are under no obligation to suspend or postpone the search until the prisoner has consulted with legal counsel.[34]

Often, investigators executing a search warrant will encounter evidence in the premises being searched that is not specified in the search warrant but is relevant to the case under investigation or that is evidence of another crime, or perhaps is something that has been used in a crime. Section 489(1) *Criminal Code* provides for the warrantless seizure of evidence located during the execution of a search warrant that is not named in the warrant. Sec. 489(2) of the *Criminal Code* signifies the "Plain View Seizure Rule" in situations where a peace officer is "lawfully on the premises" whether executing a search or not. Any such evidence seized is required to be treated in the same manner as if it had been seized under the authority of a search warrant.[35]

If the execution of a search warrant requires the assistance of civilians whose expertise is essential to the identification of evidence to be seized, such as forensic identification technicians, forensic scientists, accountants, computer experts, mechanics or tradespersons,

---

[29]*Genest v. The Queen*, [1989]1 SCR 59, 45 C.C.C. (3d) 385.

[30]*R. v. Silveira* (1995), 97 C.C.C. (3d) 450 (S.C.C.).

[31]*Convicting the Guilty: A Strategy Manual of Law and Technique for Dedicated Investigators and Prosecutors Combatting Major Crime.* Steve Sherriff (1997) p. 48.

[32]*Genest v. The Queen, supra.*

[33]*R. v. Dobney Holdings* (1985), 18 C.C.C. (3d) 238 (B.C.C.A.).

[34]*R. v. Debot* (1989), 2 S.C.R. 1140, 52 C.C.C. (3d) 193.

[35]*Criminal Code*, R.S. 1985, c. C-46, s. 489.1.

etc., they may be named on the face of the search warrant. Such persons, even if not named in the search warrant, must remain under the control of the peace officer who is accountable for the search.[36]

Not all police officers who will be involved in the search are required to be named on the face of the search warrant.[37] While the specific officer "named" in the warrant need not be present during the search, it is strongly recommended that they be present, whenever possible, as they will be held responsible for the supervision and conduct of the search.[38]

If a search warrant is issued in one territorial division, such as the province of Ontario, but is intended for execution in another territorial division, for example British Columbia, it must first be endorsed in Form 28 *Criminal Code* by a justice in the territorial division (B.C.) in which the warrant is to be executed.[39]

Once a search warrant is executed, it is presumed to have been obtained and executed lawfully unless the accused establishes, on a balance of probabilities, that the search was unreasonable. An accused person may do so in court either by attacking the search warrant information and or the facial validity of the warrant itself or the reasonableness of the execution of the warrant. The prosecution is not obliged to prove the legality of a search warrant in court unless it is challenged.[40] (Hill 1999)

8.18.1 Seizure of Things Not Named in the Warrant

Subsection 489(1) *Criminal Code* provides that if a police officer, who is executing a search warrant, finds anything that is not named in the search warrant that was obtained by, or was used in the commission of the offence(s) under investigation, or any other criminal offence, the officer is also entitled to seize the unnamed evidence.[41] This legal authority is similar to the plain-view seizure doctrine for warrantless searches that was covered in Chapter 7, and has also been embodied into the *Criminal Code*.[42]

The seizure of evidence under either of these legal authorities still has to be reported to a justice in accordance with sections 489.1(1) and 490 *Criminal Code*. (See Section 8.22 Report to a Justice)

Any one who executes a *Criminal Code* 487 warrant or 487.1 telewarrant may also seize any explosive substance that the officer suspects is intended to be used for an unlawful purpose and remove it to a place of safety. Such seizures may be retained until there is an order to deliver it to a person or disposed of it in the event of a conviction for an offence of the person from whom it was seized.[43]

---

[36]*R. v. B. (J.E.)* (1989), 52 C.C.C. (3d) 224 (N.S.C.A.).

[37]*R. v. Haley* (1986), 27 C.C.C. (3d) 454, (Ont. C.A.).

[38]*Goodbaum and The Queen* (1977), 38 C.C.C. (2d) 473 (Ont. C.A.); *Campbell v. Clough* (1979), 23 Nfld. &; P.E.I.R. 249 (P.E.I.S.C.); *R. v. Davidson* (1982), 40 N.B.R. (2d) 702 (Q.B.T.D.); and *R. and Attorney General of Canada v. Newson* (1985), 41 Alta. L.R. (2d) 375 (Q.B.).

[39]*Criminal Code*, R.S. 1985, c. C-46, Part XXVIII (Part 28).

[40]*R. v. Feldman* (1995), 93 C.C.C. (3d) 575 S.C.C.

[41]*Criminal Code*, R.S. 1985, c. C-46, s. 489(1).

[42]*Criminal Code*, R.S. 1985, c. C-46, s. 489(2).

[43]*Criminal Code*, R.S. 1985 c. C-46, s. 492(1)-(2).

8.19   SEARCH AND RIGHTS TO COUNSEL

Whenever a person is detained during a search, they are entitled to legal counsel, no different than if they were placed under arrest. The police are generally not obligated to suspend the search until the person has the opportunity to exercise their right to counsel. During the execution of a search warrant when everything is satisfactorily under control, the police are required to afford the occupant of the premises an opportunity to contact legal counsel.[44]

8.20   SEARCHES INVOLVING SOLICITOR–CLIENT PRIVILEGE

The procedures for searching law offices or seizing documents in the possession of a lawyer who claims solicitor-client privilege on behalf of a client, requires that the police officer not examine the seized documents, but seal them in a package, which must then be turned over to the local sheriff. Within fourteen days of the seizure, either party may apply to a judge to set a hearing date, at which time the court will determine whether or not the documents should be disclosed to the police.[45]

8.21   SEARCHES OF MOTOR VEHICLES

The topic of searching motor vehicles was first raised in Chapter 7 dealing with warrantless searches. The difficulty with searching motor vehicles is that by the time a search warrant is obtained, the vehicle may become mobile and may be far removed from where it was first observed. Exigent circumstances can be claimed where there are reasonable grounds to believe that evidence inside the motor vehicle may be lost or destroyed[46] or in circumstances of a motor vehicle that is either mobile, or is about to move.[47] (Sherriff 1997)

That does not mean to say that the driver of a motor vehicle has no reasonable expectation of privacy in their vehicle. Quite the opposite, in fact, unless the suspect is a passenger in a motor vehicle of which they are not the owner or lessee. If reasonable grounds exist to arrest the driver and/or the owner, if they are a person other than the driver and are an occupant of the motor vehicle, the common law warrantless authority to search the prisoner incident to arrest also extends to the motor vehicle.[48]

As with the location or outbuildings to be searched and the description of the items to be seized, the description of the motor vehicle itself must be sufficiently clear to clarify any ambiguity in the mind of an uninvolved officer who is assigned to search it. The description of a "1972 Volkswagen diesel Rabbit 4-door, Orange in colour, bearing Ontario Registration: ABCD 123 parked in the driveway next to the dwelling

[44]*R. v. Debot*, [1989] 2 S.C.R. 1140, 52 C.C.C. (3d) 193, 73 C.R. (3d) 129, *R.v. Strachan*, [1988] 2 S.C.R. 980, 46 C.C.C. (3d) 479, 67 C.R. (3d) 87 (7:0).

[45]*Criminal Code*, R.S. 1985, c. C-46, s. 488.1.

[46]*R. v. Grant* (1993), 84 C.C.C. (3d) 97 (S.C.C.).

[47]*R. v. Rao* (1984), 40 C.R. (3d) 1, 12 C.C.C. (3d) 97 (Ont. C.A.).

[48]*R. v. Belnavis* (1989), 107 C.C.C. (3d) 195, 36 C.R.R. (2d) 32, 1996 C.R.R. Lexis 241.

house situated at 45 Colborne Street, Newmarket, Ontario", is specific enough to prevent it from being mistaken for any other vehicle.

If an officer routinely stops a motor vehicle and wishes to examine the glove compartment or trunk for evidence of a crime, absent reasonable grounds to arrest the driver/occupant that would justify a search incident to the arrest, the only lawful methods to search the motor vehicle are:

1. with the consent of the driver/owner, or

2. in exigent circumstances involving articulable reasonable grounds relating to the potential loss or destruction of evidence, or

3. on the authority of a search warrant.

A warrant to search a dwelling house does not automatically authorize the search of all motor vehicles situated on that property unless they are also specifically named on the face of the search warrant as a "place to be searched". If the search of a motor vehicle is not associated to the search of another location, it is still considered to be a place, within the definition of "building, place or receptacle", as envisioned by subsection 487(1) *Criminal Code*, and a search warrant is required to search it. If there are reasonable grounds to believe that evidence of a criminal offence may be concealed in a suspect's motor vehicle, parked outside their residence, one warrant will authorize the search of the motor vehicle, if it has been included in the Information to Obtain and on the face of the search warrant itself.

If the precise location of the motor vehicle is not known when a search warrant for it is obtained, it is strongly recommended to describe the motor vehicle itself as precisely as possible and add at least some geographical description of the anticipated location, such as "within the City of Toronto" or at least within the territorial jurisdiction of the issuer, i.e., "wherever the said vehicle may be found within the Province of Ontario." (Hill, et al 1999) [49]

Police officers and students are reminded of the warrantless search authorities for motor vehicles that exist under federal legislation for weapons, ammunition, explosive substances, controlled substances in exigent circumstances,[50] and under provincial legislation for evidence in contravention of those respective acts. (See Chapter 7.)

8.22 REPORT TO A JUSTICE – SEC. 489.1(1) AND 490 *CRIMINAL CODE*

A police officer who seizes anything under the authority of any of the search warrant provisions of the *Criminal Code*, or without a warrant either incident to arrest,[51] or under the "plain view seizure rule" embodied in section 489, or in exigent circumstances as authorized by sections 117.02(1) or 487.11 *Criminal Code*, must make a Report to a Justice reporting that they have done so.[52] Making a report involves either producing the article(s) seized, and/or making a written report in Form 5.2 *Criminal Code*.

---

[49]*Search Warrants: Protection or Illusion?* p.8.

[50]*Criminal Code*, R.S. 1985, c. C-46, s. 117.02(1) and 117.04(2) *Controlled Drugs and Substances* 1996, C-19, s. 11.

[51]*R. v. Backhouse* (2005) 194 C.C.C. (3d) 1, 127 C.R.R. (2d) 1, 28 C.R. (6th) 31, 195 O.A.C. 80, CanLII 4937 (Ont. C.A.).

[52]*Criminal Code*, R.S. 1985, c. C-46, s. 489.1(1).

The justice may order the seized item(s) be returned to the rightful owner, if they are known, unless the police or prosecutor shows that the item is required for the purposes of investigation, preliminary hearing, trial or other proceeding.[53] Such an order, if granted, is only valid for a period of not more than three months from the date of original seizure[54] and contains provisions that the person in whose custody the item is detained, take "reasonable care to ensure that it is preserved".[55] A detention order may be extended for consecutive periods of three months unless in the meantime, proceedings are instituted in which the item is required as evidence.

In complex, long-term investigations where no charges have been laid, extensions of detention orders beyond one year from the day of seizure must be ordered by a judge of a superior court.[56] An item may be detained for any length of time following a detention order, granted at the time of the initial Report to a Justice if the lawful owner, or a person lawfully entitled to possess it consents, in writing, to its detention for that period.[57]

A sample of an Information to Obtain a Search Warrant, a search warrant and a Report to a Justice for a fictitious case have been included in the Appendices near the end of this textbook.

8.23 DISPOSAL OF PERISHABLE EVIDENCE

Where any thing that is perishable is seized by warrant or without warrant under the *Criminal Code,* the property may be returned to its lawful owner or the person lawfully entitled to it. A justice may also, on an *ex parte* application, authorize the disposal of the property with the proceeds to be given to the lawful owner, if they are not a party to an offence in relation to the property. If the identity of the lawful owner cannot be established, the proceeds of the sale of the item are forfeited to the Crown.[58]

8.24 INSPECTION VS. INVESTIGATION

Difficulties arise when warrantless seizures, made under the authority of search or inspection provisions of provincial (regulatory) legislation, are used as evidence in criminal proceedings against the person from whom the seizure was made. Search or inspection authorities under certain provincial statutes are intended to assist officials in gathering information for purposes other than proving criminal offences.

The purpose of such access to premises and inspections also includes special investigations such as coroner's investigations to determine the circumstances of a person's death, and to ensure compliance with the requirements of various acts of provincial and federal legislation. Environmental enforcement agencies and Revenue Canada, Fire Marshall and Coroners/Medical Examiners are just some examples of government agencies with powerful rights of inspection.

---

[53]*Criminal Code*, R.S. 1985, c. C-46, s. 490(1)(a).

[54]*Criminal Code*, R.S. 1985, c. C-46, s. 490(2).

[55]*Criminal Code*, R.S. 1985, c. C-46, s. 490(1)(b).

[56]*Criminal Code*, R.S. 1985, c. C-46, s. 490(3).

[57]*Criminal Code*, R.S. 1985, c. C-46, s. 490(3.1).

[58]*Criminal Code*, R.S. 1985, c. C-46, s. 490.01.

When the purpose of the seizing official changes from merely ensuring compliance with legislation to gathering evidence for the purpose of proving the guilt of a person for a serious offence, a search warrant must always be obtained, where practicable. Police officers and other investigative officials should not "piggy-back" one investigation on another. Evidence obtained through a warrantless inspection cannot serve to further a criminal investigation if it was obtained for a different purpose than determining a person's penal liability.[59]

Similar restrictions apply where samples of a person's blood are seized for medical purposes at a hospital and the blood or the results of blood alcohol analyses are seized, without a warrant, by the police as evidence on Impaired or Care or Control offences. The warrantless seizure of samples that are collected for medical purposes cannot be used to circumvent the necessity of obtaining a search warrant to collect evidence of criminal acts.[60]

Once blood is seized for a medical purpose, it is subject to seizure by the police under the authority of a search warrant. Knowing that the blood sample taken from an impaired driver exists in a certain location and knowing that a toxicological analysis of the sample would provide evidence in relation to an alleged offence would be all the reasonable grounds a police officer would need to obtain a warrant authorizing its seizure from a hospital. It is always better to err on the side of caution and obtain a search warrant. Seizing evidence without a search warrant, merely to save the time and effort of preparing a warrant, will surely create a *Charter* violation and will result in the exclusion of evidence at trial.

8.25 SEALING SEARCH WARRANTS

Where information is contained in a search warrant or any information relating to it that, if disclosed, would be detrimental to the administration of justice, a judge or justice of the peace may make an order prohibiting access to the documents. This procedure is referred to as sealing a warrant, or alternatively referred to as sealing the packet.

If a search warrant is executed and evidence is seized, once it is filed with the court it becomes a public document, which any member of the public has a right to examine, unless a search warrant is sealed.[61] Even if nothing is seized during the execution of a search warrant, a suspect or accused named in the warrant always has the right to inspect all documentation in relation to that warrant, unless it is sealed.[62]

Typical situations where sealing the warrant is sometimes requested, include:

1. information that would compromise the identity of a confidential informer

2. information that would compromise an ongoing investigation

3. information that would endanger a person engaged in particular intelligence-gathering techniques that would prejudice future investigations

---

[59]*R. v. Jarvis*, [2002] 3 S.C.R. 757, 2002 S.C.C. 73, also *R. v. Ling*, [2002] 3 S.C.R. 814, 2002 S.C.C. 74, also *R. v. Colarusso*, [1994] 1 S.C.R. 20, 87 C.C.C. (3d) 193, 26 C.R. (4th) 289.

[60]*R. v. Dyment*, [1988] 2 S.C.R. 417, 45 C.C.C. (3d) 244, 66 C.R. (3d) 348, also *R. v. Dersch*, [1993] 3 S.C.R. 768, 85 C.C.C. (3d) 1, 25 C.R. (4th) 88 (9:0).

[61]*Nova Scotia (Attorney General)*, [1982] 1 S.C.R. 175, 65 C.C.C. (2d) 129, 26 C.R. (3d) 193 (5:4).

[62]*R. v. Jany* (1983), 9 C.C.C. (3d) 349 (B.C.S.C.).

4. information that would prejudice an innocent person

5. any other sufficient reason[63]

Once a sealing order is made, the judge who made the order, or a judge who may preside over the proceedings into the matter, may hear an application to terminate the order or vary its terms and conditions. If a judge orders that the packet be opened and disclosed to the defence, the Crown would have the opportunity to edit the documents to delete portions that would be prejudicial to the public interest. The edited version is then supplied to the accused, who may still apply for an order to disclose the edited portion(s) of the documents. If the judge believes that disclosure of the edited portion is necessary to allow the accused to make full answer and defence, they may order such disclosure. If this were to happen, the Crown could elect to withdraw or stay the charges.[64]

SUMMARY

- A reasonable search is one that is authorized by statute law or common law, that is reasonable and is executed in a reasonable manner, or one that is pre-authorized in the form of a search warrant, or is covered by one of the six warrantless search authorities.

- A person's reasonable expectation of privacy is closely associated with – but not restricted to – their proprietary interest in a given location or thing.

- When issues of proprietary interest and reasonable expectation of privacy are vague, and a suspect might possibly have a reasonable expectation of privacy in an item to be seized, or in the building, place or receptacle to be searched, it is strongly recommended to obtain a search warrant whenever it is practicable to do so.

- The Information to Obtain a Search Warrant is a document filed in support of an application to issue a search warrant. It contains the informant's reasonable grounds for belief:
  - that an offence has been committed,
  - that the things to be seized will afford evidence of the offence,
  - that the things to be seized are at the place to be searched.

- A police officer who drafts a search warrant information must state precisely how and when they obtained their reasonable grounds being used to justify the search.

- If detached outbuildings, such as garages, sheds, or workshops on a property or motor vehicles are also to be searched in conjunction with the search of a dwelling house, they must be separately described, both on the Information to Obtain the search warrant and on the face of the warrant itself.

- Unless authorized for execution by "night" a subsection 487(1) or 487.1 *Criminal Code* search warrant must be executed by "day", that is, between the hours of 6:00 a.m. and 9:00 p.m. local time.

---

[63]*Criminal Code*, R.S. 1985, c. C-46, s. 487.3(1-2).

[64]*R. v. Garofoli*, [1990] 2 S.C.R. 1421, 60 C.C.C. (3d) 161, 80 C.R. (3d) 317 (5:2).

- Section 29(1) *Criminal Code* imposes the duty upon every one who executes a process or warrant to have it in their possession and to produce it when requested.

- Police officers executing search warrants must first knock and announce their presence and purpose, unless reasonable grounds exist to believe that to do so could result in the loss or destruction of evidence, or unless reasonable officer safety concerns exist.

- Serious and obvious defects on the face of the search warrant, such as an incorrect address, failure to specify the things to be seized or omitting the times of execution will render the warrant invalid.

DISCUSSION QUESTIONS

1. It is winter. You are investigating a break, enter and theft that occurred overnight at a local business. A cashbox containing $500 was taken. Blood at the crime scene indicates that the suspect cut his hand fairly seriously. A trail of foot-print impressions and drops of blood in the snow leads from the victimized business to a nearby house. You knock on the front door and make inquiries. The owner of the house states that his tenant who rents a downstairs bedroom came home two hours ago but has now gone to the hospital emergency room for treatment to a gash on his hand that he claimed he received in a fight. When you inform the owner of the nature of your investigation, he tells you that you have his permission to search the downstairs bedroom for the stolen cashbox and money. Is his consent valid? May you search the downstairs bedroom for the stolen property without a search warrant? Explain the rationale for your answer.

2. You have been assigned to assist in the investigation of an armed robbery. The investigating officer is tied up interviewing witnesses. He asks you to execute a search warrant on the residence of the suspect's girlfriend to seize clothing, allegedly worn by the suspect at the time of the robbery, which he left at her house, where the suspect has also been staying. You know nothing about the case except for what appears on the search warrant and that the investigating officer tells you that both the suspect and the girlfriend are being charged with the armed robbery. The investigating officer assures you that all the work has been done and that you only have to go and seize the articles of clothing named in the warrant. When you attend at the girlfriend's house, you learn that she resides with her parents. You produce the search warrant and explain your purpose to her mother. Upon inspecting the search warrant, the mother informs you that the house number in the address on the warrant is incorrect but invites you in to conduct your search in any event. What, if anything, should you do next? Explain the rationale for your answer.

3. You are investigating a sexual assault. During the investigation, you have interviewed six witnesses. Five witnesses indicate that the same person is responsible for the sexual assault. The one remaining witness states that he was with the suspect in a local restaurant during the period in which the alleged sexual assault occurred and indicates that the suspect never left his company and could therefore not have committed

the attack. This last witness produces a credit card bill indicating the purchase of two large meals and several drinks throughout the time the attack occurred. You want to prepare a search warrant for the suspect's residence and his motor vehicle. Your Sergeant tells you to just include the information given by the first five witnesses in your search warrant application and to ignore the alibi witness as the last witness is obviously lying to protect his friend. Will you follow your Sergeant's advice and selectively draft your search warrant information to exclude the contradictory witness? Whether you answered yes or no, explain the rationale for your answer.

 # WEBLINKS

http://scc.lexum.umontreal.ca/en/index.html

Supreme Court of Canada decisions, provided through the collaborative effort of the Supreme Court and the LexUM laboratory in the University of Montreal Faculty of Law. A free searchable database of Supreme Court decisions on important legal matters, including search and seizure.

www.canlii.org/en/index.html

CanLII is a non-profit organization managed by the Federation of Law Societies of Canada. Canadian Legal Information Institute provides a free searchable database of provincial and federal legislation and reported case law decisions from various levels of courts throughout Canada.

Chapter 9

Other Search Warrants and Authorizations

"In a constitutional environment of presumption of search by warrant, the implicit expectation is that the authorities responsible for dealing with search warrants will get it right."[1]

The Honourable Mr. Justice Casey Hill.

Learning Outcomes

After reading this chapter, students should be able to:

- Distinguish between types of search warrants used to seize tangible evidence and those that authorize the seizure of information and permit investigative techniques.
- Explain the requirements of prior announcement, production of a search warrant, and limitations relating to the time of execution of a search warrant.
- Describe the types of mistakes or deficiencies on the face of a warrant that would be fatal to the validity of the entire warrant.
- Explain what types of things, not mentioned on the face of a search warrant, can be lawfully seized during the execution of such a warrant.
- Compare the differences between search warrants and production orders, giving examples of when to utilize the former over the latter.

9.1   OTHER SEARCH WARRANTS

As we saw in Chapter 8, subsection 487(1) *Criminal Code* permits a justice to issue a search warrant to search a building, receptacle or place for evidence obtained by or used in the commission of a real or intended offence. Searches authorized by 487(1) *CC* authorize the search for and seizure of tangible evidence, meaning real or physical property. In addition to subsection 487(1) *Criminal Code* search warrants, there are numerous other search warrants that peace officers may utilize to seize things, gather information, gather evidence of offences or seize articles for the purpose of preventing offences.

---

[1]*Search Warrants: Protection or Illusion?*, p. 13.

In this chapter we will examine some of those additional search authorities that authorize peace officers to conduct searches or investigative procedures that, if they were not pre-authorized by a justice, would constitute unlawful search and seizure.

9.2 WARRANTS TO OBTAIN BLOOD SAMPLES

If reasonable grounds exist to believe that a person has committed a drinking and driving offence under section 253 *Criminal Code*, and was involved in an accident causing death or bodily harm to any person – including themselves – a peace officer may demand samples of the person's breath to analyze the amount of alcohol in the driver's blood. If, in the opinion of a qualified medical practitioner, the driver is unable, by reason of physical or mental condition, to consent to providing samples of their breath or blood, a justice may issue a warrant to seize samples of the suspect's blood.

The person from whom the blood samples are to be seized must have operated or had the care or control of a motor vehicle or vessel, or have assisted in the operation of an aircraft or railway equipment while their ability was impaired by alcohol or a drug or done so while their blood alcohol concentration exceeded 80 milligrams of alcohol in 100 millilitres of blood. The incident must have occurred within the preceding four hours and the samples must be taken by a medical practitioner or a qualified technician under the direction of a qualified medical practitioner – while the person is still unable to consent to provide samples of their blood. The samples may be taken from the person only if it would not endanger their life or health to do so.

An Information to Obtain a warrant to seize blood must be in Form 1 *Criminal Code* and the warrant may be in Form 5 or 5.1 *CC* The telewarrant provisions of 487.1 *CC* apply for a warrant to take blood to be applied for by telephone or other means of telecommunications. When such a warrant is executed, the peace officer must provide a copy of the warrant to the person from whom the blood samples were taken, as soon as it is practicable to do so.[2]

A qualified medical practitioner or qualified medical technician who refuses to take a sample of blood does not commit an offence by doing so, nor do they incur criminal or civil liability for anything done with reasonable care and skill in the taking of such a sample of blood.[3]

9.3 *CONTROLLED DRUGS AND SUBSTANCES ACT*, S.C. 1996 C-19

Subsection 11(1) of the *Controlled Drugs and Substances Act (CDSA)* authorizes a justice who receives information on oath (or solemn affirmation) to issue a search warrant. The same procedure applies for applying for a *CDSA* search warrant as for one under the *Criminal Code*.

An informant applying for a *CDSA* search warrant must have reasonable grounds to believe that a controlled substance, a precursor used in the manufacture of controlled substances, anything in which a controlled substance or precursor is contained, offence related property or any thing that will afford evidence of an offence under the *CDSA* will be found in a place. The informant then makes an ex parte application requesting a search warrant,

---

[2]*Criminal Code*, R.S. 1985, c. C-46, s. 256(1)-(5).

[3]*Criminal Code*, R.S. 1985, c. C-46, s. 257(1)-(2).

either in person or by telephone or other means of telecommunication under the telewarrant provisions of section 487.1 *Criminal Code*.[4] (See section 9.4, Telewarrants.)

There are no dedicated search warrant forms under the *CDSA*, as there are under the *Criminal Code*. Police officers should therefore utilize a *Criminal Code* Form 1 Information to Obtain a Search Warrant and either Form 5 or 5.1 Search Warrant, making the necessary changes.

Unlike a *Criminal Code* search warrant, however, a *CDSA* search warrant may be executed at any time, rather than just by day. No endorsement for night time execution is required on the face of a *CDSA* warrant – nor would such an endorsement render the face of a *CDSA* search warrant invalid.[5] However, stating your reasonable grounds in the Information to Obtain, indicating why it is advisable to execute a *CDSA* search warrant at night, especially one for a dwelling house, only indicates good faith on the part of the officer drafting the information and search warrant.

The same rules apply to *CDSA* search warrants as with *Criminal Code* search warrants with respect to having the actual warrant present and producing it when requested to.[6] A *CDSA* search warrant execution still requires the expectations of reasonableness on the part of the police regarding the need of prior announcement, to "knock and announce" their presence[7] and to use only as much force as necessary.[8]

The *CDSA* also allows peace officers executing search warrants to seize additional items that are not named in the search warrant if, on reasonable grounds, they will afford evidence in respect of an offence under the Act,[9] and to exercise search and seizure powers without a warrant if grounds for a warrant exist but by reason of exigent circumstances it would be impracticable to obtain one.[10] *CDSA* search warrants also authorize an officer to search persons found inside a premises being searched, if the officer executing the warrant has reasonable grounds to believe that they have a controlled substance, precursor or offence-related property on their person, and to seize that thing.[11]

As with *Criminal Code* search warrants, *CDSA* search warrants may be issued by a justice for execution in a different territorial division (province), but they must first be endorsed for execution in Form 28 *CC* by a justice in the territorial jurisdiction in which the place is situated.[12]

9.4 TELEWARRANTS – SECTION 487.1 *CRIMINAL CODE*

Crime and criminals rarely keep normal office hours. Frequently, a search warrant is required to be obtained and executed after-hours or on weekends. The *Criminal Code*

---

[4]*Controlled Drugs and Substances Act*, S.C. 1996 C. 19, s. 11(1)-(2).

[5]*R. v. Saunders* (2004), 181 C.C.C. (3d) 268, 232 Nfld. & P.E.I.R. 22 (Nfld. C.A.), aff'd [2004] 3 S.C.R. 505, 189 C.C.C. (3d) 436, 244 Nfld. & P.E.I.R. 180, see also *R. v. Dueck* (2005), 200 C.C.C. (3d) 378 (B.C.C.A.).

[6]*Criminal Code*, R.S. 1985, c. C-46, s. 29(1).

[7]*R. v. Gimson* (1990), 54 C.C.C. (3d) 232, 77 C.R. (3d) 76 (Que C.A.).

[8]*R. v. Genest*, [1989] 1 S.C.R. 59, 45 C.C.C. (3d) 385, 67 C.R. (3d) 224 (7:0).

[9]*Controlled Drugs and Substances Act*, S.C. 1996, c. C.19, s. 11(6).

[10]*Controlled Drugs and Substances Act*, S.C. 1996, c. C.19, s. 11(7).

[11]*Controlled Drugs and Substances Act*, S.C. 1996 C. 19, s. 11(5).

[12]*Controlled Drugs and Substances Act*, S.C. 1996 C. 19, s. 11(3).

provides that, "Where a peace officer believes that an indictable offence has been committed and that it would be impracticable to appear personally before a justice to make application for a [search] warrant, . . . the peace officer may submit an information on oath by telephone or other means of telecommunication to a justice designated for the purpose by the chief judge of the provincial court having jurisdiction in the matter."[13]

The information must still be sworn under oath, however, the oath may be in the form of a statement which, if transmitted electronically, "is deemed to be a statement made under oath."[14] Once issued, a telewarrant has the same legal authority as a warrant personally issued by a justice[15] and may also require the telewarrant [except 11(2) *CDSA*] to be executed by day (6:00 a.m. to 9:00 p.m.) unless specified otherwise on the face of the warrant.[16]

In addition to the information required in an ordinary search warrant application, including:

1. a statement of the alleged offence,

2. description of the place or premises to be searched,

3. description of the articles to be searched for, and

4. the officer's reasonable grounds to believe the items to be seized in respect of the offence will be found in the place or premises to be searched,

a telewarrant application must also contain the reason(s) why it is impracticable for the informant to appear personally before the justice. Typical reasons might include being in a remote location, the timing of the request being after business hours or on a weekend or holiday, the non-availability of a justice, or other circumstances that make it impracticable for the peace officer to appear personally before the justice.

An Information to Obtain the telewarrant must also disclose any information concerning instances of prior application(s) for a warrant under this section, or any other type of search warrant, of which the officer has knowledge. Applying for a telewarrant after having been refused by a different justice for another type of warrant would constitute an abuse of the telewarrant process and is highly improper.[17]

The telewarrant process is available for *Criminal Code* search warrants [s. 487(1)], blood sample warrants [ss. 256, 487.1], DNA warrants [s. 487.05(3)], impression warrants [s. 487.091(4)], general search warrants [s. 487.01(1)] and substances warrants [s. 11(2) *Controlled Drugs and Substances Act*] (Hill et al. 1999)

In every case, other than a telewarrant to obtain blood samples, a police officer executing a telewarrant shall, before or at the time of entry, provide a copy of the telewarrant to any person present who is in control of the premises being searched. If the premises being searched are unoccupied, the officer is required upon entry, or as soon thereafter as practicable, to affix a copy of the telewarrant at a conspicuous place within the premises that is searched.[18]

---

[13]*Criminal Code*, R.S. 1985, c. C-46, s. 487.1(1).

[14]*Criminal Code*, R.S. 1985, c. C-46, s. 487.1(3) and (3.1).

[15]*Criminal Code*, R.S. 1985, c. C-46, s. 487.1(5).

[16]*Criminal Code*, R.S. 1985, c. C-46, s. 487.1(5), s. 488.

[17]*Criminal Code*, R.S. 1985, c. C-46, s. 487.1(4).

[18]*Criminal Code*, R.S. 1985, c. C-46, s. 487.1 (7)-(8).

A telewarrant is only enforceable for seven days from the date of issue. No later than seven days following the issue of a telewarrant, a police officer must file a report with the clerk of the court having jurisdiction, stating the time and date of the execution of the telewarrant or a statement of reason(s) why it was not executed. Such a report to the court must also include a statement of anything seized pursuant to a telewarrant that was executed.[19]

9.5   GENERAL WARRANTS

In 1997, amendments to the *Criminal Code* provided investigators with the legal means to seek judicial authority to seize evidence, obtain information and utilize investigative techniques that had previously been held to constitute unreasonable searches and seizures, but were not included under the search warrant provisions of subsection 487(1) *Criminal Code*. General warrants may now be issued by "a provincial court judge or a judge of a superior court of criminal jurisdiction" to authorize investigative techniques, procedures, the use of devices or any thing in relation to a person or their property, which if it not authorized, would result in a section 8 *Charter of Rights* violation.[20] The general warrant provisions specifically do not permit anything that would interfere "with the bodily integrity of any person."[21]

General warrants now authorize the seizure of intangible things, such as information, biological samples for DNA analysis[22] or comparison samples of a person's hand, foot or fingerprints, of teeth impressions.[23] General warrants also permit investigators to utilize investigative techniques including the installation of tracking devices or surreptitious video surveillance installations,[24] to conduct perimeter searches, or monitor a person's mail deliveries. The issuing judge must be satisfied on oath in writing that it is in the best interests of the administration of justice to issue the warrant and may place "such terms and conditions as the justice considers advisable to ensure that any search or seizure, . . . is reasonable".[25]

In extraordinary cases, an investigation may require that a premises be surreptitiously searched without the knowledge of the person having control of the premises. Such instances might include investigations involving terrorist offences or organized crime. A general search warrant could be issued under subsection 487.01(1) to conduct a covert entry and search that would otherwise constitute a trespass.

In such rare cases, the officers executing the warrant would be excused from the requirement of prior announcement of their entry. The giving of notice of such a covert search to a person having control of the premises is only delayed, and not cancelled.

The issuing judge will decide, as part of the terms and conditions referred to in the warrant, the time period following the date of execution following which notice of the

---

[19]*Criminal Code*, R.S. 1985, c. C-46, s. 487.1 (9).

[20]*Criminal Code*, R.S. 1985, c. C-46, s. 487.01(1).

[21]*Criminal Code*, R.S. 1985, c. C-46, s. 487.01(2).

[22]*Criminal Code*, R.S. 1985, c. C-46, s. 487.05.

[23]*Criminal Code*, R.S. 1985, c. C-46, s. 487.092(1).

[24]*Criminal Code*, R.S. 1985, c. C-46, s. 487.01(4).

[25]*Criminal Code*, R.S. 1985, c. C-46, s. 487.01(3).

search must be given.[26] The time period in which the notice must be given can be extended by a judge, if it is in the interests of justice to do so, however, no extension may exceed three years from the date of the execution of the warrant.[27]

The process for obtaining and executing a general warrant is virtually the same as for a 487(1) *Criminal Code* search warrant except that general warrants are not issued by Justices of the Peace. General warrants may only be issued by a Provincial Court judge or a judge of a Superior Court of criminal jurisdiction. General warrants may also be obtained through the same telewarrant procedures as contained in section 487.1 *Criminal Code*. (See Section 9.4, Telewarrants.)

General warrants may be "backed" for execution in a different territorial division than the one in which it was issued if executing the general warrant would require entering upon private property in the other province, or involves DNA collection, tracking devices or a number recorder.[28] Any physical item seized as the result of a general warrant must also be the subject of a Report to a Justice under section 490 *Criminal Code*.

9.6 GENERAL WARRANT – VIDEO SURVEILLANCE

A general warrant may be issued by a provincial judge or a judge of a superior division court that authorizes the surveillance, by means of closed circuit television camera or similar electronic device, of a person who has a reasonable expectation of privacy in a location.[29] The judge who issues a video surveillance warrant may attach whatever terms and conditions they considers advisable to ensure that the privacy of the person named in the warrant, or any other person, is respected as much as possible.[30]

Unlike most general warrants that may be obtained for federal offences, a video surveillance warrant may only be issued for an offence listed in section 183 *Criminal Code*. This is the same subset of offences that are also designated as eligible for the interception of private communications.

The list of designated offences, which is not replicated here due to its sheer length, includes more than 140 public order, property, weapons, terrorist and crimes of violence offences in the *Criminal Code, Controlled Drugs and Substances Act, Customs Act, Excise Act* and a variety of other federal statutes. These designated offences include all the major offences that one might possibly imagine could reasonably be expected to justify the use of such invasive – and costly – investigative techniques.

9.7 GENERAL WARRANT – BODILY SUBSTANCES (DNA)

Deoxyribonucleic acid (DNA) is a molecule that makes up the 23 pairs of chromosomes in the nucleus of most cells in the human body. DNA consists of two intertwining strands that

---

[26]*Criminal Code*, R.S. 1985, c. C-46, s. 487.01(5.1).

[27]*Criminal Code*, R.S. 1985, c. C-46, s. 487.01(5.2).

[28]*Criminal Code*, R.S. 1985, c. C-46, s. 487.03(1).

[29]*R. v. Wong*, [1990] 3. S.C.R. 36, 60 C.C.C. (3d) 460, 1 C.R. (4th) 1.

[30]*Criminal Code*, R.S. 1985, c. C-46, s. 487.01(4).

resemble a spiral shaped ladder referred to as a double helix, which is composed of pairings of sugar, phosphate and nitrogenous molecules. Each human being has approximately 3 million of these base pairs of molecules which carry the person's unique genetic information, with the exception of identical twins, who always share an identical DNA profile.

It is this uniquely identifiable profile that makes DNA such a valuable tool for the investigation of crimes involving the loss or transfer of bodily fluids. The initial use of DNA by law enforcement was restricted almost exclusively to cases of homicide and sexual assault, but has now been expanded to a wide variety of other crimes of violence, and other cases in which biological evidence could be transferred.

Suspects have even been identified from DNA from the analysis of epithelial cells in their saliva, recovered from the flap of an envelope, or the back of licked postage stamps. DNA molecules may also be extracted from samples of blood, semen, saliva, teeth, bone and the root sheath of hair follicles. (Van Allen 2007)

DNA warrants may be obtained from a provincial court judge for any of the primary designated offences or secondary designated offences listed in section 487.04 *Criminal Code*. There are approximately 34 primary designated offences plus their predecessor sections from the previous version of the *Criminal Code, Revised Statutes of Canada* 1970, chapter C-34. There are an additional 19 secondary designated offences plus their respective predecessor sections.

Numerous additional primary and secondary designated offences have been added by way of amendments and are awaiting Royal Assent before coming into force and effect in law at a future date. The entire list of primary and secondary designated offences and proposed additional offences has not been replicated here due to length constraints.

A DNA warrant may be applied for where there are reasonable grounds to believe that any primary or secondary designated offence has been committed and a questioned DNA sample is found or obtained in relation to a victim's person or their personal effects, such as clothing, or at the location where the offence was committed. A DNA warrant will authorize the taking of a DNA sample from a party to the offence in order to compare it to evidence about whether the bodily substance that was recovered from the victim or location was from that person.

In the event that the person from whom DNA samples are to be taken does not wish to cooperate with the procedure, the execution of a *Criminal Code* DNA warrant authorizes the person to be detained for a reasonable period. The person may also be required to accompany a peace officer to a location, such as a police station or hospital, for the purpose of enabling the samples to be taken.[31]

DNA samples should only be taken by a police office who has the experience and training to do so or a qualified person acting under the direction of the peace officer and may be done, with reasonable care and with respect for the person's privacy, in any of the following forms:

1. "the plucking of individual hairs from the person, including the root sheath;

2. the taking of buccal swabs by swabbing the lips, tongue and inside cheeks of the mouth to collect epithelial cells; or

3. the taking of blood by pricking the skin surface with a sterile lancet."[32]

---

[31]*Criminal Code*, R.S. 1985 c. C-46, s. 487.07(2).

[32]*Criminal Code*, R.S. 1985 c. C-46, s. 487.06(1)(a)-(c).

Prior to the taking of DNA samples under the authority of a warrant under 487.05 *CC*, the person from who the samples are to be taken must be informed of the following:

"(a) the contents of the warrant, order or authorization;

(b) the nature of the investigative procedures by means of which the samples are to be taken;

(c) the purpose of taking the samples;

(d) the authority of the peace officer and any other person under the direction of the peace officer to use as much force as is necessary for the purpose of taking the samples;

(e) in the case of samples of bodily substances taken in execution of a warrant,

    i) the possibility that the results of forensic DNA analysis may be used as evidence, and

    ii) if the sample is taken from a young person, the rights of the young person to consult with and the right to have the warrant executed in the presence of counsel and a parent or, in the absence of a parent, an adult relative or, in the absence of a parent and an adult relative, any other appropriate adult chosen by the young person."[33]

As soon as is feasible following the taking of the DNA samples, the peace officer who is authorized by the warrant shall make a written report in Form 5.07 *Criminal Code* to the Provincial Court judge or the court that made the order, or to another Provincial Court judge. Such a report shall include a statement of the time and date the samples were taken and a description of the bodily substances that were taken.[34]

9.8 GENERAL WARRANT – BODILY IMPRESSIONS

Offenders who commit crimes often leave behind impressions at the crime scene in the form of fingerprints, handprints, footprints or footwear impressions. It is not uncommon to encounter teeth impressions at scenes of sexual assaults, homicides and other crimes of violence.

A police officer investigating a criminal offence may apply in writing to a justice for a warrant to cause impression evidence to be taken of the body or any part of the body of a person if the officer has reasonable grounds to believe that information concerning the offence will be obtained by the print or impression. If the justice believes that it is in the best interests of the administration of justice to do so, they may issue a warrant. Such a warrant may be obtained by the telewarrant procedures under section 487.1 *CC* if it is impracticable for the peace officer to appear personally before a justice.[35]

---

[33]*Criminal Code*, R.S. 1985 c. C-46, s. 487.07(1).

[34]*Criminal Code*, R.S. 1985 c. C-46, s. 487.057(1)-(2).

[35]*Criminal Code*, R.S. 1985, c. C-46, s. 487.092(1).

9.9   GENERAL WARRANT - TRACKING DEVICE

During the investigation of serious crimes, prior to reasonable grounds being established on which to base an arrest or charge, physical or electronic surveillance of a suspect is a sometimes valuable investigative technique. Surveillance can sometimes provide information about a suspect's movements and criminal associations, and may even lead to the location of concealed evidence.

Electronic surveillance may be used in conjunction with other forms of surveillance and other investigative methods. Electronic surveillance may be in the form of a tracking device attached to a target vehicle to record routes travelled by a suspect, either as a stand-alone method or in conjunction with mobile (physical) surveillance.

Tracking devices can be useful in circumstances where it would otherwise be difficult to observe a target without being detected by allowing the surveillance team to remain out of sight and monitor the electronic signals from a discreet distance. Global Positioning Systems (GPS) may also be used to track the routes travelled by a suspect. Tracking devices may also be inserted into items such as drug shipments, property that is vulnerable to theft or a package containing ransom money to track it to its eventual destination.

A justice may, on the sworn application of a peace officer, issue a warrant for a police officer to install, maintain, monitor or remove a tracking device to gather information, upon reasonable grounds to suspect that the subject of the investigation has committed or will commit any criminal offence.[36] A tracking device warrant is valid for a period not exceeding 60 days, but may be extended by further warrants issued by the justice.[37]

Note the relaxed wording, indicating a slightly lower standard of justification in the form of *"reasonable grounds to suspect"* rather than "reasonable grounds to believe". Whereas reasonable grounds is usually held to represent a degree of probability that exceeds mere suspicion, a tracking device warrant is less invasive than other section 8 searches, and the standard for obtaining one is therefore slightly less restrictive.

Utilization of a tracking device may only be carried out without a warrant "if the conditions for obtaining a warrant exist but by reason of exigent circumstances it would be impracticable to obtain a warrant."[38] Exigent circumstances are held to include circumstances that could result in imminent injury or death or the possible loss or destruction of evidence.[39]

9.10   GENERAL WARRANT - NUMBER RECORDER

When a peace officer has reasonable grounds to suspect that the subject of a criminal investigation has committed, or will commit an offence and that information that would assist the investigation may be obtained by establishing patterns of the suspect's

---

[36]*Criminal Code*, R.S. 1985, c. C-46, s. 492.1(1).

[37]*Criminal Code*, R.S. 1985, c. C-46, s. 492.1(2)-(3).

[38]*Criminal Code*, R.S. 1985, c. C-46, s. 487.11.

[39]*Criminal Code*, R.S. 1985, c. C-46, s. 529.3(2).

telephone communications, the officer may apply for a warrant to install a number recorder.[40]

Note the same the relaxed wording as in the case of a tracking device warrant, indicating the same slightly lower standard of justification in the form of "reasonable grounds to suspect" rather than "reasonable grounds to believe". Whereas reasonable grounds is usually held to represent a degree of probability that exceeds mere suspicion, a number recorder warrant and tracking device warrant is less invasive than other section 8 searches and the standard for obtaining one is therefore slightly less restrictive.

A number recorder is a device that is used to record the numbers of incoming and outgoing calls placed to and from a specific landline or cellular telephone. This device is sometimes referred to as a dialled number recorder (DNR) but that term is a throwback to earlier times when telephones were equipped with rotary dials to transmit the numbers, requiring each digit to be manually placed by rotating the dial a specific distance. These early devices may still be seen in museums and in old motion pictures, but have been replaced by telephones with keypads, hence the change of name to simply number recorders.

Number recorder warrants can also require a person or a body such as a telephone company, which is in possession of records of telephone calls originated by or received or intended to be received at any telephone, to supply copies of the records to a person named in the order.[41] This allows police officers to receive billing information and the names and addresses of subscribers for the telephone numbers of the incoming and outgoing calls that are recorded. It isn't much use knowing that an outgoing call was placed by the target to telephone number (416) 123-4567 if you have no way to determine the identity of the subscriber of that number.

9.11 INTERCEPTION OF PRIVATE COMMUNICATIONS

"Electronic surveillance plays an indispensable role in the detection of sophisticated criminal enterprises. Its utility in the investigation of drug related crimes, for example, has been proven time and again. But, for the reasons I have touched on, it is unacceptable in a free society that the agencies of the state be free to use this technology at their sole discretion. The threat this would pose to privacy is wholly unacceptable."

The Honourable Mr. Justice La Forest, J.J. in *R. v. Duarte*, [1990] 1 S.C.R. 30, 71 O.R. (2d) 575, 65 D.L.R. (4th) 240, 53 C.C.C. (3d) 1, 45 C.R.R. 278, 74 C.R. (3d) 281, 37 O.A.C. 322 [42]

There was a simpler time when the interception of private communication was limited to personal conversations or telephone conversations. There is now an abundance of methods that modern criminals can use to contact each other to discuss illicit matters

---

[40]*Criminal Code*, R.S. 1985 c. C-46, s. 492.2(1).

[41]*Criminal Code*, R.S. 1985 c. C-46, s. 492.2(2).

[42]scc.lexum.umontreal.ca/en/1990/1990rcs1-30/1990rcs1-30.html Retrieved: April 7, 2007.

and carry on their criminal affairs in our current high-tech world. Since the advent of electronic pagers, e-mail, wireless messaging devices and satellite communications, law enforcement has had to continually develop strategies to respond in the investigation of technology-savvy law breakers in order to meet this challenge.

Electronic surveillance in the form of surreptitious eavesdropping on private communications has been held to constitute a search or seizure within the meaning of s. 8 of the *Charter of Rights and Freedoms*.[43] It is a criminal offence to intercept a private communication using "any electro-magnetic, acoustic, mechanical or other device" unless authorized by a judge of a designated court under either section 184.2, where any party to the communication consents to its interception, or under subsection 186(1) *Criminal Code*, where no consent to intercept exists.[44]

Private communication infers that, at the time of the communication, the originator of the communication had a reasonable expectation that no one other than the intended recipient would receive it. For example, this could include a face-to-face conversation between two or more criminals in one of their residences, a car or other private place that is intercepted by means of an electronic listening device called a probe. A private communication would also include a pay-telephone call from a criminal to an associate whose residence telephone service has been "tapped" by a law enforcement agency.

Electronic surveillance utilizing a wire tap, room or car probe, or using a "body-pack" recorder involves obtaining a judicially authorized interception of private communications that may be used to gather evidence under very strict circumstances, which are set out in Part VI of the *Criminal Code*. Various criminal offences, including attempts, counselling, accessory after the fact and conspiracies to commit them, for which interception of private communications may be authorized, are contained in s. 183 *Criminal Code* and include any offence where "there are reasonable grounds to believe is a criminal organization offence or any other offence that there are reasonable grounds to believe is an offence described in paragraph (b) or (c) of the definition 'terrorism offence'. . . ."[45]

When applying for an authorization under s. 185(1) *Criminal Code*, a designated agent of the Solicitor General of Canada or the designated agent of the Attorney General of Canada or any province must establish that "other investigative procedures have been tried and have failed or why it appears they are otherwise unlikely to succeed or the urgency of the matter is such that it would be impractical to carry out the investigation of the offence using only other investigative procedures". This requirement doesn't apply to the offences of instructing, participating in the activities of, or committing offences for the benefit of a criminal organization as defined in s. 467.1 *Criminal Code*.[46]

The application made in support of an authorization is most often accompanied by the sworn affidavit of a specially trained investigator that sets out the grounds to establish why the interception of private communications is an investigative necessity.[47]

---

[43]*R. v. Duarte*, [1990] 1 S.C.R. 30, 53 C.C.C. (3d) 1, 65 D.L.R. (4th) 240.

[44]*Criminal Code*, R.S. 1985, c. C-46, s. 184(1).

[45]*Criminal Code*, R.S. 1985, c. C-46, s. 183.

[46]*Criminal Code*, R.S., 1985, c. C-46, s. 467.11 to 467.13.

[47]*Criminal Code*, R.S. 1985, c. C-46, s. 185(1).

In exceptional circumstances, a police officer may intercept private communications without an authorization to do so where there are reasonable grounds to believe that it "is immediately necessary to prevent an unlawful act that would cause serious harm to any person or to property" and that one of the parties to the conversation is either the person who would commit the harm or be the victim of it.[48] An emergency 36-hour authorization to intercept private communications may also be applied for by a small number of specially designated police officers where, because of urgent circumstances, a normal authorization could not be obtained, but such authorizations are very rare.[49] Normally the interception of private communications is authorized for a period not to exceed sixty days, but may be extended by subsequent authorizations for further periods of not more than sixty days.[50]

In recognition of the privilege relating to solicitor-client communications, no authorization to intercept private communications may be issued for any place involving the law offices or residence of a lawyer unless there are reasonable grounds to believe that the lawyer, an employee, or a person residing in their residence has been or will become a party to a designated offence.[51]

A judge may authorize the interception of the communications of known and unknown persons whose communications would assist the investigation, for a sixty day period, if they are satisfied that it ". . . would be in the best interests of the administration of justice to do so".[52] The covert installation and removal of surreptitious listening devices inside residences, cars etc., requires police officers to commit acts that would normally be unlawful. An authorization to intercept private communications, however, specifically authorizes police officers "to install, maintain or remove [the electronic devices used to intercept communications] covertly."[53]

During a drug-trafficking investigation several years ago, a particular suspect was known to conduct transactions on his yacht in the middle of a lake in the belief that his conversations were private and unheard by local law enforcement officers. We had, however, installed a probe on his boat and had to surreptitiously re-enter the boat several times over the course of the boating season to maintain the device or to remove it when we became aware that the boat required servicing by a mechanic who might have inadvertently discovered the unusual apparatus. The probe was irreparably damaged on one occasion when either a mechanic or the owner forgot to replace a transom plug before re-launching. The vessel in question sunk in five feet of water, causing absolute havoc with the boat's electronics – and ours.

The application for an authorization to intercept private communications and any documents in relation to the application are confidential and are placed in a sealed packet by the judge after the application is reviewed, whether or not an authorization is issued.[54] The only times that a packet may be opened are when an issue becomes relevant during

---

[48]*Criminal Code*, R.S. 1985, c. C-46, s. 184.4.

[49]*Criminal Code*, R.S. 1985, c. C-46, s. 188(1)-(2).

[50]*Criminal Code*, R.S. 1985, c. C-46, s. 186(4)(e) and 186(7).

[51]*Criminal Code*, R.S. 1985, c. C-46, s. 186(2).

[52]*Criminal Code*, R.S. 1985, c. C-46, s. 186(1)(a).

[53]*Criminal Code*, R.S. 1985, c. C-46, s. 186(5.2).

[54]*Criminal Code*, R.S. 1985, c. C-46, s. 187(1).

the trial that requires that the contents of the packet be examined or when, after a prosecution has commenced, an accused applies for an order to receive copies of the contents of the packet to make full answer and defence to their charge(s).[55]

Prior to turning over copies of the contents of a sealed packet to any accused, the prosecutor is entitled to edit anything that might reveal the identity of a confidential police informant, compromise any ongoing investigation or endanger the safety of persons engaged in certain intelligence-gathering techniques or that would prejudice future investigations.[56] See Box 9.1.

Any person who is the object of an intercepted private communication must be notified of the interception in writing, usually within ninety days following the expiration of the authorization, whether or not the interception resulted in the laying of charges.[57] Where charges are laid, reasonable notice of intention to produce evidence obtained as the result of such interceptions must be given to all accused persons.[58] The Solicitor General of Canada and the Attorneys General of all provinces are required by law to prepare comprehensive annual reports detailing, among other things, the numbers of authorizations applied for and issued or refused in that year.[59]

BOX 9.1	Investigative Relevance

The area of law regarding the interception of private communications is extremely technical and complex and the use of electronic interception of private communications constitutes an extraordinary and highly invasive law enforcement method that far exceeds those used in everyday investigations. While not necessarily a "last resort" investigative technique, it is a specialized investigative method that should only be reserved for exceptional circumstances and only when absolutely necessary.

Due to the considerable expense of utilizing electronic surveillance, it is a procedure that is usually reserved for major offences such as high-level drug trafficking, murder, organized crime investigations etc. Electronic surveillance should only be resorted to when, having regard to all the circumstances, conventional investigative methods have either been tried unsuccessfully or are unlikely to be successful and the success of the investigation depends upon its use.

9.12 ASSISTANCE ORDERS – SECTION 487.02 *CRIMINAL CODE*

A judge or justice who issues a warrant under the *Criminal Code* or who authorizes the interception of private communications or the installation of a number recorder may also require any person, whose assistance is necessary in the execution of the order, to provide such assistance as may be reasonably required. Assistance orders

---

[55]*Criminal Code*, R.S. 1985, c. C-46, s. 187(1.3) and 187(1.4).

[56]*Criminal Code*, R.S. 1985, c. C-46, s. 187(4).

[57]*Criminal Code*, R.S. 1985, c. C-46, s 196(1).

[58]*Criminal Code*, R.S. 1985, c. C-46, s. 189(5).

[59]*Criminal Code*, R.S. 1985, c. C-46, s. 195(1) to (5).

might be directed to employees of a telephone company to assist with the installation of surreptitious intercepting equipment or to search and compile customer billing records. Assistance orders may also be used to compel employees of Canada Post to assist with the interception of mail addressed by or to the subject of an investigation.[60]

9.13 PRODUCTION ORDERS – SECTIONS 487.012 AND 487.013 *CC*

The vast majority of evidence of criminal offences is obtained from sources or locations other than directly from the suspect or from locations in which a suspect or an accused person has a reasonable expectation of privacy. Evidence may be obtained in the form of copies of documents or data from a party other than the party under investigation. The documents or data in possession of the third party may be accessed by way of a production order issued by a justice or a judge.

If, for example, I was investigating a break in at a bank where an attack was made on the vault using oxy-acetylene welding equipment, I may wish to demonstrate that a particular person of interest had received training and was proficient in the use of such equipment. If I had information that the person of interest to my investigation had graduated from a welding course at a vocational training institute I may wish to obtain a transcript of their academic performance and a statement of the scope and degree of training received.

The vocational institute in possession of those documents either may not wish to voluntarily co-operate with the investigation, or might want to co-operate but be restricted by protection of privacy legislation. Even though the person under investigation does not have physical control over the location where the requested documents or data is kept, they still have a reasonable expectation of privacy that the institution won't release personal information about them to the police, which in turn could be used against them as evidence.

The documents requested in this situation are in the form of official college records that must remain under the control of the institute to preserve the integrity of the information. The information may not even be in hard copy format and may only exist in data form. The investigating officer would be satisfied to receive copies but such records don't actually exist until the educational institute produces them. Subsection 487(1) *Criminal Code* only authorizes the seizure of things that exist in the present, rather than evidence that only exists in a tangible form in an anticipatory sense.[61] (Hill 1999)

A business or institution may simply not have the resources to devote immediately upon receipt of such a request and may require a period of time to comply with the order. You wouldn't drop off a regular search warrant with a business and say. "I'll be back in two weeks to pick up the information."

Fortunately, the Parliament of Canada has provided law enforcement agencies with the solution to this quandary in the form of production orders under section. 487.012 *CC*

---

[60]*Canada Post Corp. v. Canada (Attorney General)* (1995), 95 C.C.C. (3d) 568 (Ont. Ct. (Gen. Div.).

[61]*Re Fleet Aerospace Corporation and The Queen* (1985), 19 C.C.C. (3d) 385 (Ont. H.C.) and *R. v. Noseworthy* (1997), 116 C.C.C. (3d) 376 (Ont C.A.).

and section 487.013 *CC*, the latter of which deals specifically with obtaining records from financial institutions. Production orders strike the necessary balance between the need for judicial pre-authorization, the effective evidence-gathering requirements of law enforcement, the need to preserve the integrity of the documents or data and the privacy interest and physical and human resource requirements of the holder of the documents.

A justice may upon information in writing and on oath or solemn affirmation, require the holder of the information, other than an actual person under investigation, to produce documents or true copies that are certified as such by affidavit, or to produce data. The *ex parte* application for a production order must contain the following information:

1. the name of the peace officer responsible for the order,

2. the criminal offence that there are reasonable grounds to believe has been or is suspected to have been committed,

3. a statement as to how the documents or data will afford evidence of the offence, and

4. the name of the person in control of the documents or data the order is to be directed to.[62]

The production order may, alternatively, require the holder of the information to prepare a document based on other documents or data already in existence.[63] The order may contain whatever terms and conditions the justice considers appropriate, including the form of the information to be supplied and the time within which that the information is to be supplied.

Whenever documents, data or reports are obtained as the result of a production order, a peace officer must make a Report to a Justice in accordance with sections 489(1) and 490 *CC* with the necessary modifications.[64] Copies of documents that are certified as true copies by affidavit are admissible as evidence in judicial proceedings and have the same weight as an original document produced in court by a witness.[65] The procedure is virtually identical for obtaining personal information about people or bank accounts from financial institutions under section 487.013 *Criminal Code*.

If the holder of the document or data is not prohibited by law from disclosing the document and consents to its release, no production order is required for it.[66] Persons, entities or financial institutions may, before the expiration of the production order, apply in writing to the judge who issued the order or another judge in the same territorial division for an exemption from producing the requested documents, data or report, as the case may be.[67]

No person is excused from complying with a production order on the ground that it may tend to incriminate them or subject them to prosecution, but no document prepared by the individual may be used in evidence against them in any proceedings except for perjury or giving contradictory evidence.[68] Any person, entity or financial institution

---

[62]*Criminal Code*, R.S. 1985, c. C-46, s. 487.012 (2)-(3).

[63]*Criminal Code*, R.S. 1985, c. C-46, s. 487.012 (1)-(2).

[64]*Criminal Code*, R.S. 1985, c. C-46, s. 487.012 (6).

[65]*Criminal Code*, R.S. 1985, c. C-46, s. 487.012 (7).

[66]*Criminal Code*, R.S. 1985, c. C-46, s. 487.014 (1).

[67]*Criminal Code*, R.S. 1985, c. C-46, s. 487.015.

[68]*Criminal Code*, R.S. 1985, c. C-46, s. 487.016.

who fails or refuses to comply with a production order is guilty of a summary conviction offence and is liable upon conviction to a fine not exceeding $250 000 or to imprisonment for a term not exceeding six months, or to both.[69]

9.14 ENTRY OF DWELLING HOUSES TO EFFECT ARRESTS – (FEENEY)

On May 22, 1997, the Supreme Court of Canada ruled that, except in cases of hot pursuit of a person who may be arrested without warrant for provincial or indictable offences [section 7.13 Hot Pursuit (Fresh Pursuit)],[70] or in exigent circumstances (section 7.14, Exigent Circumstances),[71] police officers could no longer enter dwelling houses without judicial pre-authorization to effect arrests.[72] An arrest warrant in Form 7.1 may be issued to enter a dwelling house to arrest a person if:

1. reasonable grounds exist to arrest the person without warrant for a *Criminal Code* offence, or the person has contravened or willfully failed to comply or is about to fail to comply with a court disposition, or[73]

2. a warrant for a federal offence exists for the person anywhere in Canada, or

3. grounds exist to arrest the person, without warrant, for any federal offence, other than the *Criminal Code*.

An investigator executing such a warrant must announce the entry unless, at the time of issuance, the justice is satisfied on information on oath that entry without prior announcement is necessary to prevent exposure of any person to imminent bodily harm or death or may result in imminent loss or destruction of evidence.[74] Even after receiving such an authorization for entry without prior announcement the officer still may not enter the dwelling house without making a prior announcement unless reasonable grounds of the necessity to prevent exposure to imminent bodily harm or death or loss or destruction of evidence exist immediately before the entry.[75]

9.15 WEAPONS, AMMUNITION AND EXPLOSIVE SUBSTANCES

If it is impracticable to obtain a warrant due to exigent circumstances, and a police officer has reasonable grounds to believe that a weapon,[76] imitation firearm, ammunition, prohibited device, prohibited ammunition or explosive substance[77] has been used in an

---

[69]*Criminal Code*, R.S. 1985, c. C-46, s. 487.017.

[70]*R. v. Macooh*, [1993] 2 S.C.R. 802, 105 D.L.R. (4th) 96, 82 C.C.C. (3d) 481, 16 C.R.R. (2d) 1, 22 C.R. (4th) 70.

[71]*Criminal Code*, R.S. 1985, c. C-46, s. 529.3.

[72]*R. v. Feeney* (1997), 2 S.C.R. 13, 115 C.C.C. (3d) 129, 7 C.R. (5th) 101.

[73]*Criminal Code*, R.S. 1985, c. C-46, s. 495(1)(a) and 672.91.

[74]*Criminal Code*, R.S. 1985, c. C-46, s. 529.4(1).

[75]*Criminal Code*, R.S. 1985, c. C-46, s. 529.4(2).

[76]*Criminal Code*, R.S. 1985, c. C-46, s. 2.

[77]*Criminal Code*, R.S. 1985, c. C-46, s. 84(1).

offence, or will afford evidence of an offence that has been committed under the *Criminal Code*, they may search a person, vehicle or place other than a dwelling house without warrant, and seize that thing.[78]

If a peace officer has reasonable grounds to believe any person is in possession of a weapon, prohibited device, ammunition, prohibited ammunition or an explosive substance, and that such possession is not desirable in the interests of the safety of any person, a warrant may be obtained to search a dwelling house, building, receptacle or place to seize the thing.[79] If reasonable grounds exist to obtain such a warrant to search any building, receptacle or place under section 117.04(1) *Criminal Code*, but due to exigent circumstances it is impracticable to obtain a warrant, a peace officer may enter a dwelling house, building, receptacle or place and seize weapons, prohibited devices, ammunition, or explosive substances to prevent possible danger to the safety of any person.[80]

The warrantless exigent circumstances search provisions for weapons and ammunition contained in the *Criminal Code* are commonly resorted to in cases of persons threatening suicide, incidents involving persons suffering from mental disorder and often in cases of domestic disputes. A search of dwelling houses, buildings, receptacles or places for weapons, prohibited devices, ammunition, prohibited ammunition or explosive substances conducted either with or without warrant also authorizes peace officers to seize any authorization, licence or registration certificate relating to the weapon, prohibited device, ammunition, prohibited ammunition or explosive substance in the possession of the person.[81]

The terms, "authorizations" and "licences" and "registration certificates" include any form of authorization, licence or registration certificate issued to the person to acquire, own, possess, sell or transport firearms or ammunition under the *Firearms Act*.[82] If at the time of the execution of a warrant or the warrantless seizure of the weapon, prohibited device, ammunition, prohibited ammunition or explosive substance, a peace officer is unable to seize a licence, authorization or registration certificate, they are deemed to be revoked at the time of seizure.

The revocation of these documents does not occur automatically, however, as the Chief Firearms Officer for each respective province must be notified by the involved police agency and requested to cause them to be revoked.

In Ontario, the Chief Firearms Officer may be contacted at:

Ministry of Community Safety and Correctional Services

777 Memorial Avenue

Orillia, ON L3V 7V3

Tel: (705) 329-5522 or toll free at 1-800-731-4000 within Canada and the U.S.A.

Fax: (705) 329-5623

---

[78]*Criminal Code*, R.S. 1985, c. C-46, s. 117.02(1).

[79]*Criminal Code*, R.S. 1985, c. C-46, s. 117.04(1).

[80]*Criminal Code*, R.S. 1985, c. C-46, s. 117.04(2).

[81]*Criminal Code*, R.S. 1985, c. C-46, s. 117.04(1)-(2).

[82]*Criminal Code*, R.S. 1985, c. C-46, s. 84(1).

9.16 APPLICATION TO JUSTICE FOR DISPOSITION – SEC. 117.05 *CC*

Where weapons, ammunition, prohibited devices or explosive substances are seized, either with or without a warrant, a police officer must, within 30 days of the seizure, apply to a justice for an order of disposition with respect to the thing(s) seized. The justice will set a date for a hearing and direct that notices of the hearing be given to specified persons.[83]

At the hearing, which may be held *ex parte* (outside of the presence of the person who is the subject of the application), relevant evidence is heard and the justice may make an order prohibiting the person from possessing weapons, ammunition or explosive substances for a period not exceeding five years, and order that items seized be forfeited to the Crown or otherwise disposed of in a manner directed by the court.[84]

9.17 SEARCH WARRANTS – DISORDERLY HOUSES

Another form of search warrant under the *Criminal Code* deals with disorderly houses, including gaming or betting houses where illegal gambling occurs and bawdy houses, which are locations in which prostitution occurs. A justice may issue a warrant to a peace officer who provides information on oath or solemn affirmation that there are reasonable grounds to believe that a designated offence listed in section 199(1) *CC* is being committed.

Such a warrant authorizes the peace officer to enter and search the place by day or night and to seize anything that may be evidence of one of the designated offences. This section also authorizes the taking into custody of all persons found in that place.[85] A peace officer may also obtain a subection 487(1) *CC* search warrant for any of the designated gambling or keeping a common bawdy house offences, which is probably the currently preferred method of searching illegal gambling and prostitution operations.

9.18 SEARCH WARRANTS – VALUABLE MINERALS

Unless you police in a mining area, you are not ever likely to have to resort to a search warrant that specifically authorizes the search for and seizure of valuable minerals. The theft of ore from mines, a practice known as "high-grading" by unscrupulous employees is a significant problem in mining locations. A peace officer may lay an information in writing on oath or solemn affirmation before a justice that they have reasonable grounds to believe that any valuable mineral (defined in section 2 *CC*) is deposited in a place or held by a person contrary to a criminal offence. Such a warrant, if issued, authorizes the peace officer to search the places or persons mentioned in the information.

---

[83]*Criminal Code*, R.S. 1985, c. C-46, s. 117.05(1).

[84]*Criminal Code*, R.S. 1985, c. C-46, s. 117.05.

[85]*Criminal Code*, R.S. 1985, c. C-46, s. 199(1).

While it is not specifically mentioned that execution of this type of search warrant must be carried out by day, you would be safe to presume that a constitutional application of the restrictions relating to daytime execution and having the warrant available for production if requested would be identical for this type of search warrant also. (Hill 1999)

9.19   WARRANTS – OBSCENE MATERIAL

The *Criminal Code* provides for a judge to issue a warrant to seize any publication that is kept for sale or distribution that on reasonable grounds is believed to be obscene [defined in section 163(8) *CC*], or a crime comic [defined in section 163 *CC*], child pornography, or a voyeuristic recording.[86] The procedure followed is that after seven days from the date of the seizure, the person from whom the material is seized shall be summonsed to show cause why the seized publication or thing should not be forfeited to the Crown.

The court proceedings described are what is referred to as ***in rem*** proceedings, meaning that the subject matter of the proceedings is the seized property rather than being against an individual. The owner or maker of the seized item may appear and be represented during the proceedings for the purpose of opposing the forfeiture of the seized publication or thing.[87] If the court is satisfied on a balance of probabilities that the seized publication or thing is obscene, child pornography, a crime comic or a voyeuristic recording, it may order the item forfeited.

Note that a warrant to seize obscene material, crime comics, child pornography or voyeuristic recordings may only be issued by a judge and not a justice of the peace. Authority to seize would also imply an authority to enter the premises where such items or things are displayed or kept for sale or distribution. While no restrictions are set out regarding the timing of the execution, police officers drafting such a warrant would be well advised to follow the common law that is constitutionally applied to other *Criminal Code* warrants.

9.20   SPECIAL SEARCH WARRANT – PROCEEDS OF CRIME

There is a special provision in the *Criminal Code* that allows a judge to issue a special search warrant upon the *ex parte* application in writing of an Attorney General in Form 1 *CC* to authorize a peace officer to search a building, receptacle or place for property that may be forfeited under the Proceeds of Crime sections of the *Criminal Code*.[88] Similar Proceeds of Crime legislation is contained between sections 14 and 22 of the *Controlled Drugs and Substances Act*.

Although the actual application for the special search warrant is made by the Attorney General rather than by a police officer, the types of cases where special search warrants are utilized comprise complex high-level investigations such as those involving

---

[86]*Criminal Code*, R.S. 1985 c. C-46, s. 164(1).

[87]*Criminal Code*, R.S. 1985 c. C-46, s. 164(4).

[88]*Criminal Code*, R.S. 1985 c. C-46, s. 462.32(1).

organized crime. The types of cases where special search warrants are considered involve close collaboration between the police and the Crown Attorney with all of the information required for the application being supplied by the police.

These proceedings may be initiated in relation to any "designated offence", a term that has undergone several iterations over the past decade but is now held to mean any indictable offence created in any Act of Parliament. The objective of this legislation is to seize and forfeit the fruits of crimes so that individuals who engage in criminal activities aren't permitted to enjoy the benefits or advantages of illegally obtained money or property.

For example, if a ring of individuals conspired to distribute heroin and created a successful trafficking network from which they derived several millions of dollars, they should not be allowed to live in the expensive houses and drive the luxury cars they purchased with the illegal profits of their criminal endeavours.

Proceeds of crime comprise a broad range of property, benefits and advantages. Proceeds might include real property, such as a house, condo or apartment building, money, motor vehicles, boats and airplanes. Proceeds of crime proceedings are *in rem* in nature, meaning that they are directed toward property rather than an individual.

Prior to issuing a special search warrant, a judge may require that prior notice of the seizure be given to anybody who appears to have a valid interest in the property unless to do so would result in the disappearance or devaluation of the property named in the special search warrant.[89] Any property seized must be reported within seven days from the date of seizure to the court, the person from whom the property was seized, and any other person deemed to have an interest in the property.[90]

The Attorney General may also apply for a restraint order that prohibits any person from disposing of or dealing with any interest in the property in any manner other than is allowed by the order.[91] A restraint order remains in effect until the offence-related property is either forfeited or is restored. Any person who fails to comply with such an order is guilty of a dual procedure offence and is liable to a term of imprisonment not exceeding five years.

9.21 *PROVINCIAL OFFENCES ACT, R.S.O. 1990, c. P-33*

A significant portion of the duties of police officers relate to the enforcement of **provincial statutes**, including the *Highway Traffic Act, Liquor Licence Act, Trespass to Property Act* and several others, including their equivalent Acts in other provinces and territories. The vast majority of provincial statute enforcement is accomplished without the necessity of resorting to seizing evidence by search warrants. If, however, a police officer is investigating an occurrence involving a breach of a provincial statute and requires real evidence in the form of documents or other tangible evidence to prove their case, they may not rely on any of the warrants that we have previously discussed.

---

[89]*Criminal Code*, R.S. 1985 c. C-46, s. 462.32(5).

[90]*Criminal Code*, R.S. 1985 c. C-46, s. 462.32(4)(b).

[91]*Criminal Code*, R.S. 1985 c. C-46, s. 462.33(3).

Subsection 487(1) *CC* authorizes the searches of buildings, receptacles or places and the seizure of evidence of offences against the *Criminal Code* or any other Act of Parliament. The provincial statutes of individual provinces were enacted by their respective provincial legislatures and, while they are statutes nonetheless, they do not meet the criteria of subsection 487(1), which is limited to the *Criminal Code* and other Acts of Parliament.

In Ontario, there are hundreds of provincial statutes. To include separate search warrant provisions in each and every one of them, and to create the necessary forms to carry them out would constitute an administrative nightmare for the provincial legislature, the police and the courts. Fortunately, in Ontario, there is one all-encompassing statute that provides a standardized procedure for the enforcement and prosecution of all provincial statutes.

Ontario police officers have only to rely on the search warrant provisions contained in the *Provincial Offences Act*, R.S.O, 1990, c. P-33, *(POA)* for any evidence gathering requirements where a reasonable expectation of privacy on the part of the person from whom the evidence is to be seized could exist. The benefits of having a single search and seizure authority for all provincial offences are numerous as it limits both the number of necessary legal forms and the procedures for their use.

Subsection 158(1) of the *Provincial Offences Act* reads:

"Where a justice is satisfied by information upon oath [or solemn affirmation] that there is reasonable ground to believe that there is in any building, receptacle, or place,

> a) anything upon or in respect of which an offence has been or is suspected to have been committed, or
>
> b) anything that there is reasonable ground to believe will afford evidence as to the commission of an offence,

the justice may at any time issue a warrant in the prescribed form under his or her hand authorizing a police officer or person named therein to search such building, receptacle or place for any such thing, and to seize and carry it before the justice issuing the warrant or another justice to be dealt with by him or her according to law."[92]

Every *POA* search warrant must specify an expiry date for the execution of that warrant and must be executed no later than fifteen days after the date of its issue.[93] As is the case with *Criminal Code* search warrants, it is the duty of a police officer executing the *POA* search warrant "to have the . . . warrant with him or her, where it is feasible to do so and to produce it when requested to do so."[94]

As with *Criminal Code* search warrants, there is a presumption that *POA* search warrants will be executed during daytime hours, with one important difference. *POA* search warrants must be executed between 6:00 a.m. and 9:00 p.m. Standard Time, unless the justice authorizes otherwise on the face of the warrant.[95] I have truly never

---

[92]*Provincial Offences Act*, R.S.O. 1990, c. P-33, s. 158(1).

[93]*Provincial Offences Act*, R.S.O. 1990, c. P-33, s. 158(2).

[94]*Provincial Offences Act*, R.S.O. 1990, c. P-33, s. 148(1).

[95]*Provincial Offences Act*, R.S.O. 1990, c. P-33, s. 158(3).

understood why the *POA* specifies Standard Time, other than perhaps the drafters of the Act knew that it would make for an excellent question on tests and police promotional processes.

Canada is one of the nations of the world that still, although somewhat reluctantly, observes Daylight Savings Time (DST) during the seven-month period between the second Sunday every March and the first Sunday in each November. This means that we advance our clocks one hour forward in the spring and turn them back one hour every Fall. (Remember the old adage, "Spring forward – Fall back".)

The solution to ensuring that your *POA* search warrant is being legally executed is to deduct one hour from the actual time if you plan to execute your warrant between the first Sunday in April and the last Sunday in October. In doing so, you will be within the period of 6:00 a.m. and 9:00 p.m. Standard Time, (7:00 a.m. to 10:00 p.m. Daylight Saving Time). The only other option is to never execute a *POA* search warrant before 7:00 a.m. or after 8:00 p.m., regardless of the time of year if, like me, you are never quite sure of the relationship between Daylight Saving Time and Standard Time and you experience a sharp pain across your forehead whenever you attempt to do these calculations.

While the *POA* does not specifically address the seizure of additional things, not mentioned in a search warrant, the common law relating to seizure of evidence of other offences and plain view seizure may or may not be held to provide the authority for their seizure. When dealing with *POA* search warrants – in fact with any type of search warrant – it is always advisable to obtain a new search warrant, whenever it is practicable to do so.

Amendments to the *POA* may make it possible to obtain search warrants for provincial offences through a telewarrant process similar to s. 487.1 *Criminal Code*, in situations where it isn't practicable for a police officer to appear personally before a justice. Those amendments have not yet received Royal Assent, however, nor does it appear that this is likely to occur in the near future.

Evidence that is seized during a *POA* search must be brought before a justice who shall order it to be detained in the care of a designated person or may direct it to be returned to the person from whom it was seized, the lawful owner or the person lawfully entitled to possess it. The justice may also order the examination, testing, inspection or reproduction of the thing and may set out any terms and conditions, in the opinion of the justice, are necessary for its preservation.[96]

For example, the ordering of examination, testing, inspection and reproduction could allow for motor vehicles seized under the *Highway Traffic Act* to be taken to a place to be examined by a mechanic. Substances seized under the *Liquor Licence Act* might have to be analyzed to prove they contain alcohol, or other forensic analyses may occasionally be required.

Such an order permits a person such as a civilian laboratory employee to lawfully possess a thing or a substance that they might not otherwise have a lawful authority to possess. Such an order would also permit the complete or partial dismantling of an item or causing irreversible changes to it during the testing process, which would otherwise be unauthorized.

---

[96]*Provincial Offences Act*, R.S.O. 1990, c. P-33, s. 159(1).

An order pertaining to the detention of anything seized under a *POA* search warrant is only valid for a period of three months after the time of seizure, unless a justice is satisfied that its further detention is required for a specified period of time, or legal proceedings in which the thing may be required as evidence are instituted within the initial three month detention period.[97]

9.22 *CORONERS ACT*, R.S.O. 1990, c. C-37

When we first examined the entry and inspection provisions of the *Coroners Act* in Chapter 7, it was in relation to the warrantless search authorities contained in this legislation. I feel that the practice of exercising these powers of entry, inspection and seizure using a warrant creates an overlap which requires that we review the authorities under the *Coroners Act*.

There is disagreement regarding the necessity of teaching anything about the *Coroners Act* to aspiring police officers. I am strongly of the opinion, however, that the police and the coroner need to work closely together during death investigations to ensure the interests of both are met.

Young police officers are frequently among the first to arrive at a death scene in the initial stages of an investigation and must be conversant with the fundamental principles of sudden death cases and the role of the coroner to effectively eliminate the possibility of foul play being involved in a death. As we will see shortly, a police officer involved in a death investigation may be required to exercise some of the investigative duties on behalf of the coroner.

Under the *Coroners Act*, every person who becomes aware of a death in one of the following categories is required to report the circumstances to a police officer or a coroner:

"Every person who has reason to believe that a deceased person died,

(a) as a result of,
    (i)   violence,
    (ii) misadventure,
    (iii) negligence,
    (iv) misconduct, or
    (v)   malpractice;

(b) by unfair means;

(c) during pregnancy or following pregnancy in circumstances that might reasonably be attributable thereto;

(d) suddenly and unexpectedly;

(e) from disease or sickness for which he or she was not treated by a legally qualified medical practitioner;

(f) from any cause other than disease; or

(g) under such circumstances as may require investigation,

---

[97]*Provincial Offences Act*, R.S.O. 1990, c. P-33, s. 159(2).

shall immediately notify a coroner or a police officer of the facts and circumstances relating to the death, and where a police officer is notified he or she shall in turn immediately notify the coroner of such facts and circumstances."[98]

Additionally, deaths that occur in provincial institutions, psychiatric facilities, nursing home, or homes for the aged must be reported to the coroner. If a death involves an inmate of a psychiatric facility, adult or young offender correctional institution, or police custody, or occurred at a construction project or mine, in addition to the usual investigation the coroner must also order that an inquest be held into the circumstances of the death.

In order to conduct the necessary investigation into a death, the Office of the Chief Coroner, not having any dedicated investigative resources apart from the medical doctors who are appointed as coroners, must rely upon the investigative capacity of the police in the jurisdiction in which the death occurred.[99] The Chief Coroner may also request the assistance of the Criminal Investigation Branch (CIB) of the Ontario Provincial Police, if appropriate, to assist with an investigation or an inquest.[100]

9.22.1 Investigative Powers of a Coroner

The statutory investigative powers under the *Coroners Act*, which are granted to all coroners, may also be delegated by the coroner to police officers or to medical practitioners who are not designated as coroners. The coroner's investigative powers authorize these three classifications of persons to:

- view or take possession of any dead body,

- enter and inspect (which is different from the enter, search and seize powers contained in s. 487 of the *Criminal Code*) any place where a dead body is found and any place from which the coroner has reasonable grounds to believe the body was removed,[101]

- inspect any place in which the deceased person was, or in which the coroner has reasonable grounds to believe was, before his or her death,

- inspect and extract information from records or writings relating to the deceased, and

- seize anything that there are reasonable grounds to believe is material to the investigation.[102]

Subsection 15(1) of the *Coroners Act* authorizes a coroner to issue a warrant to seize a dead body. While there is no specific statutory authority for a coroner to issue a warrant to "enter", "inspect" or "seize" evidence, common practice (in Ontario) has been for the coroner to issue a warrant, in writing, notwithstanding the absence of documentation

---

[98]*Coroners Act*, R.S.O. 1990, c. C.37, s. 10(1).

[99]*Coroners Act*, R.S.O. 1990, c. C.37, s. 9(1).

[100]*Coroners Act*, R.S.O. 1990, c. C.37, s. 9(2).

[101]*Coroners Act*, R.S.O. 1990, c. C.37, s. 16(1).

[102]*Coroners Act*, R.S.O. 1990, c. C.37, s. 16(2).

specifying the grounds for reasonable belief. Presumably, this practice began in an effort to formalize the delegation of the coroner's authority to police officers, as the grounds for believing that those actions are material and necessary must be the personal belief of the coroner – not of the police officer executing the coroner's delegated powers.

A police officer may not presume to be exercising the powers of a coroner under the *Coroners Act* when the coroner has no knowledge of the case nor any personal belief of the necessity to "enter", "inspect" or "seize" anything, material or otherwise, and where there has not been any directed delegation of the coroner's powers to the police officer(s). See Box 9.2.

Box 9.2	Investigative Relevance

A police criminal investigation must never "piggy-back" on the coroner's investigation to circumvent the requirements of obtaining judicial pre-authorization for search and seizure. There must be a sepa-ration between the role of law enforcement to investigate crime and the role of the coroner to investigate certain classes of deaths.[103]

SUMMARY

- A justice may issue a warrant to seize samples of the suspect's blood for a *Criminal Code* drinking and driving offence involving death or bodily harm if, in the opinion of a qualified medical practitioner, the driver is unable, by reason of physical or mental condition, to consent to providing samples of their breath or blood.

- The incident justifying a warrant to seize blood samples must have occurred within the preceding four hours and the samples must be taken by a medical practitioner or a qualified technician under the direction of a qualified medical practitioner – while the person is still unable to consent to provide samples of their blood and if it would not endanger their life or health to do so.

- A *Controlled Drugs and Substances Act (CDSA)* search warrant may be executed at any time, rather than just by day. No endorsement for night time execution is required on the face of a *CDSA* warrant – nor does such an endorsement render the face of a *CDSA* search warrant invalid.

- *CDSA* search warrants also authorize the search of persons found inside a premises being searched, if the officer executing the warrant has reasonable grounds to believe that they have a controlled substance, precursor or offence-related property on their person and to seize that thing.

- Once issued, a telewarrant has the same legal authority as a warrant personally issued by a justice and may also require the telewarrant [except for 11(2) *CDSA*] to be executed by day (6:00 a.m. to 9:00 p.m.) unless specified otherwise on the face of the warrant.

---

[103]*R. v. Jarvis*, [2002] 3 S.C.R. 757, 2002 S.C.C. 73, also *R. v. Ling*, [2002] 3 S.C.R. 814, 2002 S.C.C. 74, also *R. v. Colarusso*, [1994] S.C.R. 20, 87 C.C.C. (3d) 193, 26 C.R. (4th) 289.

- In addition to the information required in an ordinary search warrant application, a telewarrant application must also contain the reason(s) why it is impracticable for the informant to appear personally before the justice.

- General warrants may be issued by a Provincial Court judge or Superior Court judge to authorize investigative techniques, procedures, the use of devices or any thing in relation to a person or their property, which if it not authorized, would result in a section 8 *Charter of Rights* violation. Nothing authorized by a general warrant is permitted to interfere with the bodily integrity of any person.

- General warrants may be issued to authorize the installation, maintenance and removal of tracking devices, video surveillance cameras and number recorders.

- A DNA warrant will authorize the taking of a DNA sample from a party to a designated primary or secondary offence in order to compare it to evidence about whether the bodily substance that was recovered from the victim or location was from that person.

- When applying for an authorization to intercept private communications, it must be established that other investigative procedures have been tried and have failed or that it appears they are otherwise unlikely to succeed or that the urgency of the matter is such that it would be impractical to carry out the investigation of the offence using only other investigative procedures.

- If a peace officer has reasonable grounds to believe any person is in possession of a weapon, prohibited device, ammunition, prohibited ammunition or an explosive substance, and that such possession is not desirable in the interests of the safety of any person, a warrant may be obtained to search a dwelling house, building, receptacle or place to seize the thing and any licences, authorizations and registration certificates.

- *Provincial Offences Act* search warrants expire no later than 15 days after they are issued and must be executed between 6:00 a.m. and 9:00 p.m. Standard Time, unless the justice authorizes otherwise on the face of the warrant.

- Common practice in Ontario has been for the coroner to issue a warrant, in writing, notwithstanding the absence of documentation specifying the grounds for reasonable belief, to delegate the coroner's powers of entry, inspection and seizure in relation to death investigations.

DISCUSSION QUESTIONS

1. You are a police officer investigating a single motor vehicle accident in which an impaired driver drove into a ditch, rendering his 1972 Volkswagen Diesel Rabbit a total wreck. Only because he was wearing his seatbelt, he avoided suffering any injuries. You place him under arrest for Impaired Care or Control of a Motor Vehicle and read him the breath samples demand. Upon hearing the demand, he begins to rub his chest and says that his chest hurts. He asks you whether or not you think he could be suffering a heart attack. He won't take the breathalyzer

test until he gets a clean bill of health. You suspect that he is feigning illness to avoid giving breath samples. When you arrive at the hospital, it has been two hours since the accident. In front of your prisoner, while taking a blood sample from the driver for medical purposes, a sympathetic doctor offers to take an extra sample of blood and give it to you to analyze for blood alcohol content. Is it permissible for you to receive the sample from the doctor? Explain your answer.

2. Back at the hospital, your impaired driver moans more loudly every time hospital staff tell him they can't find anything wrong with him. It has now been three hours since the accident. Your Sergeant calls you to ascertain what the delay is and you explain your situation to him. He informs you that you should contact the telewarrant number and request a telewarrant authorizing a qualified medical practitioner to take a blood sample on the grounds that your impaired driver is pretending to be ill and is not cooperating. Will you follow the advice given by your Sergeant? Explain your answer.

3. You are a police officer working day shift in a small town. An elderly couple stops you while you are on patrol and reports that their thirty-year-old son, who lives with them, suffers from paranoid schizophrenia. His condition is normally controlled by his prescription medications but they cause him painful side-effects. As a result, he hasn't been taking his medications for a week and is becoming increasingly violent with both of them. He storms around the house, ranting and yelling at them and has hit them both within the past two days, causing minor bruising and abrasions. Their son fears that the police will come to get him and says that he won't allow himself to be taken into custody.

    Years ago, before the couple's son became ill, he was an active hunter and still has a collection of high-powered hunting rifles, including a .30-30 lever action rifle, a bolt-action .303 calibre rifle, a pump-action .30-06 rifle and a single-shot .22 rifle. He also has a .410 gauge shotgun and a 12 gauge pump shotgun. He keeps the firearms in a gun vault in his bedroom and has a large stock of ammunition for all of the weapons. The couple left their house under the pretence of going to buy him more ammunition and took the only set of keys to their son's pickup truck with them. The couple informs you that they are afraid to return home in case their son hurts them. What will you do to help them? What are your concerns, if any, regarding the firearms, and what do you propose to do? This is a true story.

 WEBLINKS

www.cfc-cafc.gc.ca/safety-surete/contacts_e.asp

Canada Firearms Centre website containing links to related resources and a directory of Chief Firearms Officers for the various provinces and territories.

scc.lexum.umontreal.ca/en/index.html

Judgments of the Supreme Court of Canada in a free searchable database provided through a collaborative effort between the Supreme Court and the LexUM laboratory of the University of Montreal's Faculty of Law.

www.canlii.org/en/index.html

The Canadian Legal Information Institute is a non-profit organization managed by the Federation of Law Societies of Canada, whose goal is to make Canadian law available for free on the internet. This website contains a free searchable database of case law and both federal and provincial statutes, including the *Criminal Code*, *Controlled Drugs and Substances Act*, and *Firearms Act* mentioned in this chapter.

Chapter 10

Admissibility of Seized Evidence

"The administration of justice does not have to be brought into disrepute on a national scale before courts may interfere to protect the integrity of the process within which they operate."[1]

The Honourable Madam Justice Louise Arbour,
in *R. v. Buhay*, [2003] 1 S.C.R. 631, 2003 SCC 30, 225 D.L.R. (4th) 624, 4 W.W.R. 1,
174 C.C.C. (3d) 97, 107 C.R.R. (2d) 240, 10 C.R. (6th) 205, 177 Man. R. (2d) 72,
177 Man. R. (2e) 72.

Learning Outcomes

After reading this chapter, students should be able to:

- Explain two main purposes that the *Charter of Rights* is intended to serve.
- Summarize the applicability of the *Charter of Rights* in relation to the various enforcement actions of police officers.
- Give specific examples of types of police misconduct that have resulted in past successful *Charter* challenges.
- Differentiate between the terms conscriptive evidence and non-conscriptive evidence and explain the difference between them with respect to the probability of admissibility.
- Describe possible remedies that might be awarded by a criminal court in response to a successful *Charter* challenge.

10.1 INTRODUCTION

In the preceding chapters of this textbook, we examined a variety of police powers relating to use of force, arrest, discretion, judicial interim release and the majority of police evidence gathering techniques relating to search and seizure. I have intentionally left this chapter, dealing with the admissibility of evidence, to the end of the book as this is

---

[1] scc.lexum.umontreal.ca/en/2003/2003scc30/2003scc30.html Retrieved: February 25, 2007.

precisely where this issue becomes relevant during a police investigation. It is at the end-stage of a successful case, in the court room, where admissibility of evidence becomes relevant in terms of potential consequences of the use of police powers, in all cases that are resolved by the laying of charges.

In a typical police investigation, either a complaint is received and the police respond to it reactively, or an investigation is commenced proactively by a police officer, having witnessed a breach of the law or in response to intelligence information concerning criminal activity. Witnesses and informants are interviewed, crime scenes are examined, persons of interest are eliminated, suspects are identified and evidence is gathered through a variety of methods.

If sufficient reasonable grounds are developed, perhaps an arrest is made and a charge is laid. The accused is either released from custody to await their trial, or they are remanded into custody until court proceedings are finalized.

At the trial of the accused, every aspect of the police investigation may become the focus of a challenge in which an accused person claims that his or her *Charter* rights have been violated in some way. The alleged violation, real or perceived, might involve the accused's rights having been infringed in some cases or denied in other cases. In any event, if the court finds that a breach or violation of the accused's rights did occur, and if evidence was obtained as the result of the breach or violation, the incriminating thing or item might possibly be excluded as evidence against the accused.

Imagine the following case. A convenience store is victimized by a robbery in which an elderly employee is struck repeatedly by a masked robber armed with a baseball bat. A transient male matching the description of the suspect is apprehended fleeing the scene. The accused does not resist arrest when he is caught, but is "taught a lesson in back alley justice" by the arresting officers for having injured the elderly store clerk. The stolen money, the mask, and the baseball bat are not recovered at the time of the arrest.

The suspect is returned to the police station where he is strip-searched by a different group of officers. The suspect is eventually turned over to a detective who persuades him that he does not really need to speak to a lawyer as the evidence is more than enough to convict him – so he "might as well start thinking about pleading guilty."

The detective obtains a confession from the suspect, who then accompanies the detective on a video-taped "show and tell", during which he leads the investigator to where he hid the stolen money and the baseball bat underneath a dumpster. A ski mask is also found that is similar in all respects to the one worn by the suspect on the in-store closed circuit security video.

The detective demands and receives DNA samples from the suspect. The known samples from the accused are then compared to the area around the mouth of the ski mask and are matched to the suspect. A charge of armed robbery is laid against the suspect. The money is photographed and after the serial numbers are recorded, it is returned to the owner of the store.

The elderly store employee is released from the hospital and is publicly grateful to the local police service for their quick and efficient response. The incident receives widespread media coverage that is very positive to the police and every officer associated with the case receives a commendation from the Chief of Police. By all accounts, this has been a very successful police investigation, wouldn't you agree?

The evidence is preserved for continuity, the Crown brief is prepared and the matter eventually makes its way to court. The accused, who has remained in custody, has now retained the services of a prominent criminal lawyer and pleads not guilty. Not guilty? In the face of overwhelming evidence of his guilt, including a full confession and a positive DNA match? How can this possibly be?

At the preliminary hearing, counsel for the defence raises certain issues and addresses the court in the following manner:

"Your Honour, may it please the court, just yesterday, my client informed me that he is only 15 years of age, a **Young Person** within the meaning of the *Youth Criminal Justice Act*. My client did not give his correct date of birth to the police as he didn't want his parents to learn of his arrest. Notwithstanding my client not being truthful to the police about his age, the police made no apparent effort to confirm his true age. This important fact was ignored by the police who did not afford my client the additional rights that are granted to Young Persons under the law."

"Your Honour, I have with me a copy of a police bulletin issued by a neighbouring police service reporting my client missing as a juvenile runaway exactly five days prior to the incident under investigation. The police circular accurately depicts my client's name, photograph and true date of birth. A copy of this circular was sent to the police service that investigated this case. I offer a copy of the police bulletin to the court as evidence of these facts and am prepared to call witnesses to testify about the circumstances. If necessary, my client's mother is prepared to testify as to his true date of birth."

"Your Honour, I also have a colour copy of the arrest photographs of the accused showing him having a blackened right eye. A black eye that my client alleges he received while he was in police custody. In fact, three independent civilians who witnessed the arrest will testify that my client did not have a black eye when he was initially apprehended by the police. Add to that the fact that my youthful client was unnecessarily strip-searched while in police custody. I assume, Your Honour, that the police weren't searching for the baseball bat and I, for one, am at a loss to explain what type of evidence they may have been searching my client's body for in a case of this nature."

"Also, Your Honour, after being taken into police custody, my client had asked to speak to a lawyer, but he was persuaded not to by the detective who convinced my client that no lawyer could help him because 'there was so much evidence against him'. Had my client been afforded the benefit of legal counsel, he would have been advised against giving a confession. Had my client availed himself of counsel, he never would have led the police to the stolen money, the baseball bat and the ski mask with the incriminating DNA evidence."

At this stage of the proceedings, the case is suddenly not looking quite as strong as it did just a few minutes earlier. The Crown prosecutor has received notice that they will now face a barrage of *Charter* challenges. If the court subsequently finds that the evidence was obtained in a manner that violated the rights of the accused, the court may impose whatever legal remedy it considers appropriate – evidence could be excluded and the accused may be acquitted or the proceedings against the accused could be stayed.

We will discuss the various remedies available to the court to resolve successful *Charter* challenges and the factors that determine how those decisions are arrived at later in this chapter.

10.2 PURPOSE OF THE *CHARTER OF RIGHTS AND FREEDOMS*

Canadian courts have long understood that law enforcement can be a very difficult job. Our courts also realize that the policing function is largely accomplished by men and women with little or no formal legal training. Complex operational decisions are often made by frontline officers with little, if any, supervision and often while under considerable stress. Decisions that must be made and acted upon in only seconds or minutes, may be dissected and analyzed by legal experts over the course of hours, days, even weeks.

Violations of individual rights are frequently inadvertently committed by well-intentioned police officers. Officers who unintentionally commit *Charter* violations act either out of a lack of training, experience or as the result of faulty interpretation of legal standards or improper systemic policies and practices. It is the duty of the courts to distinguish between what individual police officers and their police services feel is reasonable and what the *Charter* considers reasonable. (Hill et al. 1999)

The goal of the *Charter* is not to punish the police for intentionally or inadvertently breaking the rules by infringing or denying an individual's *Charter* rights – nor is it the goal of the *Charter* to reward offenders whose rights have been violated. The objective of the *Charter* is to protect the guaranteed rights of private individuals and to avoid improper actions by those who administer and enforce the law.

The common theme that I have tried to stress throughout this textbook is that the actions of the police often can and do interfere with the guaranteed rights of persons who are under investigation. The certainty of this conflict is to be expected in a situation where the rights and values of offenders are in direct opposition with the rights of society as a whole.

When society's rights to prevent crime and to apprehend offenders supercede the rights of the individual the courts will admit the evidence. When, however, the police fail to abide – intentionally or otherwise – with *Charter* expectations, that misconduct will not be tolerated by the courts, for the same reason that unlawful conduct by criminal offenders is not tolerated.

The public expects that representatives of law enforcement – individually and collectively – will abide by high standards of conduct and will respect the rights of individual citizens that the community appoints them to protect.

Later in this chapter, we will examine a number of examples of types of police misconduct that have resulted in the exclusion of evidence under the *Charter of Rights and Freedoms*.

10.3 *CHARTER* CHALLENGES

"Evidence improperly obtained is prima facie *admissible. The onus is on the person who wishes the evidence excluded to establish the further ingredient: that the admission of the evidence would bring the administration of justice into disrepute."*[2]

Seaton, J.A., quoted by The Honourable Mr. Justice Lamer J. in *R. v. Collins.*

---

[2]*R. v. Collins*, [1987] 1 S.C.R. 265, 38 D.L.R. (4th) 508, 3 W.W.R. 699, 33 C.C.C. (3d) 1, 56 C.R. (3d) 193, 13 B.C.L.R. (2d) 1.

The *Charter of Rights* applies to all aspects of the Parliament and government of Canada, the provincial and territorial legislatures and all matters within their respective authorities.[3] The *Charter*'s broad application extends to virtually every operation of government at the federal and provincial levels, any legislation passed at those levels of government and also the manner in which federal and provincial legislation is enforced. (Rock et al 2006)

Therefore, the first step in establishing a *Charter* violation during criminal proceedings is for an individual to claim that one or more of their rights has been infringed as the result of legislation or some form of government action. In policing, the majority of challenges occur as the result of warrantless searches. (Hill 1999)

In criminal or quasi-criminal trials, only an infringement of the rights of the accused can be challenged and only the accused will be granted standing to claim that a violation of their rights has occurred. The *Charter* rights of witnesses, investigators, prosecutors and defence counsel cannot be breached – only the rights of the accused.

Only the accused will suffer the consequences of the evidence used against them and this is the basis which permits them to challenge the admission of the evidence.[4] No uninvolved third party may vicariously raise a *Charter* challenge concerning an alleged breach of the rights of another person.[5]

While the guaranteed rights of any individual may be breached during any stage of an investigation, unless that person is subsequently charged with an offence, they may not initiate a challenge at trial – for without a charge, there can be no trial for illegally obtained evidence to be used against the accused. An individual who is not charged with an offence but whose constitutional rights were breached during a police investigation may still seek remedy through a civil court action.

10.4 *CHARTER* VIOLATIONS IN THE SEIZURE OF EVIDENCE

There are several areas in which police misconduct – intentional or otherwise – can result in the infringement of an accused person's *Charter* rights. In this section we will examine some of the different types of police misconduct that have resulted in successful *Charter* breaches.

This section is intended to provide more of an overview of categories of police misconduct than a definitive analysis of the issue. To attempt to cover every imaginable type of police wrongdoing is simply beyond the scope of this textbook.

My intention in drawing attention to the following examples of police misconduct is not to condone any of these forms of misbehaviour. Nor is it my intention to provide a roadmap for how to conduct damage control when an investigative mistake has been made. By highlighting mistakes that have caused investigations to falter in the past, it is my hope that the reader will become more inclined to recognize the ramifications of unacceptable behaviours and be motivated to avoid committing these types of misconduct.

---

[3]*Canadian Charter of Rights and Freedoms*, Being Part I of the *Constitution Act*, 1982, Enacted by the *Constitution Amendment Proclamation*, 1983, SI/84-102, effective June 21, 1984, s. 32(1).

[4]*R. v. Pugliese* (1992), 71 C.C.C. (3d) 295 (Ont. C.A.) and *R. v. Carosella*, [1997] 1 S.C.R. 80.

[5]*Borowski v. Canada (Attorney General)* (1989), 1 S.C.R. 342, 47 C.C.C. (3d) 1, 57 D.L.R. (4th) 231.

10.4.1 Institutional Recklessness

If a police service, knowingly for any reason, or unknowingly – but recklessly – allows their officers to repeatedly operate outside of the expected standards of the *Charter*, the police service could be found to be institutionally reckless. Every law enforcement agency needs to have an understanding of the complexity of *Charter* issues.

The policies and standing orders of a police service must reflect current policing practices that effectively guide members of the police service to remain within the bounds of the law and to respect the rights of individuals. Police services must also ensure that their respective officers have the correct level of training and experience necessary to conduct the tasks they are assigned to carry out.

For example, the principles of search warrant preparation are virtually the same for a break and enter as they are for a homicide investigation but the nature and scope of the evidence is far more complex in the latter. It hardly needs to be said that the consequences of *Charter* violations and possible exclusion of evidence are also obviously far greater with a homicide due to the severity of the offence.

Similarly, a certain skill-set is required to investigate minor thefts but a much higher level of expertise is necessary to conduct serial sexual predator investigations. The drafting of wiretap authorizations is a highly complex task that should only be undertaken by officers who have received a high level of training to develop the necessary expertise.

It isn't that some investigators just aren't capable – but neither is it the case that all police officers are equal in terms of their capabilities due to differences in their training, knowledge and experience. Police investigations vary widely in terms of their complexity, as do the skill-sets that are required to conduct them properly. Investigators should hone their investigative skills by commencing with cases requiring less expertise such as minor thefts, missing persons, break and enters, minor frauds and low level drug offences.

As an officer's expertise develops with training and with demonstrated experience, investigators may then be assigned to cases of higher complexity such as crimes of major drug trafficking, arsons, robberies, sexual assaults and suspicious deaths. Major crime, including high level drug offences and homicides should not be used by police services as a training ground for investigators. To do so invites a heightened risk of faulty prosecutions, wrongful convictions, *Charter* violations, court challenges, acquittals and lawsuits.

The irresponsible policy of assigning inexperienced investigators to cases that exceed their current capability, while having little or no concern for the possible consequences, indicates a blatant organizational disregard or at least an inappropriate indifference toward individual rights. In my opinion, such unjustifiable practices are nothing less than institutionally reckless and are as much or more the responsibility of the police service than of the individual police officer.

Effective police officers should, however, always strive to remain current regarding matters of relevant case law, prevailing legal standards and legislative amendments. If specialized training is not readily available to them through their police service, they should establish a self-learning program to develop their knowledge and expertise, utilizing whatever means are available to them.

10.4.2 Abuse of Process

"Finally, the fact that the police rode roughshod over a young offender's refusal to provide his bodily samples would certainly shock the conscience of all fair minded members of the community. The admission of the evidence would thus bring the administration of justice into disrepute." [6]

> The Honourable Justice Mr. Cory, J. commenting on the taking of a saliva sample, hair samples and dental impressions, under threat of force, from an in-custody 17-year-old murder suspect in *R. v. Stillman*.

Abuse of process involves any form of wrongdoing during the investigative or prosecutorial stage to such a degree as to contravene the community's basic sense of decency and fair play. In a 1997 Supreme Court decision involving a sexual homicide of 14-year-old Pamela Bischoff, investigating police officers violated the rights of a 17-year-old suspect by obtaining bodily samples by force and under threat of force. These samples were taken without the consent of the youthful suspect and without the knowledge of his parents or legal counsel.

The Supreme Court ruled that the search was not conducted incident to the suspect's arrest and was a clear violation of the suspect's *Charter* rights. The police, while vigorously trying to solve a shocking and violent murder of a young girl, blatantly disregarded the rights of the suspect and coerced him into providing samples of his public hair. The suspect was also forced to submit to a two hour dental procedure, during which dental impressions were taken by a dentist.

The accused's appeal was partially successful. A new trial was ordered and the hair, buccal (oral) swabs and dental impressions were declared inadmissible. A mucous stained tissue discarded by the suspect, while in police custody, that identified the suspect by his DNA was declared admissible as it existed independently of the *Charter* violation and was inevitably discoverable by the police.[7] (See section 10.9 Discoverability – the "But For" Test.)

10.4.2.1 Arrest – Rights to Counsel - Right to Silence   The actions of the police may be deemed to affect the fairness of the trial where the accused is originally arrested for one offence and then charged with a more serious offence without being informed once again of their right to counsel. An accused person must be informed of the jeopardy they face.[8] In some cases, prisoners have been questioned without even having been informed of their right to counsel or their right to silence. Prisoners who have been arrested must also be informed of the existence and availability of duty counsel and legal aid.[9]

When an accused person indicates a desire to speak to legal counsel, police officers are required to refrain from questioning the suspect until they have had an opportunity to do so.[10]

---

[6]*R. v. Stillman*, [1997] 1 S.C.R. 607, 185 N.B.R. (2d) 1, 185 N.B.R. (2e) 1, 144 D.L.R. (4th) 193, 113 C.C.C. (3d) 321, 42 C.R.R. (2d) 189, 5 C.R. (5th) 1.

[7]*R. v. Stillman*, supra.

[8]*R. v. Black*, [1989] 2 S.C.R. 138, 50 C.C.C. (3d) 1, 70 C.R. (3d) 97 *R. v. Evans*, [1991] 1 S.C.R. 869, 63 C.C.C. (3d) 289, 4 C.R. (4th) 144.

[9]*R. v. Brydges*, [1990] 1 S.C.R. 190, 53 C.C.C. (3d) 330, [1990] 2 W.W.R. 220.

[10]*R. v. Manninen*, [1987] 1 S.C.R. 1233, 41 D.L.R. (4th) 301, 34 C.C.C. (3d) 385, 38 C.R.R. 37, 58 C.R. (3d) 97, 21 O.A.C. 192.

Where a prisoner has indicated to the police a desire to remain silent, the police must not attempt to elicit incriminating evidence from them.[11]

This also applies to the use of undercover police officers during the detention of the accused.[12] There are absolutely no restrictions on eliciting information from persons who are not in custody, even though they may have indicated their intention to remain silent to the police.[13]

10.4.2.2 Verbal and Physical Abuse

"If a person is subjected to inhumane conditions, such that they confess purely out of desire to escape those conditions, then the resulting confession will not be voluntary."

Morrissey, J. referring to *R v. Hoilett*,
1999 CanLII 3740 (ON C.A.) (1999), 136 C.C.C. (3d) 449 (Ont.C.A.).[14]

Criminal courts take a very dim view of police officers engaging in an abuse of their official powers to threaten, coerce, insult or menace prisoners. This type of oppressive behaviour on the part of law enforcement officers is totally unacceptable even when it does not result in prejudice to the accused or affect the outcome of the trial.

Such unprofessional behaviour on the part of police officers is not only grossly improper, it will always be seen to have an adverse impact on the administration of justice – amounting to an abuse of process. Even where actual physical violence is not involved, verbal insults and the use of profanity toward prisoners in custody is sufficient to result in a successful abuse of process challenge.[15] Marathon interrogations of sleep-deprived prisoners, withholding food for lengthy periods and depriving prisoners of clothing and blankets are other examples of abuse toward individuals in police custody.[16]

In cases where actual unjustified physical violence is used by the police toward a person in custody, it constitutes not only criminal behaviour on the part of the offending officer – it is a form of extra-judicial punishment. That is to say that the prisoner is being punished by agents of the state (police) before being convicted of an offence through due process of law.

Incidents involving pepper-spraying incapacitated prisoners[17] and even minor forms of assault, such as the slapping of the hand of a prisoner attempting to light a cigarette,[18] have resulted in cases being lost. Unwarranted aggression on the part of police officers is beneath the standard of behaviour that is expected by the public and would prejudice the integrity of the judicial system if it were to be allowed by the courts.

---

[11]*R. v. Broyles*, [1991] 3 S.C.R. 595, 68 C.C.C. (3d) 308, [1992] 1 W.W.R. 289 (7:0).

[12]*R. v. Hebert*, [1990] 2 S.C.R. 151, 57 C.C.C. (3d) 1, 77 C.R. (3d) 145.

[13]*R. v. Hicks*, [1990] 1 S.C.R. 120, 54 C.C.C. (3d) 575, 73 C.R. (3d) 204 (7:0) aff'g 42 C.C.C. (3d) 394, 64 C.R. (3d) 68 (Ont. C.A.).

[14]Quoted by The Honourable Mr. Justice W.P. Sullivan in *R. v. Wiegand* (2003), 11 C.R. (6th) 356, 2003 ABQB 283 (CanLII).

[15]*R. v. McCrea* (2004), 185 C.C.C. (3d) 222, 120 C.R.R. (2d) 85 (B.C.C.A.).

[16]*R. v. Hoilett* (1999), 136 C.C.C. (3d) 449, 26 C.R. (5th) 332, 121 O.A.C. 391, 1999 CanLII 3740 (ON C.A.).

[17]*R. v. Spannier* (1996), CanLII 978 (BC S.C.).

[18]*R. v. Woodland*, 2001 BCPC 255 (CanLII).

10.4.3 Reasonable Expectation of Privacy

Considerable attention was paid to the issue of an individual's expectation of privacy throughout chapters 7, 8 and 9 of this textbook. Suffice it to say, however, that a great number of *Charter* challenges could be avoided if police officers adhered strictly to the legal requirement of pre-judicial authorization. In any search and seizure situation where a person under investigation may have a reasonable expectation of privacy, a police officer should obtain the appropriate warrant or authorization, where it is feasible to do so. (See Chapter 8 – Search Warrants and Chapter 9 – Other Search Warrants and Authorizations.)

Warrantless searches must only be carried out where they are authorized by common law or by statute law, if the law itself is reasonable and if the search is conducted in a reasonable manner. (See Chapter 7 – Warrantless Search and Seizure.)

10.4.3.1 Police Trespass   Several court decisions have established that when police officers commit a trespass, without invitation or judicial authorization, or in the absence of reasonable grounds, they infringe upon the guaranteed rights of an individual to be free from unreasonable search and seizure. Past incidents have involved investigators conducting "perimeter searches" of an accused's property to conduct visual, olfactory (smell) and aural (sound) observations of a location in order to develop reasonable grounds to obtain a warrant.

Once armed with a valid search warrant, the officers returned to the accused's property and seized evidence of a marijuana growing operation. One particular *Charter* challenge and a later similar case were successful because the reasonable grounds to obtain the warrants were illegally obtained and to admit the seized evidence would have brought the administration of justice into disrepute.[19]

In a 1998 decision of the British Columbia Supreme Court, police officers being aware of the Supreme Court of Canada restrictions against trespassing on an accused's property to conduct warrantless perimeter searches trespassed on adjoining neighbours' property. In this case, the police still had no legal authorization to be there, nor did they obtain the consent of the respective property owners.

After developing reasonable grounds through the making of sensory observations, the police applied for and received a search warrant, which they executed, and seized a variety of marijuana growing equipment. The BC Supreme Court did not allow the accused's challenge to exclude the evidence on the grounds that the accused's privacy rights were not infringed upon and that she had no standing to claim an infringement of the rights of her neighbours.

The court further ruled that the conduct of the police did not amount to an abuse of process.[20] Readers are recommended to resort to such a practice with considerable caution, if at all, however, as the officers in this case, admittedly committed an unlawful act through their unauthorized trespass on the neighbouring properties and in doing so, could face legal sanctions for their actions.

---

[19]*R. v. Kokesch*, [1990] 3 S.C.R. 3, [1991] 1 W.W.R. 193, 61 C.C.C. (3d) 207, [1991] 50 C.R.R. 285, 1 C.R. (4th) 62, 51 B.C.L.R. (2d) 157; also *R. v. Grant*, [1993] 3 S.C.R. 223, 8 W.W.R. 257, 84 C.C.C. (3d) 173, 17 C.R.R. (2d) 269, 24 C.R. (4th) 1.

[20]*R. v. Vereczki*, 1998 CanLII 1996 (BC S.C.).

10.4.4 Tricks vs. Dirty Tricks

"The authorities, in dealing with shrewd and often sophisticated criminals, must sometimes of necessity resort to tricks or other forms of deceit and should not through the [exclusionary] rule be hampered in their work."[21]

The Honourable Mr. Justice Lamer, March 2, 1981,
prior to the proclamation of the *Charter of Rights*,
in *Rothman v. The Queen*, [1981] 1 S.C.R. 640, 59 C.C.C. (2d) 30, 121 D.L.R. (3d) 578, 1981 CanLII 23 (S.C.C.).

Numerous court decisions have recognized that it is unfair to hold the police to strict rules as to how an accused must be treated during the investigation of each and every major crime. Many police activities are conducted in a covert, undercover manner and must be believable to the suspect if they are to be successful. Inherent in any undercover police operation is a certain amount of deceit if the undercover officer is to conceal their true identity and collect sufficient evidence upon which to convict or exclude the person under investigation from suspicion.

The courts will likely condone behaviour on the part of the police that is intended simply to trick or deceive the subject of an investigation. What our courts will not condone is behaviour that amounts to "dirty tricks" – police behaviour that is so unfair, indecent, unacceptable or outrageous that it would shock the community's sense of fair play and decency or would prejudice the accused's right to a fair trial.[22]

In the 1990 British Columbia Supreme Court decision of *R. v. Cretney*, undercover police officers supplied a person suspected of murder with alcoholic beverages, knowing that he was a heavy drinker. After reviewing the police conduct, the court ruled that the liquor was used only as an investigative aid to bolster the cover and credibility of the undercover officer and did not undermine the administration of justice.[23]

Lying to a suspect to overemphasize the effectiveness of a polygraph during an interrogation and blaming the victim for provoking an offence under investigation has been held to be oppressive behaviour on the part of the police that exceeded acceptable limits.[24] As long as a ruse used by the police to obtain evidence is not seen to affect the voluntariness of the suspect's actions, however, the evidence may still be admissible.

The police have significantly more latitude in dealing with suspects who are not under arrest or detention than with those who are in police custody. The voluntariness of an in-custody prisoner's actions is already influenced to a significant extent due to the increased control that the police have over them and they are more likely to be deprived of their free will in the face of coercion or trickery.

For example, lying to a suspect who is not in custody to obtain a confession, by intentionally misleading them about the strength of evidence against them would constitute a trick, but any admission or confession obtained would still likely be admissible. **Propping** is a form of ruse that involves the strategic placement of artifacts intended to

---

[21]www.canlii.org/en/ca/scc/doc/1981/1981canlii23/1981canlii23.html Retrieved: May 11, 2007.

[22]*R. v. Mccreery*, 1996 CanLII 1073 (BC S.C.).

[23]*R. v. Cretney*, 1999 CanLII 6350 (BC S.C.).

[24]*R. v. Black*, 1996 CanLII 7018 (SK Q.B.).

be observed by the suspect to impress upon them the gravity of the offence and the strength of the evidence against them.

Propping may include conspicuous signage, photographs, wall-charts and file cabinets bearing the suspect's name on the drawer fronts. Case Managers have even displayed mannequins dressed to resemble a victim in abduction/homicide cases. Such behaviour is not at a level of conduct that would shock the community's sense of fair play, nor does it deprive the suspect of free will. (Van Allen 2007)

A police officer posing as a member of the clergy to obtain an in-custody suspect's "confession" would be an example of a "dirty trick". Another example of a "dirty trick" would be a plain-clothes officer posing as an attorney and giving false advice to a suspect to cooperate with a police investigation by telling the police everything they know.

Both forms of behaviour would be certain to shock the conscience of the community and any evidence resulting from either practice would be excluded.[25] A police officer pretending to be a drug user to gather evidence of drug trafficking from suspects who are not in custody would, however, not tend to shock the community due to the acceptable investigative techniques required to investigate different classes of crime.[26]

The making of disparaging comments intended to undermine the reliability of a suspect's choice of attorney, made by the police in order to convince the suspect to confess, has also been held to constitute unacceptable behaviour likely to affect the fairness of a confession and the integrity of the trial of the accused.[27]

10.4.5 Disclosure

"Crown counsel is under a duty to disclose [to the defence] all information in his or her possession relevant to the guilt or innocence of the accused . . . whether favourable or unfavourable to the accused . . . which is not clearly irrelevant.[28]

The Honourable G. Arthur Martin, OC., O. Ont., LL.D.,
The Attorney General's Advisory Committee on Charge Screening, Disclosure and Resolution

Disclosure refers to the legal obligation on a prosecutor to make known all relevant information in their possession, whether favourable or unfavourable to the accused, about a case to allow the accused to make full answer and defence to the charge(s) against them.

While there may be privilege relating to certain evidence gathered during a police case, there is never any ownership in the findings of the investigation. Once a criminal charge has been laid, evidence gathered during the course of the investigation doesn't belong solely to the police or to the Crown. If evidence can be said to be owned at all, it is the property of the effective administration of justice. (Van Allen 2007)

---

[25]*Rothman v. The Queen*, [1981] 1 S.C.R. 640, 59 C.C.C. (2d) 30, 121 D.L.R. (3d) 578.

[26]*R. v. Miller* (1991), 5 O.R. (3d) 678, 68 C.C.C. (3d) 517, 9 C.R. (4th) 347, 50 O.A.C. 282, 1991 CanLII 2704, (ON C.A.).

[27]*R. v. Burlingham*, [1995] 2 S.C.R. 206, 124 D.L.R. (4th) 7, 97 C.C.C. (3d) 385, 38 C.R. (4th) 265, 1995 CanLII 88 (S.C.C.).

[28]The Martin Report (1993) - Recommendation 41 at p. 7.

Disclosure of evidence allows accused persons to prepare their defence to the charge(s) against them by making all relevant evidence – **inculpatory** as well as **exculpatory** – available to the defence prior to the commencement of the trial. The benefits to the justice system in disclosing evidence include:

1. It helps to ensure against the possibility of wrongfully convicting persons by allowing accused persons the opportunity to investigate and rebut false or erroneous evidence.

2. It allows for the resolution of non-contentious issues of evidence that a well-informed defence may stipulate (agree to).

3. Accused persons may elect to waive preliminary hearings or shorten the duration of their trials.

4. Accused persons may plead guilty to offence(s) against them when they are aware of the strength of the evidence against them.[29]

The 1993 Martin Report recommended that the defence is entitled to disclosure of the following types of evidence, including:

1. A copy of the charges contained in the information or indictment

2. A complete synopsis prepared by the investigating police agency setting out the circumstances of the alleged offences committed by the accused

3. Written statements or 'Will Say' statements of all persons, including statements of co-accused persons, interviewed during the police investigation, whether or not the Crown intends to call them as witnesses, and any police reports or notes from which they were prepared or in relation to interviews where no statements were taken

4. The defence shall be given an opportunity to view or listen to the original copy of electronically recorded statements in private. Copies or transcripts of such electronically recorded statements may be disclosed at the discretion of the Crown

5. The criminal record of the accused

6. A copy of any written statement of the accused, including transcripts, corresponding police reports or notes or the opportunity to view or listen to the original copy of an electronically recorded statement in private

7. Copies of any police occurrence report and supplementary report

8. Copies of forensic, medical or laboratory reports relating to the offence

9. Copies of documents, photographs, audio or video recordings of anything other than a statement of a person

10. Copies of search warrants and lists of seized items

11. Copies of judicial authorizations to intercept private communications

12. Upon request, copies of criminal records relating to proposed Crown or defence witnesses

---

[29]The Martin Report 1993.

13. All information relating to the visual identification of the accused where identity is an issue

14. Any material relevant to the credibility of any proposed Crown witness

The 1991 Supreme Court of Canada landmark ruling in the *Stinchcombe* decision set out similar guidelines for disclosure of relevant inculpatory or exculpatory evidence in the possession of the Crown.[30] The *Stinchcombe* decision and the recommendations of the Martin Report have since been entrenched in section 603 *Criminal Code*. As yet, there is no statutory authority for the defence to disclose relevant defence evidence to the Crown.

Section 603 *Criminal Code* reads:

"An accused is entitled, after he has been ordered to stand trial or at his trial,

(a) to inspect without charge the indictment, his own statement, the evidence and the exhibits, if any; and

(b) to receive, on payment of a reasonable fee determined in accordance with a tariff of fees fixed or approved by the Attorney General of the province, a copy

i) of the evidence

ii) of his own statement, if any, and

iii) of the indictment

but the trial shall not be postponed to enable the accused to secure copies unless the court is satisfied that the failure of the accused to secure them before the trial is not attributable to lack of diligence on the part of the accused."[31]

As the investigating police agency is the primary source of the disclosable evidence, the obligation of the Crown to evaluate and disclose relevant evidence to the defence can only be met if the police fully disclose the findings of the case to the Crown in a timely fashion. Investigators must make full and timely disclosure of their case to the Crown Attorney and for greater certainty, should maintain detailed records of what evidence was disclosed to the Crown and when it was disclosed. (Van Allen 2007)

The intentional failure to disclose evidence by "keeping a trump card hidden", the inadvertent failure to disclose evidence through careless investigative practices, or concealing evidence that is favourable to the defence can all cause prejudice to the accused. The prejudice could result in additional legal expense to an accused to defend themselves, interfere with their right to have their trial conducted within a reasonable time or may impair the accused's ability to make full answer and defence to the charges against them. It is inherently unfair when an accused is not made aware of the scope and magnitude of the Crown evidence against them until immediately before, or during their trial.

In cases where the Crown at one time had evidence in their possession that was subsequently lost or misplaced, they still have an obligation to explain what happened to it. Inherent in the Crown's duty to disclose evidence is a duty to preserve all evidence that is relevant. Therefore the relevance placed on the evidence by the police prior to its loss is an important factor.

---

[30]*R. v. Stinchcombe*, [1991] 3 S.C.R. 326, 68 C.C.C. (3d) 1, 9 C.R. (4th) 277 (7:0).

[31]*Criminal Code*, R.S. 1985 c. C-46, s. 603.

Courts have realized that the relevance of a piece of evidence is not always apparent in the early stages of a police investigation. The type of conduct involved in the loss or destruction of evidence will also be examined for evidence of negligence or intentional purging. In the end, the Crown has a duty to disclose information about anything that was ever in their possession, but can only disclose evidence actually in their possession or information of which they have knowledge.[32]

Copies of confidential information, such as a victim's medical records, the originals of which are held by third parties, may also be required to be disclosed by the Crown. Factors to be considered in the disclosability of such evidence would include if the information is determined to be of a probative value and if the rights of the accused to make full answer and defence to the charge(s) against them outweigh the privacy rights of the complainant. Another key factor requiring the Crown to disclose such confidential information includes whether or not the information sought could be obtained by the accused through any other reasonable means.[33]

The Crown prosecutor has considerable latitude in deciding what to disclose to the defence so that the privacy rights and privilege of victims, witnesses and informers are protected. The Crown must always be made aware of the total evidence gathered during a police investigation in order to make informed disclosure on such issues.

10.4.6 Deliberate or Reckless Misrepresentation of Facts

Police officers have a professional, moral and legal obligation to present facts fairly and accurately at all stages of a police investigation. This includes the writing of investigative notes, submission of official reports and Crown Briefs and preparation of legal documents such as applications for search warrants and authorizations to intercept private communications.

A police officer's reasonable grounds for belief in such documents must disclose all known facts for the issuing justice or the trier of fact to evaluate the reliability of those grounds. A high degree of accuracy on the part of the drafting police officer is expected by the courts in the preparation of search warrant informations – accuracy, but not necessarily perfection.

Inadvertent errors made during the drafting of search warrant informations are not necessarily fatal. But, where the incorrect information is the result of intentional errors, fraudulent misrepresentation of facts or a deliberate attempt to mislead the court, a finding of misrepresentation is certain to follow and the warrant will be quashed.[34]

It is one thing to make a mistake, but where the errors are so numerous or so egregious (notoriously bad) in nature, they indicate a total lack of respect for the rights of the accused. The court will, in all likelihood, rule in favour of excluding evidence.

On occasion, search warrant applications have failed to disclose that the police had already entered the premises to be searched without a warrant. On two occasions, one

---

[32]*R. v. La*, [1997] 2 S.C.R. 680.

[33]*R. v. O'Connor*, [1995] 4 S.C.R. 411.

[34]*R. v. Sismey* (1990), 55 C.C.C. (3d) 281, 1 C.R.R. (2d) 381, 1990 CanLII 1483 (BC C.A.).

involving a death and the other a drug search, the court ruled that the breach of the accused's *Charter* rights was not serious enough to warrant declaring the searches unlawful.[35]

Officers who draft search warrant applications must exercise care in correctly stating the facts of the investigation. Exaggeration of facts, and the formation of conclusions for which there is no factual basis, are both examples of material misstatements that have been proven false by a correct analysis of the evidence. Stating only those facts which support a certain investigative theory and ignoring exculpatory evidence not only tends to paint a picture of unfairness on the part of the police, but can have a damaging effect on the remaining evidence in the case.

In an Ontario case, drug officers received an anonymous tip of unknown reliability about a marijuana growing operation.[36] They obtained records of the hydroelectric consumption of the suspect. The police also compared the neighbours' power consumption rates to that of the suspect's residence, presumably for the purpose of corroborating the anonymous tip. The actual power consumption of the suspect was somewhat exaggerated and no valid comparative analysis was made between the suspect's power consumption and those of his neighbours, which might have explained any disparity due to lifestyle or other potential factors.

The police maintained surveillance on traffic arriving at and leaving from the suspect's home and reported observing persons carry packages away from the residence. The implication was clear – the packages contained drugs. The court ruled that as the police had taken no steps to determine the contents of the packages that were carried away, it was improper to allow the presentation of those facts as corroboration of the anonymous tip.

The suspect was checked for prior criminal convictions but was found not to have any previous record. The police failed to disclose the suspect's lack of a criminal record in the information to obtain the search warrant, thereby depriving the issuing justice of the fact that the accused had not previously been convicted of any prior criminal offence, but especially of any previous drug offences. While this is a small point, it is one that weighs in favour of the accused that was not disclosed by the police.

Although the search warrant was executed by the police and resulted in the seizure of incriminating evidence of marijuana cultivation, the court ruled that the warrant had been improperly issued. The successful results of a search cannot, ***ex post facto*** (retroactively, or after the fact) provide evidence of reliability of the information that was presented as the original basis for the search.[37]

Once again, it is not the purpose of courts that make such rulings to punish the police by letting guilty suspects go free – society as a whole does not benefit from the guilty going unpunished. The objective of such rulings is to prevent the administration of justice from coming into disrepute by allowing offenders to be convicted by way of unlawfully obtained evidence.[38]

---

[35]*R. v. Turner* (1995), 170 N.B.R. (2d) 345, 170 N.B.R. (2e) 345, 1995 CanLII 3891 (NB Q.B.), and *R. v. Silveira*, [1995] 2 S.C.R. 297, 23 O.R. (3d) 256, 124 D.L.R. (4th) 193, 97 C.C.C. (3d) 450, 28 C.R.R. (2d) 189, 38 C.R. (4th) 330, 81 O.A.C. 161, 1995 CanLII 89 (S.C.C.).

[36]*R. v. Philpott* (2002), 101 C.R.R. (2d) 87, 2002 CanLII 25164 (ON S.C.).

[37]*R. v. Garofoli*, [1990] 2 S.C.R. 1421, 60 C.C.C. (3d) 161, 1990 CanLII 52 (S.C.C.).

[38]*R. v. Sismey*, supra.

10.4.7 Entrapment

Entrapment is another form of police misconduct, but it is uniquely different from the previous examples of wrongdoing, in terms of court procedure and consequences. Entrapment is the inappropriate inducement of a reluctant individual to commit a crime that they would not otherwise have committed through excessively forceful and unrelenting persuasion by an **agent provocateur**.

Key to the defence of entrapment is the fact that the conduct of the police was without any prior basis of reasonable grounds to believe the involved individual was involved in criminal activity or that the location involved is one in which the illegal activity under investigation is likely to be occurring. Courts have ruled that untargeted and indiscriminate police enforcement amounts to **random virtue testing** and is an improper use of police powers. (Van Allen 2007)

Even where an accused person is known to have been previously involved in criminal activity, where the conduct of the police is so forceful or persistent or induced by reward or threat to such an extent that community opinion would not condone it, a claim of entrapment may still be successful.

Unlike most criminal defences which could result in an acquittal, or finding of not guilty, entrapment may only be raised as a defence once the accused has been found guilty for the offence they are charged with. When a claim of entrapment is made by the accused, their guilt or innocence is no longer at stake – they will already have been proven guilty beyond a reasonable doubt of the essential elements of the charge(s) against them.

In the 1988 Supreme Court decision of *R. v. Mack*, the accused, a former drug trafficker, was approached by an agent provocateur in the employ of the police who offered to purchase narcotics – the accused refused. Over the next several months, the accused was approached 12-13 more times and was the subject of a veiled threat involving the display of a handgun. When the accused again refused to supply drugs, he was again threatened and was forcefully told to get his act together. A subsequent drug transaction occurred in which the accused supplied narcotics to the police agent.

Even though the accused possessed the necessary intent to commit the offence, to convict him for a crime he committed on the basis that he had no other reasonable choice available to him was deemed by the court to be unjust. Although the actions of the accused in the *Mack* case were unjustified, they were excused as being reasonably unavoidable.[39]

10.5 ENFORCEMENT OF *CHARTER* RIGHTS – REMEDIES

No discussion of the *Charter* would be complete without an explanation of how tainted (contaminated) evidence is dealt with in court when it is determined that the *Charter* rights of an accused person have been violated. Where an accused believes that their rights or freedoms have been infringed or otherwise denied, they may apply to a court for appropriate "judicial remedy". Section 24 of the *Charter* deals with how persons

---

[39]*R. v. Mack*, [1988] 2 S.C.R. 903, [1989] 1 W.W.R. 577, 44 C.C.C. (3d) 513, [1989] 37 C.R.R. 277, 67 C.R. (3d) 1, 1988 CanLII 24 (S.C.C.).

may challenge an alleged *Charter* violation and, if such a breach or infringement is confirmed, how the courts may deal with the matter. Section 24 of the *Charter* states:

> "24(1)   Anyone whose rights or freedoms, as guaranteed by this Charter, have been infringed or denied may apply to a court of competent jurisdiction to obtain such remedy as the court considers appropriate and just in the circumstances.
>
> 24(2)   Where in proceedings under subsection (1), a court concludes that evidence was obtained in a manner that infringed or denied any rights or freedoms guaranteed by this Charter, the evidence shall be excluded if it is established that, having regard to all the circumstances, the admission of it in the proceedings would bring the administration of justice into disrepute."

For example, such situations might involve an incriminating statement where the accused's rights to counsel under subsection 10(b) were denied, or where real evidence was improperly seized in contravention of the accused's rights against unreasonable search and seizure guaranteed by section 8 of the *Charter of Rights*. Where the court finds that incriminating evidence was obtained as the result of a *Charter* breach, the remedy sought by the accused will most likely be to have the evidence excluded, meaning that if the challenge is successful, the evidence will be declared inadmissible.[40]

Where no tainted evidence was obtained but proceeding with a trial, in the face of a *Charter* breach, would bring the administration of justice into disrepute, the appropriate remedy may be to stay the proceedings (a procedure whereby a charge is discontinued by the Crown for a period of up to one year and if not recommenced during that time, must be re-laid).[41] A stay of proceedings is the appropriate remedy for findings of abuse of process and for successful entrapment defences.

It is still possible that evidence might be admitted even in cases where it is determined that an accused's *Charter* rights have been violated. The test that will be used by the court to determine whether the evidence should be admitted or excluded is whether or not the introduction or exclusion of the evidence obtained as the result of a *Charter* breach could bring the administration of justice into disrepute, meaning that to admit the evidence would render the trial unfair.[42]

Factors that are used by courts to determine whether or not admission of improperly obtained evidence should be excluded include:

1. the type of evidence that was obtained

2. how and when the evidence was discovered

3. the *Charter* right of the accused that was denied or infringed upon

4. the severity of the *Charter* breach

5. whether or not the *Charter* breach was intentional

6. the existence of exigent circumstances

---

[40]*Canadian Charter of Rights and Freedoms*, Being Part 1 of the *Constitution Act, 1982*, Enacted by the *Canada Act 1982* (U.K.) c. 11; proclaimed in force April 17, 1982, s. 24.

[41]*Criminal Code*, R.S., 1985 c. C-46, s.579.

[42]*R. v. Collins*, supra.

7. whether or not the evidence would likely have been found through other investigative methods

8. the severity of the offence (the more serious the charge, the more likely that the admission of tainted evidence could bring the administration of justice into disrepute)

9. the necessity of the evidence to prove the charge (whether or not the exclusion of the evidence would render the charge impossible to prove)

10. whether or not other remedies are available to the accused[43]

10.6 CONSCRIPTIVE VERSUS NON-CONSCRIPTIVE EVIDENCE

When determining the impact of evidence on the fairness of a trial, a court will first assess whether or not the evidence is **conscriptive** or **non-conscriptive** based largely on how the evidence was obtained. The best way to explain this difference is that conscriptive evidence involves the participation of the accused in some way in its creation or discovery, meaning that the accused was involuntarily "conscripted" (compelled) to supply evidence against themselves.

An example of conscriptive evidence might involve an accused voluntarily providing a self-incriminating statement or providing a blood sample to police after being denied their *Charter* rights to counsel. Conscriptive evidence that did not exist prior to the *Charter* violation, and which would not otherwise have been discovered, such as an illegally obtained confession, will almost always be deemed to be inadmissible and excluded by the court.

Conscriptive evidence also includes real evidence, such as a murder weapon, that is discovered as the result of an illegally obtained confession made by a suspect (**derivative evidence**). Non-conscriptive evidence is evidence where the accused does not participate in its creation or discovery. The admission of conscriptive evidence would almost always be deemed to affect the fairness of the trial, whereas non-conscriptive evidence is usually seen to not affect the fairness of the trial.

If the evidence is determined to be conscriptive in nature, the court must determine if it could have been discovered in a non-conscriptive way, had the *Charter* breach not occurred. If, on a balance of probabilities, conscriptive evidence would have been discovered anyway by non-conscriptive means, the admission of the evidence would probably not render the trail unfair if the evidence were to be admitted. The court must still assess the severity of the *Charter* breach and whether or not the admission or exclusion of the evidence would bring the administration of justice into disrepute.

If conscriptive evidence would, on a balance of probabilities, not have been discovered by non-conscriptive means, the court will normally exclude the evidence.[44] (Van Allen 2007)

---

[43]*R. v. Collins*, supra.

[44]*R. v. Stillman*, [1997] 1 S.C.R. 607, 113 C.C.C. (3d), 5 C.R. (5th) 1.

10.7 EXCLUSIONARY RULE

Evidence that is improperly or illegally obtained as the result of a violation of the rights and freedoms guaranteed to an individual shall be excluded as evidence at the trial of the accused, if the admission of that evidence would bring the administration of justice into disrepute.[45] This is a legal doctrine that is referred to as the **exclusionary rule**.

In determining whether or not to exclude evidence that was obtained by a *Charter* violation and in deciding whether or not the admission of that evidence would bring the administration of justice into disrepute, a court will examine three main issues:

1. Whether or not the admission of the impugned evidence would affect the fairness of the trial of the accused

2. The severity of the *Charter* violation. Serious and blatant violations will tend to cause the evidence to be excluded, while violations of a technical nature or inadvertent or motivated by urgency or good faith tend toward admission of the evidence

3. The effect that excluding the evidence would have on the public perception of the administration of justice. If a simple violation resulted in excluding evidence on a serious charge, the effect of doing so might have a greater impact on the administration of justice than admitting the evidence.[46] (Schmalleger et al 2004)

10.8 "FRUIT OF THE POISONED TREE"

What happens when illegally obtained evidence results in the discovery of other evidence? For example, a suspect may confess to their role in a crime to the police after having been denied the opportunity to obtain legal counsel upon their arrest. From information obtained directly through the confession, such as the location of stolen property, police obtain a search warrant and successfully recover the property.

The **"fruit of the poisoned tree"** doctrine deals with derivative evidence that results from improperly or illegally obtained evidence. In this analogy of a tree, if the confession ("the tree") was obtained as the result of a violation of the suspect's rights, it will be considered tainted by the *Charter* breach and will be excluded. Derivative evidence, such as the stolen property ("the fruit") will also be considered tainted and may also be excluded.

10.9 DISCOVERABILITY – THE "BUT FOR" TEST

In determining whether or not to exclude illegally derived evidence, the court may also apply the **"but for"** test. If the evidence could not have been discovered by the police through independent means – but for the *Charter* violation – it should be considered tainted and excluded.

---

[45]*Canadian Charter of Rights and Freedoms*, Being Part 1 of the *Constitution Act, 1982*, Enacted by the *Canada Act 1982* (U.K.) c. 11; proclaimed in force April 17, 1982, s. 24 (2).

[46]*R. v. Collins*, supra.

If the derivative evidence could have been wholly or even partially discovered by the police, independently of the *Charter* breach, using proper investigative methods, the evidence may still be admitted. Another factor that may be considered by a court is whether or not the strength of any link between the *Charter* violation and the discovery of the evidence has become diminished by other factors, such as the passage of time or the suspect's access to legal counsel.

For example, if an accused's rights to counsel are violated, such a serious *Charter* violation would render any subsequent confession inadmissible. As the result of the illegally obtained confession, police learn of the location of a firearm used in the crime that was stored in a storage locker at a bus station. A search warrant is obtained and the evidence is seized out of the locker. Under the fruit of the poisoned tree doctrine, the derivative evidence may also be declared inadmissible.

If, however, a witness, a police informer or an accomplice provides the police with information about the incriminating firearm, its seizure may pass the discoverability test as it was obtained through an independent source and its discovery by the police was inevitable. It must always be remembered that a failure to obtain evidence independently when proper means are available "tends to indicate a blatant disregard for the Charter, which is a factor supporting the exclusion of the evidence."[47]

SUMMARY

- The objective of the *Charter* is to protect the guaranteed rights of private individuals and to avoid improper actions by those who administer and enforce the law.

- When society's rights to prevent crime and to apprehend offenders supercede the rights of the individual, the courts will admit the evidence.

- Police misconduct – intentional or otherwise – that fails to comply with *Charter* expectations, will not be tolerated by the courts for the same reason that unlawful conduct by criminal offenders is not tolerated.

- The *Charter of Rights* applies to all aspects of the Parliament and government of Canada, the provincial and territorial legislatures and all matters within their respective authorities.

- In criminal or quasi-criminal trials, only an infringement of the rights of the accused can be challenged and only the accused will be granted standing to claim that a violation of their rights has occurred.

- No uninvolved third party may vicariously raise a *Charter* challenge concerning an alleged breach of the rights of another person.

- Examples of police misconduct that has resulted in successful *Charter* challenges include institutional recklessness, abuse of process, verbal and physical abuse of prisoners, violation of an individual's reasonable expectation of privacy, arrest violations, denial of rights to counsel, "dirty tricks", misrepresentation of facts, nondisclosure of evidence and entrapment.

---

[47]*R. v. Collins*, supra., also *R. v. Burlingham*, [1995] 2 S.C.R. 206, 124 D.L.R. (4th) 7, 97 C.C.C. (3d) 385, 38 C.R. (4th) 265.

- Where the court finds that incriminating evidence was obtained as the result of a *Charter* breach, the remedy sought by the accused will most likely be to have the evidence excluded, meaning that if the challenge is successful, the evidence will be declared inadmissible.

- Where no tainted evidence was obtained but proceeding with a trial, in the face of the *Charter* breach, would bring the administration of justice into disrepute, the appropriate remedy may be to stay the proceedings (a procedure whereby a charge is discontinued by the Crown for a period of up to one year and if not recommenced during that time, must be re-laid).

- Conscriptive evidence involves the participation of the accused in some way in its creation or its discovery, meaning that the accused was involuntarily conscripted (compelled) to supply evidence against themselves.

- Non-conscriptive evidence does not involve the participation of the accused in its creation or discovery.

- Evidence that is improperly or illegally obtained as the result of a violation of the rights and freedoms guaranteed to an individual shall be excluded as evidence at the trial of the accused, if the admission of that evidence would bring the administration of justice into disrepute.

- The fruit of the poisoned tree doctrine deals with derivative evidence that results from improperly or illegally obtained evidence. If the original source is inadmissible, derivative evidence may also be inadmissible unless it meets certain criteria.

- If the derivative evidence could have been wholly or even partially discovered by the police, independently of the *Charter* breach, using proper investigative methods, the evidence may still be admitted.

DISCUSSION QUESTIONS

1. An accused with a history of violent criminal convictions is charged with a despicable assault against an elderly female victim. At his trial, the accused raises a challenge that his *Charter* rights were violated. The court hears evidence and determines that a serious police misconduct during the investigation of the crime amounted to an abuse of process. The incriminating evidence the Crown relied upon to obtain a conviction is declared inadmissible. In the absence of other evidence, the accused is acquitted. The victim, police and the media are all critical of the accused's acquittal "on a technicality". What was the basis for the judge's decision in terms of the objective of the *Charter of Rights*? Was the judge's decision fair? Explain your answer.

2. During the trial of an accused, it comes to the attention of the defence that a witness to the crime was interviewed by the police, and provided a physical description of the person responsible for the crime that is totally inconsistent with the description of the accused. Counsel for the defence objects that because the accused was not provided with information in the possession of the police that points toward the accused's innocence, the *Charter* rights of the accused have been irreparably violated. What is

the term that refers to the automatic sharing of relevant evidence by the Crown? What is the rationale for requiring the Crown to provide evidence to the defence? If the court finds that the accused's rights were violated, what is a possible remedy the court may apply to this situation? Do you agree with this practice? Explain your answer.

3. Explain the difference between conscriptive and non-conscriptive evidence. What is the difference in the way these types of evidence are dealt with by the courts in violations of the *Charter* rights of the accused?

4. Explain what is meant by the legal doctrine of the fruit of the poisoned tree, in relation to derivative evidence and its admissibility in court. Explain how derivative evidence may still survive the discoverability test and be admitted as evidence against the accused.

WEBLINKS

www.scc-csc.gc.ca/Welcome/index_e.asp

Website of the Supreme Court of Canada. In our criminal justice system of constitutional supremacy, the Supreme Court is the highest court of the land, giving effect to Canadian law and serving as the last recourse of appeal for all criminal and civil legal matters. Leave to appeal to the Supreme Court must be applied for and granted, unless where an acquittal has been overturned or in the case of a person convicted of a criminal offence, where one judge of a panel dissented with the ruling of the court. This website provides a wealth of information including the role, jurisdiction, history and cases of the Supreme Court.

www.ontariocourts.on.ca/appeal.htm

Website of the Ontario Court of Appeal, the highest court in the province of Ontario This website includes a description of the court, biographical information concerning the judges of the court, and case statistics and information. This website also provides access to the motions and decisions relating to the appeal of Steven Murray Truscott in relation to his contentious 1959 conviction for the murder of Lynn Harper.

www.cbc.ca/news/background/truscott/video.html

Canadian Broadcasting Corporation (CBC) website containing courtroom video coverage of the actual appeal proceedings of the Ontario Court of Appeal, held between January 31 and February 14, 2007, relating to the historic appeal of Steven Truscott. The Truscott appeal was the first appeal to be televised in Canadian history, commencing a new era of transparency and accountability in the criminal justice system.

www.aidwyc.org

Association in Defence of the Wrongfully Convicted website. A Canadian volunteer organization dedicated to the prevention and rectifying of wrongful convictions. This website contains information regarding the association's current cases and their status.

CONSENT TO SEARCH

DATE: _____ TIME: _____

LOCATION: _____

In order to cooperate with an investigation being conducted by the

_____ Police Service,

I, _____ (Name)

of _____ (Address)

do hereby authorize _____ (officer) of the

_____ Police Service to search my

_____

_____

(detailed description and location of place, dwelling, vehicle, etc. to be searched)

and its contents, which are owned or controlled by me and to remove any items pertinent to their investigation, providing a detailed receipt is furnished to me for any items that are removed by the police.

I have been advised that any items taken by the police may be used in their investigation, subjected to possible forensic testing and may be introduced as evidence in a court proceeding.

No promise, nor inducement, nor threat, nor coercion of any kind has been made to or against me by the police and I have been advised of my right to refuse to consent to this search and of my right to withdraw my consent to search at any time.

I have been advised of my right to retain and instruct legal counsel prior to the signing of this document and make this consent voluntarily and of my own free will.

_____   _____
Signature of Person Consenting   Witness Officer

INFORMATION TO OBTAIN A SEARCH WARRANT
DÉNONCIATION EN VUE D'OBTENIR UN MANDAT DE PERQUISITION

Form 1 Section 487
Formule (Article)

	)	INFORMATION of **Detective John Smith**
CANADA	)	*Les présentes consitituent LA DENONCIATION de*
PROVINCE OF ONTARIO	)	of **Greater Sudbury Police Service**
PROVINCE DE L'ONTARIO	)	*de*
North	)	**Peace Officer**

REGION/RÉGION) (Occupation)/(*Profession*)

herein called the informant, taken / *ci-après appelé le dénonciateur, portée devant moi.*

The informant says that he/she has reasonable and probable grounds to believe and does believe that there is (are) in a certain building, receptacle or place, namely,
Le dénonciateur déclare qu'il (qu'elle) a des motifs raisonnables de croire qu'il y a dans un certain bâtiment, contenant ou lieu, savoir:

Dwelling House and detached single garage
(Dwelling -House, Building, Receptacle, or Place)
(habitation, bâtiment, contenant ou lieu)

of/de

Robert Alan Jones
(Owner or Occupant of Dwelling-House, Building, etc.)
(propriétaire ou occupant de l'habitation, bâliment, etc.)

1452 Danforth Avenue, Sudbury, ON

At (Address or Location of Dwelling-House, Building, etc) in the said region,
à/au *(adresse ou emplacement de l'habitation, du bâtiment, etc)* *dans ladite région*

(Describe things to be searched for) *(décrire les choses à rechercher)* **See "Appendix A" attached hereto**

which there are reasonable grounds to believe * will afford evidence with respect to the commission of an offence against the Criminal Code, namely, the offence of:
*dont on a des motifs raionnavles de croire * qu'elles fourniront une preuve touchant la perpétration d'une infraction au Code criminel, savoir:*

(Describe offence in respect to which search is to be made) **See "Appendix B" attached hereto**
(décrire l'infraction à l'égard de laquelle la perquisition doit être effectuée)

and that his/her grounds for so believing are that: / *et que ses soupçons sur les motifs suivants:*

(State grounds of belief) *(énoncer les motifs)* **See "Appendix C" attached hereto**

WHEREFORE the informant prays that a search warrant may be granted to search the said
IN CONSEQUENCE, le dénonciateur demands qu'un mandat de perquisition soit accorde pour perquisitionner dans ledit/ladite

Dwelling House and detached single garage

for the said thing(s). (Dwelling-House, Building, etc.) *vue*
de trouver lesdites choses. *(habitation, bâtiment, etc.)*

Sworn before me at **The City of Greater Sudbury** in the said Region, this **22nd** day of **March, 2007**
Assermenté devant moi, à/au *de/du* *dans ladite région ,* *ce* *jour de*

[Signature of Informant]

A Justice of the Peace in and for the Province of Ontario Informant
juge de paix dans et pour la province de l'Ontario *Dénonciateur*

*or " is (are) intended to be used for the purpose of committing an offence against the person may which be arrested without warrant, namely, the offence of
ou " sont destinées à servir aux fins de la perpetration d'une infraction conte une personne, pour laquelle un individu peut être arrêté sans mandat, savoir:

This is Appendix 'A' as referred to in the Information to Obtain a Search Warrant of Detective John Smith dated at the City of Greater Sudbury this 22nd day of March, 2007.

"Description of things to be searched for:"

1. Acme cheque writing machine, Model: 240, serial number: unknown, brown in colour, having a cracked red plastic knob on the handle. Partial cardboard box containing sequentially numbered, perforated blank cheques, each comprising of a cheque-stub plus the written portion of the cheque. The cheques are in batches of fifty and are blue in colour with black printing. All cheques are made out to the account of "Fly By Night Motors", 6700 Kingsway Boulevard, Sudbury, Ontario, and are drawn on account #015-23456 of the 47 Barrydowne Road, Sudbury branch of the Bank of Cayman Islands.

2. Portable combination floor safe, Make: Chubb, Model: Fort Knox, serial number: 67854, grey in colour. Safe stands on four legs, each with a rolling metal caster.

3. White canvas money deposit bag bearing the business logo of "Fly By Night Motors", 6700 Kingsway Boulevard, Sudbury, ON, measuring approximately 30 cm X 30 cm.

4. Canadian currency totalling $25 640.00 in the following denominations:

   10 X $1 000.00 bills = $10 000.00
   50 X $100.00 bills   = $ 5 000.00
   200 X $50.00 bills   = $10 000.00
   32 X $20.00 bills   = $ 640.00

5. 2006 Chevrolet Blazer 4-door Black in colour VIN: 123GM67FX345SUV6869

6. Ignition key for 2006 Chevrolet Blazer, above, on black leather key fob bearing the inscription of "Fly By Night Motors", 6700 Kingsway Boulevard, Sudbury, ON.

7. Blue metal pry bar or like instrument, having a flat-bladed surface measuring approximately 30 mm in width.

This is Appendix 'B' as referred to in the Search Warrant issued to Detective John Smith dated at the City of Greater Sudbury this 22nd day of March 2007.

"Which there are reasonable grounds to believe will afford evidence with respect to the commission of an offence against the Criminal Code, namely, the offence of:"

That Robert Alan Jones, on or about the 20th day of March, 2007 at the City of Greater Sudbury in the North Region did unlawfully break and enter a certain place, to wit: Fly by Night Motors, situated at 6700 Kingsway Boulevard, Sudbury, Ontario, and did commit therein the indictable offence of theft, contrary to Paragraph 348(1)(e) of the *Criminal Code of Canada*.

This is Appendix 'C' as referred to in the Information to Obtain a Search Warrant of Detective John Smith dated at the City of Greater Sudbury this 22nd day of March, 2007.

"The informant states that his/her grounds for so believing are that . . . "

1. The informant in this matter is Detective John Smith of the Greater Sudbury Police Service, Criminal Investigation Department. The informant has been a peace officer since August 28th, 1995. Since January 3, 2005, the informant has been assigned to the Criminal Investigation Department and holds the rank of Detective.

2. On March 20, 2007, the informant was assigned to investigate an alleged break, enter and theft at Fly By Night Motors, situated at 6700 Kingsway Boulevard, Sudbury, ON. The break and enter was reported by the owner, Fred Swindler, when he showed up for work on March 20, 2007 at 8:00 A.M. According to Mr. Fred Swindler, his business is not equipped with an intrusion alarm system. The informant believes this information to be true.

3. Upon arriving at the location, the informant personally observed that the front door had been forcibly entered by prying it open with a pry-bar, or other like instrument, having a flat blade measuring approximately 30 millimetres in width. Tool-mark impressions were made by the instrument and traces of blue paint were visible in scratches on the aluminium door frame.

4. The informant personally interviewed Fred Swindler, owner of Fly By Night Motors, and learned that the front door had not been damaged when he locked up the business at 8:00 PM March 19, 2007. Mr. Swindler states that he always secures the business at the end of the business day and did so that night. Mr. Swindler states that the floor safe was missing from his office. Mr. Swindler described the safe as a portable combination floor safe, Make: Chubb, Model: Fort Knox, serial number: 67854, grey in colour. Safe stands on four legs, having rolling metal casters.

5. Mr. Swindler stated that the missing safe contained the day's business receipts comprising: Canadian currency totalling $25 640.00 in the following denominations:

   10 X $1 000.00 bills = $10 000.00
   50 X $100.00 bills = $ 5 000.00
   200 X $50.00 bills = $10 000.00
   32 X $20.00 bills = $ 640.00

   Mr. Swindler was certain of the amount of stolen money and denominations as he had counted the receipts himself as his regular book-keeper, Penny Pilferer, had called in sick that day. According to Mr. Swindler, when he placed the money into the safe, the money was contained in a white canvas money deposit bag, measuring approximately 30 cm square, bearing the business logo of "Fly By Night Motors".

6. Mr. Swindler stated that he noticed that his cheque-writing machine was also missing from his office and described it as an Acme cheque writing machine, Model: 240, serial number: unknown, brown in colour, having a cracked red plastic

knob on the handle. Mr. Swindler knows the handle was broken as his visiting grandchildren knocked the machine to the floor on a previous visit to his business, breaking the knob of the handle. Mr. Swindler is certain that he can positively identify it. Also missing from his office was a partial cardboard box containing sequentially numbered, perforated blank cheques, each comprising of a cheque-stub plus the written portion of the cheque. The cheques are in batches of fifty and are blue in colour with black printing. All cheques are made out to the account of "Fly By Night Motors, 6700 Kingsway Boulevard, Sudbury, Ontario, and are drawn on account #015-23456 of the 47 Barrydowne Road, Sudbury branch of the Bank of Cayman Islands.

7. Mr. Swindler personally stated to the informant that he caused an inventory of the business to be done and noticed that a 2006 Chevrolet Blazer 4-door Black in colour VIN: 123GM67FX345SUV6869 was missing from the sales lot. Swindler further stated that the keys to the vehicle were missing from his office and had been attached to a black leather key fob bearing the business logo of "Fly By Night Motors", which was hanging from a key rack in his office. Mr. Swindler stated that nothing else had been disturbed.

8. The informant believes that the information provided by Fred Swindler in his signed statement is reliable and the informant believes it to be true.

9. On March 21, 2007, the informant received a telephone call from a reliable and confidential informer who stated that Bobby Jones was responsible for the break in at "Fly By Night Motors" that occurred on March 20, 2007. The informer further stated that Bobby Jones is the boyfriend of one Penny Pilferer, the bookkeeper of Fly By Night Motors. The informer stated that Jones was attempting to sell a newer model black Chevy Blazer, that Jones said was stored in a garage behind his residence situated at 1452 Danforth Avenue, Sudbury, ON.

10. The informant stated that Jones was bragging about the heist at the Intergalactic Hotel situated on Katherine Street, Sudbury, during the afternoon of March 21, 2007 and that he was buying rounds of drinks for all the patrons present with $50.00 and $100.00 bills. According to the informer, every time Jones would buy a round he would say, "This one's on Swindler, boys!"

11. The confidential informer has previously provided information to the informant that has resulted in the July 16, 2006 conviction of Adam Dube, for two counts of Break, Enter & Theft, section 348(1)(a) *Criminal Code*, for which Dube was sentenced to six months imprisonment and resulted in the recovery of $15 000.00 in stolen property. The informant has reasonable grounds to believe that the facts provided by the confidential informer are reliable and accurate and he believes them to be true.

12. At 9:00 P.M., March 21, 2007, the informant walked past the residence situated at 1452 Danforth Avenue, Sudbury. From the municipal sidewalk in front of the house, the informant personally observed three male persons inside the detached garage situated behind the dwelling house. The garage door, facing Danforth Avenue, was open and lights were on inside the garage. From a distance of approximately 30 metres, the informant clearly observed the three males inspecting under the hood of a newer model, black, sport utility vehicle that was either a GMC Jimmy or a Chevrolet Blazer.

13. The informant states that he recognized one of the men as Robert Alan Jones, DOB: July 14, 1980, of 1452 Danforth Avenue, Sudbury, as he has had dealings with him on previous occasions.

14. The informant personally conducted inquiries of the records of the Ministry of Transportation of Ontario (MTO). The informant is aware that information relating to driver and vehicle licencing within the province of Ontario is contained within the MTO database. The informant is aware that persons seeking to obtain an Ontario Driver's Licence, or register motor vehicles, are required to provide certain information to the Ministry of Transportation including their current residential address. The informant believes the MTO database to be an accurate and reliable source of information.

15. The informant states that as the result of his inquiries that he learned that Robert Alan Jones is not currently the registered owner of any black sport utility vehicles in the province of Ontario.

16. The informant has personal knowledge that within the Canadian Police Information Centre (C.P.I.C.) database, information is kept in relation to criminal records, outstanding criminal charges, warrants for arrest, details of probation orders, and other personal information as it may relate to individuals. The informant has personal knowledge that information contained in the C.P.I.C. database which is entered by the various Canadian police services that may have had involvement with a particular individual. The informant has personal knowledge that information relating to a person's criminal record is entered on C.P.I.C. by the R.C.M.P. after submission of a court disposition from accredited Canadian police services. The informant believes the C.P.I.C. database to be an accurate and reliable source of information.

17. The informant personally conducted inquiries with the C.P.I.C. database and learned that an individual by the name of Robert Alan Jones, DOB: July 14, 1980, FPS: 12345C has the following criminal convictions associated to him:

Oct 17, 2000 Sudbury, ON Theft Under $5 000.00 12 months probation
Nov 5, 2002 Sudbury, ON Break enter with intent 90 days imprisonment
Jan 22, 2004 Sudbury, ON Break enter and theft 9 months imprisonment

18. The informant personally made discreet inquiries with Mr. Fred Swindler, owner of "Fly By Night Motors" and learned that the home address of his book-keeper, Penny Pilferer, is listed as 1452 Danforth Avenue, Sudbury, ON. Mr. Swindler advised the informant that Ms. Pilferer recently attempted to gain employment for her boyfriend, Bobby Jones, at "Fly By Night Motors", however, no positions were available at that time. The informant believes the information related to him by Fred Swindler relating to Penny Pilferer and Bobby Jones to be true.

19. The informant has reasonable grounds to believe and does believe that the sport utility vehicle that he observed in the garage behind the dwelling house at 1452 Danforth Avenue, Sudbury, is the one referred to by the confidential informer and is the vehicle stolen from "Fly By Night Motors". The informant has reasonable grounds to believe that the vehicle was stolen to transport the stolen floor safe. The vehicle will provide direct physical evidence in relation to the offence under investigation as referred to in Appendix "B" of this information.

20. The informant has reasonable grounds to believe that the missing portable combination floor safe, Make: Chubb, Model: Fort Knox, serial number: 67854, grey in colour, with rolling metal casters will be located at 1452 Danforth Avenue, Sudbury, and will afford evidence of the offence under investigation as referred to in Appendix "B" of this information.

21. The informant has reasonable grounds to believe that the money and canvas deposit bag will be located at 1452 Danforth Avenue, Sudbury, and will afford evidence of the offence under investigation as referred to in Appendix "B" of this information.

22. The informant has reasonable grounds to believe and does believe that the pry bar as described in Appendix "A" of this information will be found at 1452 Danforth Avenue, Sudbury, ON, and may be matched forensically to the tool mark impression and trace evidence of blue paint recovered from the scene of the break in at 6700 Kingsway Boulevard, Sudbury. Forensic testing will provide direct physical evidence of the method of entry of the offence under investigation as referred to in Appendix "B" of this information.

23. The informant has reasonable grounds to believe and does believe that the Acme cheque writing machine, Model: 240, serial number: unknown, brown in colour, having a cracked red plastic knob on the handle and sequentially numbered, perforated blank cheques made out to the account of "Fly By Night Motors", 6700 Kingsway Boulevard, Sudbury, ON, will be found at 1452 Danforth Avenue, Sudbury, ON, and will provide direct physical evidence of the offence under investigation as referred to in Appendix "B" of this information.

WARRANT TO SEARCH
MANDAT DE PERQUISITION

Form/*Formule* 5 C.C.
(Section/*Article*

CANADA
PROVINCE OF
ONTARIO
PROVINCE DE L'ONTARIO

North

Region/*Région*

}

To the Peace Officers in the said Region, and in the Province of Ontario or to the
Aux agents de la paix dans ladite région, et dans la province de l'Ontario

Greater Sudbury Police Service

(insert named public officers/*indiquez le nom des fonctionnaires publics*)

WHEREAS it appears upon the information of
ATTENDU OU'il appert de la dénonciation de

Detective John Smith – Greater Sudbury Police Service

that there are reasonable grounds to believe that there are in
qu'il existe des motifs raisonnables de croire qu'il y a dans

Dwelling House and detached single garage

of Robert Alan Jones

at/à/au 1452 Danforth Avenue., C

City of Greater Sudbury

, herein called
ci-après appelé(e)

the premises, certain things namely:
les lieux, certaines choses, savoir:

Refer to "Appendix A" attached hereto

that being sought as evidence in respect to the commission, suspected commission or intended commission of an
qui sont recherchées comme preuve en ce qui concerne une infraction, présumée ou en voie d'être perpétrée, au Code

offence against the Criminal Code, namely:
criminel, savoir:

Refer to "Appendix B" attached hereto

THEREFORE, this is to authorize and require you, between the hours of   11:00 AM – 9:00 PM   to enter into
À CES CAUSES, les présentes ont pour objet de vous autoriser et obliger à entrer, entre les heures de   *dans*

the premises and to search for and seize the above things, and to bring them before me or some other justice to be dealt with
lesdits fieux at de rechercher lesdites choses at de les apporter devant moi ou devant tout autre juge de paix afin qu'il en soit

according to law.
disposé selon la loi.

DATED this   day of March   , yr. 2007   , at City of Greater Sudbury
FAIT le   *jour de*   *an*   *à/au*

_____
Judge or Justice of the Peace in and for the Province of Ontario
Juge ou juge de paix dans et pour la province de l'Ontario

Executed on the _____ day of _____ , yr. _____
Exécuté le _____ jour de _____ an

by _____ , P.C. _____ , Division _____
par _____ C.P. _____ Division

Seizure under: ☐ section 487;   ☐ section 489   ☐ no seizure
Saisie aux termes de :   art. 487;   art. 489,   aucune saisie

Return made before _____ , on the
Rapport effectué devant _____ le

_____ day of _____ , yr. _____ , at _____
jour de _____ an _____ à/au

This is Appendix 'A' as referred to in the Search Warrant issued to Detective John Smith dated at the City of Greater Sudbury this 22nd day of March, 2007.

"Description of things to be searched for:"

1. Acme cheque writing machine, Model: 240, serial number: unknown, brown in colour, having a cracked red plastic knob on the handle.

   Partial cardboard box containing sequentially numbered, perforated blank cheques, each comprising of a cheque-stub plus the written portion of the cheque. The cheques are in batches of fifty and are blue in colour with black printing. All cheques are made out to the account of "Fly By Night Motors", 6700 Kingsway Boulevard, Sudbury, Ontario, and are drawn on account #015-23456 of the 47 Barrydowne Road, Sudbury branch of the Bank of Cayman Islands.

2. Portable combination floor safe, Make: Chubb, Model: Fort Knox, serial number: 67854, grey in colour. Safe stands on four legs, each with a rolling metal caster.

3. White canvas money deposit bag bearing the business logo of "Fly By Night Motors", 6700 Kingsway Boulevard, Sudbury, ON, measuring approximately 30 cm X 30 cm.

4. Canadian currency totalling $25 640.00 in the following denominations:

10 X $1 000.00 bills	=	$10 000.00
50 X $100.00 bills	=	$ 5 000.00
200 X $50.00 bills	=	$10 000.00
32 X $20.00 bills	=	$ 640.00

5. 2006 Chevrolet Blazer 4-door Black in colour

   VIN: 123GM67FX345SUV6869

6. Ignition key for 2006 Chevrolet Blazer, above, on black leather key fob bearing the inscription of "Fly By Night Motors", 6700 Kingsway Boulevard, Sudbury, ON.

7. Blue metal pry bar or like instrument, having a flat-bladed surface measuring approximately 30 mm in width.

This is Appendix 'B' as referred to in the Information to Obtain a Search Warrant of Detective John Smith dated at the City of Greater Sudbury this 22nd day of March 2007.

"Which there are reasonable grounds to believe will afford evidence with respect to the commission of an offence against the Criminal Code, namely, the offence of:"

That Robert Alan Jones, on or about the 20th day of March, 2007 at the City of Greater Sudbury in the North Region did unlawfully break and enter a certain place, to wit: Fly by Night Motors, situated at 6700 Kingsway Boulevard, Sudbury, Ontario, and did commit therein the indictable offence of theft, contrary to Paragraph 348(1)(e) of the *Criminal Code of Canada*.

REPORT TO A JUSTICE / *RAPPORT À UN JUGE DE PAIX*
(Section 489.1 Criminal Code/*l'article 489.1 du Code criminel*)

CANADA PROVINCE OF ONTARIO *PROVINCE DE L'ONTARIO*	)))	To the justice who issued a warrant to the undersigned pursuant to section 256, 487 or 487.1 of the Criminal Code, or any other justice for the same territorial division or, if no	*Au juge de paix qui a décerné un mandat au soussigné en vertu de l'l'article 256, 487, ou 487.1 du Code criminel, ou autre juge de paix pour la même circonscription territoriale et,*
North Region/*Région*	))	warrant was issued, to any justice having jurisdiction in respect of the matter.	*si aucun mandat n'a été décerné, tout juge de paix ayant compétence en la matière.*

I   Detective John Smith, C.I.D. Greater Sudbury Police Service   have:
Je soussigné(e)   (name of Peace Officer or other person making report / *nom de l'agent de la paix ou autre auteur du rapport*)

☒ acted under the authority of a warrant issued pursuant ☐ section / *l'article 256*   ☒ section / *l'article 487*   ☐ section / *l'article 487.1*
to
ai exécuté un mandat décerné aux termes de   (check one / *cocher la case appropriée*)

of the Criminal Code,   J.P. Madeline Laforest   on   March 22nd   200   7
by
du Code criminel, par   (insert name of issuing Justice/*nom du juge de paix qui a décerné le*   *le*   (insert date warrant issued / *date où a été*
               mandat)   *décerné le mandat*)

at   City of Greater Sudbury
à/au   (insert location from which warrant was issued / *inscrire le nom de l'endroit où a été décerné le mandat*)

☐ acted under the authority of section 489 of the Criminal Code in the execution of a warrant issued under
section
ai exécuté un mandat décerné aux termes de l'article 489 du Code   (487 or / *ou 487.1*)

of the Criminal Code by   on   200
criminel, par   (insert name of issuing Justice / *nom du juge de paix qui a décerné le mandat*)   *le*   (insert date warrant issued / *date où a été*
                                                       décerné le mandat)

at
à/au   (insert location from which warrant was issued / *inscrire le nom de l'endroit où a été décerné le mandat*)

☐ acted otherwise in the execution of my duties under the Criminal Code or any other act of Parliament:
ai exécuté un mandat autrement dans l'exercice des fonctions prévues en vertu du Code criminel ou d'une autre loi fédérale:

                    (specify statutory authority / *préciser la loi*)

and have conducted a search, the specific details of which are as follows (specify the exact nature of the search, including the premises, place, or person searched, the specific location of the search, and the specific date and time that the search was conducted)	☐	*et ai effectué une perquisition comme suit: (préciser les circonstances exactes de la perquisition, y compris les lieux, l'endroit ou les personnes ayant fait l'objet de la perquisition, ainsi que la date et l'heure exactes auxquelles la perquisition s'est effectuée)*

A search warrant issued under s. 487 CC was executed upon the residence of Robert Alan Jones, situated at 1452 Danforth Avenue, Sudbury, ON. The warrant was executed between 1:15 P.M. and 4:30 P.M. Thursday, March 22, 2007 by Detective John Smith and other members of the Greater Sudbury Police Service.

During the course of the search, certain items (listed below) which were named in the warrant were seized and are presently detained at the Greater Sudbury Police Service Headquarters. Mr. Robert Alan Jones was arrested for Break Enter and Theft and was released from custody on his Undertaking Given To a Justice on Friday, March 23, 2007.

Robert Alan Jones is to appear in court to answer to his charge on Monday, April 9, 2007

Further, in conducting this search, I have seized the following things and have dealt with them in the following way: I have seized the following things and returned them to the persons lawfully entitled to their possession, as indicated in the attached receipts: (list items returned, where additional space is required, attach additional page(s) marked as exhibit) I have seized the following things and detained them at	☐	*De plus, en effectuant la perquisition, j'ai saisi les biens suivants et en ai disposé de la façon suivante:* *J'ai saisi les biens suivants et les ai remis à la personne ayant droit à leur possession, ainsi qu'en témoignent les reçus suivants: (décrire chaque bien remis; au besoin, annexer une ou plusieurs pages supplémentaires et les coter)* *J'ai saisi les biens suivants et les détiens à/au*

       Greater Sudbury Police Service, Seized Property Unit, 190 Brady St., Sudbury, ON
       (state location at which things are being detained / *préciser l'endroit où les biens sont détenus*)

to be dealt with according to law (list the items detained; where additional space is required, attach additional page(s) marked as exhibit)	*pour qu'il en soit disposé conformément à la loi (décrire chaque bien rapporté; au besoin annexer une ou plusieurs pages supplémentaires et les coter)*

REPORT TO A JUSTICE CONT'D
(Section 489.1 Criminal Code)

ACME cheque writing machine, Model 240, Serial: X23B7, Colour: Brown with cracked red plastic knob on handle
200 sequentially numbered perforated blank cheques bearing logo of "Fly By Night Motors" 6700 Kingsway Blvd., Sudbury
White canvas money deposit bag bearing the logo of "Fly By Night Motors" 6700 Kingsway Blvd., Sudbury
Canadian Currency totalling $10 400.00 in denominations of $50.00 and $20.00 bills
2006 Chevrolet Blazer 4-door Colour: Black VIN: 123GM67FX345SUV6869
Ignition key fitting the ignition of above 2006 Chevrolet Blazer bearing logo of "Fly By Night Motors"

(In the event that a warrant was issued pursuant to section 487.1 of the Criminal Code, the following portion of the report must be completed.)

(Dans le cas d'un mandat décerné aux termes de l'article 487.1 du Code, criminel, remplir la partie suivante du rapport.)

Further, I, _____ make the following statements:
De plus, je soussigné(e) (insert name of the Peace Officer or other person making report / *nom de l'agent de la paix ou de l'auteur du rapport*) *déclare que:*

(In the event that the warrant was executed, complete the following)

(Dans le cas d'un mandat exécuté, remplir ce qui suit)

the following things were seized in addition to the things mentioned in the warrant:
(list all of the items seized which are not mentioned in the warrant: where additional space is required, attach additional page(s) marked as exhibit)

☐ *les biens suivants ont été saisis en plus des biens mentionnés dans le mandat:*
(décrire chaque bien saisi qui n'est mentionné dans le mandat; au besoin, annexer une ou plusieurs pages supplémentaires et les coter)

the things which were seized in addition to the things mentioned in the warrant are
being held at

☐ *les biens saisis en plus des biens mentionnés dans le mandat sont détenus à/au*

_____
(specify location / *préciser l'endroit*)

the grounds for believing that the things which were seized in addition to the things
mentioned in the warrant, had been obtained by, or used in, the commission of an offence, are as follows: (specify the reasonable grounds for this belief; where additional space is required, attach additional page(s) marked as exhibit)

☐ *les motifs de croire que les biens qui ont été saisis en plus des biens mentionnés dans le mandat, avaient été obtenus ou utilisés en perpétrant une infraction, sont les suivants: (préciser les motifs raisonnables de croire ainsi; au besoin, annexer une ou plusieurs pages supplémentaires et les coter)*

(In the event that the warrant was not executed, complete the following)
The warrant was not executed for the following reasons (specify reasons):

(En cas de non exécution d'un mandat, remplir la partie suivante)
Le mandat n'a pas été exécuté pour les raisons suivantes:(préciser ces raisons) :

_____

_____

_____

Dated this /*Fait le*   26   day of / *jour de*   March

200 7   at / *à/au* _____ City of Greater Sudbury _____

_____
Signature of Peace Officer or other person/
Signature de l'agent de la paix ou autre personne

Absolute Jurisdiction	A classification of criminal offence designated as being the exclusive entitlement of a particular level of court to try, or to deal with in matters of interim judicial release and trial. Sec. 553 *Criminal Code* offences, which are the absolute jurisdiction of the Provincial Court, also impose limitations upon a police officer's powers of arrest without warrant where the public interest has been met.
Accused	A person against whom one or more charges have been formally laid. Alternatively referred to in court as a defendant. (See: **defendant**)
Actus Reus	(L. = guilty act) Any offence committed by an act or omission that is prohibited by statute law. (See: **statute law**)
Adjective Law (Procedural Law)	A law or part of a law that does not prescribe an offence but provides rules to govern legal procedures or practice. (See antonym: **substantive law**)
Agent Provocateur (Agent)	One who is in the employ of the police who takes an active role in the investigation to gather evidence or to facilitate the commission of offences through the justifiable offering (on the basis of reasonable suspicion) of the opportunity for individuals to commit crimes. The term "agent" is broadly considered to include undercover police officers, however, most often refers to non-police officers in the employ of the police.
Arbitrary Arrest	An unlawful or improper arrest. Whether or not an arrest was arbitrary will be determined by analysis of the existence or absence of articulable cause to make the arrest, the scope and extent of the arrest itself and the conduct of the person(s) making the arrest. (See: **arrest; articulable cause**)
Arraignment	The official reading of the charges contained in the information or indictment to the accused in court. Depending upon the classification of the offence, arraignment is followed by the Crown election of the mode of trial and election by the accused as to which court he or she wishes their trial to be held.
Arrest	The detention of a person, or restriction of their liberty, whether or not by physical force, by a person acting under lawful authority either for investigative purposes including the need to prevent the commission of an alleged offence, or to compel a person's attendance in court. (See: **arbitrary arrest; investigative detention**)

Articulable Cause	Legal justification expressed in the form of reasonable grounds exceeding mere suspicion, to use force, to arrest or detain an individual, or to conduct a search for evidence.
	Police officers must develop the ability to verbalize their observations, conclusions and justification for their actions, including arrests and searches in terms of the legal requirements of their action. It is not sufficient to merely state, in a report or while testifying in court, that you believed that a particular action was necessary. A skilled police officer must be able to articulate why they believed that their action was necessary and justify their belief in terms of the specific facts, information or circumstances of the event or investigation consistent with existing law.
Bail	(See: **judicial interim release; show cause hearing**)
Beyond a Reasonable Doubt	The standard of proof in criminal or quasi-criminal judicial proceedings that must be attained before a person may be convicted of any offence. Guilt beyond a reasonable doubt does not mean beyond any doubt, but to an objective standard where there is high degree of moral certainty regarding the guilt of the accused.
Breach of the Peace	Any incident of disorderly conduct that involves, or is likely to result in, harm to persons, damage to property, or which may provoke such behaviour in others. The term breach of the peace is not defined in Canadian law and does not constitute an offence. Everyone is authorized to use reasonable and proportional force in such situations to prevent the commission or continuance of a breach of the peace or to prevent any person from joining in a breach of the peace. (For example, a "blow struck in anger" is considered to be a breach of the peace.)
"But For" Test	A test applied by a criminal court in determining whether or not to exclude derivative evidence resulting from information obtained by a *Charter* violation. If the evidence could not have been discovered by the police by independent means – but for the *Charter* violation – it should be considered tainted and excluded. If the evidence would still have been wholly or partially discovered by the police, independently of the *Charter* breach, using proper investigative methods, the evidence may be admitted.
	(See: **derivative evidence; fruit of the poisoned tree; discoverability; exclusionary rule**)
Case Law	Originated in Middle Ages in England and is still an accepted part of western jurisprudence. Case law is established by previous court decisions and is based on the rule of precedent. Case law serves as a starting point for adjudicating cases of a similar nature in future court proceedings.
	(See: **rule of precedent**)

Common Law

Unwritten laws which are based on custom, tradition and practice, rather than originating from court decisions or statute law. Common law refers to practices which have become so entrenched in our legal system that everyone is familiar with their existence (for example, police officer's power to search a prisoner incident to arrest).

Community Safety Division [Formerly known as Policing Services Division (P.S.D.)]

Division of the Ministry of Community Safety and Correctional Services responsible for developing professional standards and policies for Ontario police services. Community Safety Division conducts systematic inspections of police services to ensure compliance with adequacy and effectiveness standards. The division works with police services to develop community safety and crime prevention initiatives.

Compelling Document

A legal form in writing (appearance notice, promise to appear, undertaking before an officer in charge, summons or arrest warrant) that commands an accused to appear in court in a specified location and at a specified time and date.

Conscriptive Evidence

Conscriptive evidence is obtained in breach of the accused's *Charter* rights and involves the participation of the accused in its creation or discovery, meaning that the accused is involuntarily conscripted (compelled) to supply evidence, such as a confession that is intended to be used against them.

(See antonym: **non-conscriptive**)

Consent

The voluntary and informed permission given by an individual to conduct an examination, search or some other action that would normally require prior judicial authorization (i.e., search warrant). To be valid consent, the guidelines of the decision of *R. v. Wills* must be followed, namely:

1. actual consent, express or implied;
2. consenter must have legal right to consent;
3. consent must be voluntary and not coerced;
4. person must be aware of nature of police conduct;
5. person must be aware of right to refuse to consent; and
6. person must be aware of consequences of action

Constabulary Independence

The doctrine that holds that the police must be free to operate with independence and be free from political interference.

Count

A single charge against an accused person. Every charge or offence alleged in an information is referred to as a count and is usually differentiated numerically. (e.g., count 1, count 2, etc.)

Criminal Law

Federally enacted statute law (passed by the Parliament of Canada) which is in force nation-wide, (e.g., *Criminal Code, Youth Criminal Justice Act,* etc.)

(See synonym: **federal statute**)

Criminal Offence	A breach or violation of any federal statute (e.g., *Controlled Drugs and Substances Act*, *Income Tax Act*, *Criminal Code*, etc.).
Defendant	A person against whom one or more charges are formally laid. Alternatively referred to as the accused. (See synonym: **accused**)
Derivative Evidence	Evidence of any type that is obtained or discovered as the direct result of other illegally obtained evidence. Derivative evidence could include stolen property recovered as the result of a breach or violation of the accused's *Charter* rights, such as a confession obtained through denying the accused's rights to legal counsel. Derivative evidence is generally inadmissible under the legal doctrine known as the **fruit of the poisoned tree**. If the original source of the evidence is contaminated, so will any resulting evidence. (See: **fruit of the poisoned tree; "but for" test; discoverability; exclusionary rule**)
Deterrence	Discouragement of unlawful behaviour through the punishment of offenders. Specific deterrence is the discouragement of an offender to engage in repeat criminal behaviour while general deterrence is to discourage all members of society from engaging in similar criminal behaviour through the fear of potential punishment.
Disclosure	The legal obligation on a prosecutor to make known all relevant information in his or her possession, whether favourable or unfavourable, to the accused about a case to allow the accused to make full answer and defence to the charge(s) against them.
Discoverability	(See: **"but for" test; derivative evidence; fruit of the poisoned tree; exclusionary rule**)
Discretion	Professional discretion is "[t]he freedom or authority to make reasonable [and fair] decisions while carrying out one's professional responsibilities."[1]
DNA (Deoxyribonucleic Acid)	A molecule found in the 26 pairs of chromosomes within the nucleus of human cells that has been referred to as the "fingerprint of life". Every human being inherits half of his or her DNA from each parent (except for mitochondrial DNA which is found throughout the body, not only in nucleated cells and is inherited only from the mother). DNA determines a person's physical characteristics, including as gender, height, hair colour, and is a valuable investigative aid in the identification of persons through recovered biological material from crime scenes.
Dual Procedure (Hybrid) Offence	A criminal offence that specifies punishment either by way of summary conviction or by indictment. The Crown prosecutor

---

[1] Bjorkquist at p. 147.

has the exclusive election on which procedure he or she wishes to prosecute that charge. Crown election occurs following the arraignment or reading of the charge to the accused but before the accused enters a plea to the charge against them.

(See: **summary conviction offence; indictable offence**)

Entrapment

The inappropriate inducement of a reluctant individual to commit a crime that they would not otherwise have committed through excessively forceful and unrelenting persuasion by an agent provocateur. Key to a finding of entrapment is the fact that the conduct of the police was without any basis of prior reasonable grounds to believe the involved individual was involved in criminal activity. The correct remedy for a successful defence of entrapment is a stay of proceedings. An accused may only raise the defence of entrapment after they have been found guilty.

(See: **agent provocateur; stay of proceedings; random virtue testing**)

Ex Parte

A legal application or hearing involving only one side of a matter or dispute, in the absence of and usually without prior notice having been given to the other side.

Ex Post Facto

Retroactively, or after the fact.

Exclusionary Rule

A legal doctrine which states that evidence that is improperly or illegally obtained as the result of a violation of the rights and freedoms of an individual shall be excluded as evidence at the trial of the accused, if the admission of that evidence would bring the administration of justice into disrepute.

(See: **fruit of the poisoned tree; derivative evidence; discoverability; "but for" test**)

Exculpatory

Evidence in any form that tends to exonerate or free a suspect or an accused person from blame.

(See antonym: **inculpatory**)

Exigent Circumstances

Where reasonable grounds exist to obtain a search warrant but emergency conditions make it impracticable to obtain a warrant, a peace officer may entry a building, receptacle or place and may seize evidence as if he or she were acting under a search warrant. Exigent circumstances involve emergent instances where there is a reasonable belief of imminent loss, removal or destruction of evidence, or imminent bodily harm or death to any person. Exigent circumstances also permit peace officers to enter dwelling houses without warrant to make an arrest where there is a reasonable belief of imminent death or bodily harm to any person.

Anything seized without warrant under exigent circumstances must be treated in the same manner as if it was seized under the authority of a search warrant.

Facts in Issue

The essential elements of a specific offence, all of which must be exist, before a person may be arrested and charged, and which must be proven before an accused is found guilty in court.

Federal Statute

Federally enacted legislation that is passed (by the Parliament of Canada) and is in force nation-wide (e.g., *Criminal Code, Canada Evidence Act, Controlled Drugs and Substances Act,* etc.).

(See synonym: **criminal law**)

Feeney Warrant

An endorsement on a Form 7.1 *Criminal Code* arrest warrant that authorizes peace officers to enter into dwelling houses to make arrests in all cases except those involving exigent circumstances.

(See: **exigent circumstances**)

Fresh Pursuit

(See synonym: **hot pursuit**)

Fruit of the Poisoned Tree

An extension of the exclusionary rule that renders evidence obtained as the result of original unlawfully obtained evidence inadmissible. Using this analogy, if "the tree" the original seizure, is poisoned or tainted, the secondary evidence, "the fruit" that results from the original source is likewise tainted unless it falls into one of three exemptions.

(See: **exclusionary rule; derivative evidence**)

Habeas Corpus

(L. = you have the body) A method by which a prisoner or someone on their behalf can challenge the lawfulness of their detention. A writ of *habeas corpus* requires the production of the prisoner to appear before a court for a hearing to determine the legality of the detention or whether the prisoner should be released.

Hearsay Evidence

Oral testimony of a witness that is third person in nature and not from the witness's direct knowledge (i.e., the witness hears [then repeats] words spoken by another person, who is not called to testify).

Hot Pursuit

A common law concept that allows peace officers to enter private premises, including residential dwellings to arrest people for provincial or indictable offences for which they may be arrested without warrant providing the occurrence, the pursuit and the arrest are so closely related as to form one single transaction. The peace officer must have lawful authority to arrest without warrant, must have reasonable grounds to believe the person being pursued is within the premises to be entered, and must announce his presence and entry. Also referred to as "fresh pursuit".

Hybrid Offence

(See: **dual procedure offence, summary conviction offence, indictable offence**)

In Rem

A category of judicial proceedings that are against a thing rather than against a person, such as proceedings to forfeit seized publications that are obscene, child pornography, a crime comic or a voyeuristic recording as set out in section 164 *Criminal Code* or Proceeds of Crime legislation.

Inculpatory

Evidence in any form that tends to incriminate or prove the guilt of a suspect or an accused person.

(See antonym: **exculpatory**)

Indictable offence

The most serious classification of criminal offence. The accused is entitled to have a preliminary inquiry if they elect to be tried by a Superior Division court judge or a jury. The general penalty section for indictable offences is 5 years but specific penalties include 2, 5, 10, 14 years or life imprisonment. A police officer may arrest a person for an indictable offence on reasonable grounds that the person has committed or is about to commit the offence.

(See: **summary conviction offence; dual procedure offence**)

Information

A charging document that is laid in writing and on oath or solemn affirmation before a justice. An information may be laid by anyone for an indictable offence or summary conviction offence. The information contains the name of the informant and the accused, and states the charge(s) alleged to have been committed. A *Criminal Code* information must be in Form 2 and may either confirm an appearance notice or promise to appear or require the issuance of a summons or arrest warrant to compel the attendance of the accused in court.

Informed Consent

(See: **consent**)

Investigative Detention

The common law right of police officers to briefly detain and investigate individuals where there are reasonable grounds to suspect they have been involved in a particular recent crime. Investigative detention is not defined in statute law and exists when police temporarily restrict the liberty of an individual for investigative purposes in the absence of reasonable grounds to make a formal arrest. A detained individual may be subjected to a "pat-down" or "frisk" search of their person if the police officer has reasonable grounds to believe it necessary to do so to ensure officer safety.

Investigative detention is not to be confused with formal arrest nor the common law right to search and arrested person incident to arrest for evidence, weapons or tools of escape.

(See: **arrest**)

Judicial Interim Release

Bail, or judicial interim release, is a form of conditional release of an accused charged with an offence to the community, prior to trial or sentencing. Release can be granted by the police at the time of an arrest, following an arrest but before a charge is laid, or by a justice after the person has been charged with one or more offences. Release methods vary with different classifications of offences.

(See: **show cause hearing; reverse onus**)

Laws	Bodies of rules designed to regulate the conduct of members of a given society which are both recognized and enforced by the government of that society at any given time. Laws are amended from time to time to reflect the changing will and values of the society that creates them. (See: **adjective law, case law; common law; criminal law; statute law; substantive law**)
Mens Rea	(L. = guilty mind) The degree of criminal intent required to commit a specific offence, (i.e., the difference between a willful or intentional act and an accident).
Ministry of Community Safety and Correctional Services	The Ministry of Community Safety and Correctional Services provides overall governance for Ontario police services, ensuring that adequate and effective services are provided and minimum policing standards are maintained.
Non-conscriptive Evidence	Evidence obtained as the result of a breach of the accused's *Charter* rights that did not involve the participation of the accused in the creation or discovery of the evidence. (See antonym: **conscriptive evidence**)
Offence	A breach or violation of prohibited behaviour (either by way of an act or by an omission) prescribed by statute law.
Ontario Civilian Commission on Police Services (OCCPS)	An independent quasi-judicial civilian agency that operates under the Ministry of Community Safety and Correctional Services with a mandate to investigate matters related to policing, hear appeals from police disciplinary hearing decisions and provide oversight to Ontario police services boards.
Paedophile (also: pedophile)	An adult who is sexually attracted to a child.
Person in Authority	Any person formally involved at any stage of the investigation, arrest, detention, examination or prosecution of a person suspected or charged with an offence and who the accused believes to have such authority.
Person of Interest	A person whose background, relationship to the victim, or opportunity to commit the offence may warrant further inquiry but at that time no other grounds exist to suggest culpability (blameworthiness) in the commission of the crime being investigated. A person of interest is not a suspect and should never be identified as such. (Definition from the Ontario Major Case Management (MCM) Manual) (See: **suspect**)
Police Services Board	A civilian police agency providing oversight and general management policy development for municipal police services. Police services boards appoint police service members, establish guidelines for and review of both the administration of public complaints and secondary employment applications.

Police services boards are forbidden to direct the Chief of Police on specific operational decisions or with respect to the day-to-day operations of the police service.

Policing Services Division (P.S.D.)

Former name of the Community Safety Division of the Ministry of Community Safety and Correctional Services.

(See: **Community Safety Division**)

Prima Facie

(L. = at first look) Sufficient evidence, which if not contradicted, will prove one or more facts in issue or will result in a finding of guilt.

Procedural Law

(See: **adjective law**)

(See antonym: **substantive law**)

Proportional

In a ratio of perhaps unequal but relative, matching or corresponding measurable characteristic such as size or degree when compared to another item, thing or concept.

For example, a person whose height and weight are proportional. If the two observable characteristics (height and weight) agree or correspond rather than disagree, they are proportional to each other.

Propping

Propping is a form of ruse or trickery that is involved at the arrest or interrogation phase of an investigation and occurs within a police facility to which a suspect is brought or arrives at for an interrogation. Propping involves the strategic placement of artifacts intended to be observed by the suspect to impress upon them the gravity of the offence and the strength of the evidence against them. Propping may include items such as conspicuous signage, photographs, wall-charts and file cabinets bearing the suspect's name on the drawer fronts.

Provincial Statute

Provincially enacted statute law that is in force only in the province in which it was passed (e.g., *Liquor Licence Act, Highway Traffic Act, Trespass to Property Act* etc.).

Public Interest

Anything that concerns the general welfare of the public at large and where the interests of the wider society come before the interests of an individual person. Within the general context of law enforcement, the public interest involves the efficient detection and investigation of crime and the apprehension and charging of offenders. Within the specific context of judicial interim release, the public interest focuses on the prevention of additional offences, protection from harm and the prosecution of offenders.

Random Virtue Testing

The inappropriate inducement of one or more persons to commit a crime without a reasonable suspicion that the person is already engaged in illegal activity, such as drug trafficking, or that the location involved is one in which the illegal activity under investigation is likely to be occurring.

(See: **entrapment**)

Reasonable	Within the limits of objectively sound judgement.
	(See: **reasonable person**)
Reasonable Expectation of Privacy	The legal standard intended to prevent unwarranted intrusion by the law enforcement agents of the state into the confidential affairs of individuals. An individual may claim a reasonable expectation of privacy relating to any personal, spatial or informational matter affecting their confidentiality, integrity, dignity or autonomy. An individual's expectation of privacy is greatest within their own home and least when openly travelling in public places.
Reasonable Grounds	A set of facts or circumstances, which if true, would lead an ordinary, prudent, cautious individual to have a strong belief that exceeds mere suspicion.
	(See: **beyond a reasonable doubt**)
Reasonable Person	A legal standard involving a fictitious, prudent and cautious individual who always exercises good judgement and does not act recklessly or emotionally. The reasonable person concept is used to determine negligence in civil court proceedings and in criminal courts to evaluate the objective reasonableness of arrests, searches or seizures of evidence.
Reverse Onus	An accused, charged with an offence under any of the circumstances listed in section 515(6) *Criminal Code*, must be remanded in custody by a justice unless the accused can show cause why their continued detention is not necessary. Usually the onus or responsibility lies with the Crown to show cause why an charged individual should remain in custody. It is this shifting of responsibility to the accused that creates a situation of reverse onus.
	(See: **judicial interim release; show cause**)
Royal Assent	The traditional final stage of the legislative process involving the symbolic consent of the monarchy as the sovereign head of state to the passing of a legislative bill. The vice-regal representative of the reigning monarch, (e.g., Governor General, Lieutenant Governor, or their designate) is present in Parliament or the legislature, respectively, and nods in consent when the name of the bill being passed is read aloud. The bill in question then becomes law, either on that date or on a later specified date.
Rule of Precedent	(L. *stare decisis* "to stand by the decision")
	A fundamental principle upon which case law is based that dictates that lower courts must be bound by the decisions of higher courts. Equal or higher courts than the court rendering the decision may take the decision into consideration when making judgements, but aren't obliged to do so.

Search	Any type of official examination by agents of law enforcement seeking evidence of illegal activity, or to prevent the commission of an offence or to ensure officer safety in certain circumstances. A search may be conducted without a warrant if it is authorized by law or may be pre-authorized by a search warrant.
	(See: **seizure; reasonable expectation of privacy**)
Seizure	The non-consensual taking or removal of information or an article of evidence in which a suspect or accused has a reasonable expectation of privacy, for the purpose of proving illegal activity or for the purpose of furthering an investigation.
	(See: **search; reasonable expectation of privacy**)
Show Cause Hearing	An accused person brought before a justice must be released from custody unless the prosecutor can show cause why their continued detention is necessary, having regard to all the circumstances. In most cases the onus (responsibility) to justify the continued detention of the accused is on the Crown. A Show Cause hearing is also referred to as a bail hearing.
	(See: **judicial interim release; reverse onus**)
Special Investigations Unit (SIU)	A civilian law enforcement agency that reports to the Ontario Ministry of the Attorney General and is authorized under the *Police Services Act* to conduct investigations into circumstances involving police and civilians that have resulted in serious injury, including sexual assault, or death. The SIU operates independently of both the police and government.
Stare Decisis	(See: **rule of precedent**)
Statute Law	Codified (written) laws enacted by a legislative body that have received Royal Assent prior to coming into force in law. In Canada, statutes may be passed by the federal parliament or a provincial or territorial legislative assembly. Statutes are in power in the jurisdiction of the legislative body enacting them.
Statute of Limitations	The specified maximum time period following an offence or incident during which a charge may be laid. In Canada, summary conviction offences have a statute of limitations of six months, while there is no statute of limitations for indictable offences.
Stay of Proceedings	A process by which judicial proceedings are stayed or suspended for a period of up to one year. If the proceedings are not recommenced within the year, the proceedings shall be deemed never to have commenced. A stay of proceedings is the proper remedy to a successful defence of entrapment or where the Attorney General of a province or the Attorney General of Canada intervenes in judicial proceedings.
Subject Officer	A police officer whose conduct appears, in the opinion of the Special Investigations Unit director, to have caused death or

serious injury to a member of the public, and who is under investigation by the SIU.

(See: **Special Investigations Unit (SIU); witness officer**)

Substantive Law

Statute law that is used to administer the law. An example of substantive law would be a section prohibiting a specific act or omission that creates criminal liability for an offence.

(See antonyms: **adjective law; procedural law**)

Summary Conviction Offence

The least serious classification of offence in Canadian jurisprudence. Because the majority of charges laid are dealt with by summary conviction, the trial will be held in the lower courts, the accused may not elect trial by a Superior Division court judge nor by a jury. The accused is not entitled to a preliminary inquiry. The general punishment for summary conviction offences is $2 000 or 6 months imprisonment or both, unless the offence provides a specific penalty that exceeds the general punishment. A police officer must find the person committing a summary conviction offence to be authorized to arrest that person.

(See: **indictable offence; dual procedure (hybrid offence)**)

Surety/Sureties (pl.)

A person who assumes legal responsibility for the deposit of bail money, or for the default or delinquency of a person in custody to assure the other person's release from custody.

(See: **judicial interim release**)

Suspect

A person [whom] an investigator reasonably believes may possess a degree of culpability [i.e., criminal liability, blameworthiness] in the commission of the criminal offence being investigated and there [exists] some incriminating information linking the person to the crime. (Definition from the Ontario Major Case Management (MCM) Manual)

(See: **person of interest**)

Tort

A wrongful or injurious misconduct, occurring outside of the context of a contract, which results in loss or damage to a party and for which the person who committed it may be held civilly liable for damages.

Witness Officer

A police officer who, in the opinion of the Special Investigations Unit director, is involved but is not a subject officer in an incident involving death or serious injury to a member of the public and that is under investigation by the SIU.

(See: **Special Investigations Unit (SIU); subject officer**)

Young Person

A person who is between 12 and 17 years of age, inclusive, at the time they commit an offence for which they are charged under the *Youth Criminal Justice Act* or any preceding legislation.

Arcaro, Gino. (2003). *Basic Police Powers: Arrest & Search Procedures*, (3rd edition) Toronto: Nelson.

Aveni, Thomas J., The Force Continuum Conundrum, The Police Policy Studies Council Website. Retrieved: October 23, 2006, from www.theppsc.org/Staff_Views/Aveni/The%20Force%20Continuum%20Conundrum.pdf

Bjorkquist, Bruce D. (2002). *The Principles of Ethical Reasoning: Ethics and Policing in a Modern Society.* Toronto: Pearson Education Canada Inc.

deC. Cory, Hon. Mr. Justice Peter, The Inquiry Regarding Thomas Sophonow. Retrieved: March 17, 2007, from www.gov.mb.ca/justice/publications/sophonow/intro/therole.html

Canadian Police Institute, Canadian Police College. *Social Order and Disorder in Canada: A Summary of the Facts,* (1996) Ottawa. (LeBeuf and Souliere), Retrieved: October 22, 2006, from www.cpc.gc.ca/rcd/order_e.pdf

Canadian Sports Riots 1933-1994. Retrieved: October 22, 2006, from www.macleans.ca/culture/books/article.jsp?content=20051222_140516_2124.

Center on Juvenile and Criminal Justice (California) report. Shattering "Broken Windows": An analysis of San Francisco's alternative crime policies. Retrieved: January 25, 2007, from www.cjcj.org/pubs/windows/windows.html

Cicero, Marcus T. Retrieved: Dec 5, 2006, from www.quotationsbook.com/subjects/684/Justice

Constitution Act, 1867 (formerly the *British North America Act* 1867), 30 &; 31 Victoria, c. 3. Retrieved: March 7, 2006, from www.solon.org/Constitutions/Canada/English/ca_1867.html

Constitution Act, 1982, being Schedule B to the *Canada Act* 1982 (U.K.), 1982, c. 11, Accessed: March 7, 2006. Retrieved: May 10, 2006, from www.canlii.org/ca/const_en/const1982.html

Definition: Common Law Retrieved: September 2, 2005, from www.pearsoned.ca/crimcjpolicing/glossaryc.html.

Definition: *Habeas Corpus*. Retrieved: May 12, 2006, from www.lectlaw.com/def/h001.htm

Definition: Royal Assent. Retrieved: March 7, 2006, from www.parl.gc.ca/information/about/process/info/ParliamentFAQ02-e.htm

Douglas, William O. Retrieved: November 20, 2006, from www.angelfire.com/az/sthurston/morequotes.html

Equipment and Use of Force, R.R.O. 1990, Reg. 926 - Police Services Act, R.S.O. 1990, c. P. 15. Retrieved: March 7, 2006, from www.canlii.org/on/laws/regu/1990r.926/20060115/whole.html

Ericson, Richard V. (1982). *Reproducing Order: A Study of Police Patrol Work*. Toronto: University of Toronto Press in association with the Centre of Criminology.

Fairburn, Michal. (1998). "Litigating the Warranted Search: A Practical Overview" in *Search and Seizure: New Developments*. Toronto: Law Society of Upper Canada.

Giuliani, Rudolph W. (2002). *Leadership*. New York: Miramax Books, Hyperion Publishing.

Groot, Norman J. (2001). *Canadian Law & Private Investigations*. Toronto: Irwin Law Inc.

Halifax Riot (VE-Day 1945). Retrieved: October 22, 2006, from www.civilization.ca/cwm/newspapers/canadawar/halifax_e.html

Heafey, Shirley, Chair of Commission for Public Complaints against the RCMP Retrieved: May 26, 2006, from www.cpc-cpp.gc.ca/DefaultSite/Archive/index_e.aspx?articleid=474

Higley, Dahn D. (1984). *O.P.P. The History of the Ontario Provincial Police Force*. Toronto: The Queen's Printer in right of the Province of Ontario.

Hill, The Hon. Mr. Casey (1999). *Warranted Searches: A Practical Perspective*. Toronto: N.P.

Hill, The Hon. Mr. Casey, Hutchinson, Scott and Pringle, Leslie (1999). *Search Warrants: Protection or Illusion?* Toronto: N.P.

Horner, Jessie J. (2007). *Canadian Law and the Canadian Legal System*. Toronto: Pearson Education Canada Inc.

Hutchinson, Scott C. (1996). *Issues in Search and Seizure Law in Canada*, Toronto: N.P.

Kaufman, The Hon. Mr Fred. (1998) *The Commission on proceedings involving Guy Paul Morin*. Toronto: Ontario Ministry of the Attorney General.

LeBeuf, Marcel Eugène, and Soullière, Nicole. (1996). *Social Order and Disorder in Canada: A Summary of the Facts*. Ottawa: N.P. Canadian Police Institute, Canadian Police College.

Martin, Dianne L. (2004) "The Canadian Review of Policing Research, Lessons about Justice from the Laboratory of Wrongful Convictions: Tunnel Vision, the Construction of Guilt and Informer Evidence" *University of Missouri-Kansas City Law Review,* 70/4: p. 847. Retrieved: April 28, 2005, from crpr.icaap.org/issues/issue1/dmartin.html.

McKenna, Paul F. (2002). *Police Powers I*. Toronto: Pearson Education Canada Inc.

McKenna, Paul F. (2003). *Police Powers II*. Toronto: Pearson Education Canada Inc.

Ministry of the Attorney General – News Release – May 15, 2007 "New System Means Increased Confidence and Respect of Public and Police". Retrieved: May 17, 2007, from www.attorneygeneral.jus.gov.on.ca/english/news/2007/20070515-bill-103-nr.asp

More, Hannah. Retrieved: January 12, 2007, from www.giga-usa.com/quotes/topics/discretion_t002.htm

Ontario Civilian Commission on Police Services – Annual Report 2004, Public Complaint statistics. Retrieved: October 24, 2006, from www.occps.ca/englishwebsite/aboutoccps/annualreport2004.pdf

Ontario Ministry of the Solicitor General Policing Standards Manual (Feb 2000), LE-024 Domestic Violence Occurrences. Retrieved: January 28, 2007, from www.lawc.on.ca/PDF_Files_Reports/Domestic%20Violence%20Occurrences.pdf

Pascal, Blaise. Retrieved: December 21, 2006, from www.wisdomquotes.com/cat_justice.html

Peel, Sir Robert. *Principles of Policing.* Retrieved: September 15, 2006, from www.edmontonpolicecommission.com

Pitt, William, Retrieved: February 25, 2007, from quotes.libertytree.ca/quote/william_william_pitt_quote_a246

Police Services Act, R.S.O. 1990 c. P-15. Retrieved: September 1, 2006, from www.e-laws.gov.on.ca

Report of the Ontario Attorney General's Advisory Committee on Charge Screening, Disclosure and Resolution Discussions (The Martin Report) (1993). Toronto: Queen's Printer for Ontario.

Report on the Police Complaints System in Ontario April 22, 2005, The Honourable Patrick J. Lesage, Q.C. Retrieved: May 26, 2006, from www.attorneygeneral.jus.gov.on.ca/english/about/pubs/LeSage/en-fullreport.pdf

Rock, Nora and Valerie Hoag. (2006). *Foundations of Criminal and Civil Law in Canada* (2nd edition). Toronto: Emond Montgomery Publications Ltd.

The Role of the Police (Griffiths & Verdun-Jones, 1994, pp. 70–71) – Chapter 1. Retrieved: March 15, 2006, from www.johnhoward.ab.ca/PUB/C52.htm

Royal Canadian Mounted Police Act, R.S. 1985, c. R-10. Retrieved: September 24, 2006, from www.canlii.org/ca/sta.

Salhany, The Honourable Mr. R.E., Q.C. (1989). *Canadian Criminal Procedure.* (5th edition). Aurora, ON: Canada Law Book Company.

Schmalleger, Frank, and David MacAlister and and Paul F. McKenna. (2004). *Canadian Criminal Justice Today* (2nd edition). Toronto: Pearson Education Canada Inc.

Schmalleger, Frank and Rebecca Volk. (2005). *Canadian Criminology Today: Theories and Applications* (2nd Edition). Toronto: Pearson Education Canada Inc.

Sher, Julian. (2002). *Until You are Dead: Steven Truscott's Long Ride into History.* Toronto: Random House of Canada Ltd.

Sherriff, Steve (1997) *Convicting the Guilty: A Strategic Manual of Law and Technique for Dedicated Investigators and Prosecutors Combating Major Crime*, N.P.

Social order and disorder in Canada: a summary of the facts (1996) Ottawa N.P. (LeBeuf and Souliere) Canadian Police Institute, Canadian Police College. Retrieved: October 22, 2006, from www.cpc.gc.ca/rcd/order_e.pdf

Statistics Canada, *The Daily,* Monday, June 23, 2006, Family Violence statistics. Retrieved: January 28, 2007, from www.statcan.ca/Daily/English/030623/d030623c.htm

Statistics Canada, *The Daily,* Monday Nov 21, 2005 Study: Referral and Convictions in Youth and Criminal Courts. Retrieved: January 23, 2007, from www.statcan.ca/Daily/English/051121/d051121b.htm

Statistics Canada, *The Daily,* Thursday, July 20, 2006, Impaired Driving statistics. Retrieved: January 28, 2007, from www.statcan.ca/Daily/English/060720/d060720b.htm

Van Allen, Bill. (2007). *Criminal Investigation: In Search of the Truth*. Toronto: Pearson Education Canada Inc.

Victims' Bill of Rights, S.O. 1995 c. 6. Retrieved: September 12, 2007, from http://www.elaws.gov.on.ca/navigation?file=browseStatutes&reset=yes&menu=browse&lang=en.

Walma, Mark W. and Leigh West. (2002). *Police Powers and Procedures*. Toronto: Emond Montgomery Publications Ltd.

R. v. Backhouse, (2005) 194 C.C.C. (3d) 1, 127 C.R.R. (2d) 1, 28 C.R. (6th) 31, 195 O.A.C. 80, CanLII 4937 (Ont C.A.). Use of hearsay in forming reasonable grounds for search warrant. Also, return to justice, in writing, must be made for all evidence seized by warrantless searches, just as if it was seized by a warrant. Retrieved: March 17, 2007, from www.canlii.org/on/cas/onca/2005/2005onca10186.html

R. v. Black, 1996 CanLII 7018 (SK Q.B.) Oppressive behaviour by police during interrogation by lying about the effectiveness of the polygraph and blaming the victim. Retrieved: May 11, 2007, from www.canlii.org/eliisa/highlight.do?text=dirty+tricks&language=en&searchTitle=Search+all+CanLII+Databases&path=/en/sk/skqb/doc/1996/1996canlii7018/1996canlii7018.html.

R. v. Collins, [1987] 1 S.C.R. 265, 38 D.L.R. (4th) 508, 3 W.W.R. 699, 33 C.C.C. (3d) 1, 56 C.R. (3d) 193, 13 B.C.L.R. (2d) 1. Factors to be weighed in determining whether or not to exclude evidence. Retrieved: April 7, 2007, from scc.lexum.umontreal.ca/en/1987/1987rcs1-265/1987rcs1-265.html

R. v. Cretney, 1999 CanLII 6350 (BC S.C.) Use of alcohol during undercover operation not a dirty trick. Retrieved: May 1, from 2007 www.canlii.org/eliisa/highlight.do?text=dirty highlight.do?text=dirty+tricks&language=en&searchTitle=Search+all+CanLII+data-bases bases&path=/en/bc/bcsc/doc/1999/1999canlii6350/1999canlii6350.html

R. v. Feeney, [1997] 2 S.C.R 13. Entry of Dwelling Houses to Effect Arrests acknowledged the exemption in cases of hot pursuit. Retrieved: April 6, 2007, from scc.lexum.umontreal.ca/en/1997/1997rcs2-13/1997rcs2-13.html

R. v. Golden, [2001] 3 S.C.R. 679, 2001 S.C.C. 83. Strip-search Incident to Arrest. Retrieved: Feb 26, 2007, from scc.lexum.umontreal.ca/sccliisa/highlight?language=en&path=http://scc.lexum.umontreal.ca/en/2001/2001scc83/2001scc83.html&query=%2Bsearch+%2Bincident+%2Bto+%2Barrest

R. v. Grant, [1993] 3 S.C.R. 223, 8 W.W.R. 257, 84 C.C.C. (3d) 173, 17 C.R.R. (2d) 269, 24 C.R. (4th) 1 Warrantless perimeter search – police trespass – Sec. 8 CH. Retrieved: May 1, 2007, from www.canlii.org/eliisa/highlight.do?text=search&language=en&searchTitle=Search+all+CanLII+databases&path=/en/ca/scc/doc/1993/1993canlii68/1993canlii68.html

R. v. Hamill (1987) S.C.C. Unconstitutionality of writs of assistance. Retrieved: April 5, 2006, from www.canlii.org/ca/cas/scc/1987/1987scc13.html

R. v. Hoilett, (1999) 136 C.C.C. (3d) 449, 26 C.R. (5th) 332, 121 O.A.C. 391,1999 CanLII 3740 (ON C.A.). Depriving prisoner of clothing and blankets prior to questioning. Retrieved: May 11, 2007, from www.canlii.org/en/on/onca/doc/1999/1999canlii3740/1999canlii3740.html

R. v. Kokesch, [1990] 3 S.C.R. 3, [1991] 1 W.W.R. 193, 61 C.C.C. (3d) 207, [1991] 50 C.R.R. 285, 1 C.R. (4th) 62, 51 B.C.L.R. (2d) 157 Warrantless perimeter search – police trespass – Sec 8 CH. Retrieved: May 1, 2007, from www.canlii.org/eliisa/highlight.do?language=en&searchTitle=Search+all+CanLII+databases&path=/en/ca/scc/doc/1990/1990canlii55/1990canlii55.html

R. v. La, [1997] 2 S.C.R. 680. Duty of Crown to disclose evidence that has been lost or destroyed and to explain what happened to it. Retrieved: May 14, 2007, from scc.lexum.umontreal.ca/en/1997/1997rcs2-680/1997rcs2-680.html

R. v. Laplante (1987), 48 D.L.R. (4th) 615, 40 C.C.C. (3d) 63, [1988] 33 C.R.R. 15, 59 Sask. R. 251, CanLII 209 (Sask. C.A.). Search of out-buildings not part of dwelling house incident to execution of search warrant for dwelling house. Retrieved: March 24, 2007, from www.canlii.org/eliisa/highlight.do?language=en&searchTitle=Saskatchewan&path=/en/sk/skca/doc/1987/1987canlii209/1987canlii209.html

R. v. Ling, [2002] 3 S.C.R. 814, 2002 S.C.C. 74, also R. v. Jarvis, [2002] 3 S.C.R. 757, 2002 S.C.C. 73. Evidence seized under regulatory warrantless search authorities not to be used as evidence of penal liability. Retrieved: February 25, 2007, from scc.lexum.umontreal.ca/en/2002/2002scc74/2002scc74.html

R. v. Macooh, [1993] 2 S.C.R. 802 Hot pursuit for indictable or provincial offences for which the suspect may be arrested without warrant [decided Feb 26/93]. Retrieved: April 6, 2007, from scc.lexum.umontreal.ca/en/1993/1993rcs2-802/1993rcs2-802.html

R. v. Mann, [2004] 3 S.C.R. 59, 2004 SCC, 52 (CanLII), Investigative Detention. Retrieved: November 19, 2006, from www.canlii.org/ca/cas/scc/1985/1985scc41.html

R. v. McCreery, 1996 CanLII 1073 (BC S.C.) Allegation of dirty tricks by undercover police officers to obtain incriminating evidence of suspect not in custody. Retrieved: May 11, 2007, from www.canlii.org/en/bc/bcsc/doc/1996/1996canlii1073/1996canlii1073.html

R. v. Miller, (1991) 5 O.R. (3d) 678, 68 C.C.C. (3d) 517, 9 C.R. (4th) 347, 50 O.A.C. 282, 1991 CanLII 2704, (ON C.A.), Obtaining handwriting samples through the employer of an out-of-custody murder suspect by the use of a ruse. Retrieved: May 11, 2007, from www.canlii.org/en/on/onca/doc/1991/1991canlii2704/1991canlii2704.html

R. v. O'Connor, [1995] 4 S.C.R. 411. Disclosure of confidential third-party records by the Crown. Retrieved: May 14, 2007, from scc.lexum.umontreal.ca/en/1995/1995rcs4-411/1995rcs4-411.html

R. v. Philpott, (2002), 101 C.R.R. (2d) 87, 2002 CanLII 25164 (ON S.C.). Wilful non-disclosure of facts in Information to Obtain Search Warrant. Retrieved: May 14, 2007, from www.canlii.org/en/on/onsc/doc/2002/2002canlii25164/2002canlii25164.html

R. v. Sismey (1990), 55 C.C.C. (3d) 281, 1 C.R.R. (2d) 381, 1990 CanLII 1483 (BC C.A.) Material misrepresentation of reasonable grounds to obtain search warrant. Retrieved: May 14, 2007, from www.canlii.org/en/bc/bcca/doc/1990/1990canlii1483/1990canlii1483.html

R. v. Spannier (1996), CanLII 978 (BC S.C.) Abuse of Process, prisoner in custody pepper-sprayed by police. Retrieved: May 1, 2007, from www.canlii.org/

eliisa/highlight.do?text=pepper+spray&language=en&searchTitle=Search+all+CanLII+
databases&path=/en/bc/bcsc/doc/1996/1996canlii978/1996canlii978.html

R. v. Stillman, [1997] 1 S.C.R. 607, 185 N.B.R. (2d) 1, 185 N.B.R. (2e) 1, 144 D.L.R.
(4th) 193, 113 C.C.C. (3d) 321, 42 C.R.R. (2d) 189, 5 C.R. (5th) 1. Taking of bodily
samples from prisoner under threat of force. Retrieved: April 7, 2007 scc.lexum.
umontreal.ca/en/1997/1997rcs1-607/1997rcs1-607.html

R. v. Turner, (1995), 170 N.B.R. (2d) 345, 170 N.B.R. (2e) 345, 1995 CanLII 3891
(NB Q.B.), Material non-disclosure of previous warrantless entry of premises to
be searched. Retrieved: May 14, 2007, from www.canlii.org/en/nb/nbqb/doc/1995/
1995canlii3891/1995canlii3891.html

R. v. Vereczki, 1998 CanLII 1996 (BC S.C.) Warrantless perimeter of third parties'
property – police trespass – Not a Sec. 8 CH violation. Retrieved: May 1, 2007, from
www.canlii.org/eliisa/highlight.do?text=search&language=en&searchTitle=Search+
all+CanLII+databases&path=/en/bc/bcsc/doc/1998/1998canlii1996/1998canlii1996.html

R. v. Wiegand, (2003), 11 C.R. (6th) 356, 2003 ABQB 283 (CanLII) Police oppression in
interrogation of suspects. Retrieved: May 11, 2007, from www.canlii.org/en/ab/
abqb/doc/2003/2003abqb283/2003abqb283.html

R. v. Woodland, 2001 BCPC 255 (CanLII) Abuse of Process, physical violence toward
prisoner. Retrieved: May 1, 2007, from www.canlii.org/eliisa/highlight.do?text=
police&language=en&searchTitle=Search+all+CanLII+databases&path=/en/bc/bcpc/
doc/2001/2001bcpc255/2001bcpc255.html

R. v. Zundel, [1992] 2 S.C.R. 731, 1992 CanLII 75 S.C.C. Definition of public interest.
Retrieved: December 28, 2006, from www.canlii.org/ca/cas/scc/1992/1992scc72.html

Chapter 1

p. 10 Bill Van Allen; p. 12 Bill Van Allen; p. 13 Bill Van Allen

Chapter 2

p. 30 Bill Van Allen; p. 33 Reproduced with the permission of the Director, Special Investigations Unit, Ministry of the Attorney General; p. 35 Dave Tamblyn; p. 41 Reproduced with the permission of the Director, Ontario Police College, Ministry of Community Safety and Correctional Services

Chapter 4

p. 101 Bill Van Allen; p. 102 (top, bottom) Bill Van Allen; p. 103 (top, bottom) Bill Van Allen; p. 105 Bill Van Allen; p. 106 (top, bottom) Bill Van Allen; p. 107 (top, bottom) Bill Van Allen; p. 108 (top, bottom) Bill Van Allen; p. 109 (top, bottom) Bill Van Allen

Chapter 7

p. 172 Bill Van Allen; p. 174 Bill Van Allen; p. 176 Bill Van Allen

Inside Back Cover

© Queen's Printer for Ontario, 2004. Reprinted with permission. The *Ontario Use of Force Model (2004)* was developed through consultation between the Ministry of Community Safety and Correctional Services and its stakeholders. The Model has been amended by and is endorsed by the Ministry.

Notes

Notes